CERES™
Celestial Legend
Volume 11: Maiden

STORY & ART BY YUU WATASE

Editor's Note: At the author's request, the spelling of Ms. Watase's first name has been changed from "Yû,"
as it has appeared on previous VIZ publications, to "Yuu."

English Adaptation/Gary Leach

Translation/Lillian Olsen
Touch–Up Art & Lettering/Melanie Lewis
Cover & Graphic Design/Hidemi Sahara
Editor/Avery Gotoh
Supervising Editor/Frances E. Wall

Managing Editor/Annette Roman
Director of Production/Noboru Watanabe
Editorial Director/Alvin Lu
Sr. Director of Acquisitions/Rika Inouye
Vice President of Sales & Marketing/Liza Coppola
Executive Vice President/Hyoe Narita
Publisher/Seiji Horibuchi

Printed in Canada

Published by VIZ, LLC
P.O. Box 77010 • San Francisco CA 94107

Shôjo Edition

10 9 8 7 6 5 4 3 2 1

First printing, April 2005

store.viz.com

www.viz.com

www.animerica-mag.com

VIZ GRAPHIC NOVEL

CERES

Celestial Legend

Vol. 11: Maiden

Story and Art by
Yuu Watase

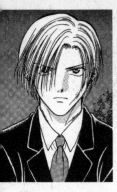

AKI MIKAGE: Aya's twin brother and host to (or hostage of, more like) the angry, Ceres-obsessed "Progenitor." Although Aya still believes that, somewhere deep inside, her brother still exists, the longer he is exposed to the insane love of the Progenitor for Ceres (who of course inhabits Aya), the less the real Aki remains.

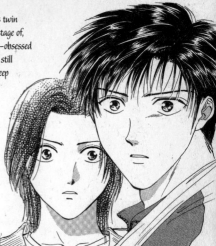

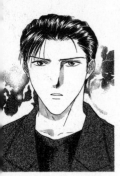

KAGAMI MIKAGE: Scion of the family empire and founder of the nefarious "C-Project." His passion mistaken by Aki/The Progenitor as lust for Ceres, the true purpose behind Kagami's search for Ceres' hagoromo is slowly being revealed.

SHURO: A woman who once passed as a man (as part of the wildly popular Japanese pop duo GeSANG), Shuro is yet another conflicted celestial, ambiguous not only about her powers, but also her sexuality.

YÛHI AOGIRI: Once it hurt just to look at her, but gradually Yûhi is learning to accept (if not understand) the love Aya bears for his rival, Tôya. Another benefit? The knowledge that he can still care for and love—without necessarily being in love with—someone.

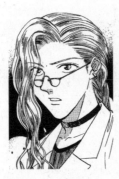

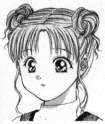

CHIDORI KURUMA: A seeming grade-school student who's actually a high-school aged seventeen years old, Chidori (like others) possesses celestial DNA and therefore also has some amount of celestial power. These days, though, the only power Chidori wants is the power to make Yûhi notice her...even if she says she doesn't, which naturally means she does.

HOWELL: A brilliant research scientist working in the Mikage labs directly accountable to Kagami himself, Alexander Howell ("Alec") spends what little time he doesn't spend in the lab watching anime, playing video games, collecting action figures...a real otaku, in other words.

DR. KUROZUKA: A gruff-talking country doctor who's also endlessly kind, "Kurozuka-sensei" is there with open arms to welcome both Tôya and Aya into their new lives as a self-supporting couple...or mostly self-supporting, anyway.

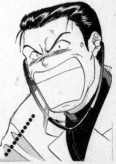

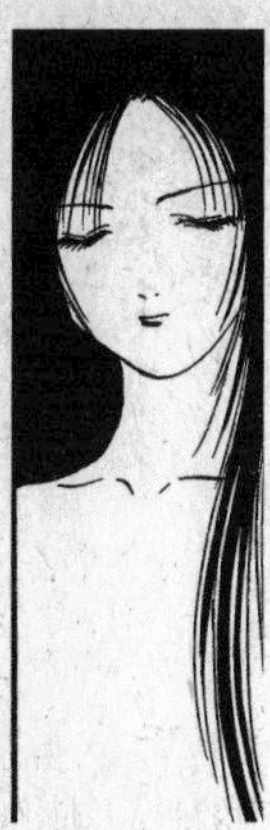

CERES: A ten'nyo or "celestial being" prevented from returning to the heavens after her hagoromo or "celestial robes" were stolen, Ceres bears little love for the descendants born of her forced union with a mortal male—the being known as "the Progenitor."

TÔYA: It isn't just about what you've done, but what you'll do—this is the realization Tôya makes on the eve of his reunion with his beloved Aya. And yet...was it the right thing to do, taking his love away from her friends, what's left of her family, her other life...?

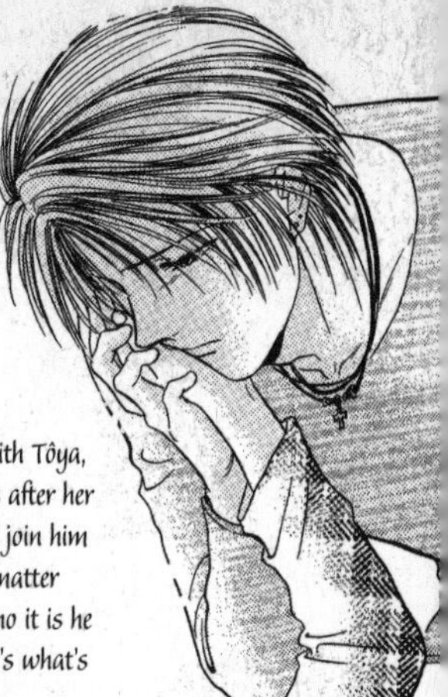

AYA MIKAGE: Reunited with Tôya, her mysterious lover, Aya resolves after her liberation from the Mikage labs to join him in the search for his identity. No matter what it is he's done, no matter who it is he once was, she loves him, and that's what's important.

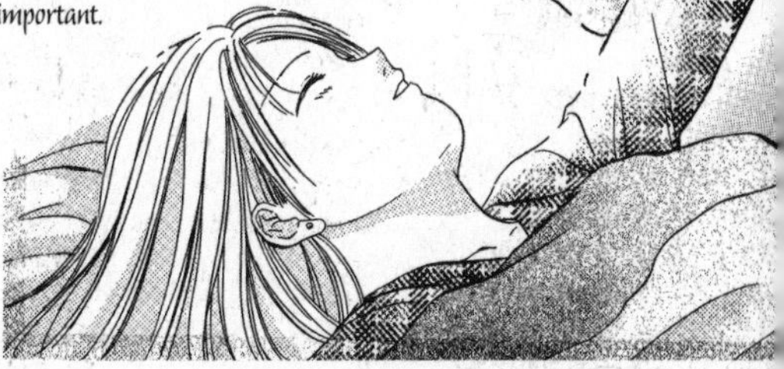

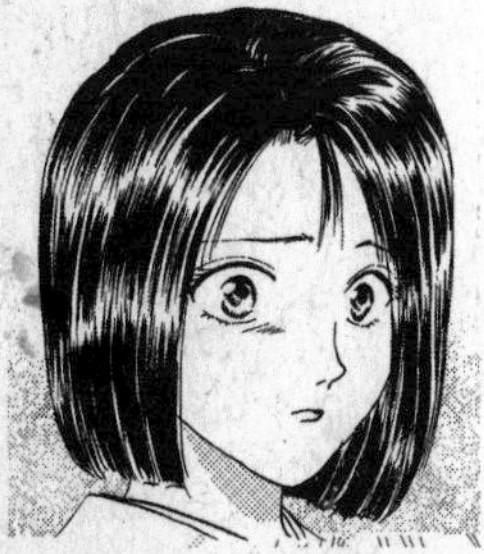

SUZUMI AOGIRI: Current head of the Aogiri household (after her husband, Yûhi's half-brother, passed away) and possessor of some ten'nyo or "celestial" blood herself. A "big sister" figure to both Yûhi and to Aya, from the start Suzumi's protection and support has meant a great deal...maybe even the difference between Aya's life and death.

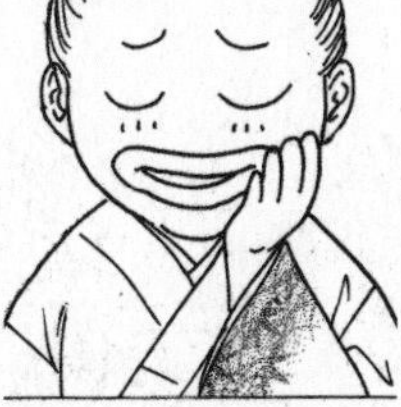

MRS. Q (ODA-KYÛ): Eccentric yet loyal-to-a-fault servant (?) to the Aogiri household...and not without a few secret powers of her own.

You may have noticed some unfamiliar people and things mentioned in CERES. VIZ left these Japanese pop-culture references as they originally appeared in the manga series. Here's an explanation for those who may not be so J-Pop savvy:

Page 35: "OTAKU" With anime and manga no longer the cryptic hobbies they once were in the U.S., otaku (which is generally taken to mean "fan") now seem to come in all shapes and sizes, all countries and colors. What differentiates an otaku from a regular ol', garden-variety "fan"...? If you can answer that question, you yourself probably are one.

Page 101: TEXT OF CHIDORI'S LETTER "I'm happy for you, Aya! You needed to find happiness [Text obscured—Ed.] ...time I made some progress with my own love life! (Yeah, right.) I'll visit when I can—call anytime!"

Page 129: "KOGAL" Its etymology uncertain, most likely this term for high-school age Lolitas (what Humbert Humbert would have called "nymphets") descends from the Japanese word for "high-school student"—kôkôsei—and the English cognate gyaru, for "girl" or "gal." Possibly unrelated is the feminine diminutive suffix -ko (Mariko, Eriko, etc.) which of course can also be used as a nominative ("A-ko"="Girl 'A'").

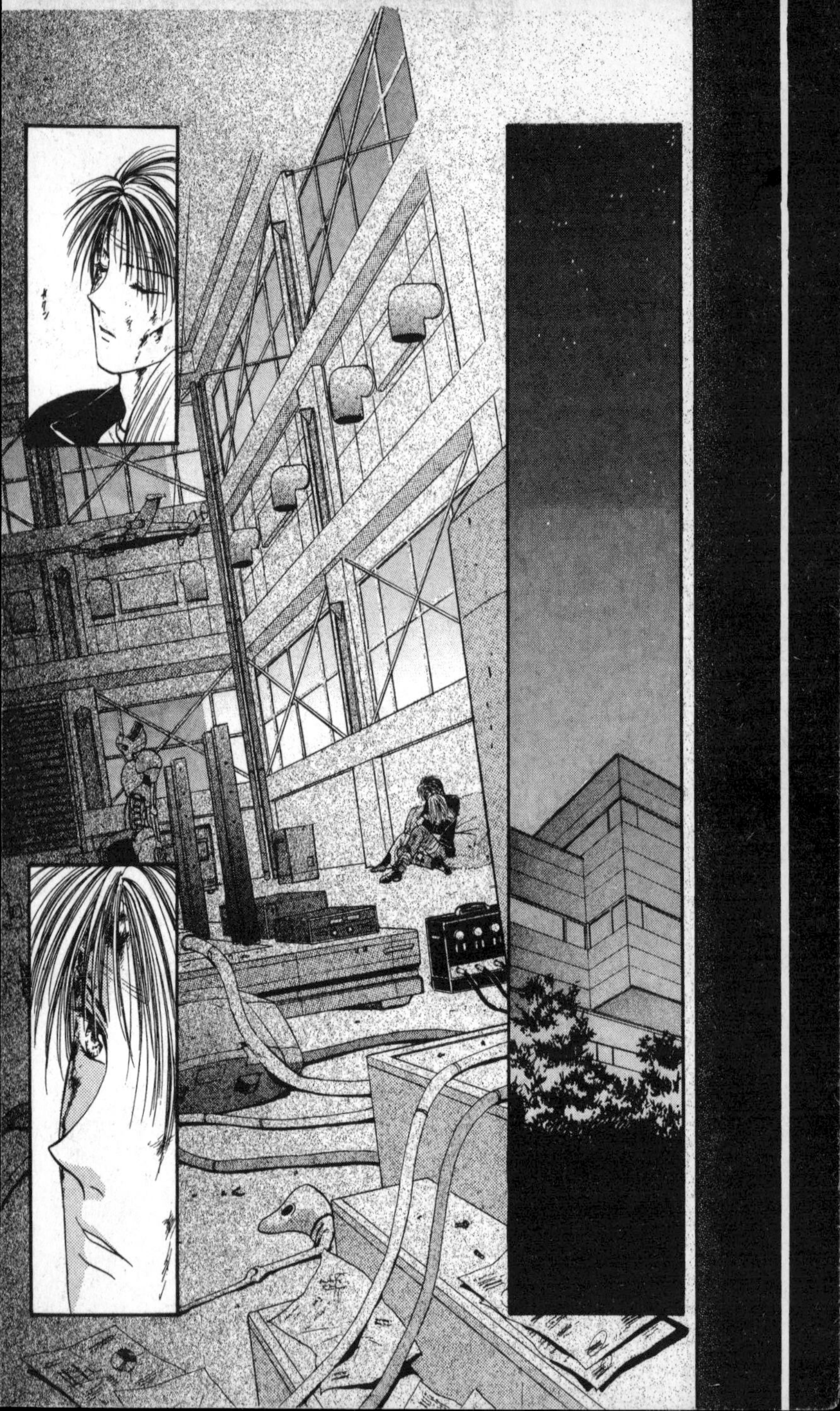

Ceres: 11

Hi, Watase here!! I'm actually writing this on a plane. Where did I go? I'll never tell. ♥ (Not that it was like a big deal, or anything....)

I hear there's still a lot of **Fushigi Yûgi** fans looking for CD dramas, videos, music CDs, etc., so here's some info. Before anything else: the first **FY** artbook has been reprinted [in Japan], so it should be easier to find now. (You'll probably have a harder time finding the second one—it had images from the anime, and was full of stuff like a chat between me and two of the voice-actors, production designs, and illustrations that weren't in the first artbook.) For info on other anime-related videos, CDs, etc., please inquire below:

- FOR VIDEOS and LDs:
  Bandai Visual (03)5828-3001
- FOR CDs:
  Bandai Music Entertainment
  (03)5379-3517
- OTHER MERCHANDISE:
  Pierrot Project (0422)70-3453
- For artbooks and drama CDs (Volumes 4-6 are still in stock), you'll have to order through a bookstore, or contact the Shogakukan Sales Department directly at (03)3230-5749.

I don't sell any of this myself, so please don't send your orders to me! The only stuff I have is for my own, personal collection. ☺ I'm not in charge of merchandise production either, so please contact the companies listed above directly. Please refrain also from sending me money with your letters, because I can't do anything about it...though it **is** nice to know so many people are eager for my stuff.

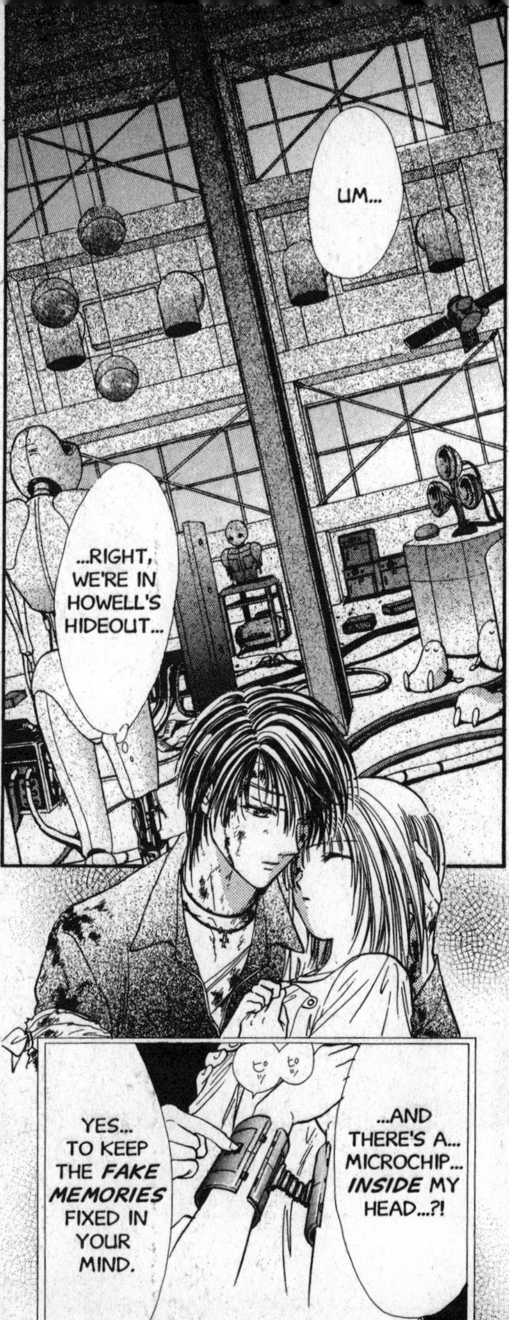
UM...
...RIGHT, WE'RE IN HOWELL'S HIDEOUT...
...AND THERE'S A... MICROCHIP... *INSIDE* MY HEAD...?!
YES... TO KEEP THE *FAKE MEMORIES* FIXED IN YOUR MIND.

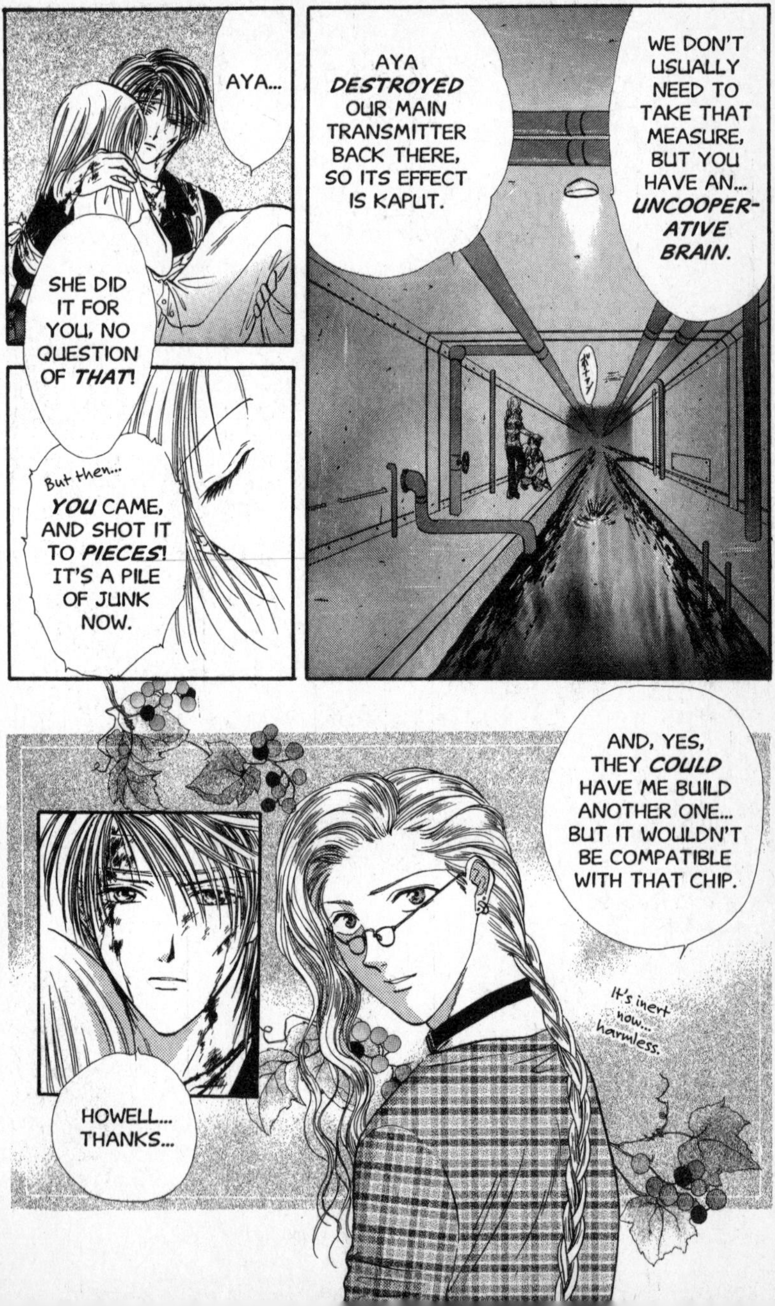
WE DON'T USUALLY NEED TO TAKE THAT MEASURE, BUT YOU HAVE AN... *UNCOOPERATIVE BRAIN.*
AYA *DESTROYED* OUR MAIN TRANSMITTER BACK THERE, SO ITS EFFECT IS KAPUT.
AYA...
SHE DID IT FOR YOU, NO QUESTION OF *THAT*!
But then...
YOU CAME, AND SHOT IT TO *PIECES*! IT'S A PILE OF JUNK NOW.
AND, YES, THEY *COULD* HAVE ME BUILD ANOTHER ONE... BUT IT WOULDN'T BE COMPATIBLE WITH THAT CHIP.
It's inert now... harmless.
HOWELL... THANKS...

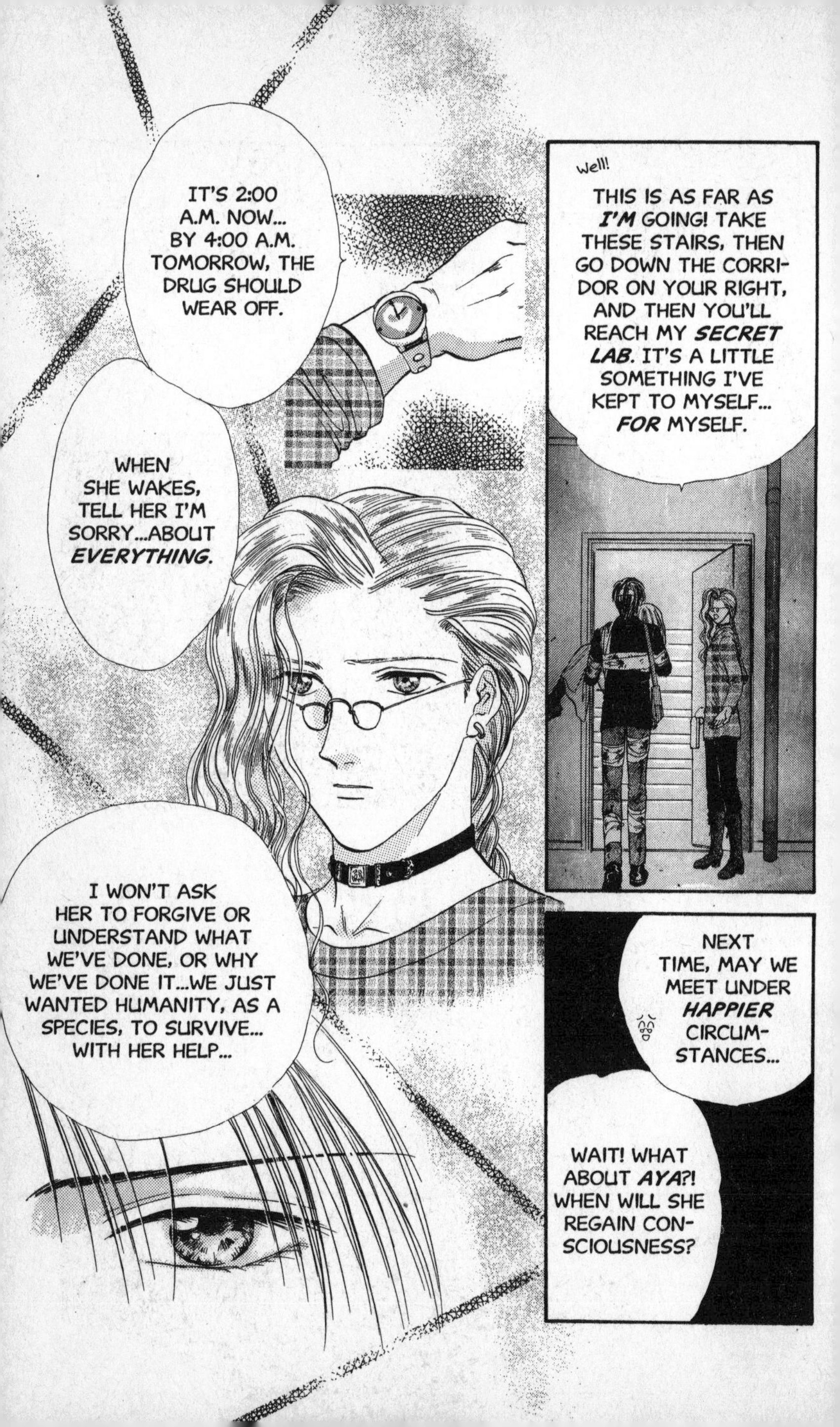
Well!
THIS IS AS FAR AS I'M GOING! TAKE THESE STAIRS, THEN GO DOWN THE CORRIDOR ON YOUR RIGHT, AND THEN YOU'LL REACH MY SECRET LAB. IT'S A LITTLE SOMETHING I'VE KEPT TO MYSELF... FOR MYSELF.
NEXT TIME, MAY WE MEET UNDER HAPPIER CIRCUMSTANCES...
WAIT! WHAT ABOUT AYA?! WHEN WILL SHE REGAIN CONSCIOUSNESS?
IT'S 2:00 A.M. NOW... BY 4:00 A.M. TOMORROW, THE DRUG SHOULD WEAR OFF.
WHEN SHE WAKES, TELL HER I'M SORRY...ABOUT EVERYTHING.
I WON'T ASK HER TO FORGIVE OR UNDERSTAND WHAT WE'VE DONE, OR WHY WE'VE DONE IT...WE JUST WANTED HUMANITY, AS A SPECIES, TO SURVIVE... WITH HER HELP...

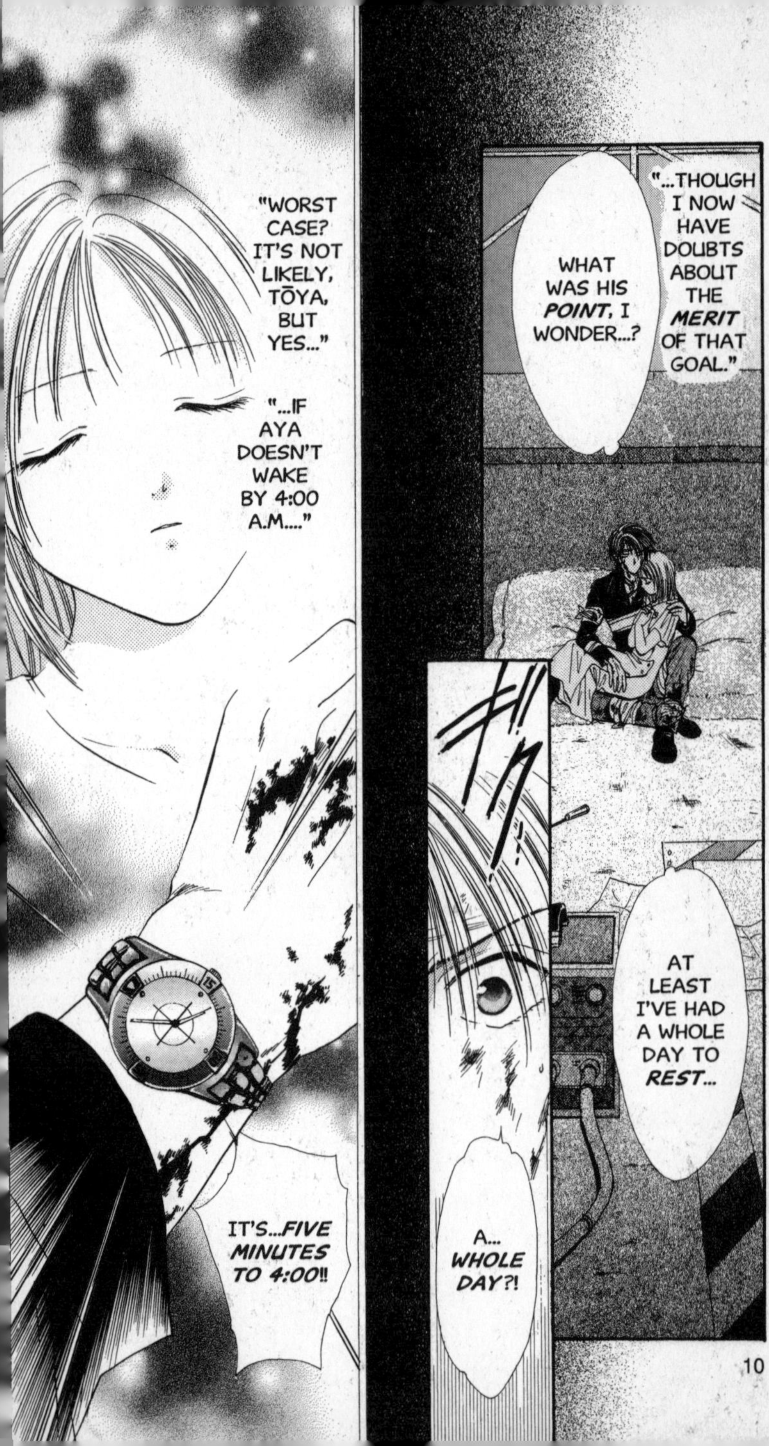
"...THOUGH I NOW HAVE DOUBTS ABOUT THE *MERIT* OF THAT GOAL."
WHAT WAS HIS *POINT*, I WONDER...?
AT LEAST I'VE HAD A WHOLE DAY TO *REST*...
A... *WHOLE DAY*?!
"WORST CASE? IT'S NOT LIKELY, TŌYA, BUT YES..."
"...IF AYA DOESN'T WAKE BY 4:00 A.M...."
IT'S...*FIVE MINUTES TO 4:00*!!

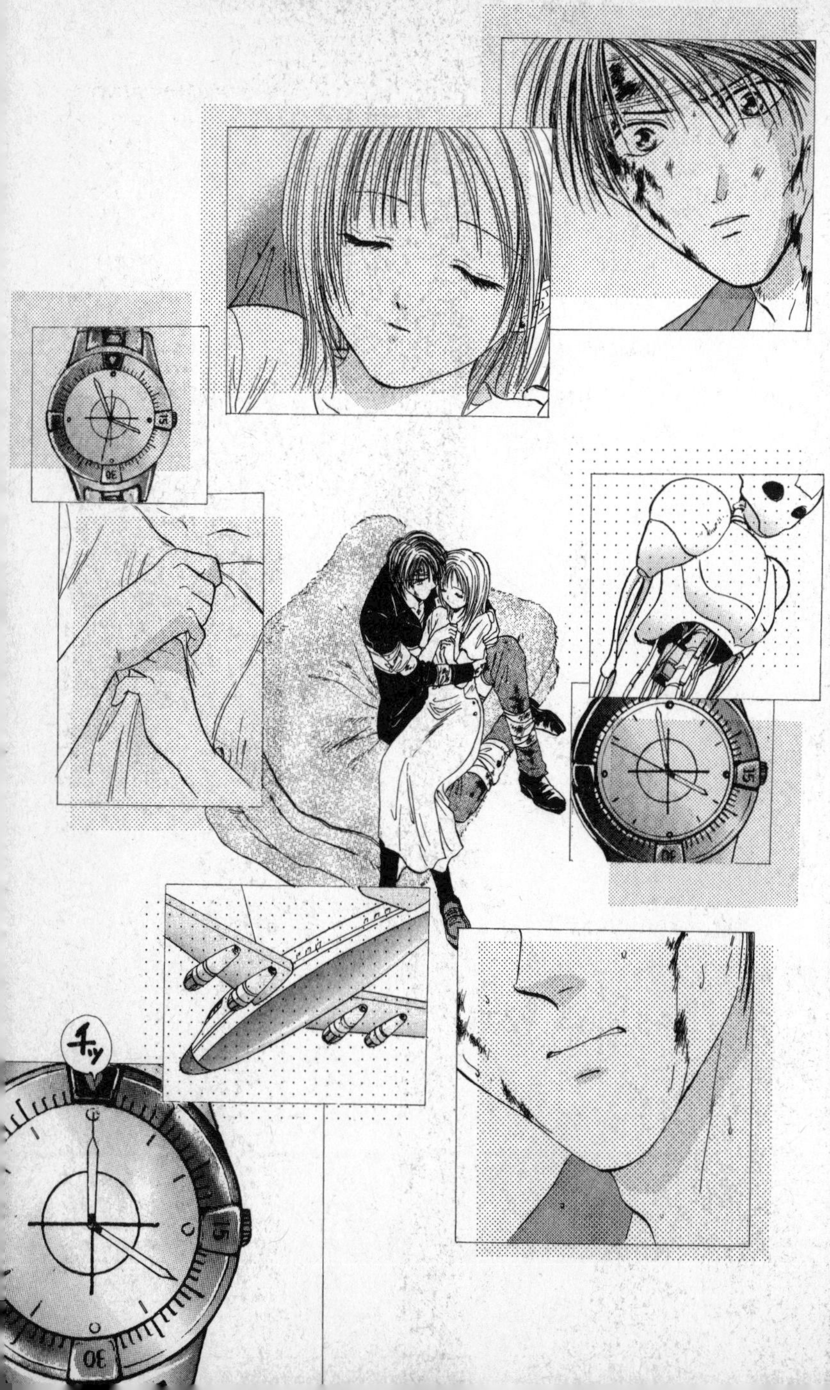
チッ

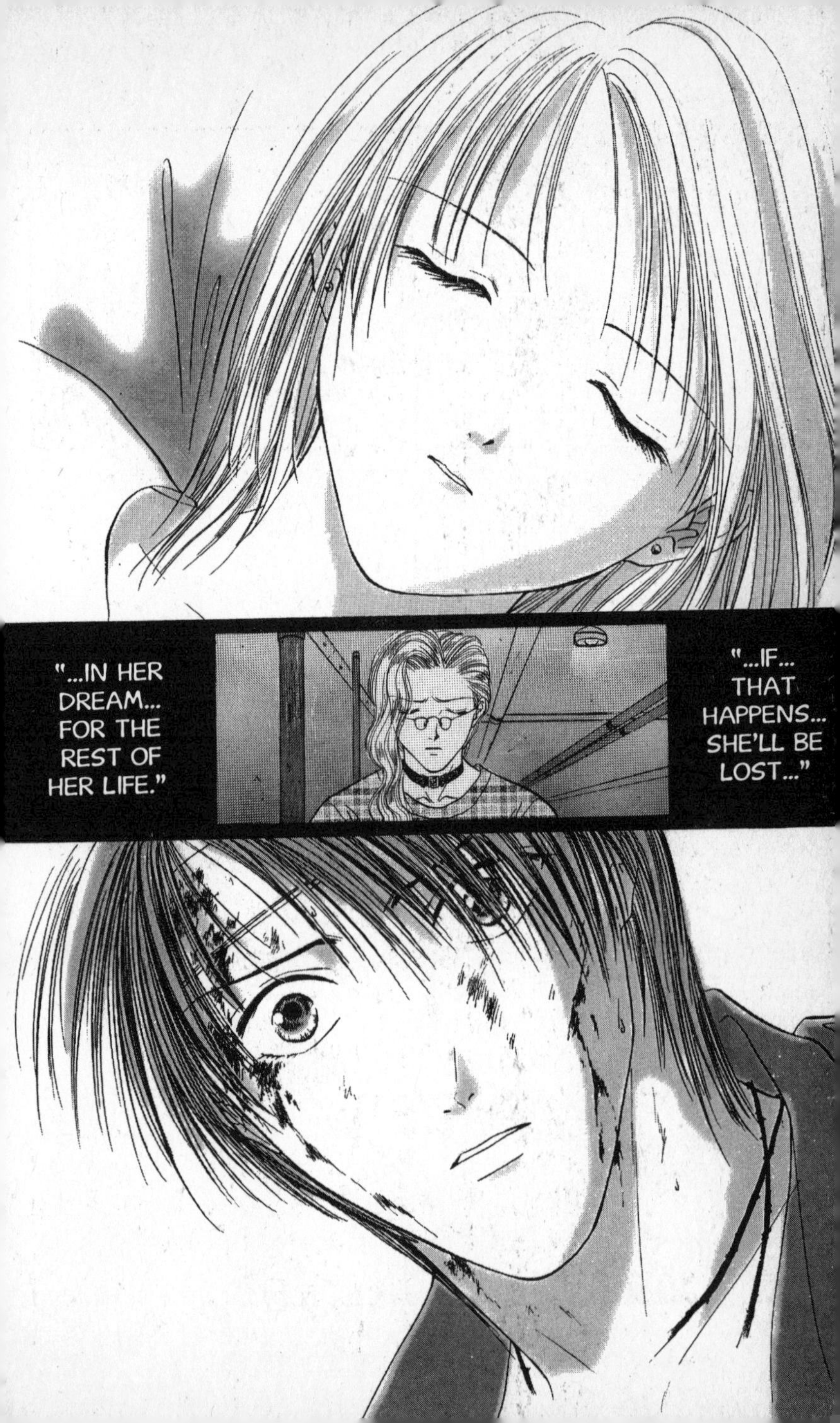
"...IF... THAT HAPPENS... SHE'LL BE LOST..."
"...IN HER DREAM... FOR THE REST OF HER LIFE."

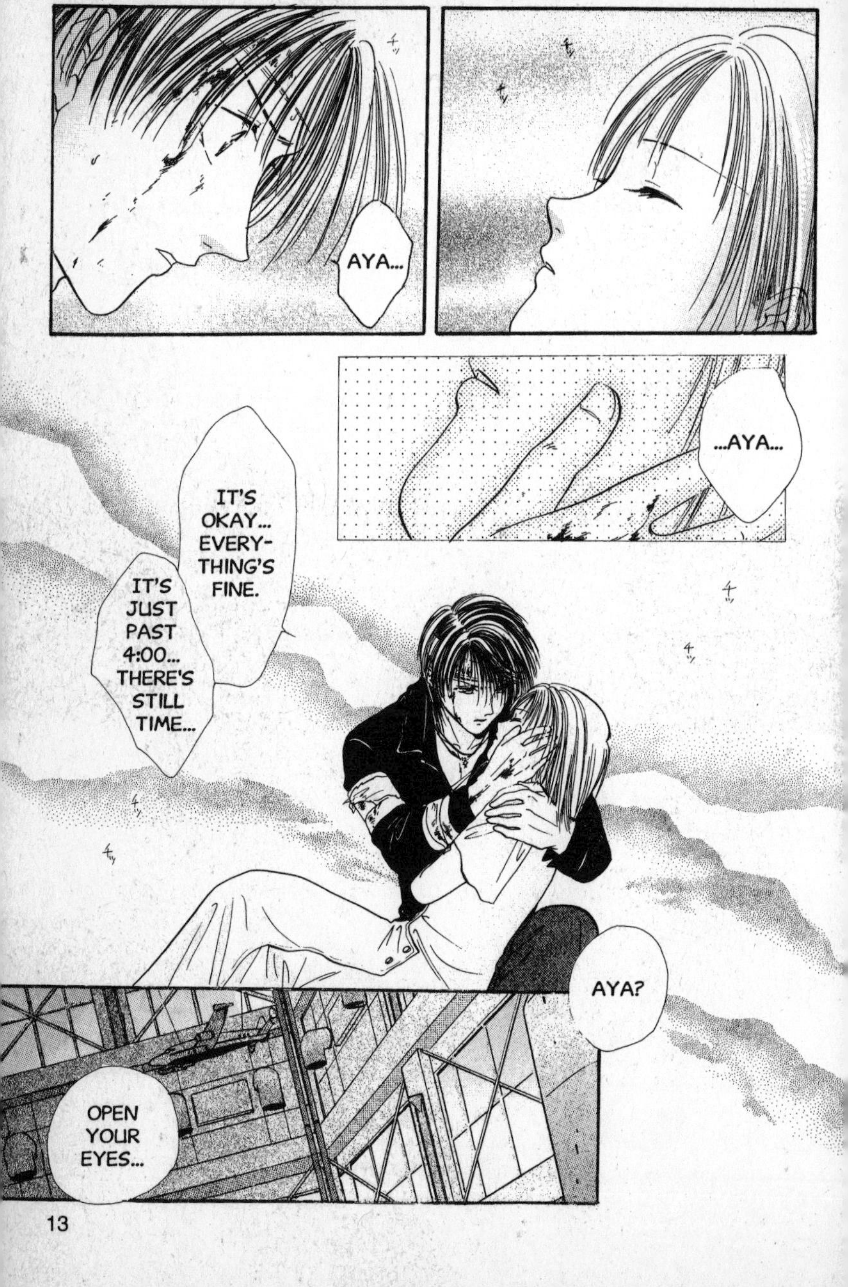
AYA...
...AYA...
IT'S OKAY... EVERYTHING'S FINE.
IT'S JUST PAST 4:00... THERE'S STILL TIME...
AYA?
OPEN YOUR EYES...

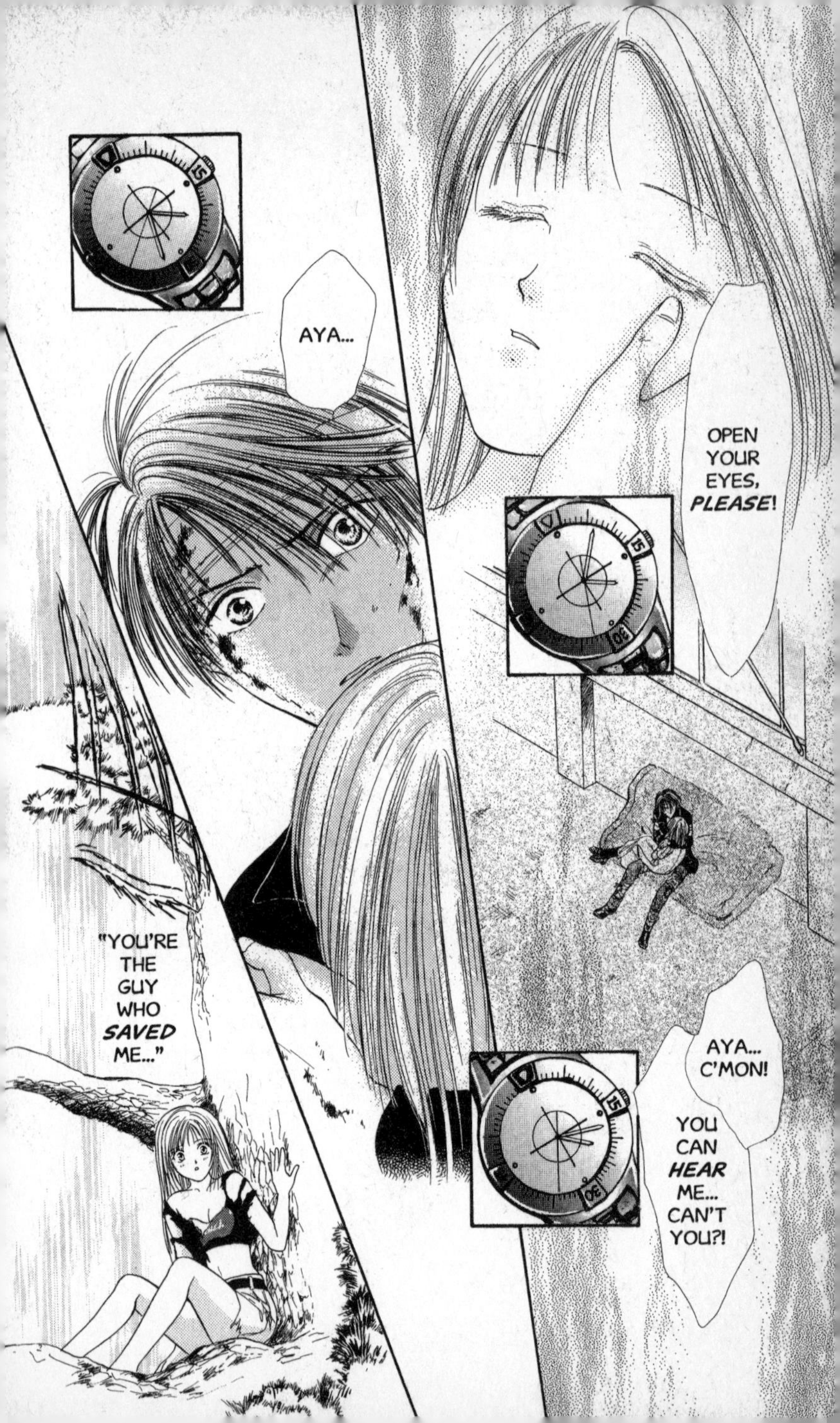
OPEN YOUR EYES, PLEASE!
AYA... C'MON!
YOU CAN HEAR ME... CAN'T YOU?!
AYA...
"YOU'RE THE GUY WHO SAVED ME..."

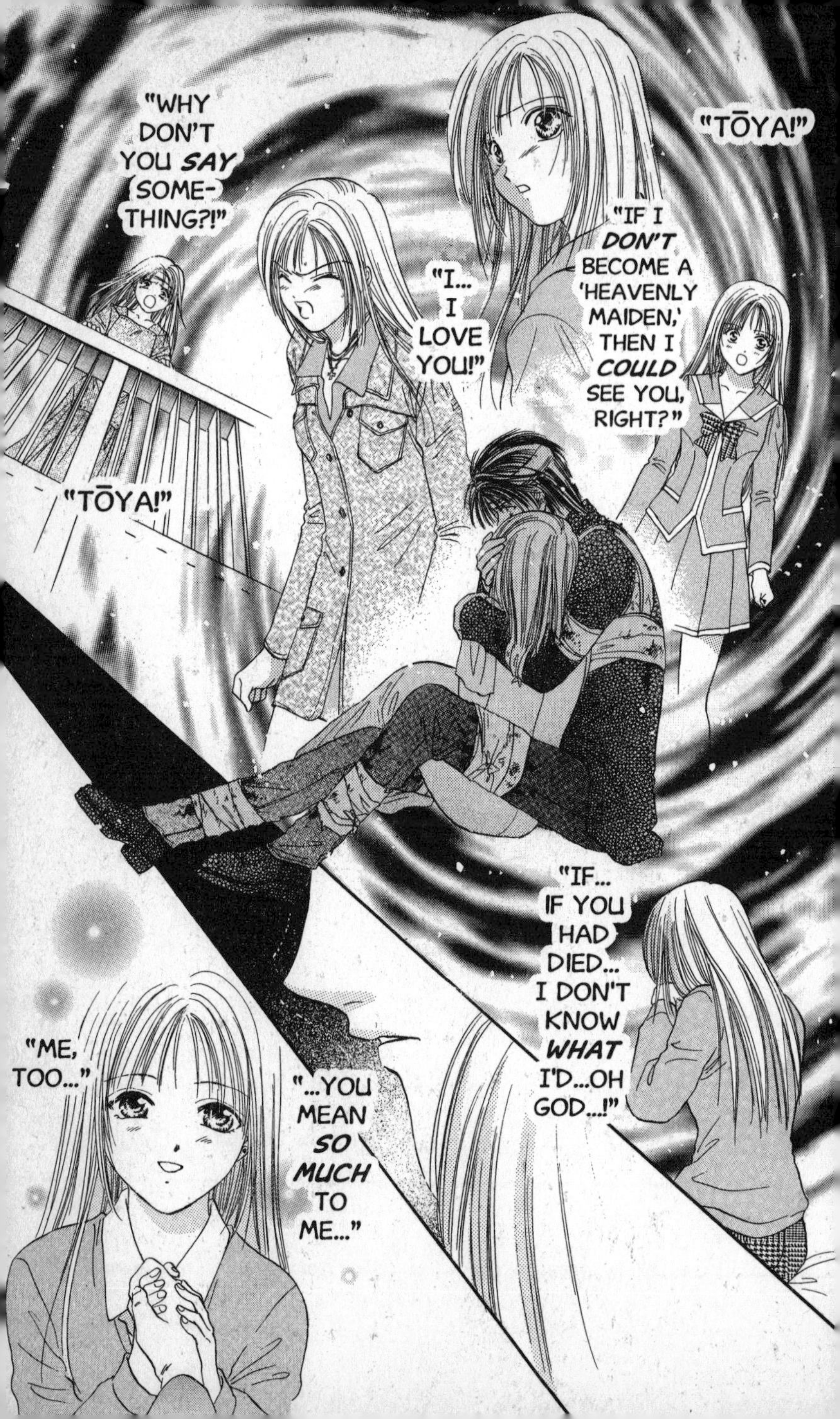
"TŌYA!"
"IF I DON'T BECOME A 'HEAVENLY MAIDEN,' THEN I COULD SEE YOU, RIGHT?"
"I... I LOVE YOU!"
"WHY DON'T YOU SAY SOME-THING?!"
"TŌYA!"
"IF... IF YOU HAD DIED... I DON'T KNOW WHAT I'D...OH GOD...!"
"...YOU MEAN SO MUCH TO ME..."
"ME, TOO..."

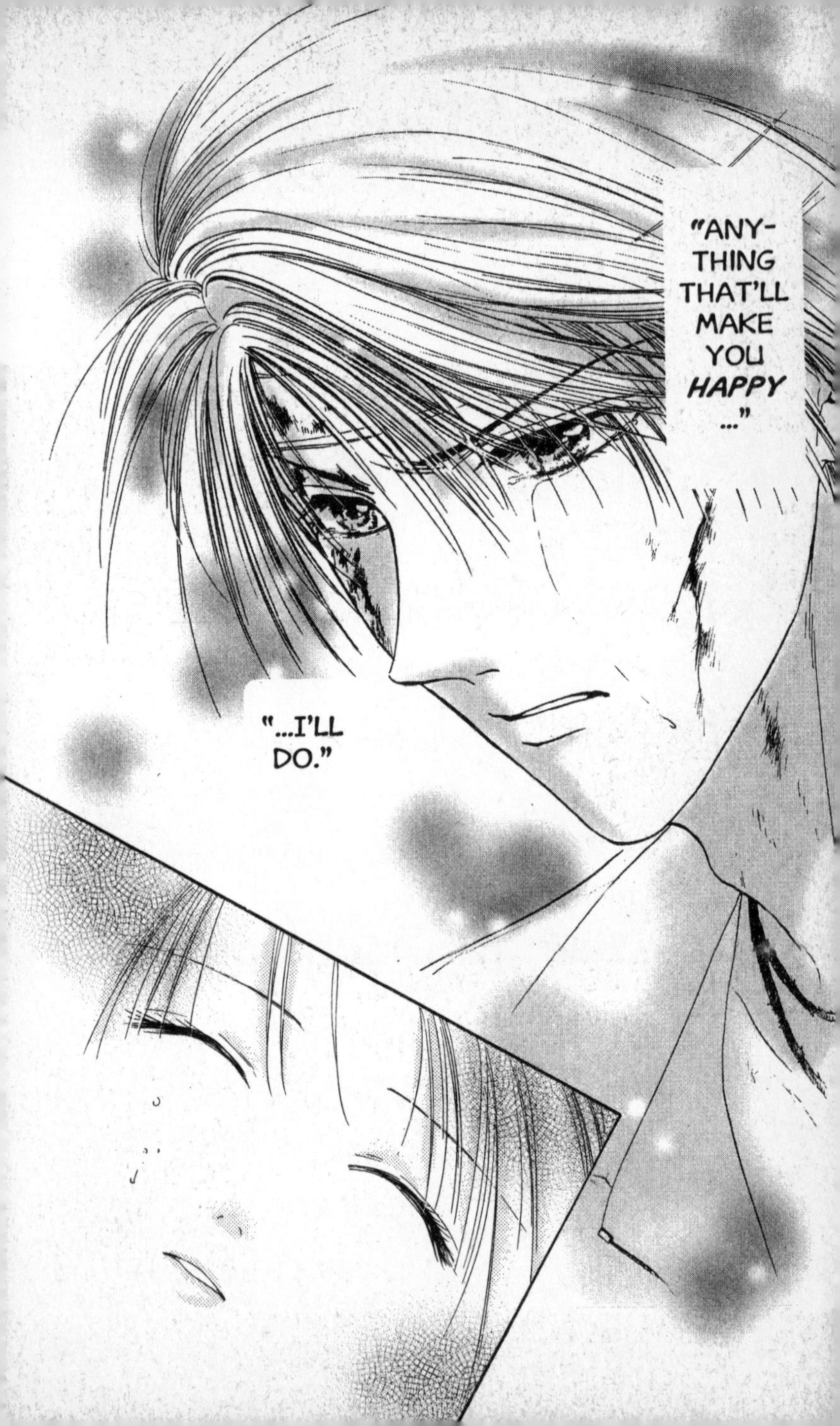
"ANY-THING THAT'LL MAKE YOU *HAPPY* ..."
"...I'LL DO."

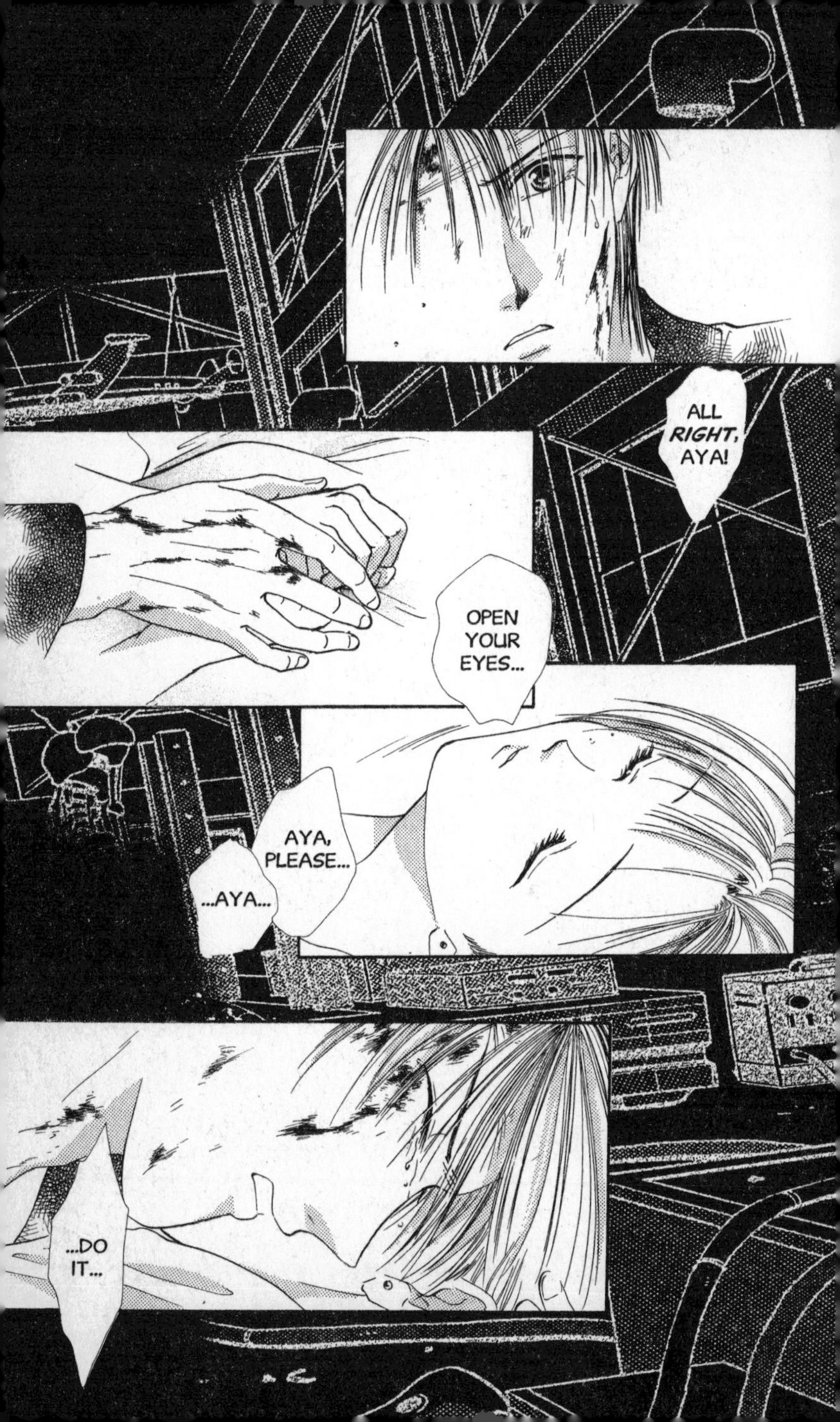
ALL RIGHT, AYA!
OPEN YOUR EYES...
AYA, PLEASE...
...AYA...
...DO IT...

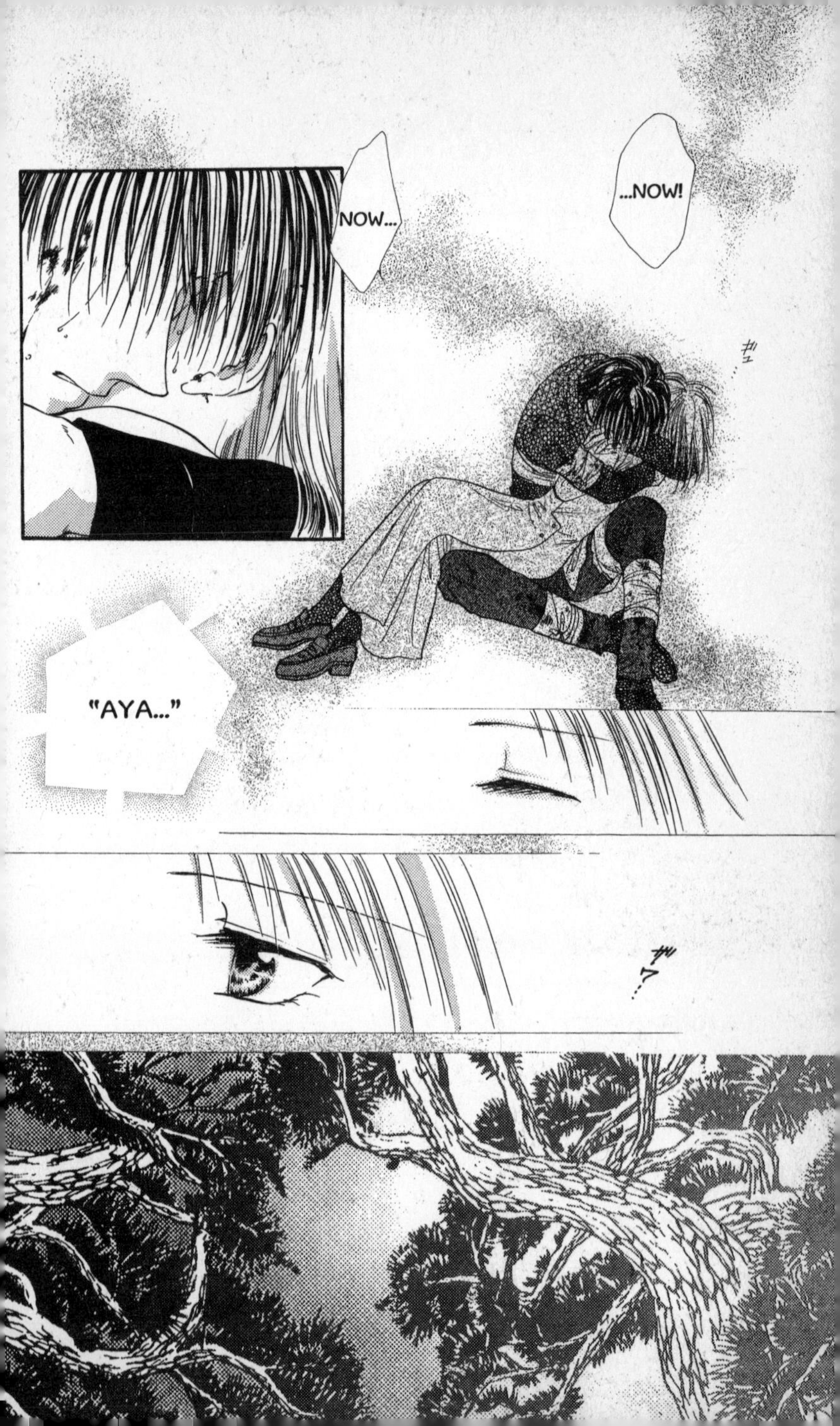
...NOW!
NOW...
"AYA..."

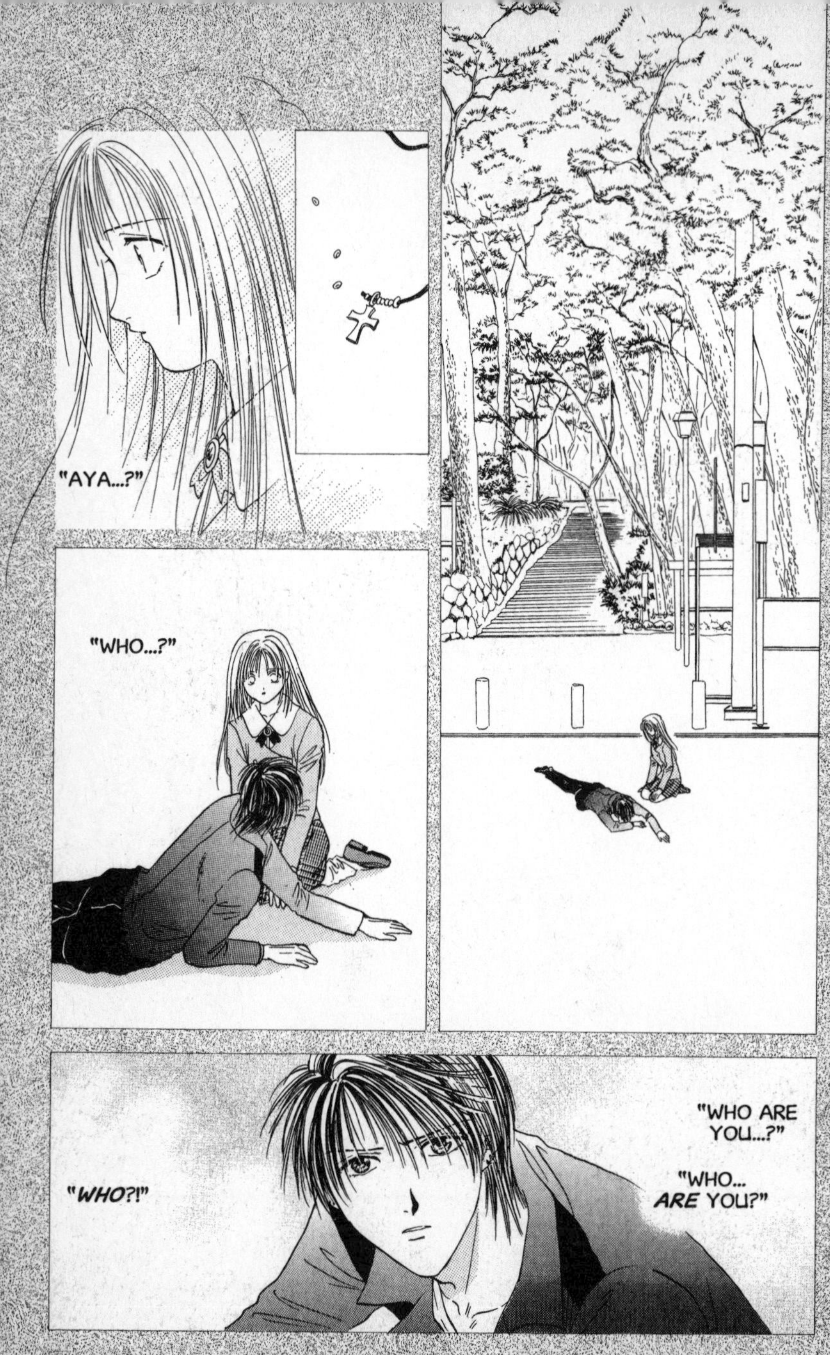
"AYA...?"
"WHO...?"
"WHO ARE YOU...?"
"WHO... *ARE* YOU?"
"*WHO?!*"

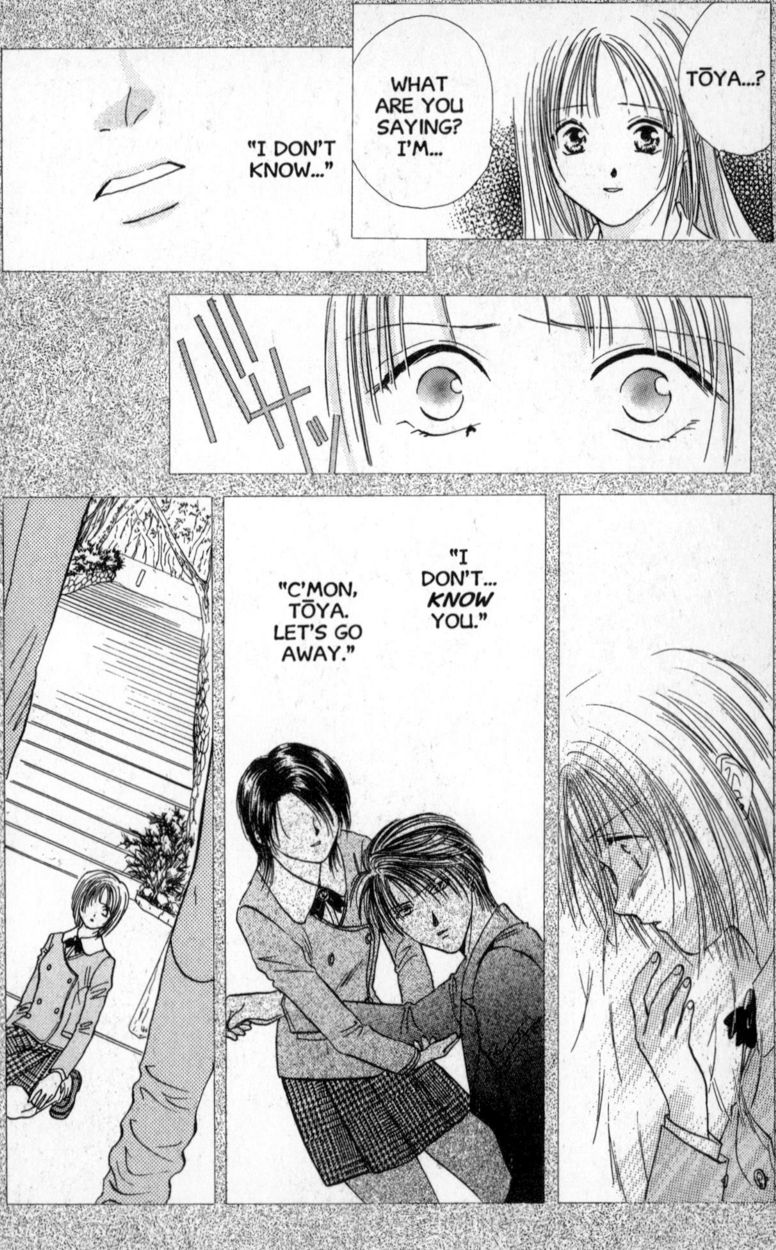
TŌYA...?
WHAT ARE YOU SAYING? I'M...
"I DON'T KNOW..."
"I DON'T... *KNOW* YOU."
"C'MON, TŌYA. LET'S GO AWAY."

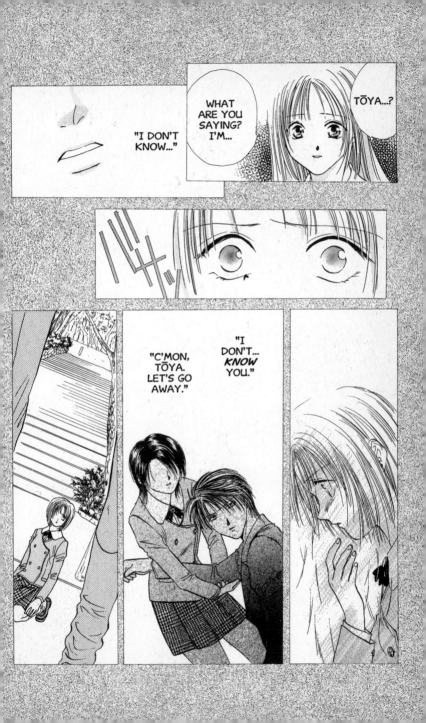

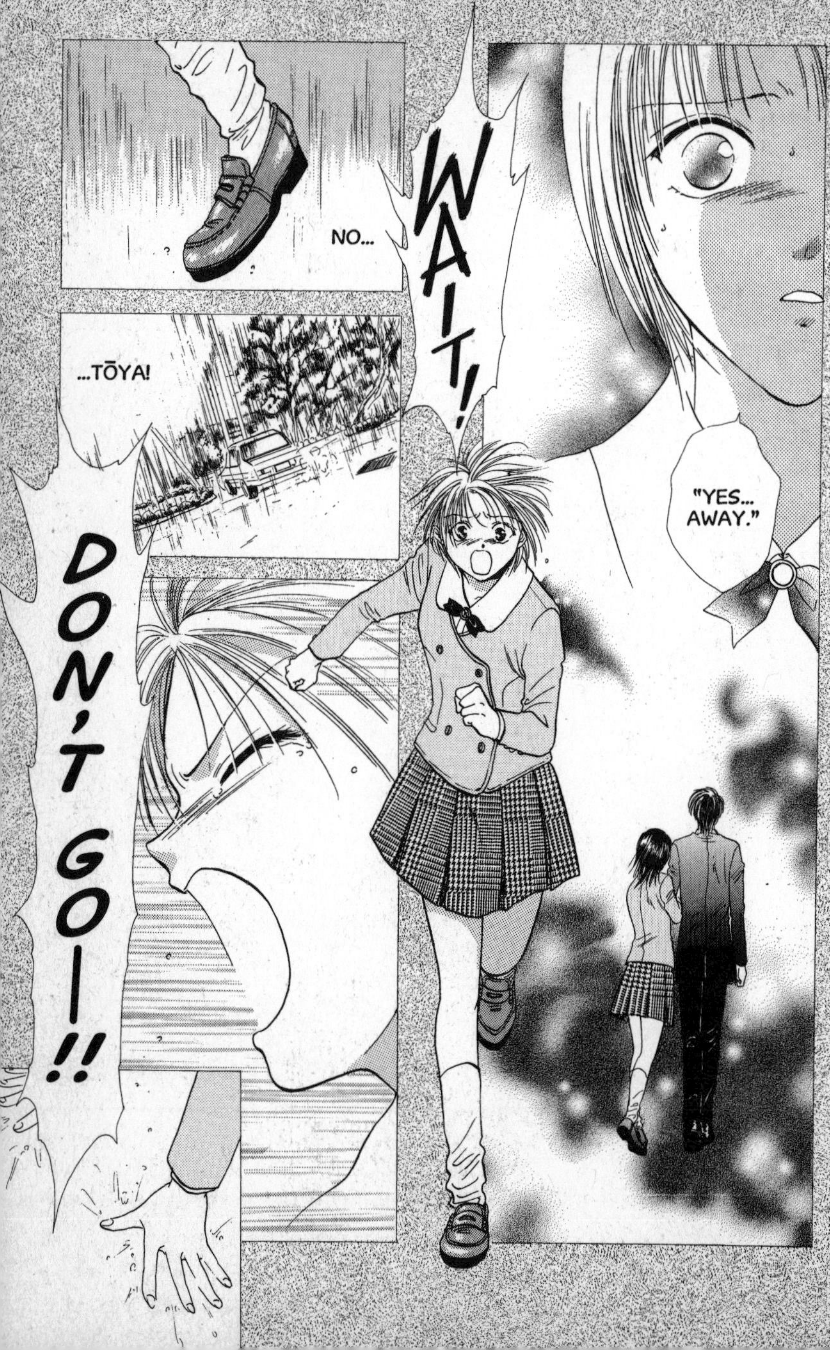
"YES... AWAY."
WAIT!
NO...
...TŌYA!
DON'T GO!!

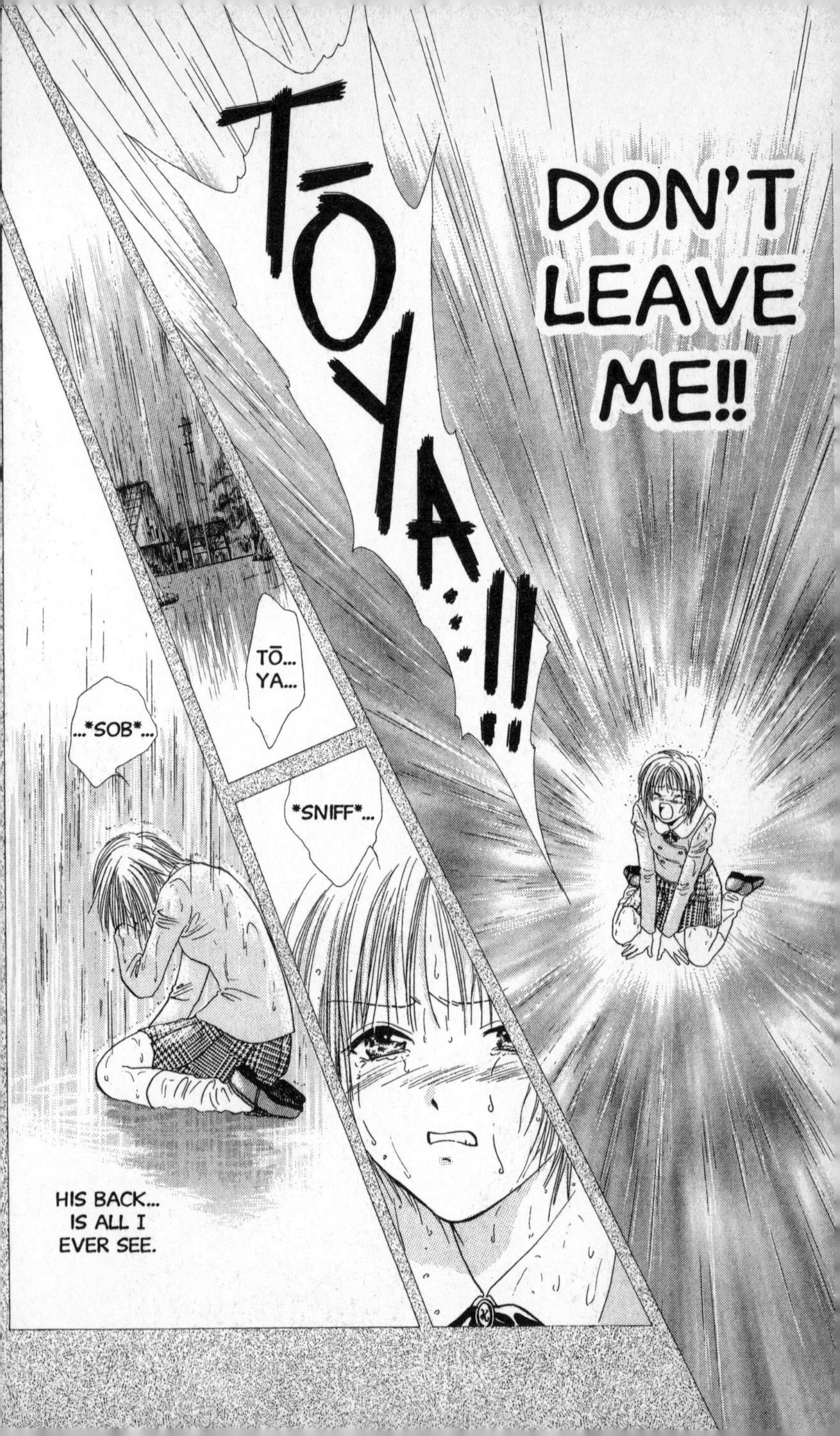
DON'T LEAVE ME!!
TŌYA...!!
TŌ... YA...
SNIFF...
...*SOB*...
HIS BACK... IS ALL I EVER SEE.

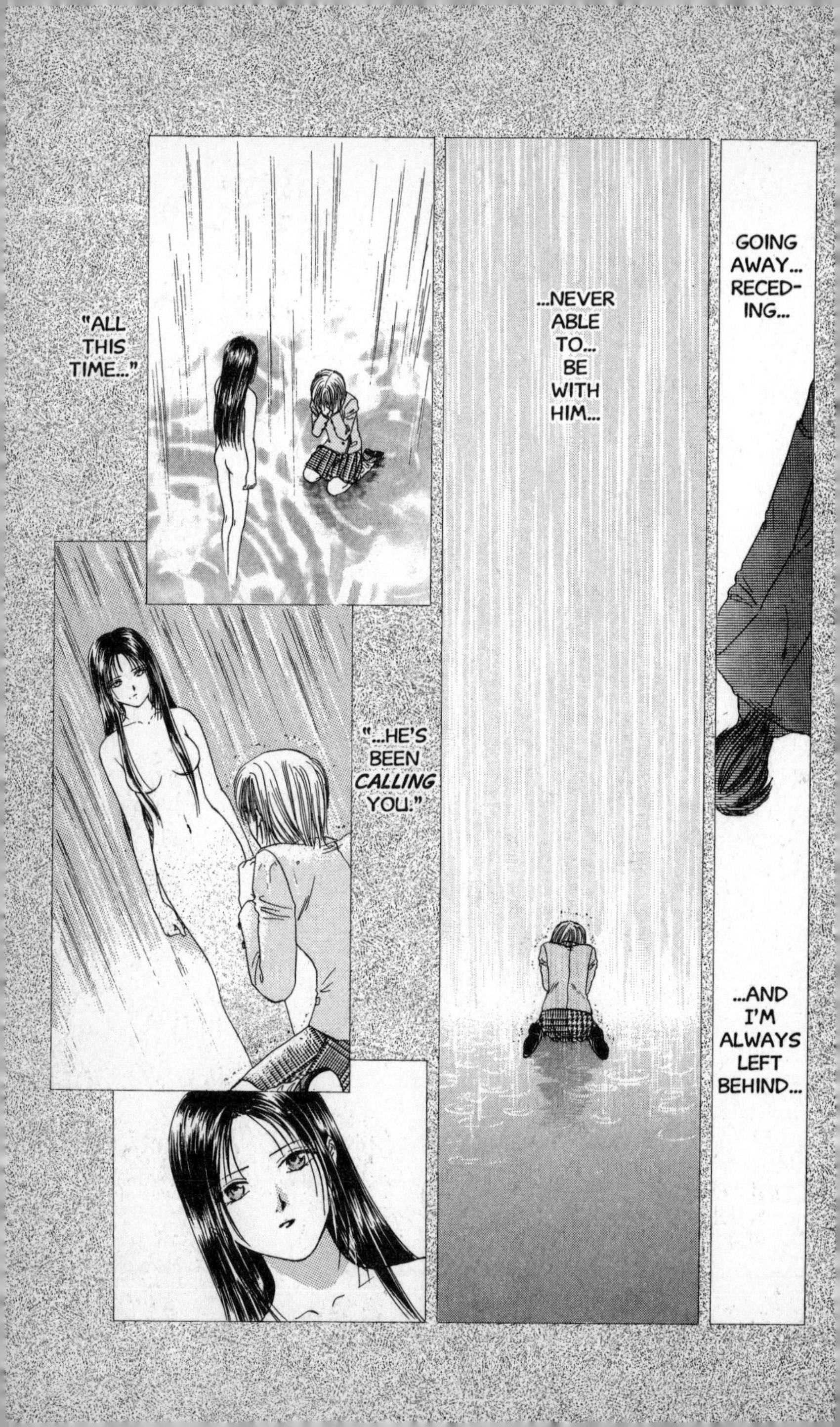
GOING AWAY... RECEDING...
...AND I'M ALWAYS LEFT BEHIND...
...NEVER ABLE TO... BE WITH HIM...
"ALL THIS TIME..."
"...HE'S BEEN CALLING YOU."

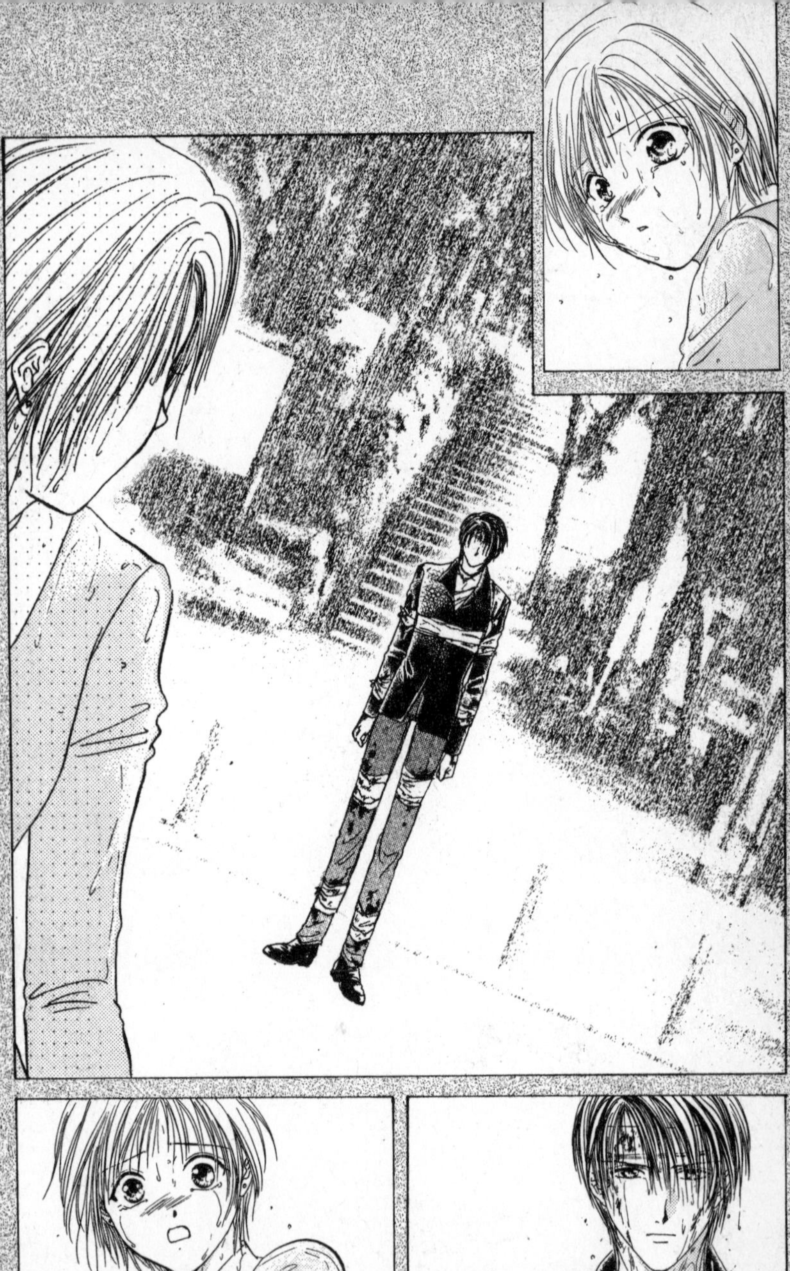

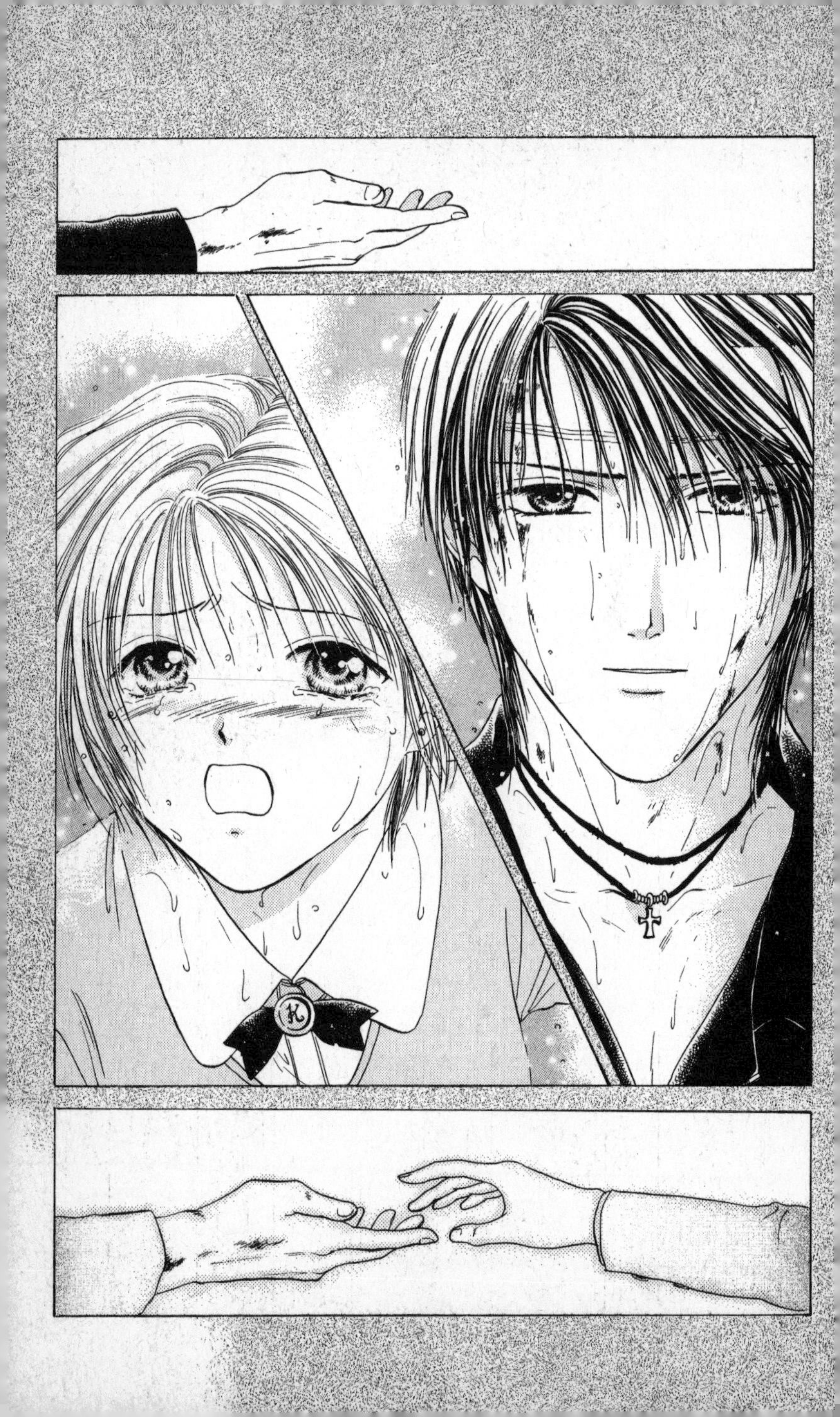

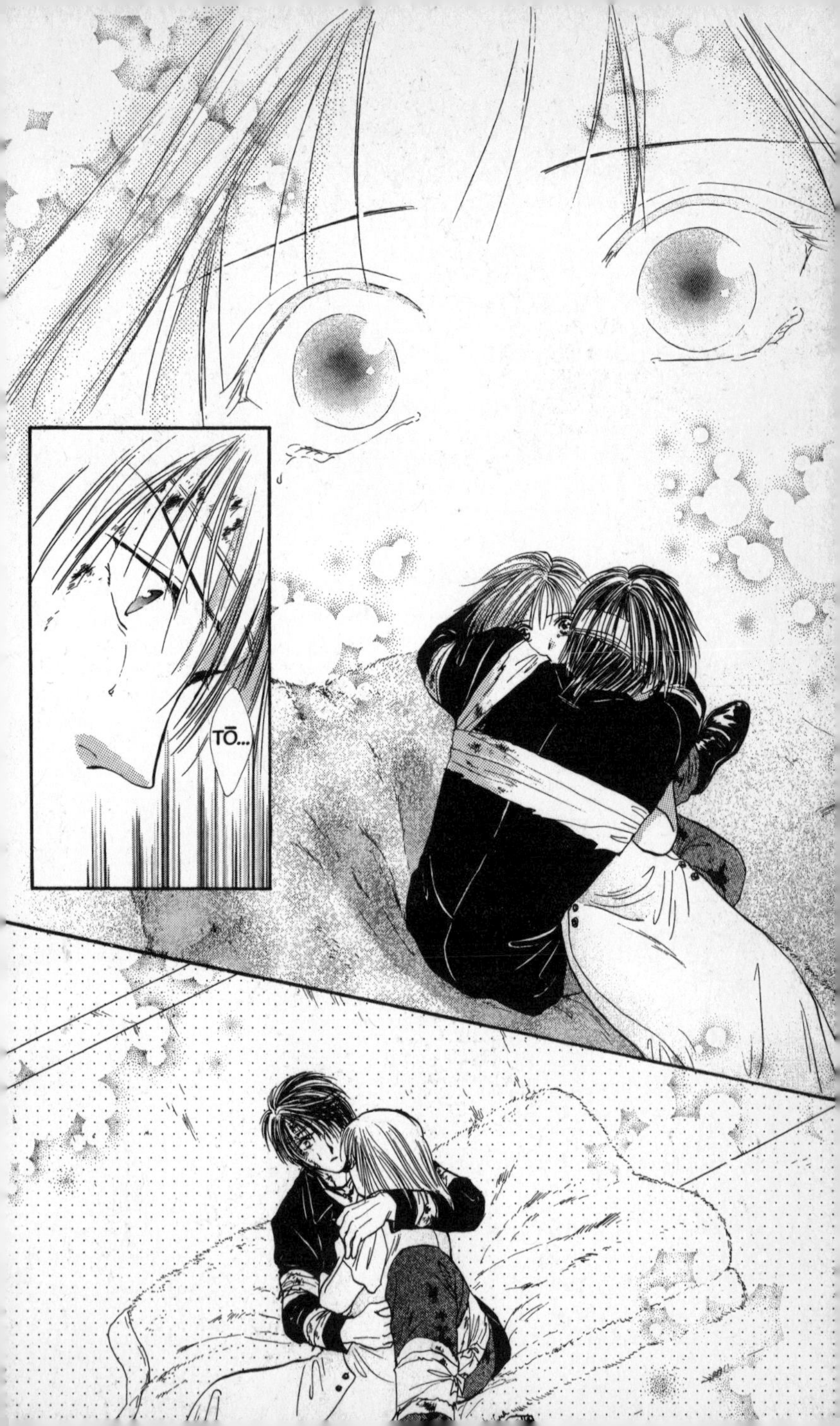
TŌ...

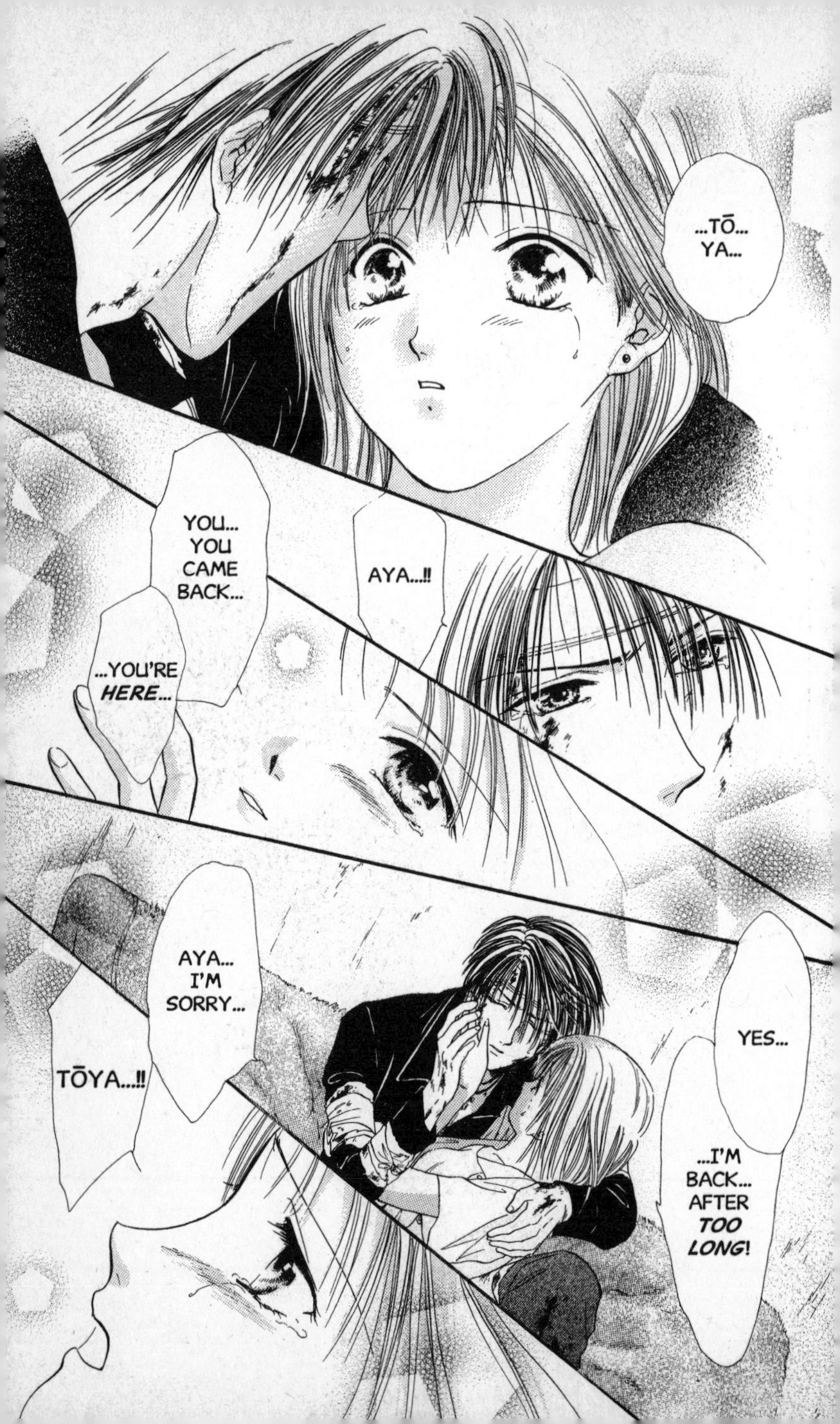
...TŌ... YA...
AYA...!!
YOU... YOU CAME BACK...
...YOU'RE *HERE*...
YES...
...I'M BACK... AFTER *TOO LONG*!
AYA... I'M SORRY...
TŌYA...!!

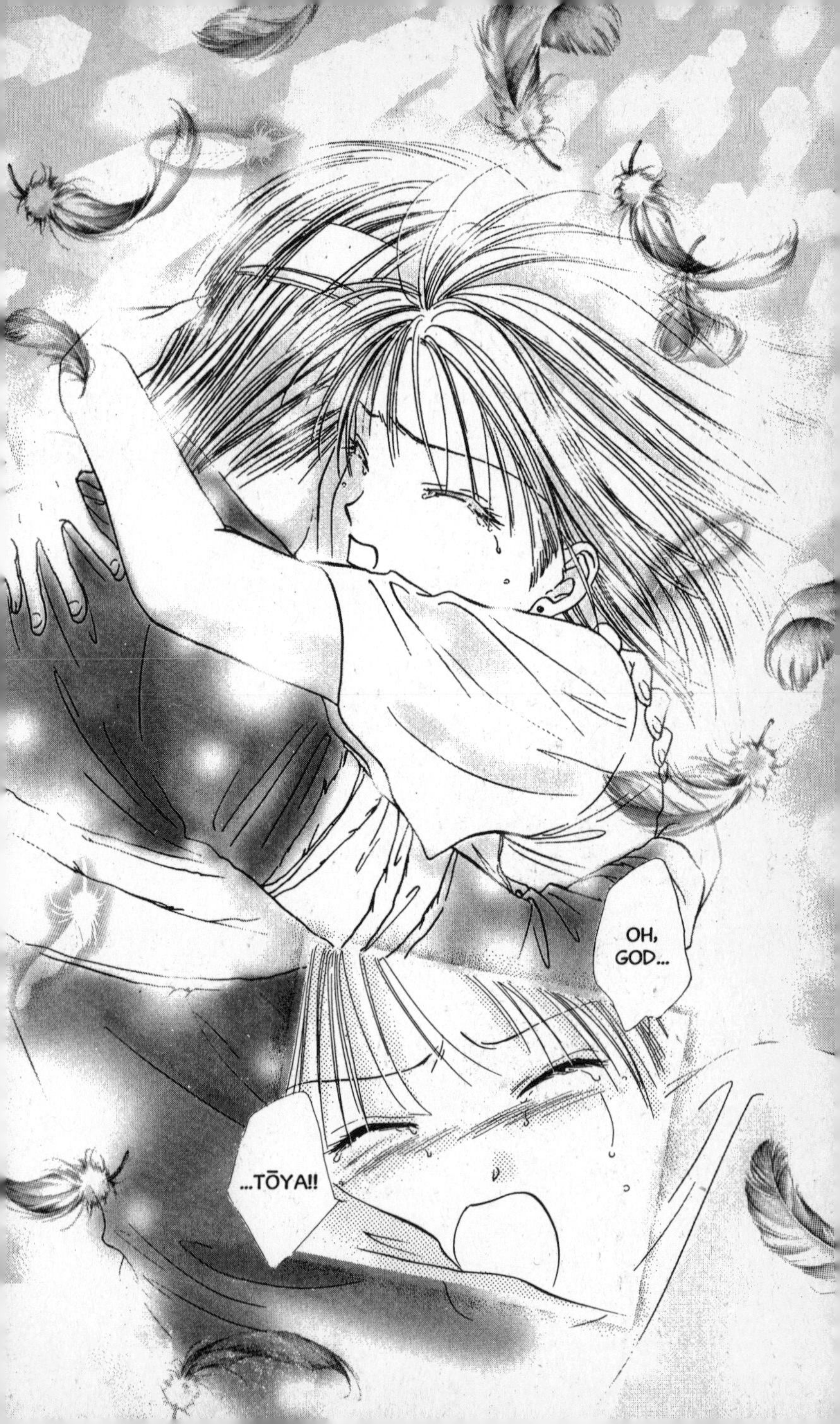
OH, GOD...
...TŌYA!!

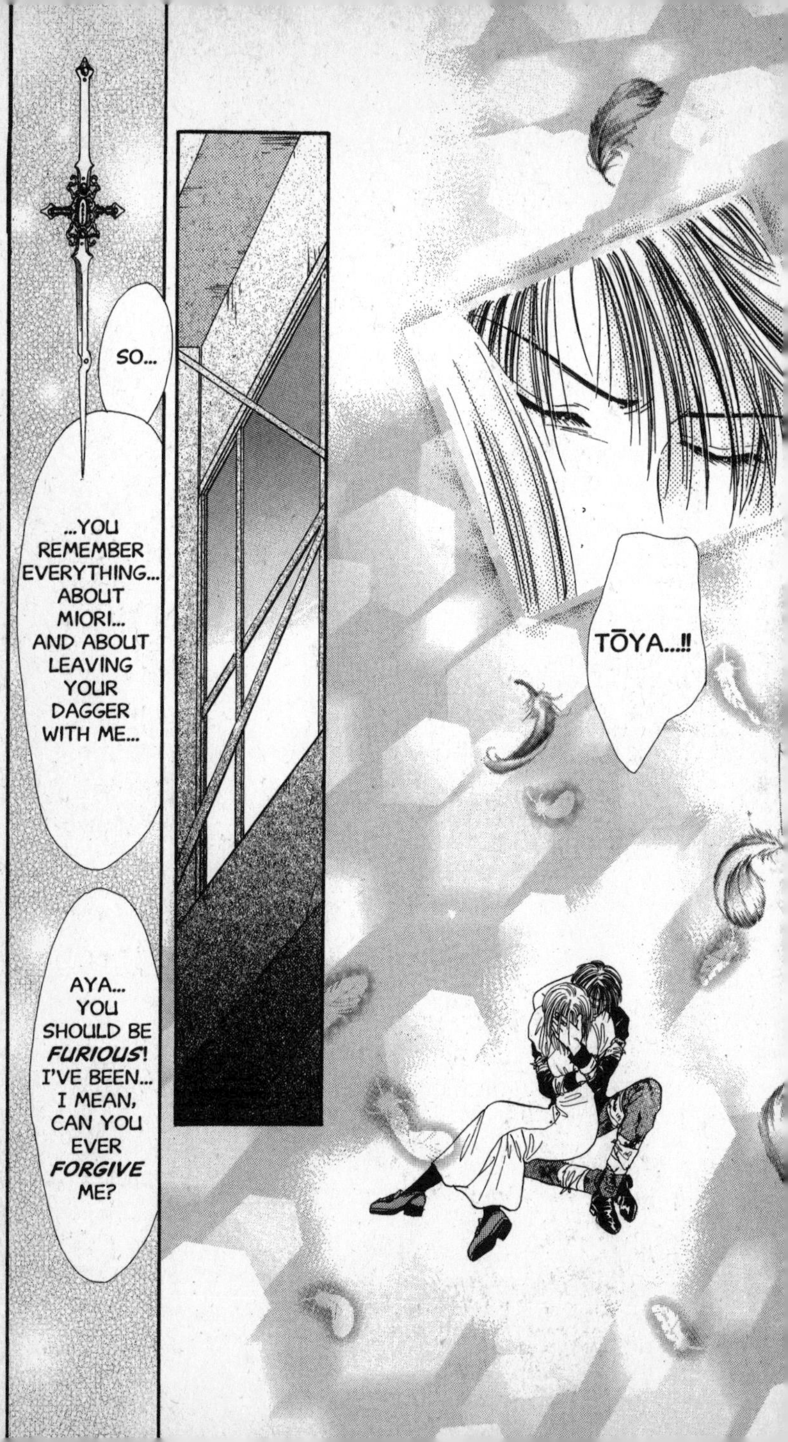
TŌYA...!!
SO...
...YOU REMEMBER EVERYTHING... ABOUT MIORI... AND ABOUT LEAVING YOUR DAGGER WITH ME...
AYA... YOU SHOULD BE ***FURIOUS***! I'VE BEEN... I MEAN, CAN YOU EVER ***FORGIVE*** ME?

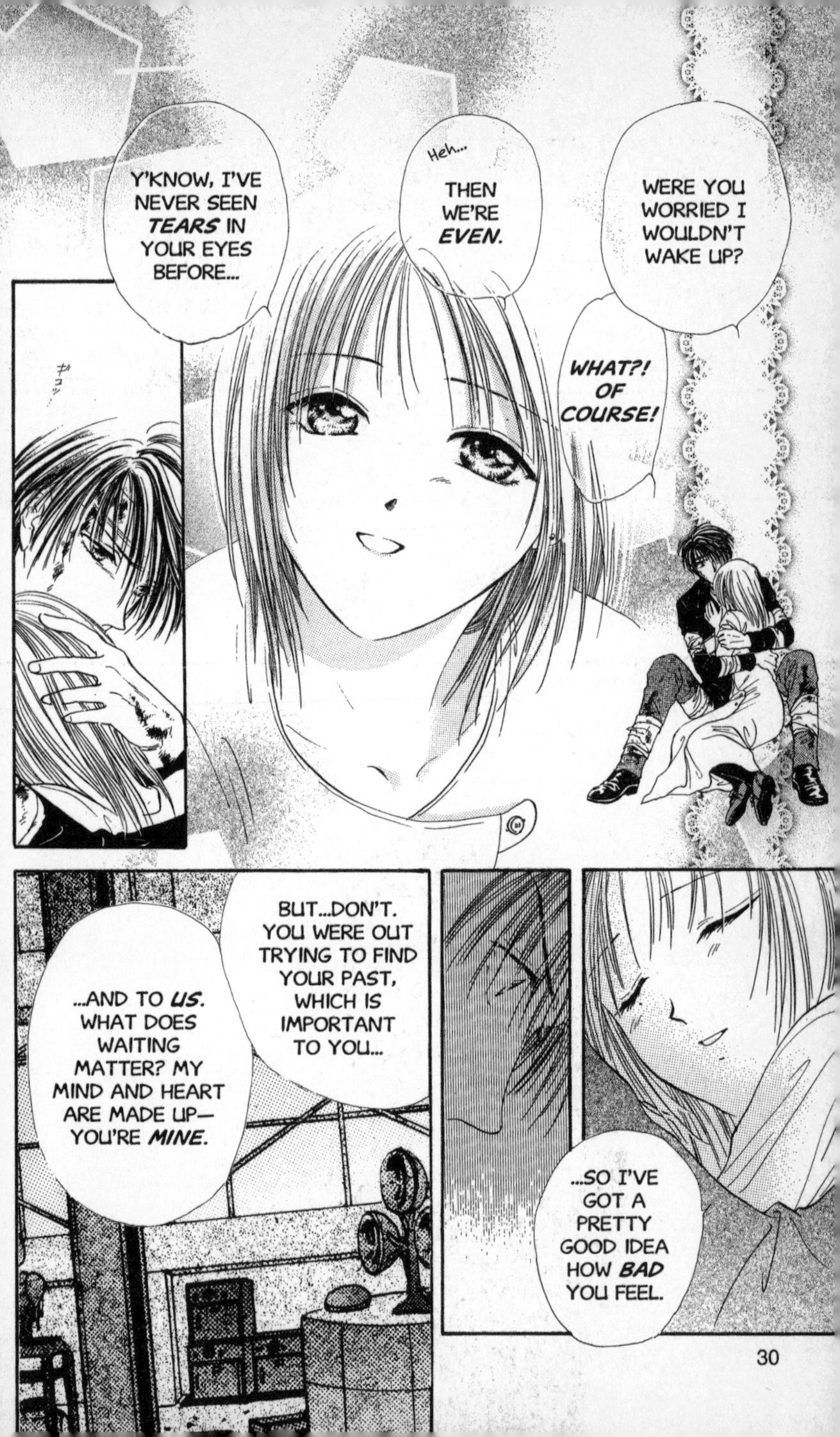
WERE YOU WORRIED I WOULDN'T WAKE UP?
WHAT?! OF COURSE!
Heh...
THEN WE'RE EVEN.
Y'KNOW, I'VE NEVER SEEN TEARS IN YOUR EYES BEFORE...
...SO I'VE GOT A PRETTY GOOD IDEA HOW BAD YOU FEEL.
BUT...DON'T. YOU WERE OUT TRYING TO FIND YOUR PAST, WHICH IS IMPORTANT TO YOU...
...AND TO US. WHAT DOES WAITING MATTER? MY MIND AND HEART ARE MADE UP— YOU'RE MINE.

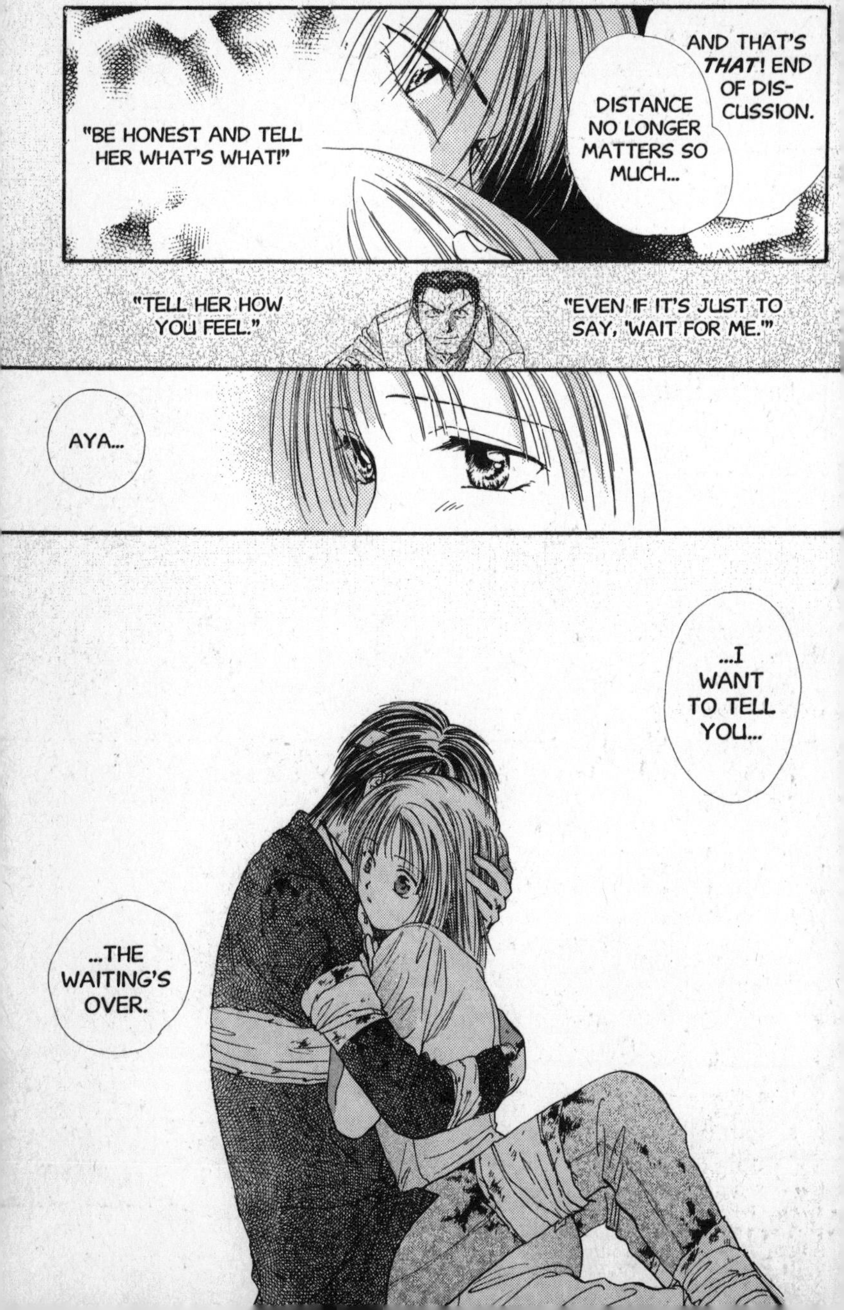
AND THAT'S *THAT*! END OF DIS-CUSSION.
DISTANCE NO LONGER MATTERS SO MUCH...
"BE HONEST AND TELL HER WHAT'S WHAT!"
"EVEN IF IT'S JUST TO SAY, 'WAIT FOR ME.'"
"TELL HER HOW YOU FEEL."
AYA...
...I WANT TO TELL YOU...
...THE WAITING'S OVER.

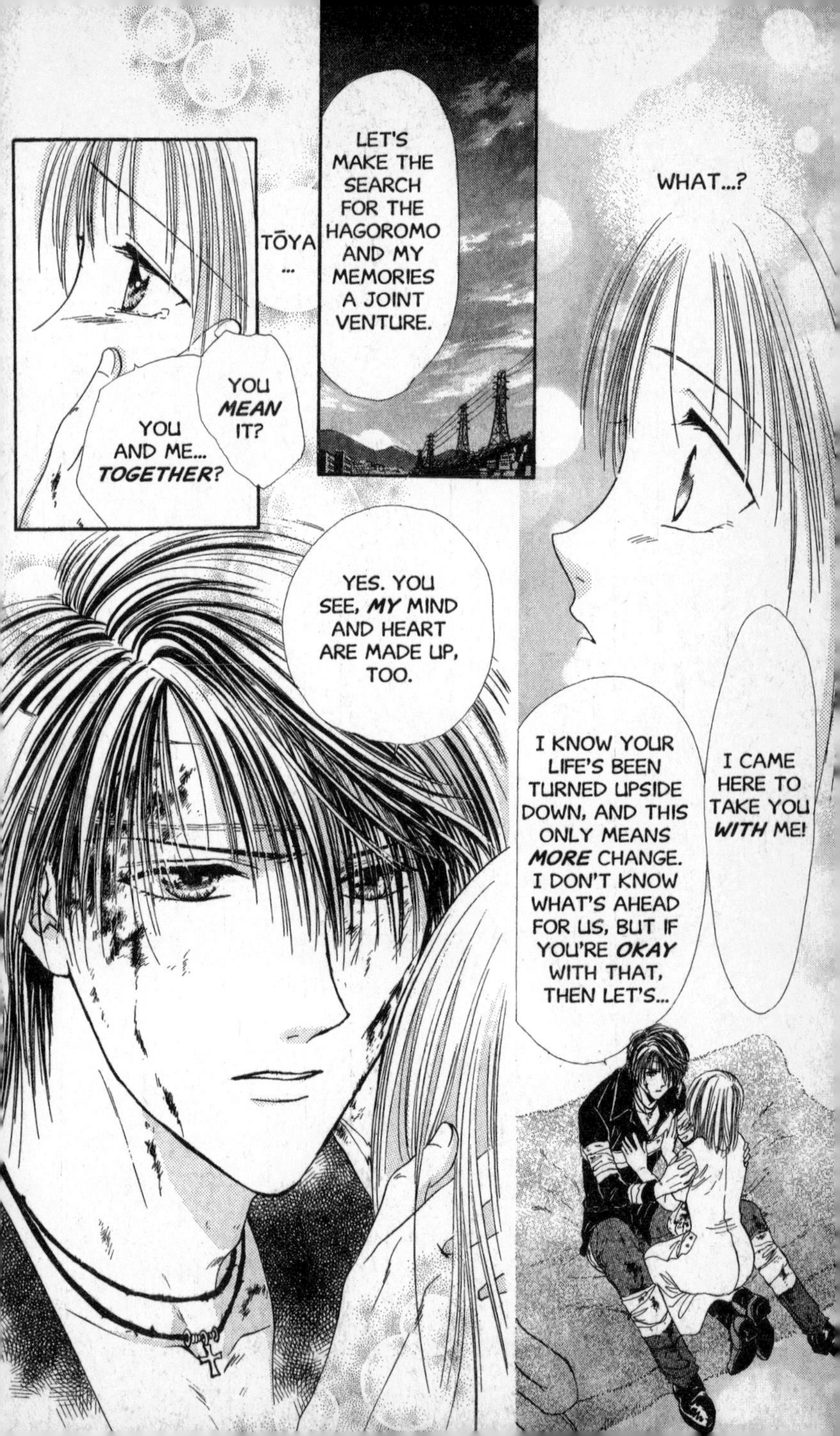
WHAT...?
I CAME HERE TO TAKE YOU *WITH* ME!
I KNOW YOUR LIFE'S BEEN TURNED UPSIDE DOWN, AND THIS ONLY MEANS *MORE* CHANGE. I DON'T KNOW WHAT'S AHEAD FOR US, BUT IF YOU'RE *OKAY* WITH THAT, THEN LET'S...
LET'S MAKE THE SEARCH FOR THE HAGOROMO AND MY MEMORIES A JOINT VENTURE.
TŌYA ...
YOU *MEAN* IT?
YOU AND ME... *TOGETHER*?
YES. YOU SEE, *MY* MIND AND HEART ARE MADE UP, TOO.

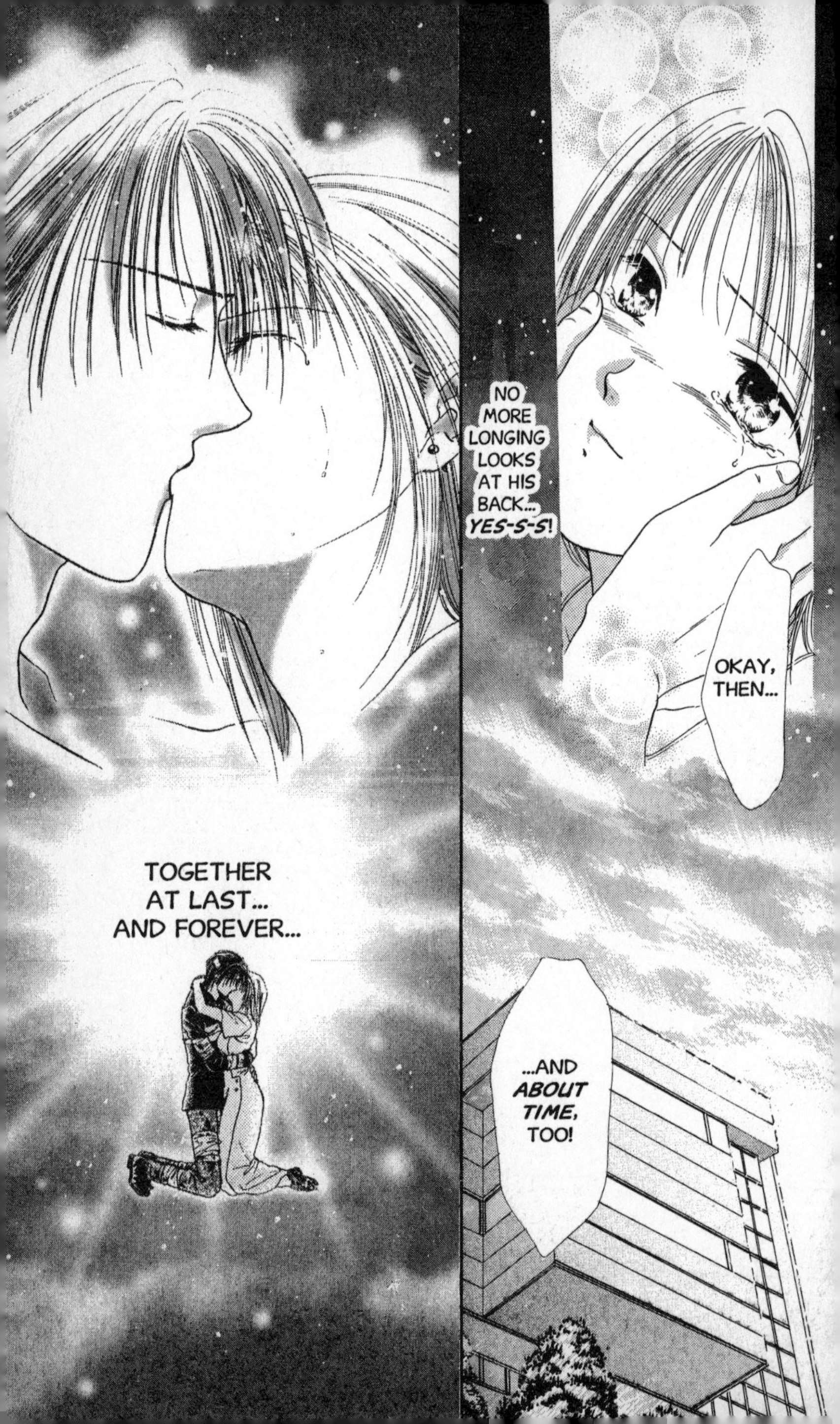
NO MORE LONGING LOOKS AT HIS BACK... *YES-S-S!*
OKAY, THEN...
...AND *ABOUT TIME,* TOO!
TOGETHER AT LAST... AND FOREVER...

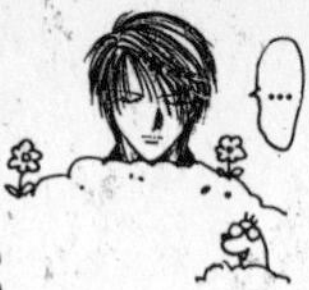

...

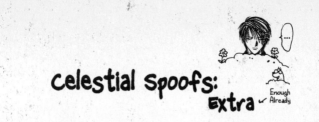

Celestial Spoofs: Extra

Enough Already

Here by special arrangement are some doodles by Assistant "H." Try and keep an open mind....

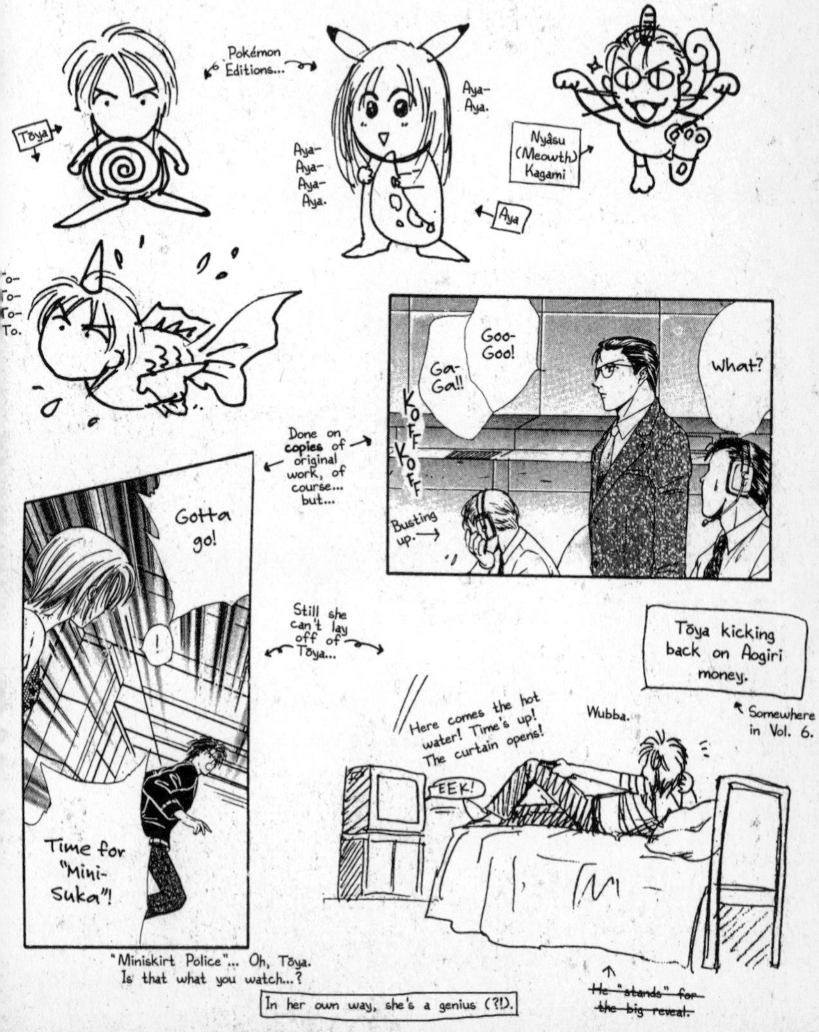

Pokémon Editions...
Tōya
Aya-Aya-Aya-Aya.
Aya-Aya.
Aya
Nyāsu (Meowth) Kagami
To-To-To-To.
Done on copies of original work, of course... but...
What?
Goo-Goo!
Ga-Ga!!
KOFF KOFF
Busting up.
Gotta go!
!
Time for "Mini-Suka"!
"Miniskirt Police"... Oh, Tōya. Is that what you watch...?
In her own way, she's a genius (?!).
Still she can't lay off of Tōya...
Tōya kicking back on Aogiri money.
Somewhere in Vol. 6.
Here comes the hot water! Time's up! The curtain opens!
Wubba.
EEK!
~~He "stands" for the big reveal.~~

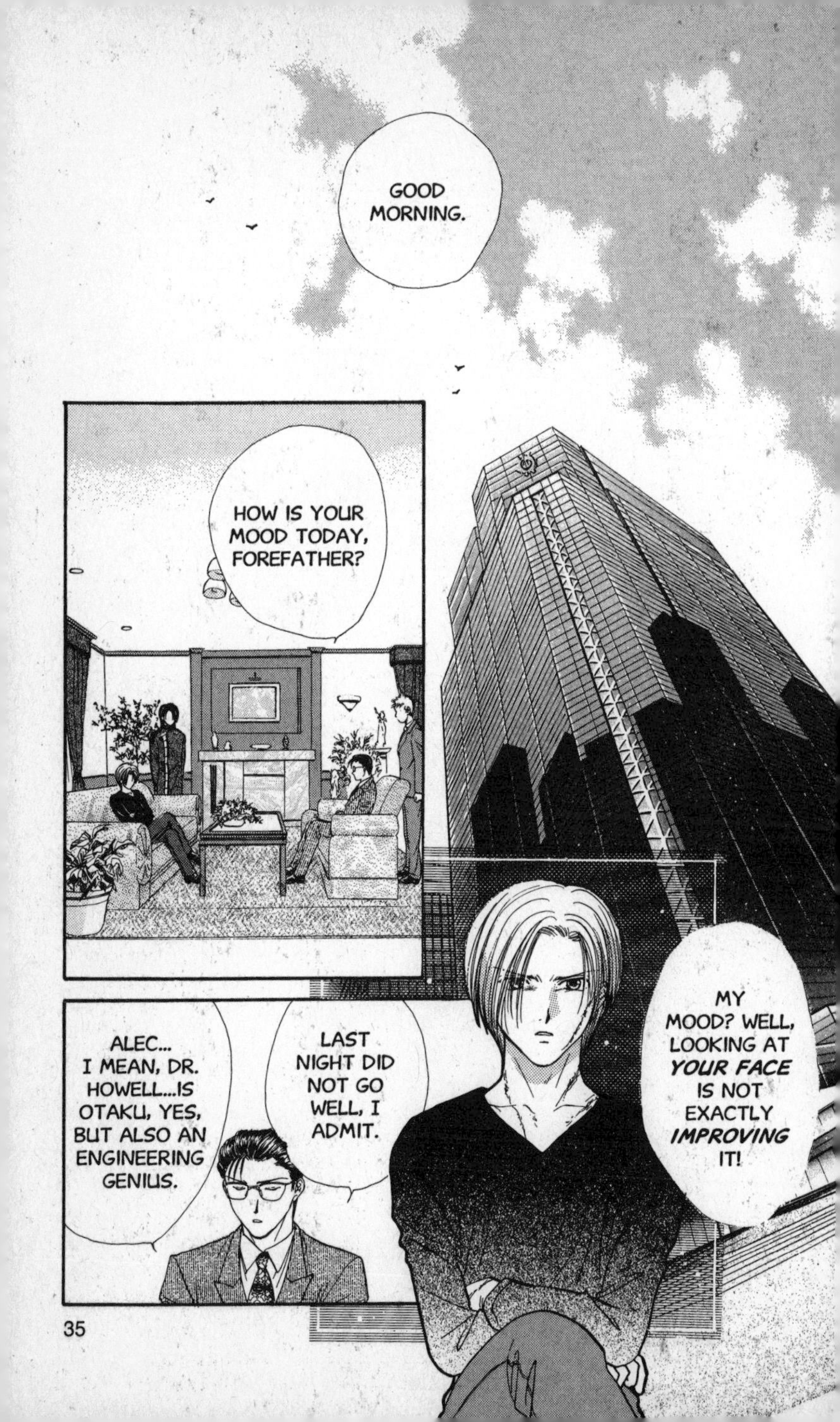
GOOD MORNING.
HOW IS YOUR MOOD TODAY, FOREFATHER?
MY MOOD? WELL, LOOKING AT *YOUR FACE* IS NOT EXACTLY *IMPROVING* IT!
LAST NIGHT DID NOT GO WELL, I ADMIT.
ALEC... I MEAN, DR. HOWELL...IS OTAKU, YES, BUT ALSO AN ENGINEERING GENIUS.

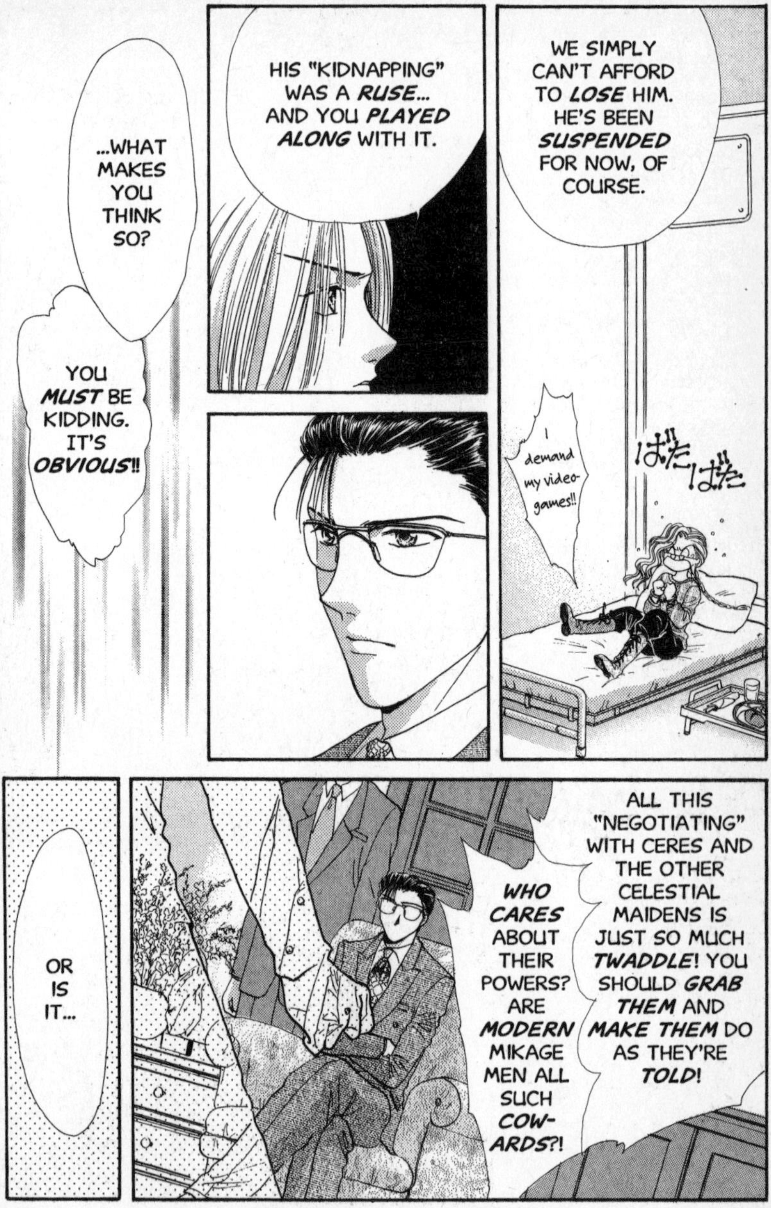
WE SIMPLY CAN'T AFFORD TO *LOSE* HIM. HE'S BEEN *SUSPENDED* FOR NOW, OF COURSE.
HIS "KIDNAPPING" WAS A *RUSE*... AND YOU *PLAYED ALONG* WITH IT.
...WHAT MAKES YOU THINK SO?
I demand my video-games!!
ばだばだ
YOU *MUST* BE KIDDING. IT'S *OBVIOUS*!!
ALL THIS "NEGOTIATING" WITH CERES AND THE OTHER CELESTIAL MAIDENS IS JUST SO MUCH *TWADDLE*! YOU SHOULD *GRAB THEM* AND *MAKE THEM* DO AS THEY'RE *TOLD*!
WHO CARES ABOUT THEIR POWERS? ARE *MODERN* MIKAGE MEN ALL SUCH *COW-ARDS*?!
OR IS IT...

Ceres: 11

Some people have been disappointed that more merchandise hasn't been made available. But the example of the artbook shows that, when there's enough demand, the companies will think about making more...or, maybe not. The numbers may need to hit the 10,000 range before they take note. ◡̈ It's people like you who make things happen. (That's why there are petitions.) It's more effective to make your requests directly to the companies, rather than by writing to me. Another good thing to do is to support the artists.... ◡̈ Filling out the surveys in magazines, buying the graphic novels...stuff like that. (What am I getting at, right?) Everything's up to the readers/consumers. I couldn't do it without you.

× × ×

So, Volume 10! Some pretty brutal stuff. As expected, there were lots of letters angry about the Progenitor, saying how thought-provoking they found it. I was trying to overdo it on purpose in that volume, so I hope you male readers can forgive me. ◡̈ Although some may not be able to convincingly deny it.... Others wrote that there was no need for me to have gone that far. Maybe not, but it was still part of my subject matter.

In any event, it was the younger readers who empathized most readily—who said "He can't get away with it!" and "Poor Aya!"—and it was the "grown-ups" who wrote in with more carefully reasoned arguments. Something to consider.

There are several people whose mothers also read **Ceres**, and so I'm hoping maybe the series can be used as a platform for discussion (too much to ask?). It's sure made **me** think a lot of stuff over.... Oops, out of space. To be continued.

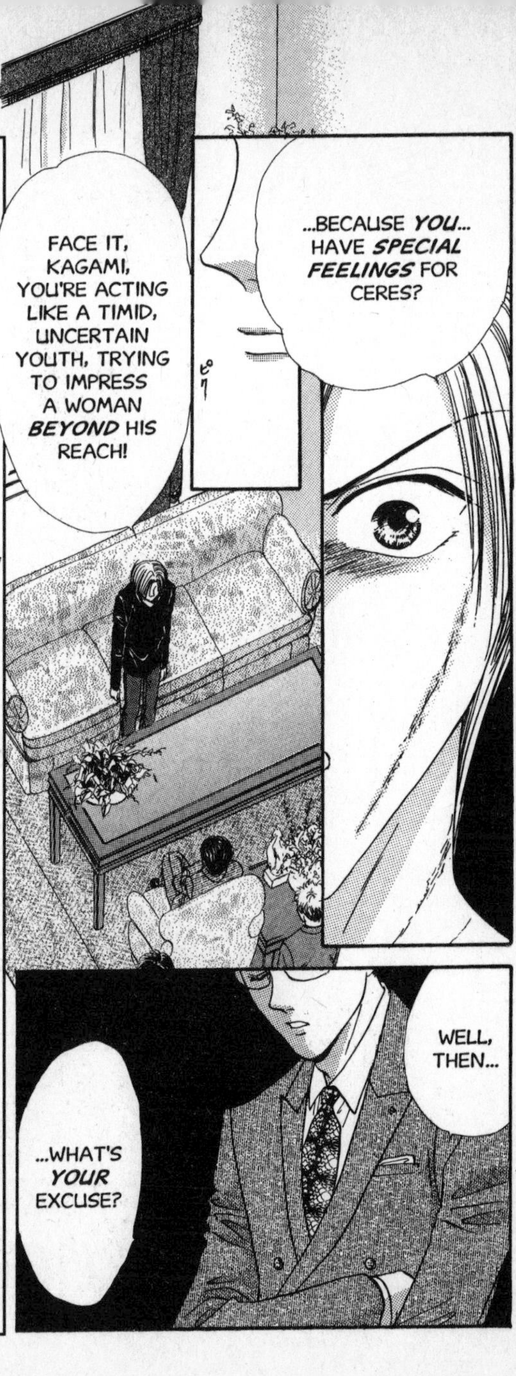
FACE IT, KAGAMI, YOU'RE ACTING LIKE A TIMID, UNCERTAIN YOUTH, TRYING TO IMPRESS A WOMAN *BEYOND* HIS REACH!
ピク
...BECAUSE *YOU*... HAVE *SPECIAL FEELINGS* FOR CERES?
WELL, THEN...
...WHAT'S *YOUR* EXCUSE?

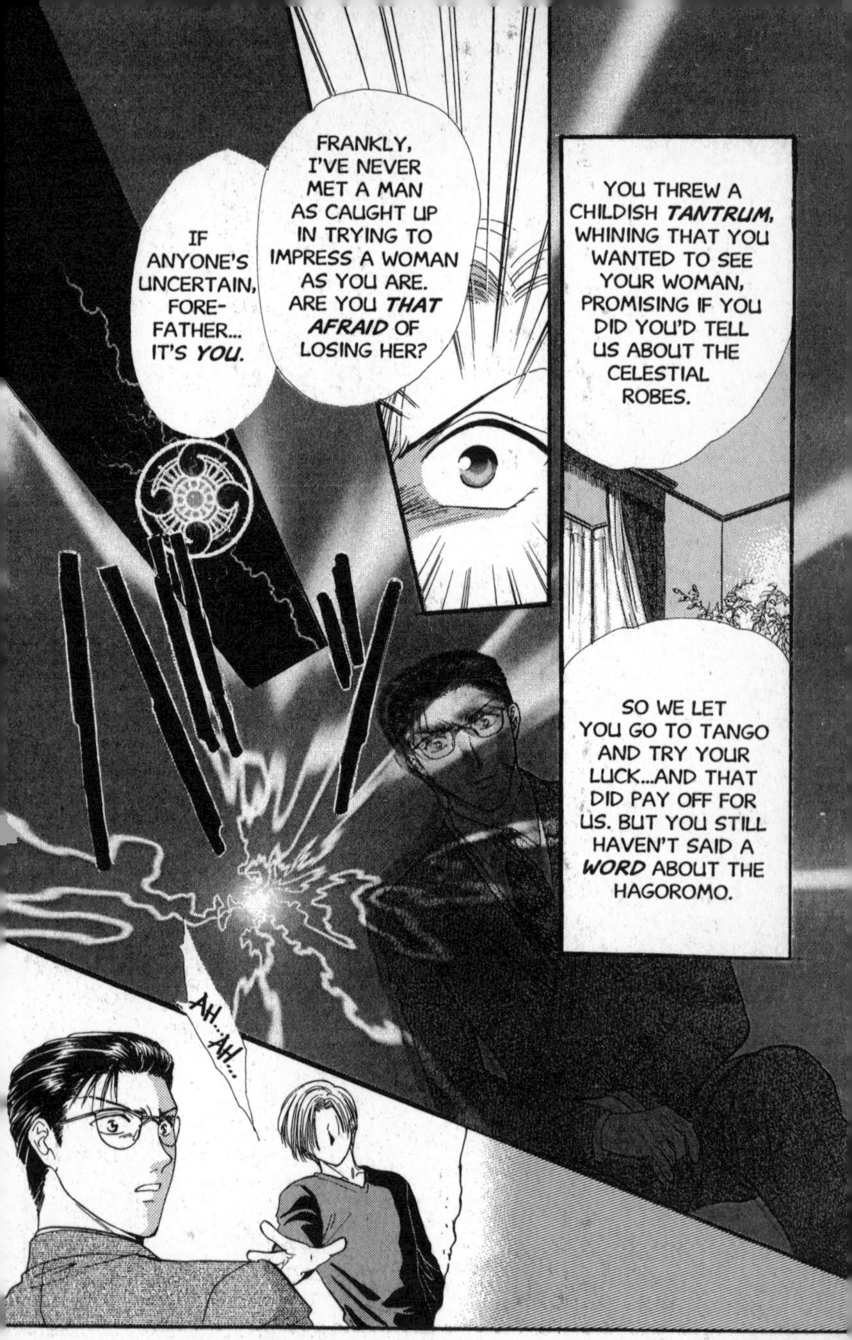
YOU THREW A CHILDISH *TANTRUM*, WHINING THAT YOU WANTED TO SEE YOUR WOMAN, PROMISING IF YOU DID YOU'D TELL US ABOUT THE CELESTIAL ROBES.
SO WE LET YOU GO TO TANGO AND TRY YOUR LUCK...AND THAT DID PAY OFF FOR US. BUT YOU STILL HAVEN'T SAID A *WORD* ABOUT THE HAGOROMO.
FRANKLY, I'VE NEVER MET A MAN AS CAUGHT UP IN TRYING TO IMPRESS A WOMAN AS YOU ARE. ARE YOU *THAT AFRAID* OF LOSING HER?
IF ANYONE'S UNCERTAIN, FORE-FATHER... IT'S *YOU*.
AH... AH...

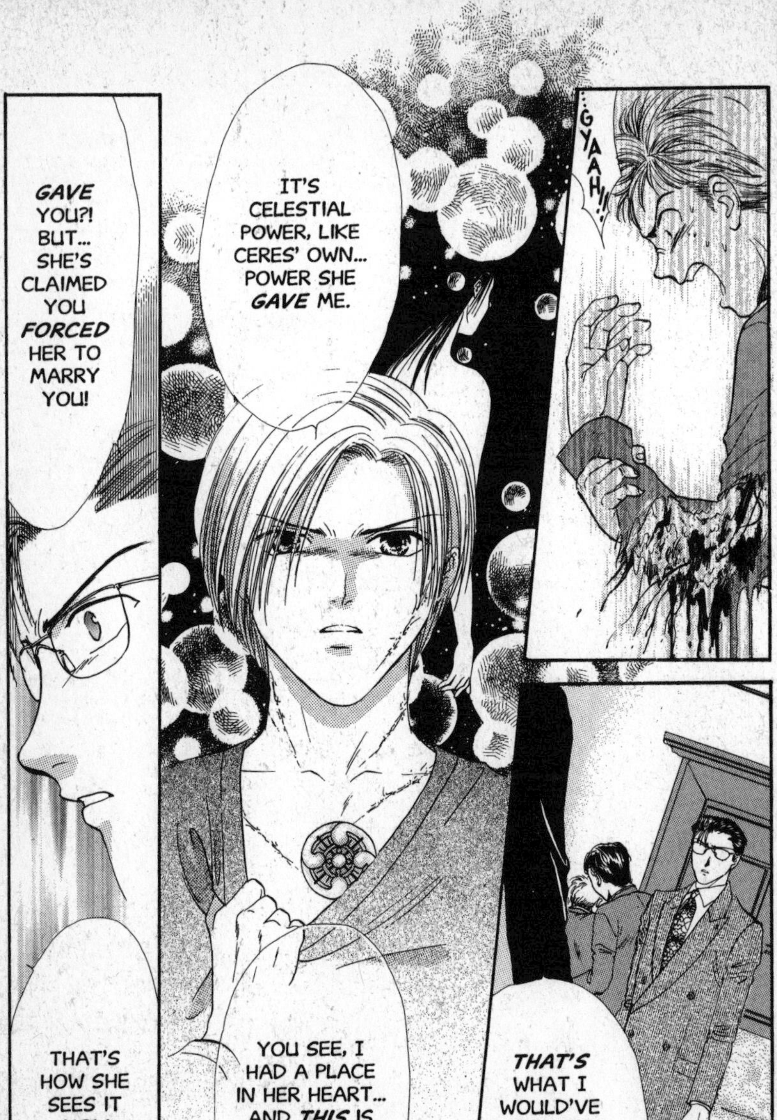
...GYAAH!!
THAT'S WHAT I WOULD'VE DONE TO TŌYA—ONLY WORSE!—IF YOU HADN'T INTERFERED.
IT'S CELESTIAL POWER, LIKE CERES' OWN... POWER SHE GAVE ME.
YOU SEE, I HAD A PLACE IN HER HEART... AND THIS IS THE PROOF THAT SHE BELONGS TO ME.
GAVE YOU?! BUT... SHE'S CLAIMED YOU FORCED HER TO MARRY YOU!
THAT'S HOW SHE SEES IT NOW. WOMEN ARE LIKE THAT.

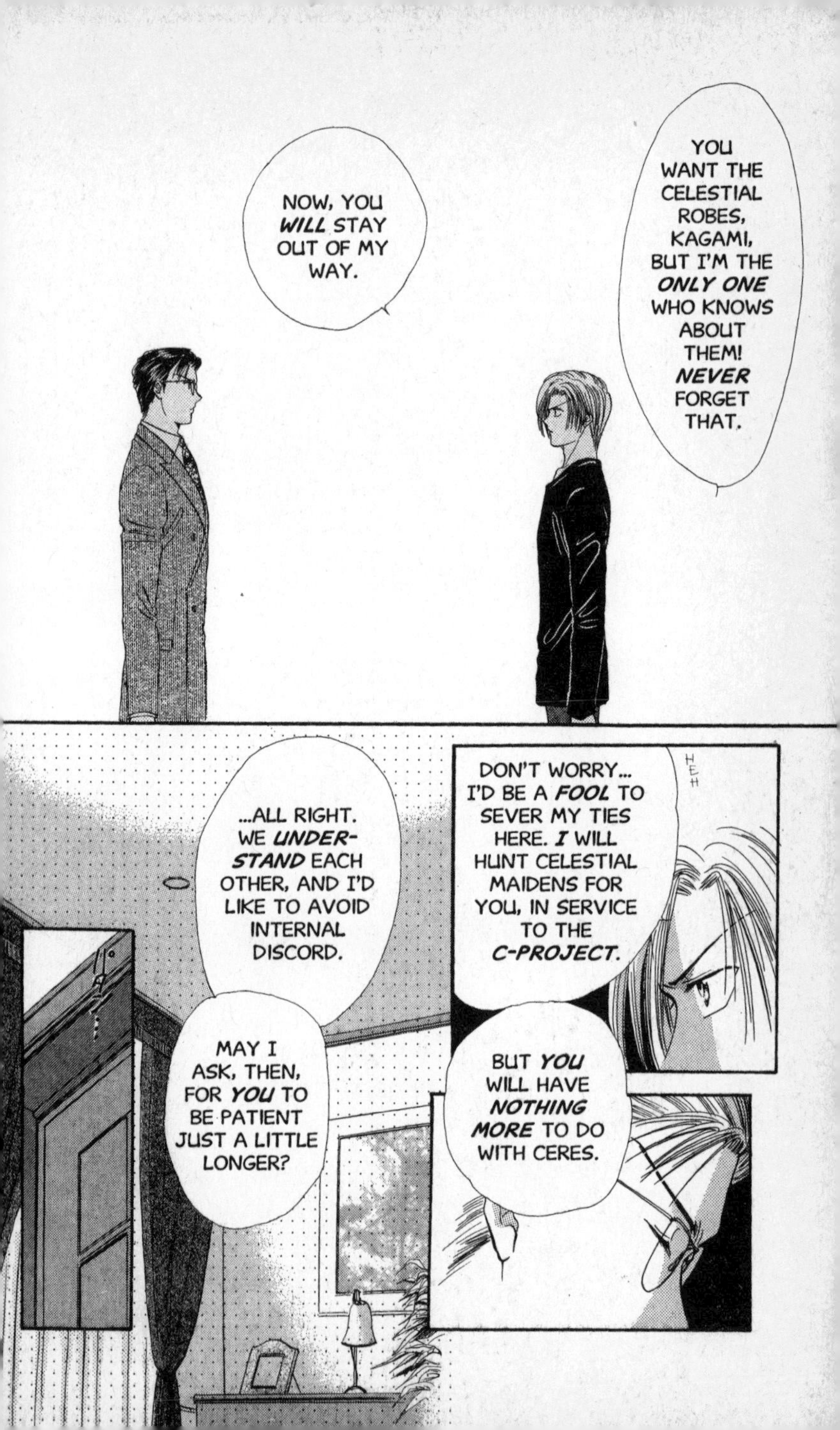
YOU WANT THE CELESTIAL ROBES, KAGAMI, BUT I'M THE ONLY ONE WHO KNOWS ABOUT THEM! NEVER FORGET THAT.
NOW, YOU WILL STAY OUT OF MY WAY.
...ALL RIGHT. WE UNDER-STAND EACH OTHER, AND I'D LIKE TO AVOID INTERNAL DISCORD.
MAY I ASK, THEN, FOR YOU TO BE PATIENT JUST A LITTLE LONGER?
HEH
DON'T WORRY... I'D BE A FOOL TO SEVER MY TIES HERE. I WILL HUNT CELESTIAL MAIDENS FOR YOU, IN SERVICE TO THE C-PROJECT.
BUT YOU WILL HAVE NOTHING MORE TO DO WITH CERES.

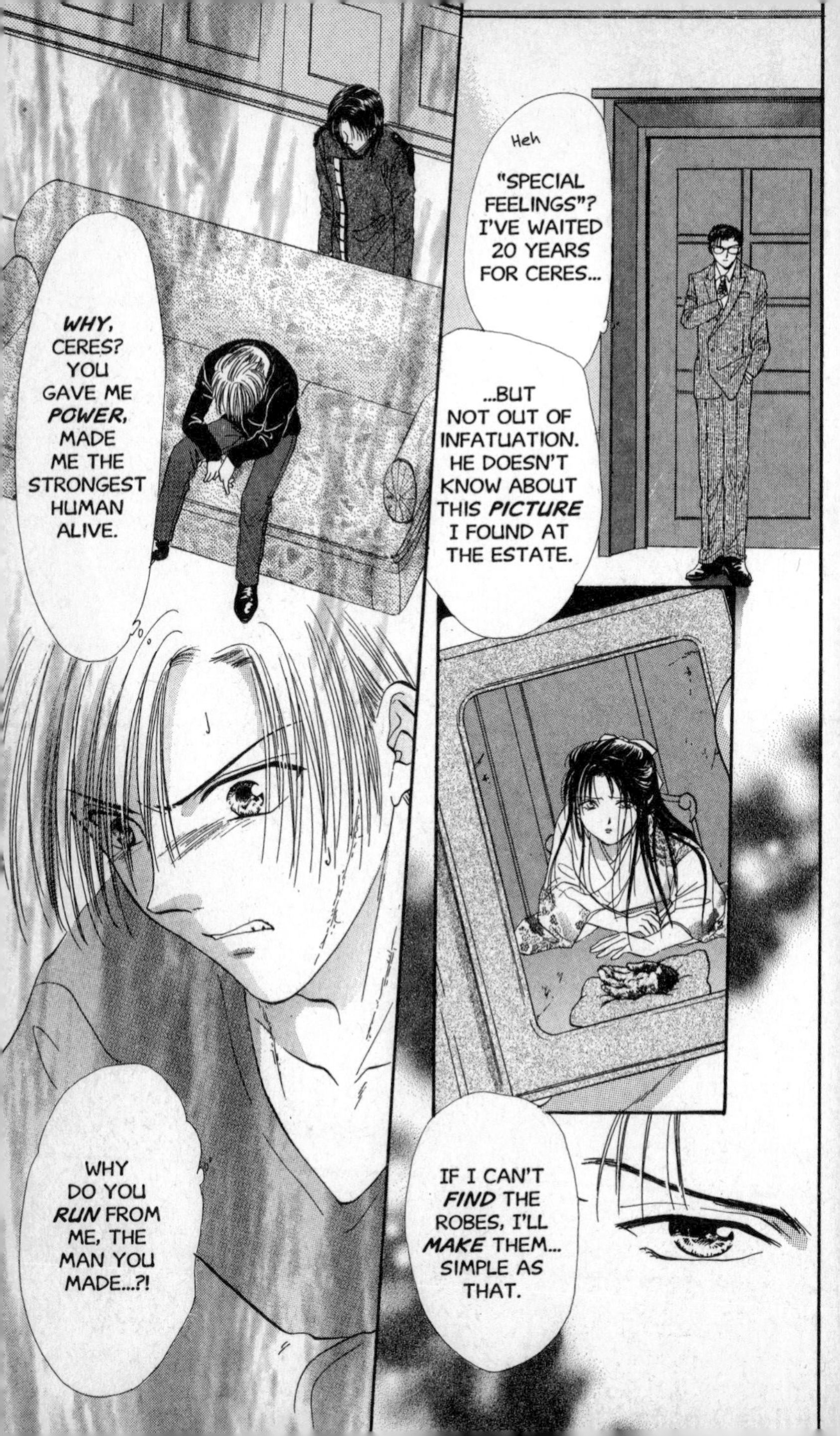
Heh
"SPECIAL FEELINGS"? I'VE WAITED 20 YEARS FOR CERES...
...BUT NOT OUT OF INFATUATION. HE DOESN'T KNOW ABOUT THIS PICTURE I FOUND AT THE ESTATE.
IF I CAN'T FIND THE ROBES, I'LL MAKE THEM... SIMPLE AS THAT.
WHY, CERES? YOU GAVE ME POWER, MADE ME THE STRONGEST HUMAN ALIVE.
WHY DO YOU RUN FROM ME, THE MAN YOU MADE...?!

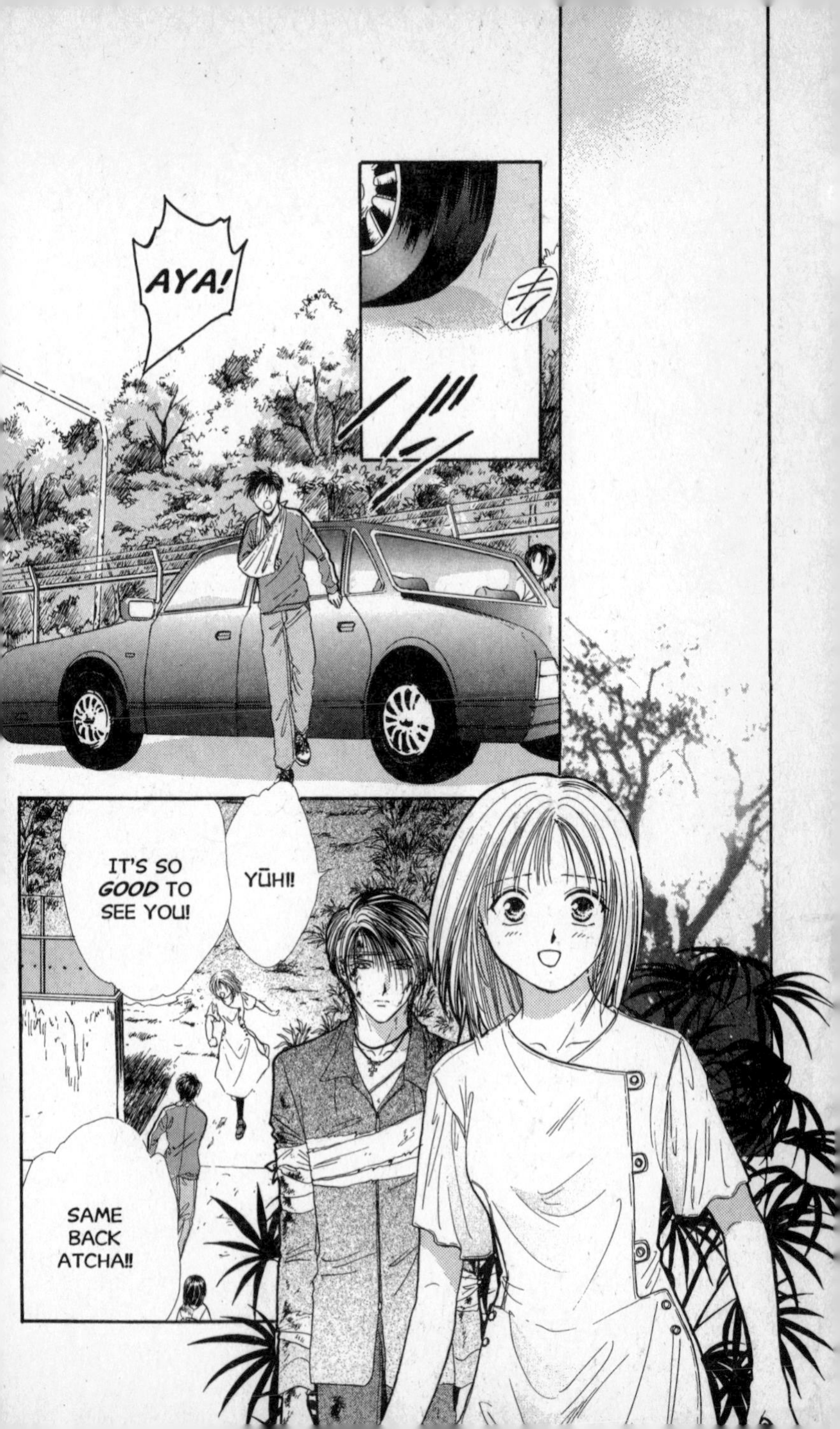
AYA!
YŪHI!
IT'S SO *GOOD* TO SEE YOU!
SAME BACK ATCHA!!

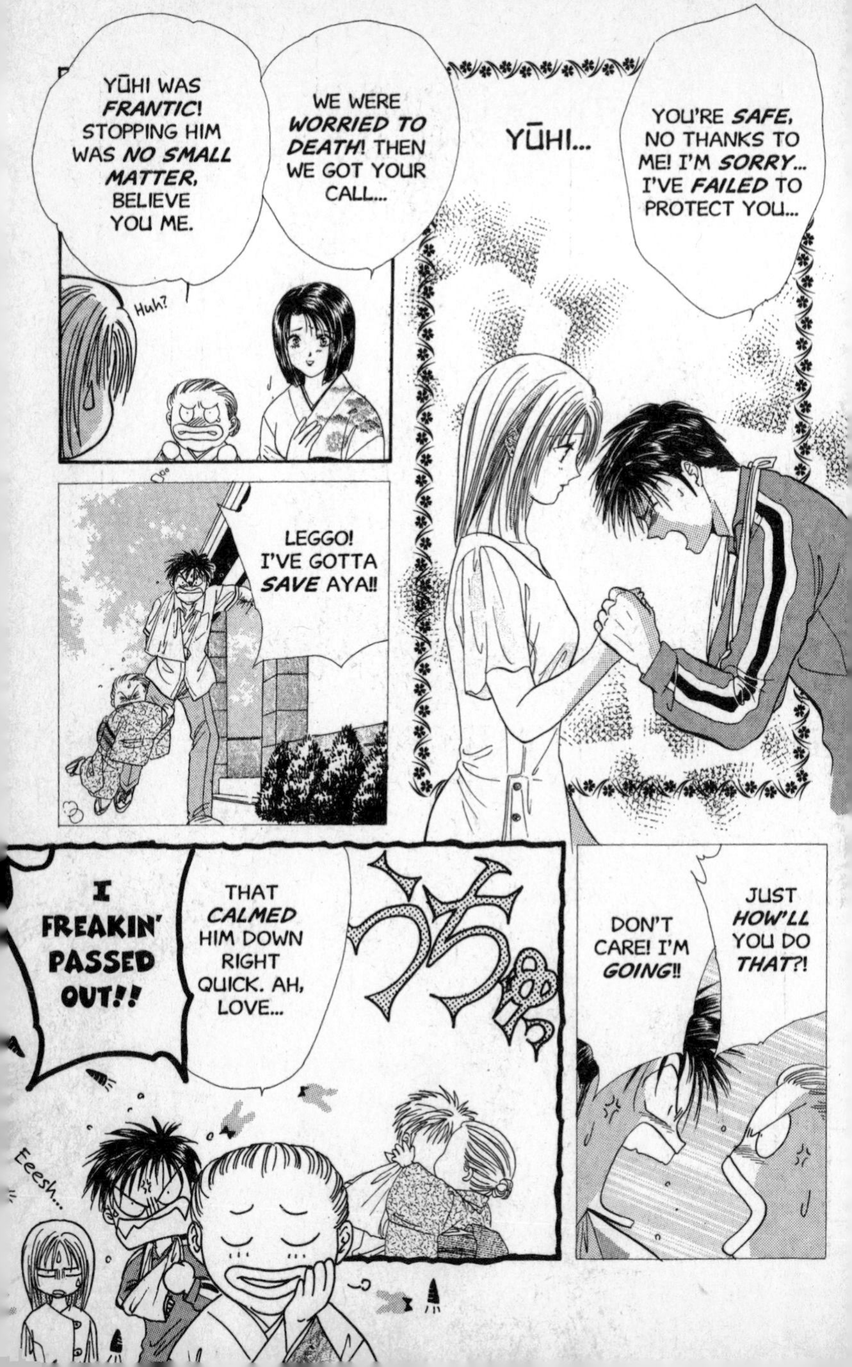
YOU'RE SAFE, NO THANKS TO ME! I'M SORRY... I'VE FAILED TO PROTECT YOU...
YŪHI...
WE WERE WORRIED TO DEATH! THEN WE GOT YOUR CALL...
YŪHI WAS FRANTIC! STOPPING HIM WAS NO SMALL MATTER, BELIEVE YOU ME.
Huh?
LEGGO! I'VE GOTTA SAVE AYA!!
JUST HOW'LL YOU DO THAT?!
DON'T CARE! I'M GOING!!
THAT CALMED HIM DOWN RIGHT QUICK. AH, LOVE...
I FREAKIN' PASSED OUT!!
Eeesh...

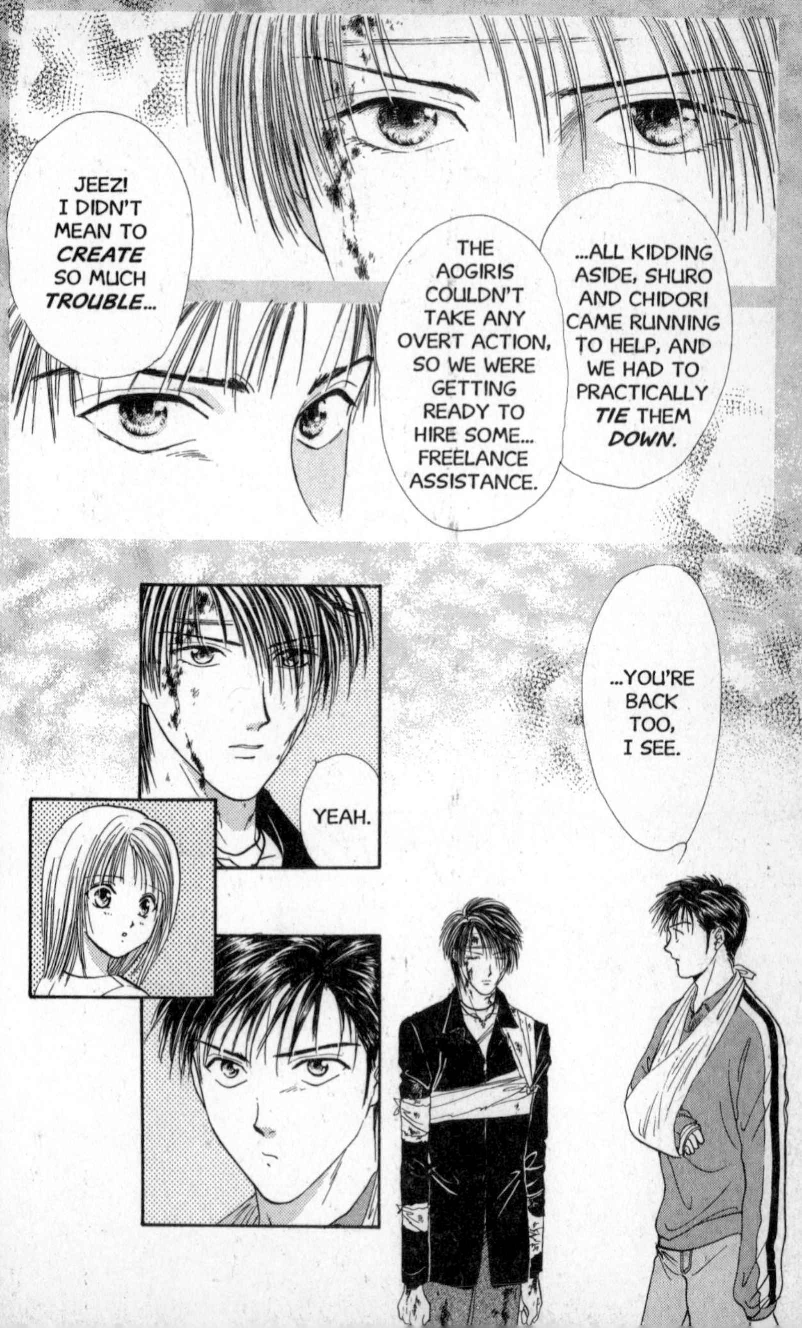
...ALL KIDDING ASIDE, SHURO AND CHIDORI CAME RUNNING TO HELP, AND WE HAD TO PRACTICALLY TIE THEM DOWN.
THE AOGIRIS COULDN'T TAKE ANY OVERT ACTION, SO WE WERE GETTING READY TO HIRE SOME... FREELANCE ASSISTANCE.
JEEZ! I DIDN'T MEAN TO CREATE SO MUCH TROUBLE...
...YOU'RE BACK TOO, I SEE.
YEAH.

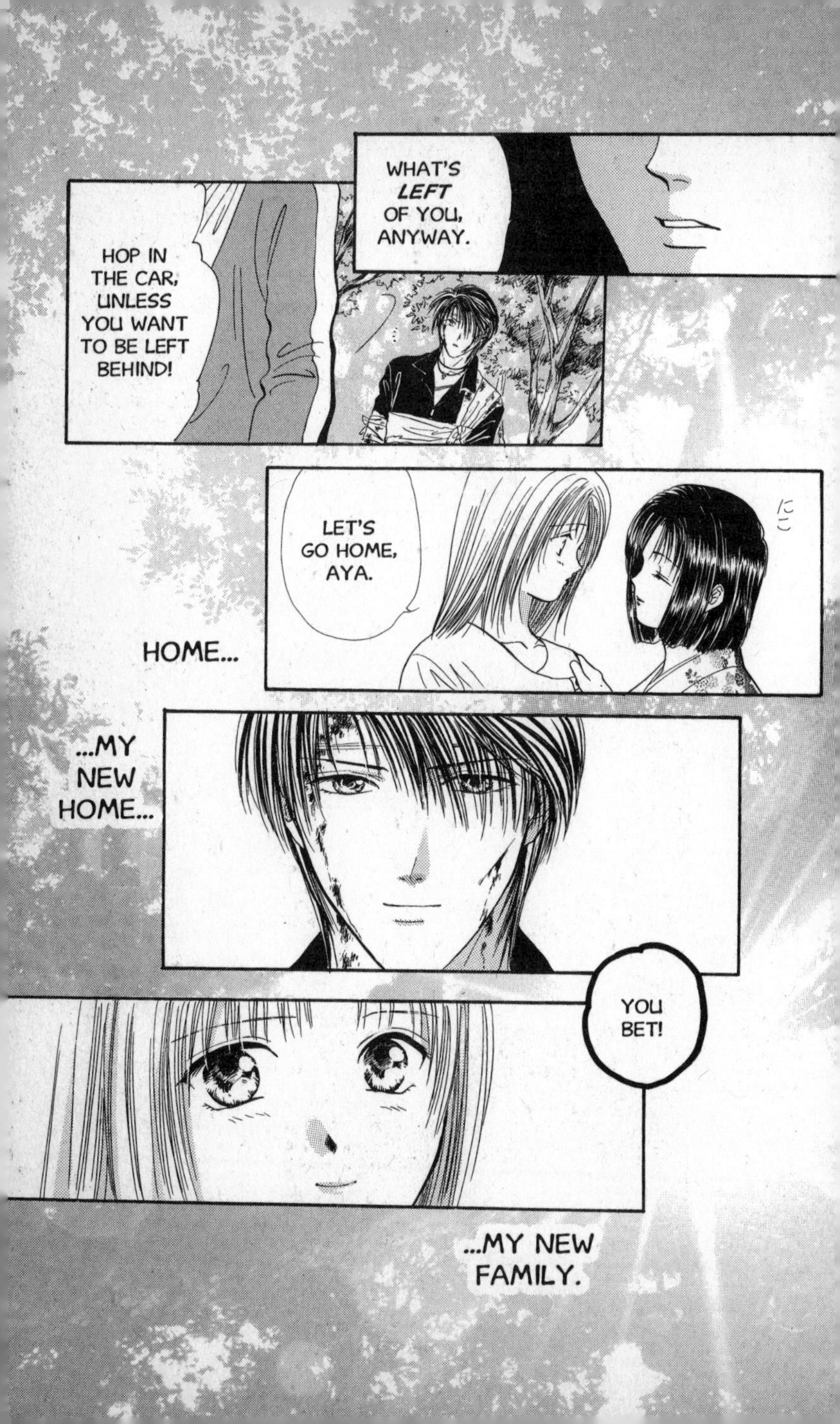
HOP IN THE CAR, UNLESS YOU WANT TO BE LEFT BEHIND!
WHAT'S *LEFT* OF YOU, ANYWAY.
LET'S GO HOME, AYA.
にこ
HOME...
...MY NEW HOME...
YOU BET!
...MY NEW FAMILY.

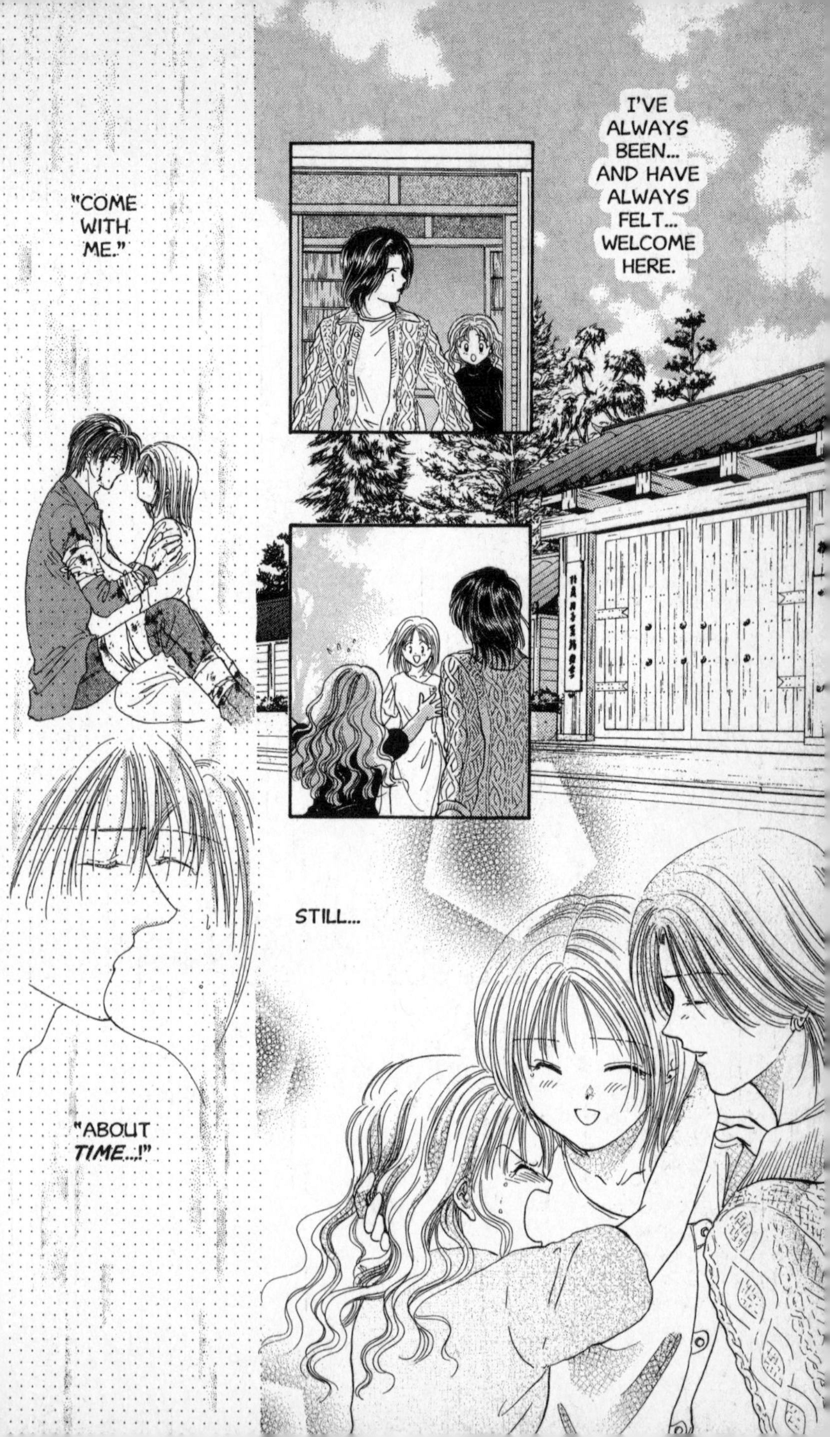
I'VE ALWAYS BEEN... AND HAVE ALWAYS FELT... WELCOME HERE.
STILL...
"COME WITH ME."
"ABOUT TIME...!"

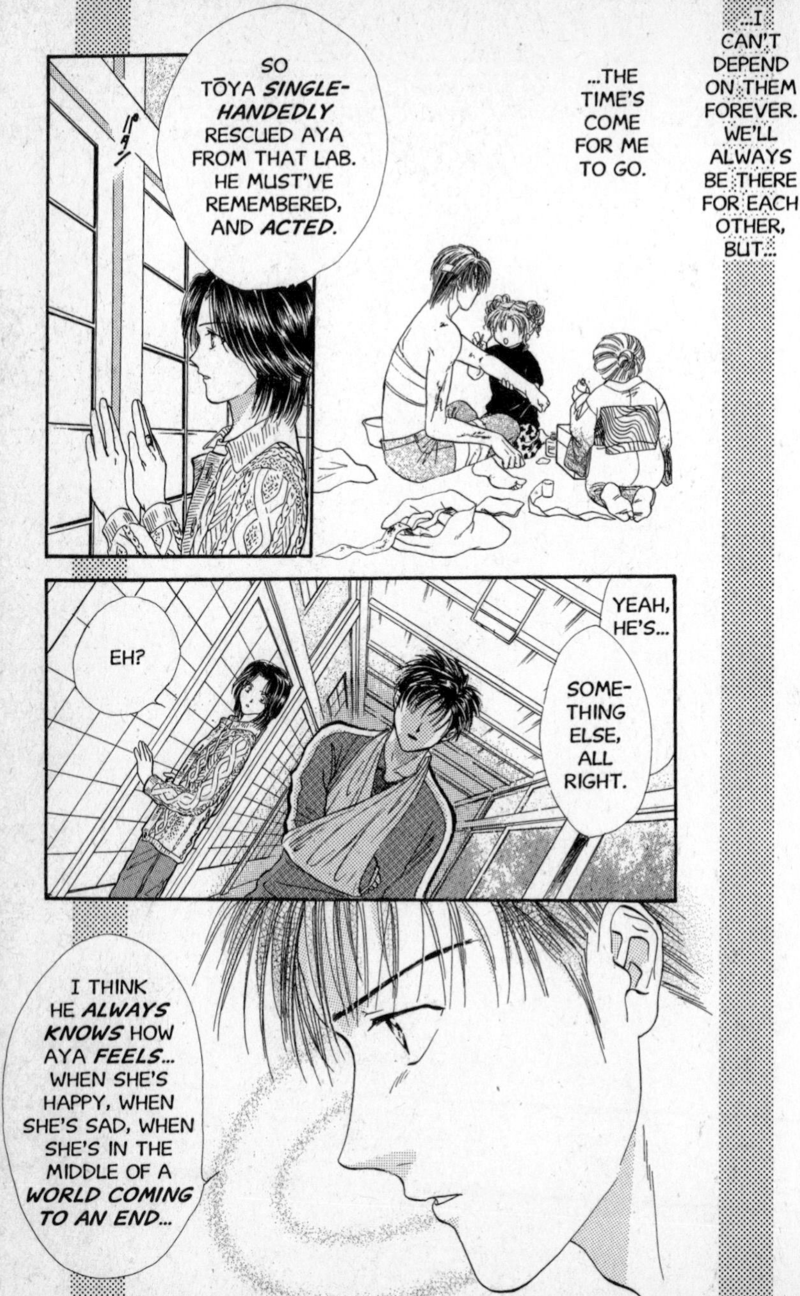
...I CAN'T DEPEND ON THEM FOREVER. WE'LL ALWAYS BE THERE FOR EACH OTHER, BUT...
...THE TIME'S COME FOR ME TO GO.
SO TŌYA *SINGLE-HANDEDLY* RESCUED AYA FROM THAT LAB. HE MUST'VE REMEMBERED, AND *ACTED*.
YEAH, HE'S...
SOMETHING ELSE, ALL RIGHT.
EH?
I THINK HE *ALWAYS KNOWS* HOW AYA *FEELS*... WHEN SHE'S HAPPY, WHEN SHE'S SAD, WHEN SHE'S IN THE MIDDLE OF A *WORLD COMING TO AN END*...

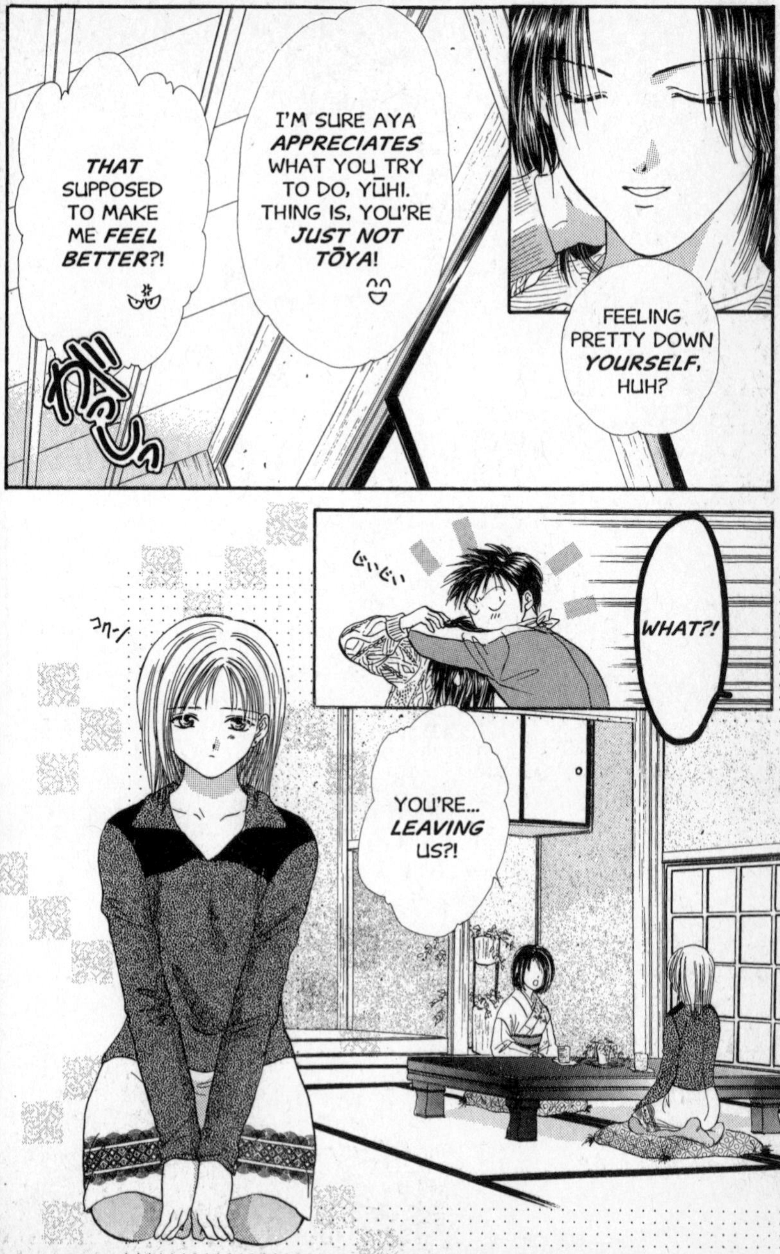
FEELING PRETTY DOWN *YOURSELF,* HUH?
I'M SURE AYA *APPRECIATES* WHAT YOU TRY TO DO, YŪHI. THING IS, YOU'RE *JUST NOT TŌYA*!
THAT SUPPOSED TO MAKE ME *FEEL BETTER*?!
WHAT?!
YOU'RE... *LEAVING* US?!

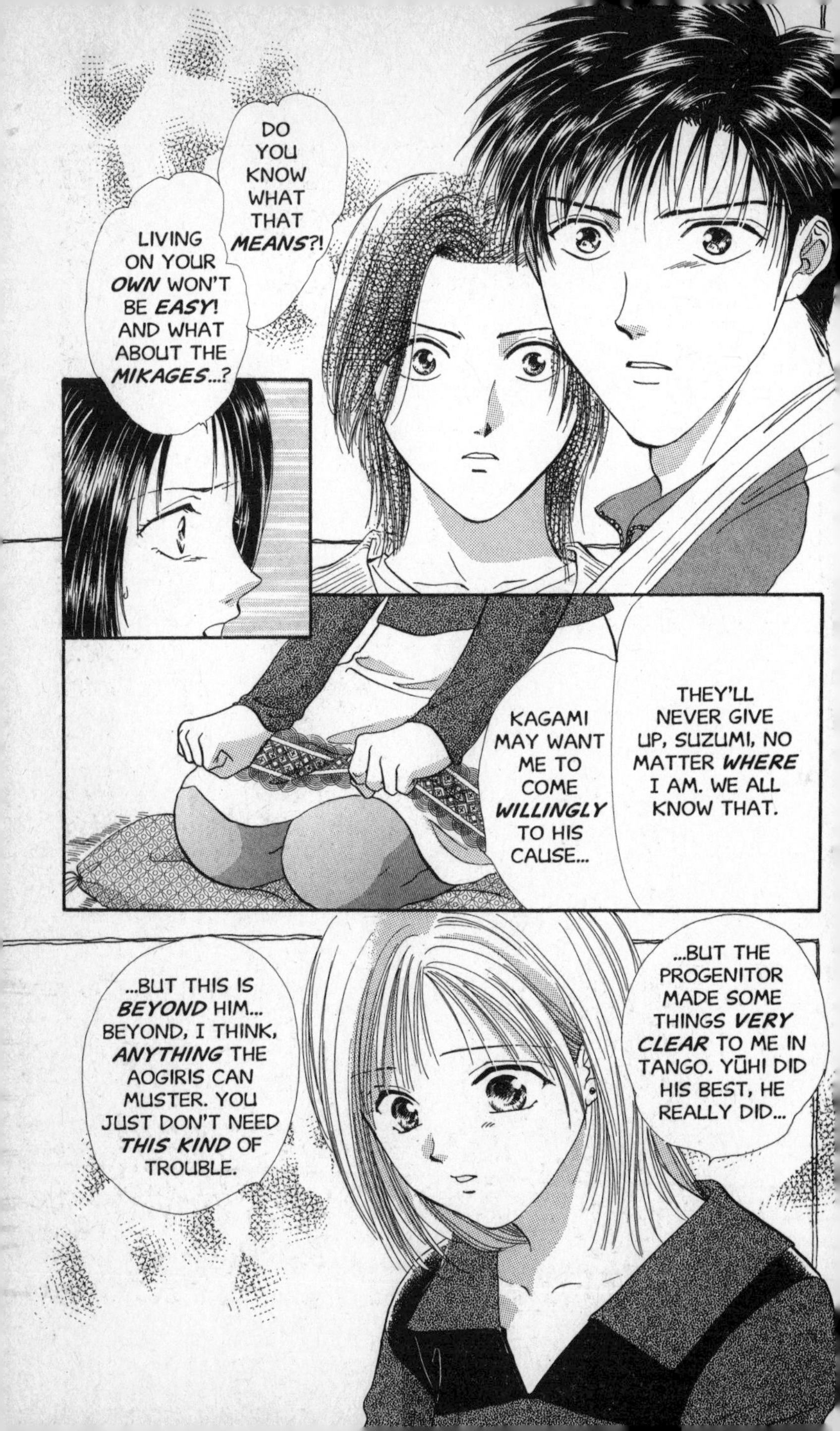
DO YOU KNOW WHAT THAT MEANS?!
LIVING ON YOUR OWN WON'T BE EASY! AND WHAT ABOUT THE MIKAGES...?
THEY'LL NEVER GIVE UP, SUZUMI, NO MATTER WHERE I AM. WE ALL KNOW THAT.
KAGAMI MAY WANT ME TO COME WILLINGLY TO HIS CAUSE...
...BUT THE PROGENITOR MADE SOME THINGS VERY CLEAR TO ME IN TANGO. YŪHI DID HIS BEST, HE REALLY DID...
...BUT THIS IS BEYOND HIM... BEYOND, I THINK, ANYTHING THE AOGIRIS CAN MUSTER. YOU JUST DON'T NEED THIS KIND OF TROUBLE.

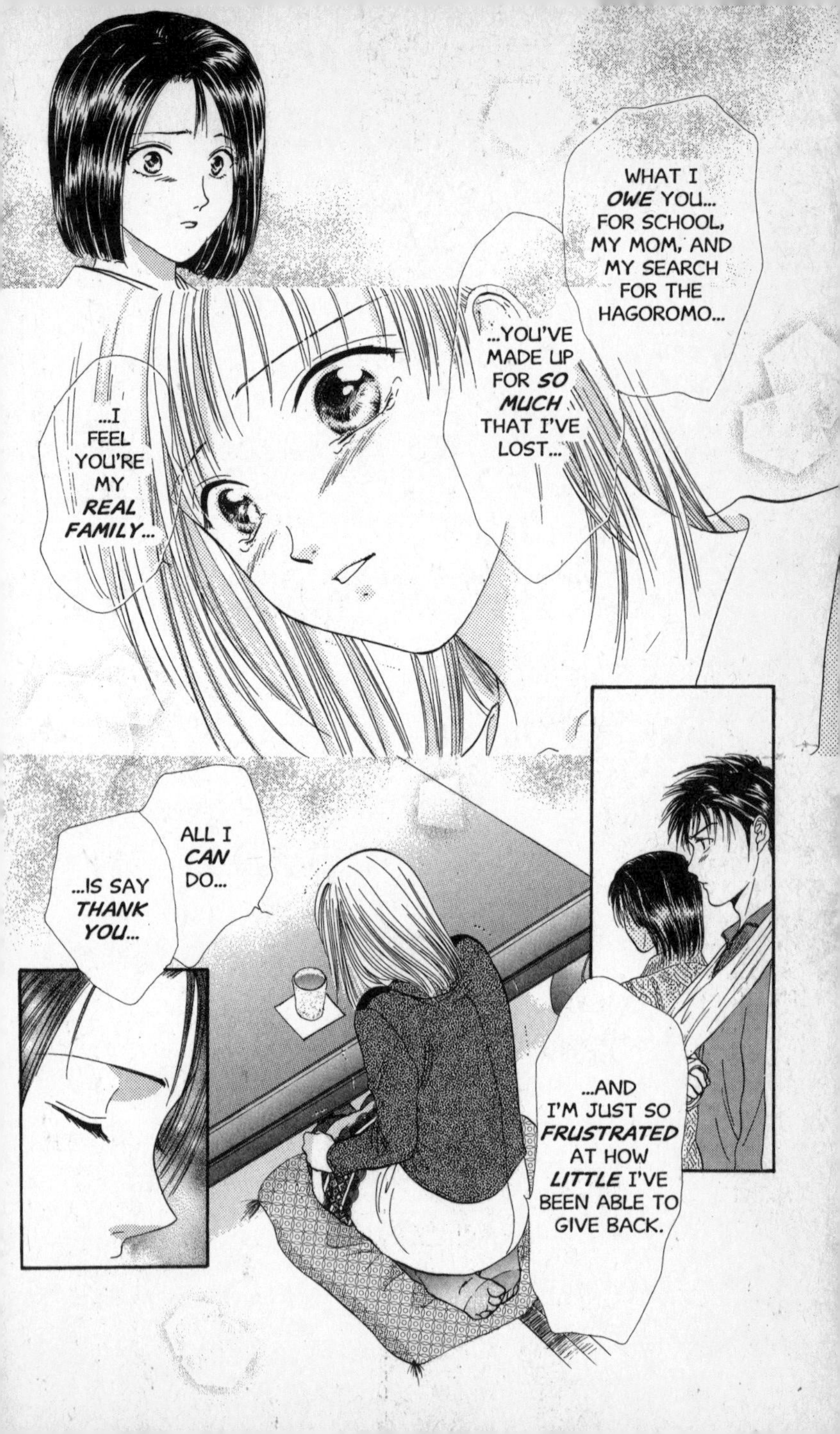
WHAT I OWE YOU... FOR SCHOOL, MY MOM, AND MY SEARCH FOR THE HAGOROMO...
...YOU'VE MADE UP FOR SO MUCH THAT I'VE LOST...
...I FEEL YOU'RE MY REAL FAMILY...
...AND I'M JUST SO FRUSTRATED AT HOW LITTLE I'VE BEEN ABLE TO GIVE BACK.
ALL I CAN DO...
...IS SAY THANK YOU...

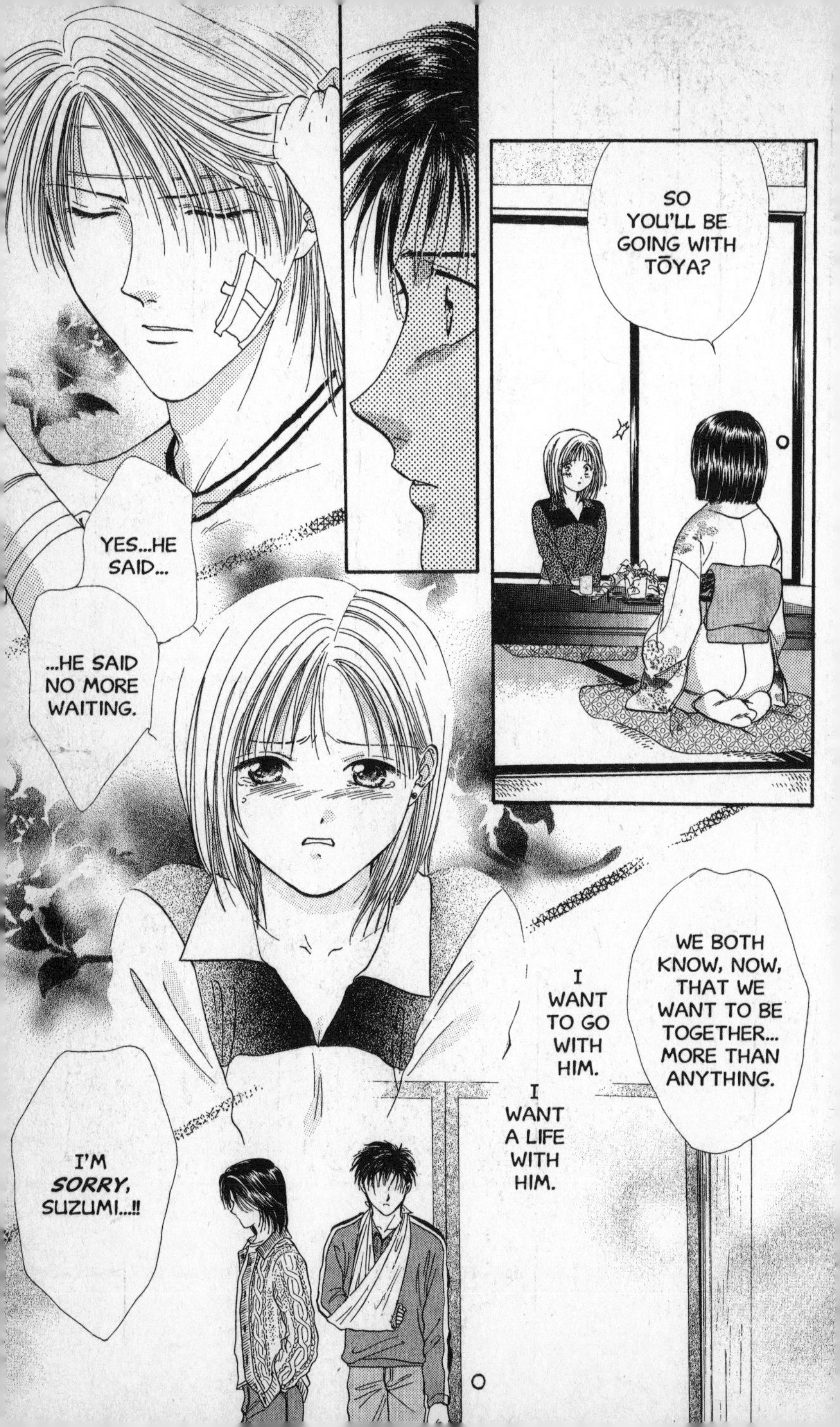
SO YOU'LL BE GOING WITH TŌYA?
YES...HE SAID...
...HE SAID NO MORE WAITING.
WE BOTH KNOW, NOW, THAT WE WANT TO BE TOGETHER... MORE THAN ANYTHING.
I WANT TO GO WITH HIM.
I WANT A LIFE WITH HIM.
I'M *SORRY*, SUZUMI...!!

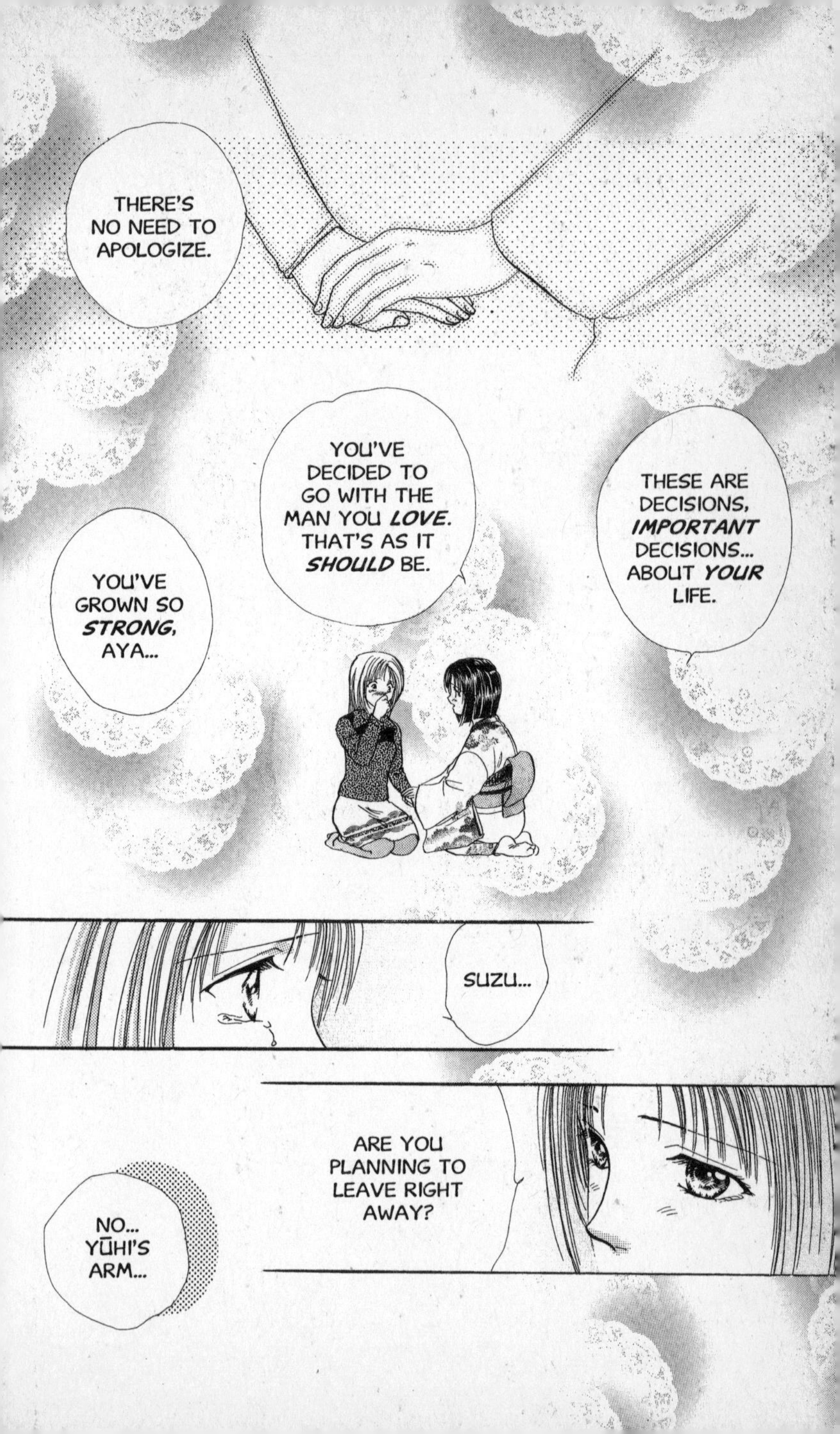
THERE'S NO NEED TO APOLOGIZE.
THESE ARE DECISIONS, *IMPORTANT* DECISIONS... ABOUT *YOUR* LIFE.
YOU'VE DECIDED TO GO WITH THE MAN YOU *LOVE*. THAT'S AS IT *SHOULD* BE.
YOU'VE GROWN SO *STRONG*, AYA...
SUZU...
ARE YOU PLANNING TO LEAVE RIGHT AWAY?
NO... YŪHI'S ARM...

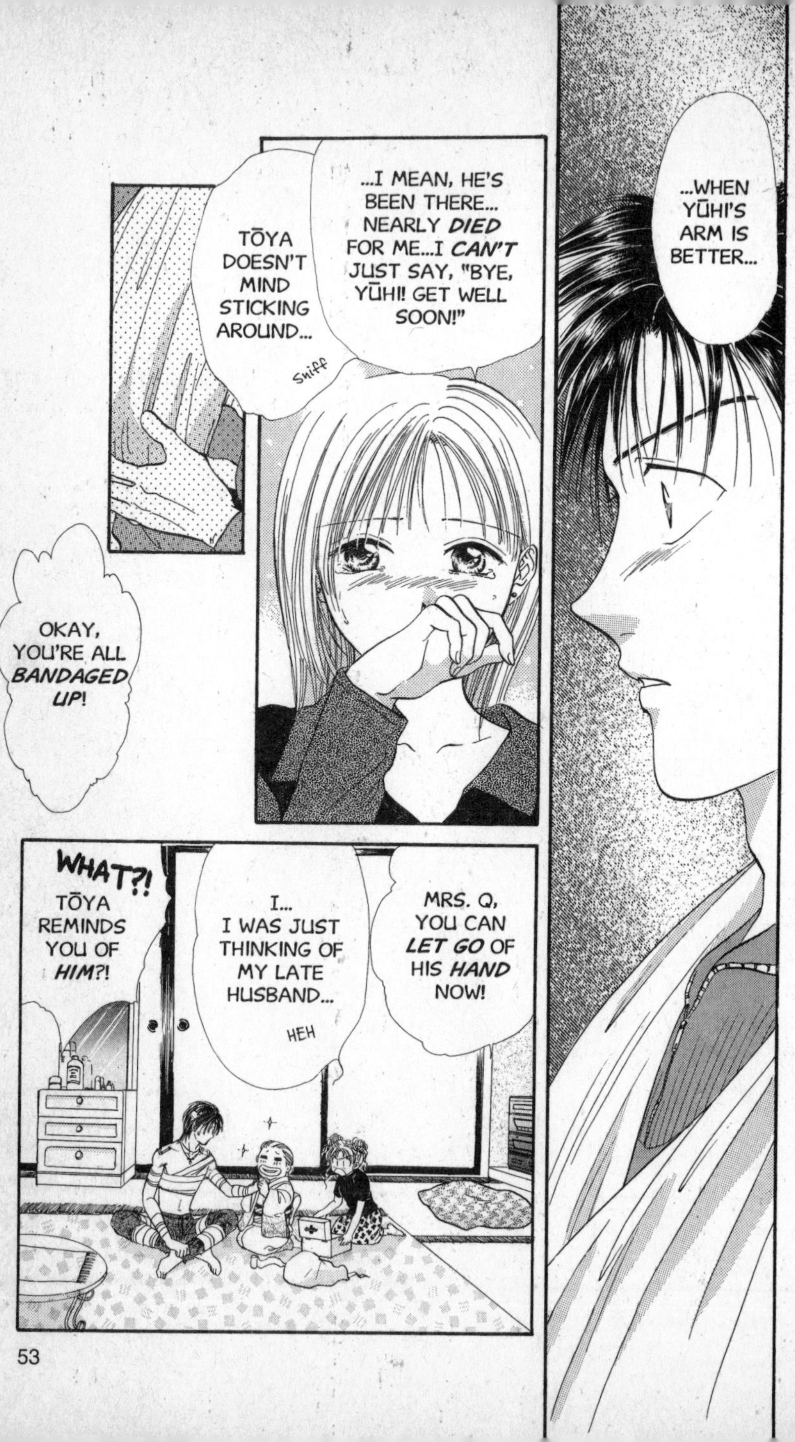
...WHEN YŪHI'S ARM IS BETTER...
...I MEAN, HE'S BEEN THERE... NEARLY *DIED* FOR ME...I *CAN'T* JUST SAY, "BYE, YŪHI! GET WELL SOON!"
TŌYA DOESN'T MIND STICKING AROUND...
Sniff
OKAY, YOU'RE ALL *BANDAGED UP*!
MRS. Q, YOU CAN *LET GO* OF HIS *HAND* NOW!
I... I WAS JUST THINKING OF MY LATE HUSBAND...
HEH
WHAT?!
TŌYA REMINDS YOU OF *HIM*?!

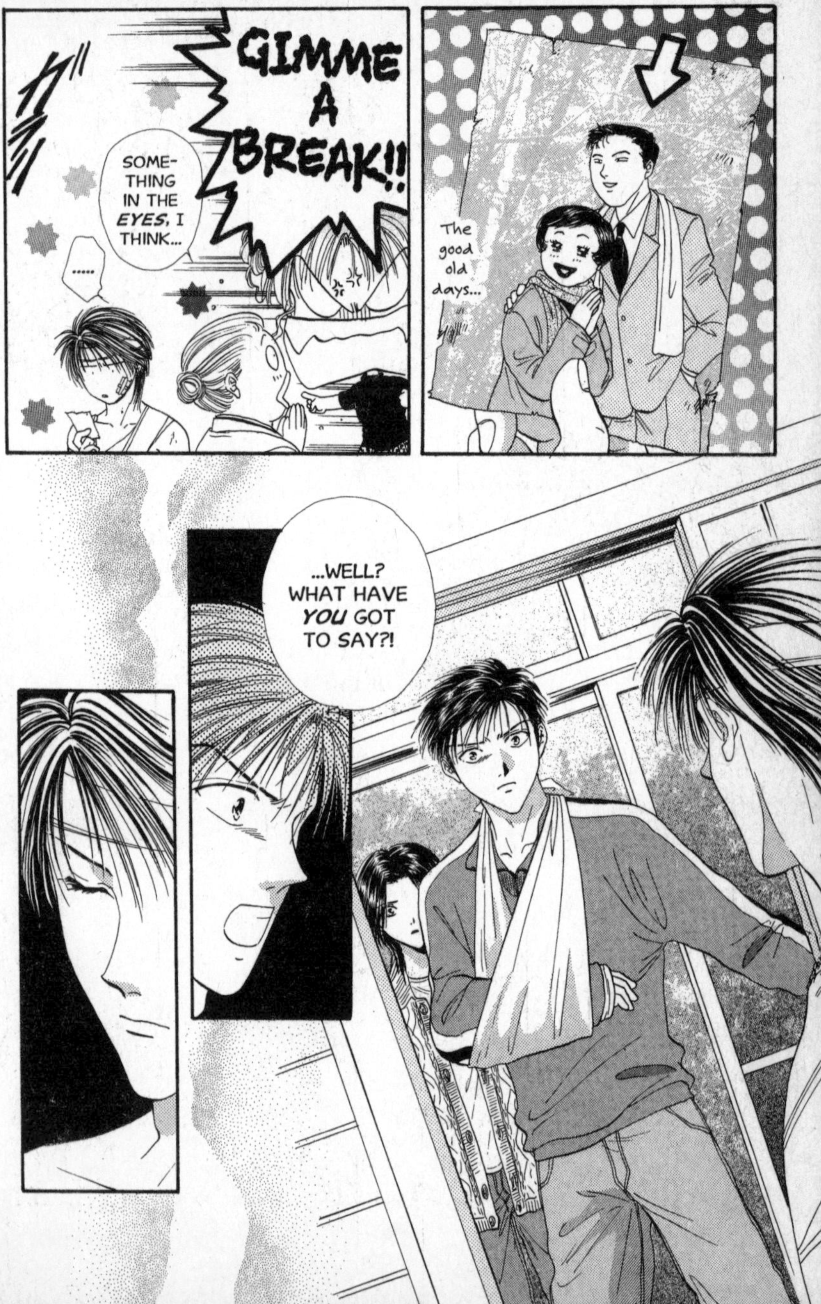
The good old days...
GIMME A BREAK!!
SOME-THING IN THE *EYES*, I THINK...
......
...WELL? WHAT HAVE *YOU* GOT TO SAY?!

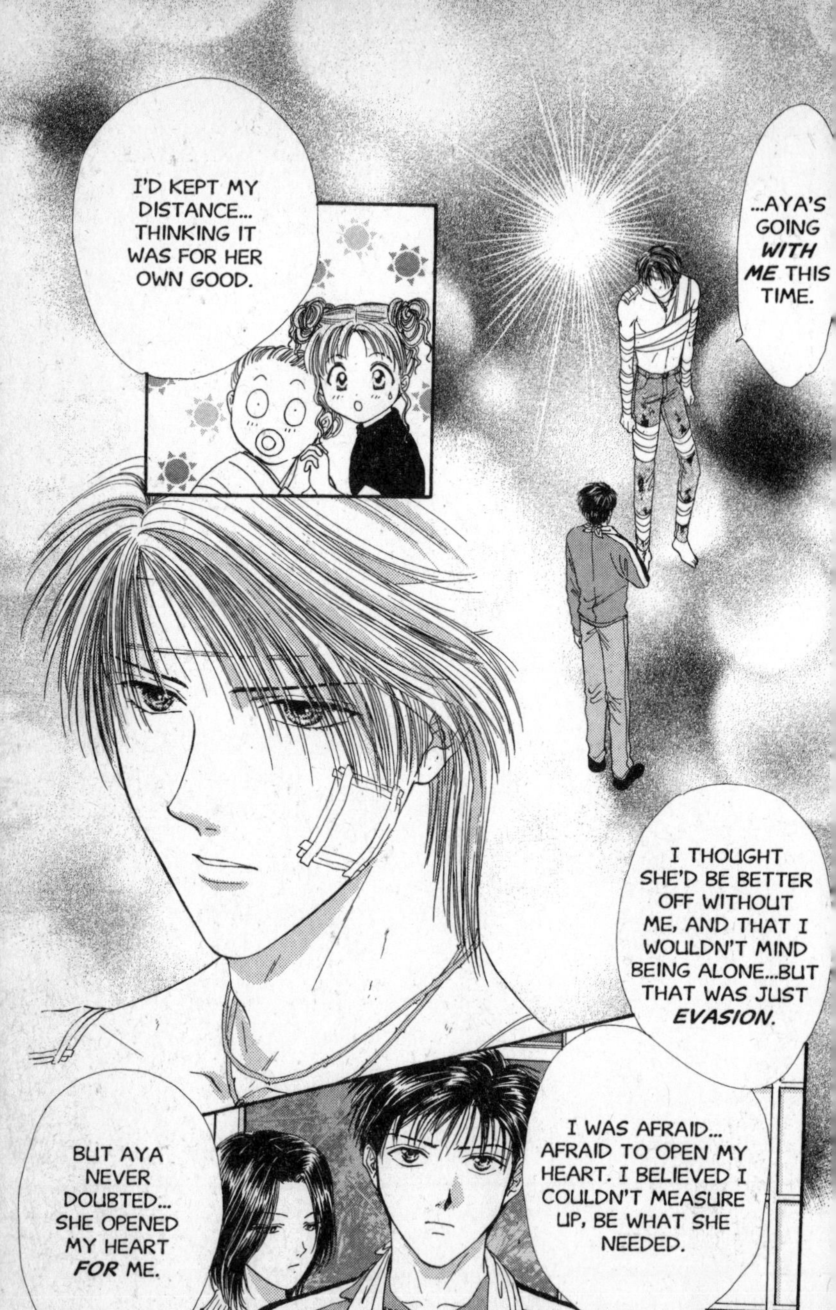
...AYA'S GOING *WITH ME* THIS TIME.
I'D KEPT MY DISTANCE... THINKING IT WAS FOR HER OWN GOOD.
I THOUGHT SHE'D BE BETTER OFF WITHOUT ME, AND THAT I WOULDN'T MIND BEING ALONE...BUT THAT WAS JUST *EVASION*.
I WAS AFRAID... AFRAID TO OPEN MY HEART. I BELIEVED I COULDN'T MEASURE UP, BE WHAT SHE NEEDED.
BUT AYA NEVER DOUBTED... SHE OPENED MY HEART *FOR* ME.

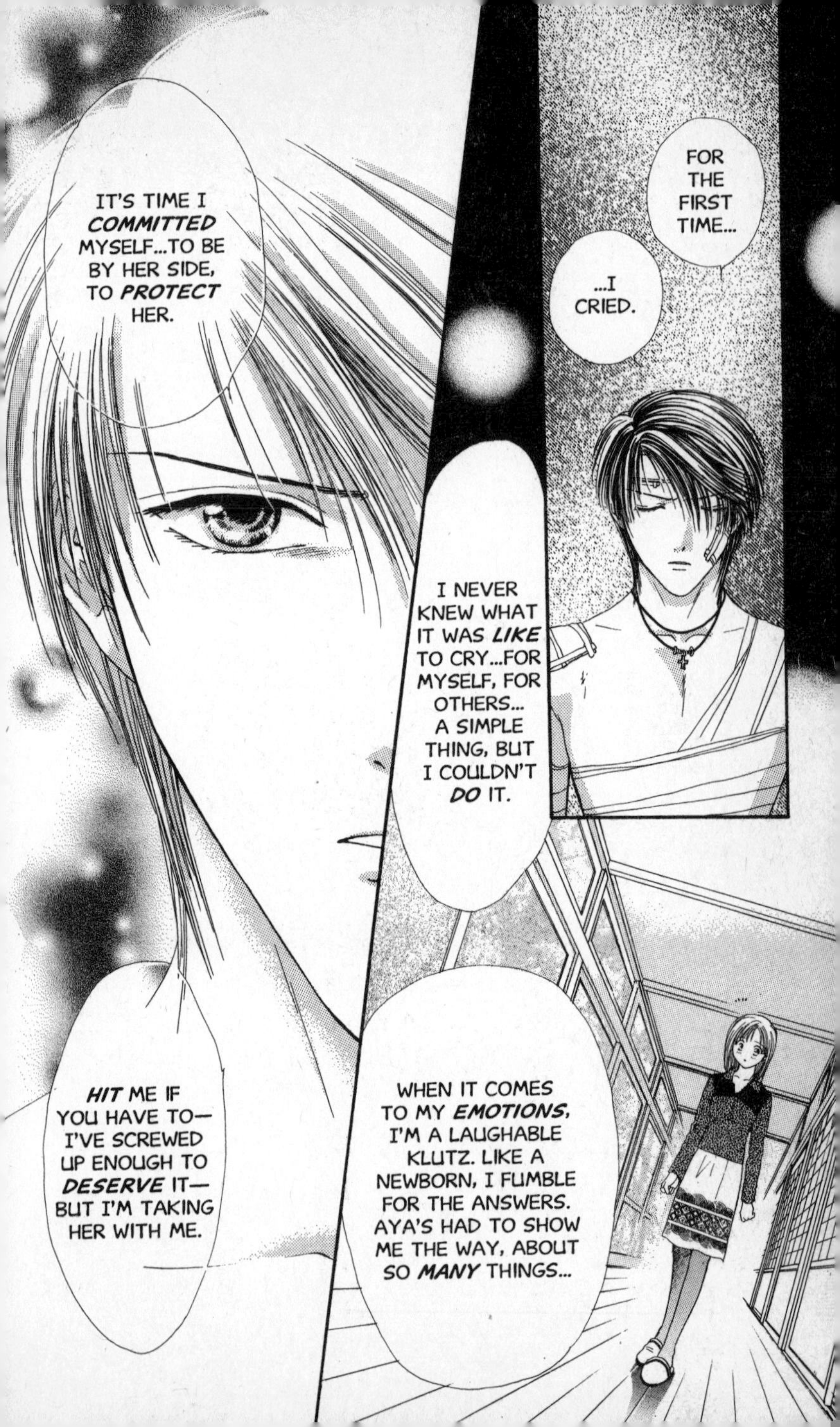
FOR THE FIRST TIME...
...I CRIED.
I NEVER KNEW WHAT IT WAS *LIKE* TO CRY...FOR MYSELF, FOR OTHERS... A SIMPLE THING, BUT I COULDN'T *DO* IT.
...
WHEN IT COMES TO MY *EMOTIONS*, I'M A LAUGHABLE KLUTZ. LIKE A NEWBORN, I FUMBLE FOR THE ANSWERS. AYA'S HAD TO SHOW ME THE WAY, ABOUT SO *MANY* THINGS...
IT'S TIME I *COMMITTED* MYSELF...TO BE BY HER SIDE, TO *PROTECT* HER.
HIT ME IF YOU HAVE TO—I'VE SCREWED UP ENOUGH TO *DESERVE* IT—BUT I'M TAKING HER WITH ME.

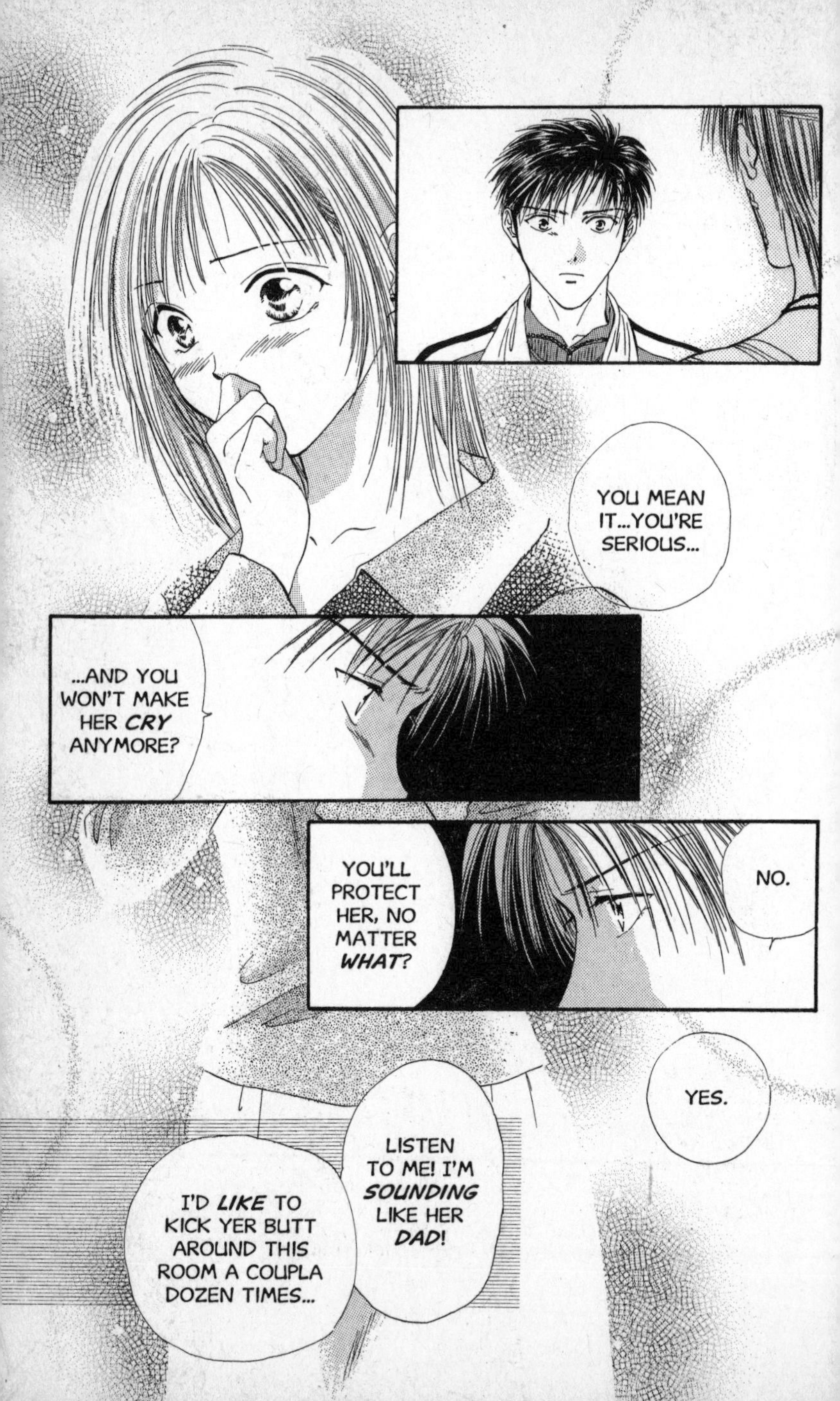
YOU MEAN IT...YOU'RE SERIOUS...
...AND YOU WON'T MAKE HER *CRY* ANYMORE?
NO.
YOU'LL PROTECT HER, NO MATTER *WHAT*?
YES.
LISTEN TO ME! I'M *SOUNDING* LIKE HER *DAD*!
I'D *LIKE* TO KICK YER BUTT AROUND THIS ROOM A COUPLA DOZEN TIMES...

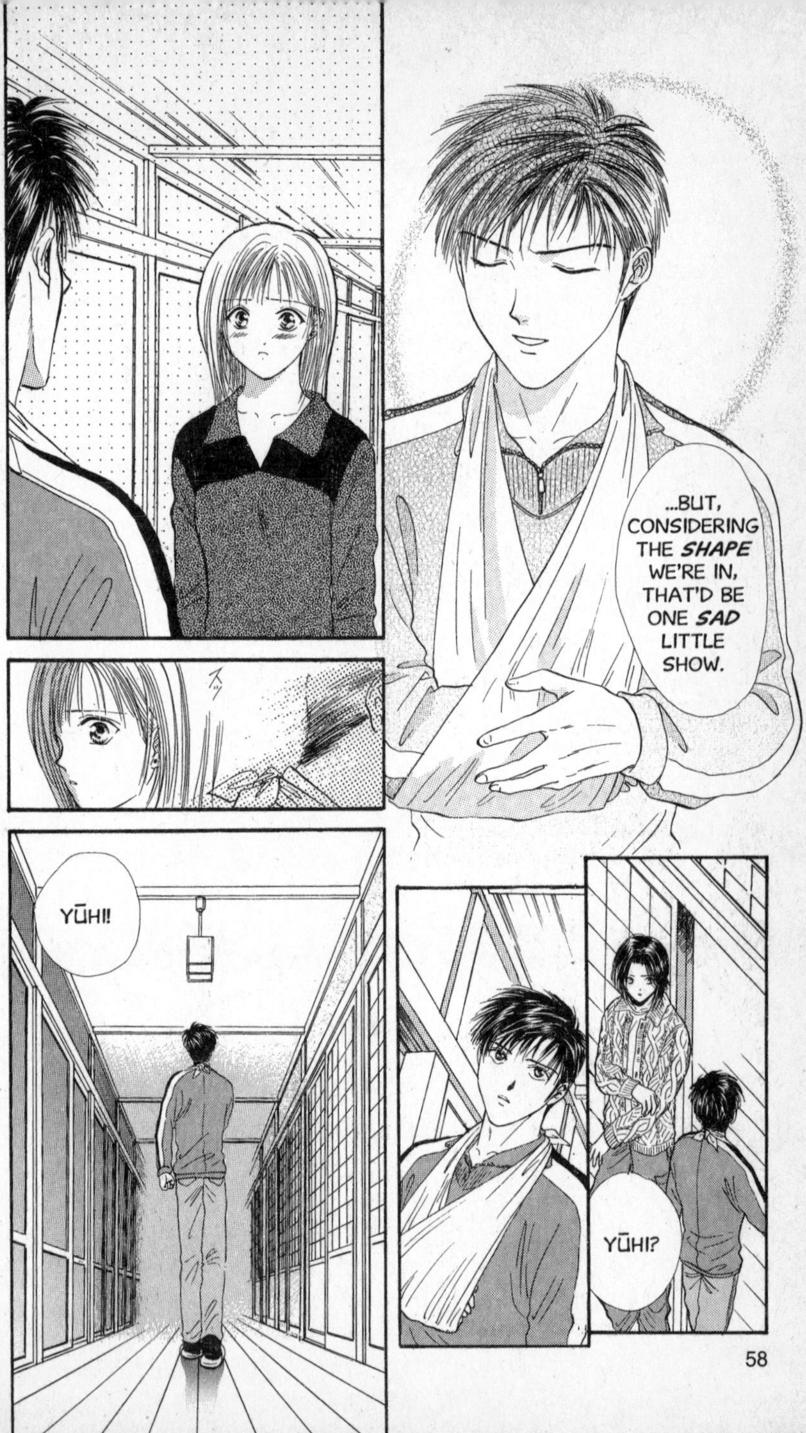
...BUT, CONSIDERING THE *SHAPE* WE'RE IN, THAT'D BE ONE *SAD* LITTLE SHOW.
YŪHI?
YŪHI!

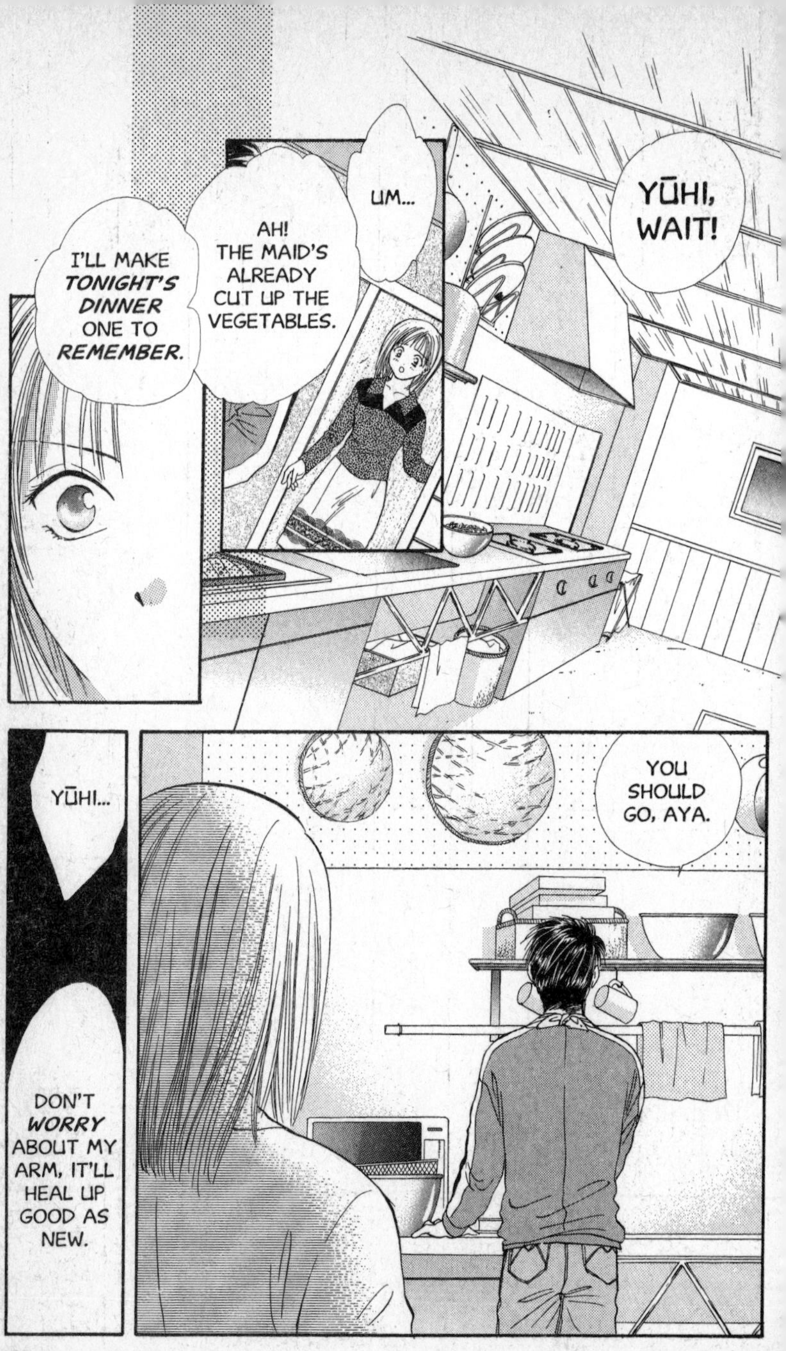
YŪHI, WAIT!
UM...
AH! THE MAID'S ALREADY CUT UP THE VEGETABLES.
I'LL MAKE TONIGHT'S DINNER ONE TO REMEMBER.
YOU SHOULD GO, AYA.
YŪHI...
DON'T WORRY ABOUT MY ARM, IT'LL HEAL UP GOOD AS NEW.

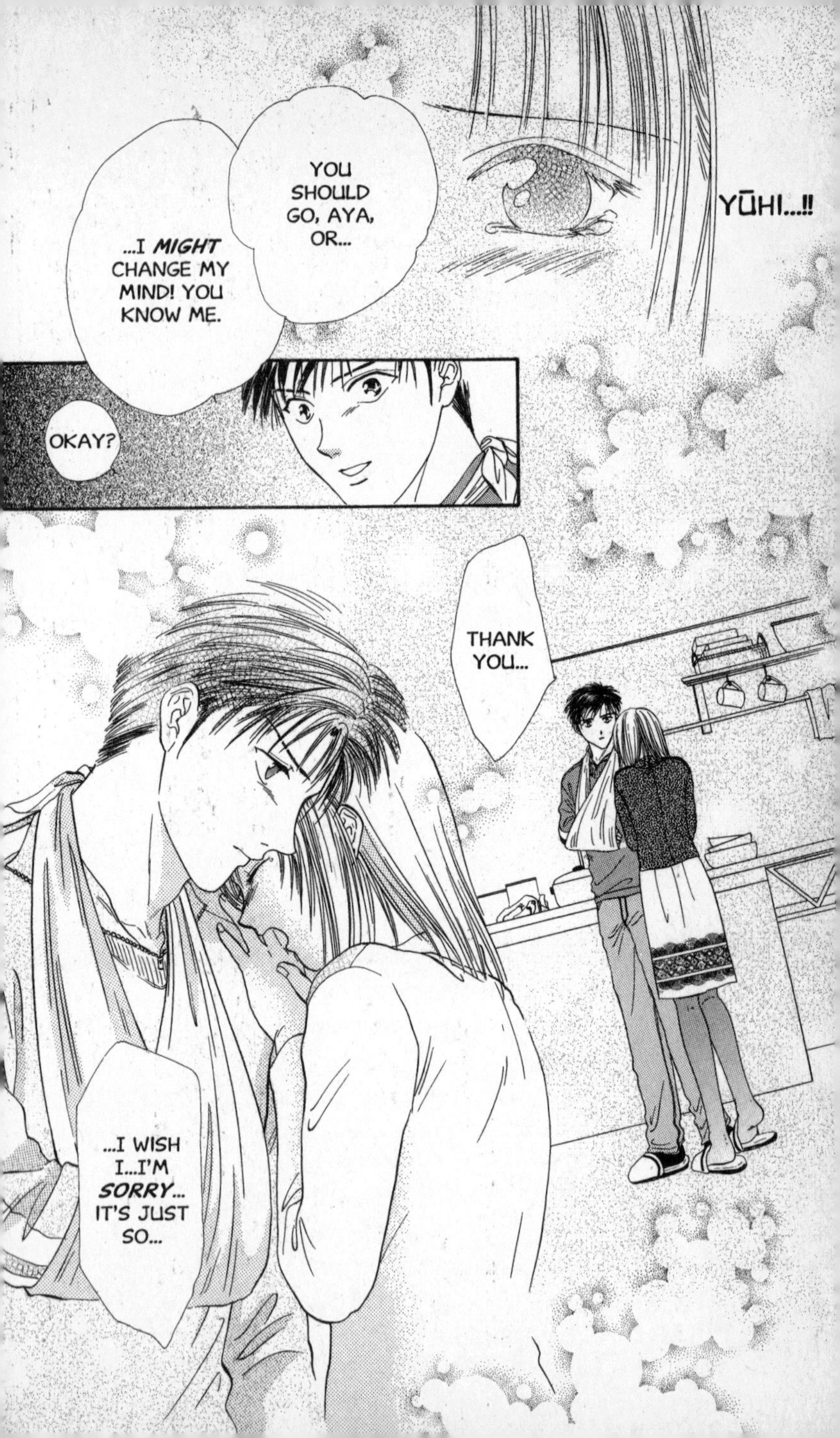
YŪHI...!!
YOU SHOULD GO, AYA, OR...
...I *MIGHT* CHANGE MY MIND! YOU KNOW ME.
OKAY?
THANK YOU...
...I WISH I...I'M *SORRY*... IT'S JUST SO...

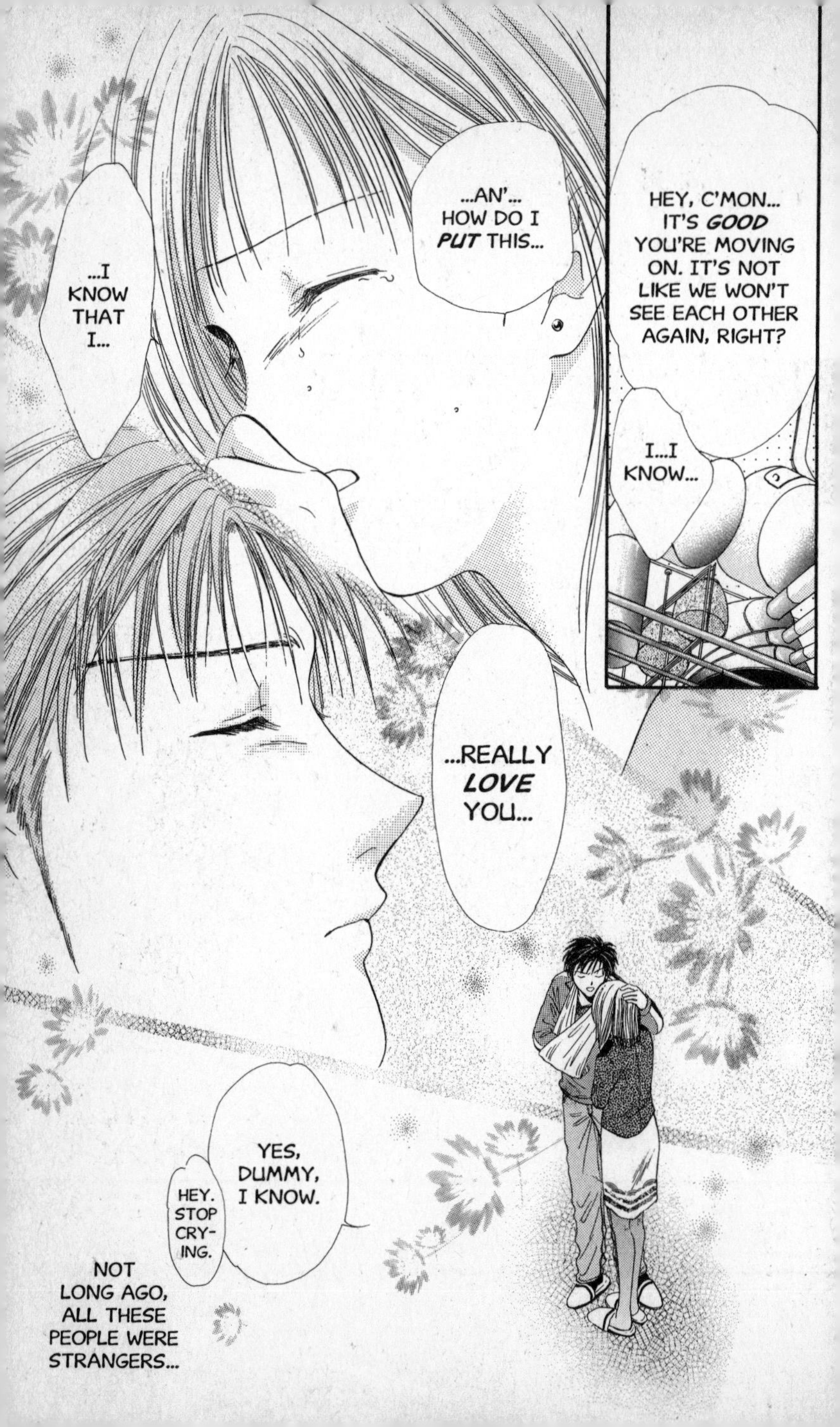
HEY, C'MON... IT'S *GOOD* YOU'RE MOVING ON. IT'S NOT LIKE WE WON'T SEE EACH OTHER AGAIN, RIGHT?
I...I KNOW...
...AN'... HOW DO I *PUT* THIS...
...I KNOW THAT I...
...REALLY *LOVE* YOU...
YES, DUMMY, I KNOW.
HEY. STOP CRY-ING.
NOT LONG AGO, ALL THESE PEOPLE WERE STRANGERS...

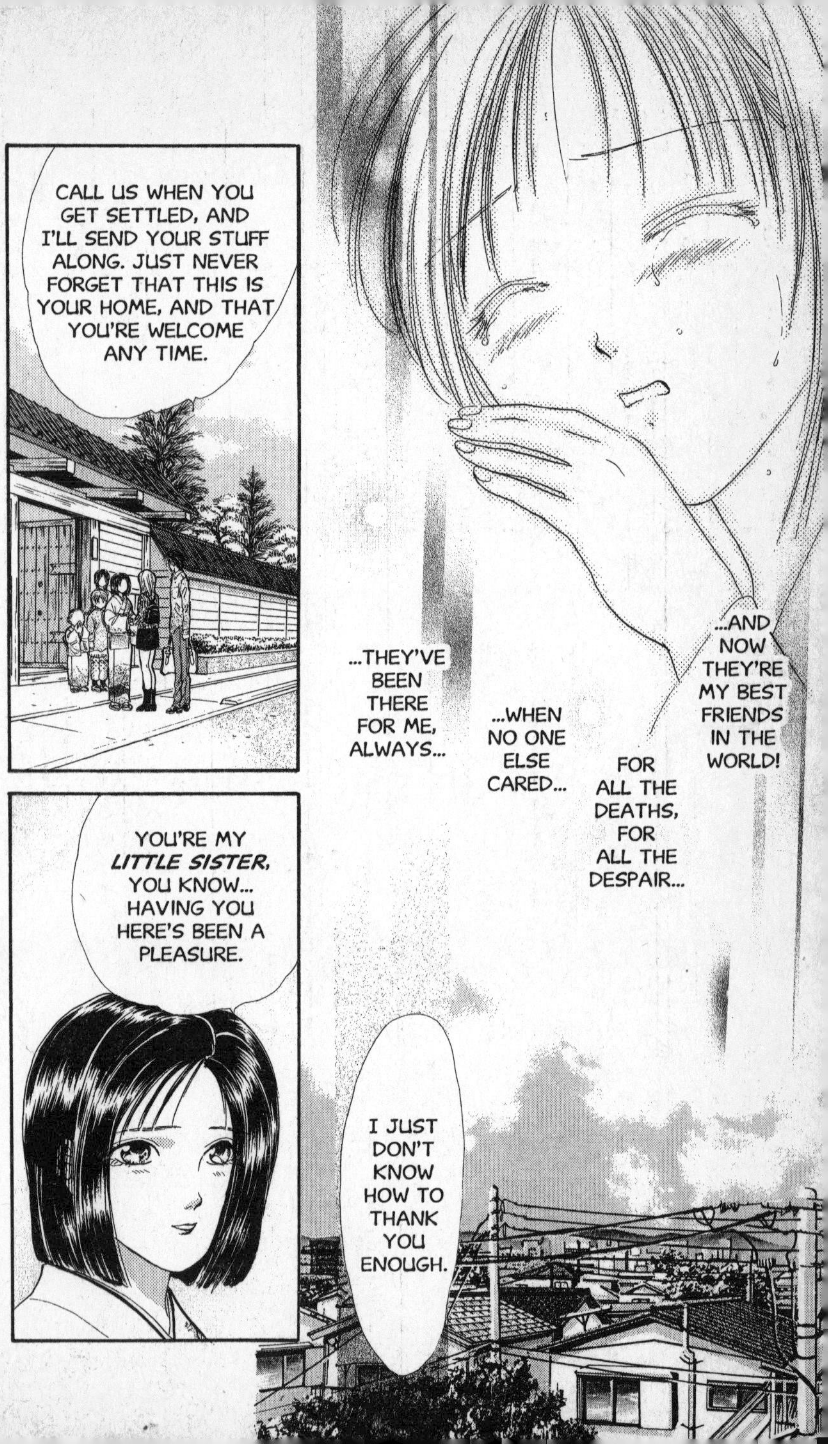
CALL US WHEN YOU GET SETTLED, AND I'LL SEND YOUR STUFF ALONG. JUST NEVER FORGET THAT THIS IS YOUR HOME, AND THAT YOU'RE WELCOME ANY TIME.
YOU'RE MY *LITTLE SISTER*, YOU KNOW... HAVING YOU HERE'S BEEN A PLEASURE.
...THEY'VE BEEN THERE FOR ME, ALWAYS...
...WHEN NO ONE ELSE CARED...
FOR ALL THE DEATHS, FOR ALL THE DESPAIR...
...AND NOW THEY'RE MY BEST FRIENDS IN THE WORLD!
I JUST DON'T KNOW HOW TO THANK YOU ENOUGH.

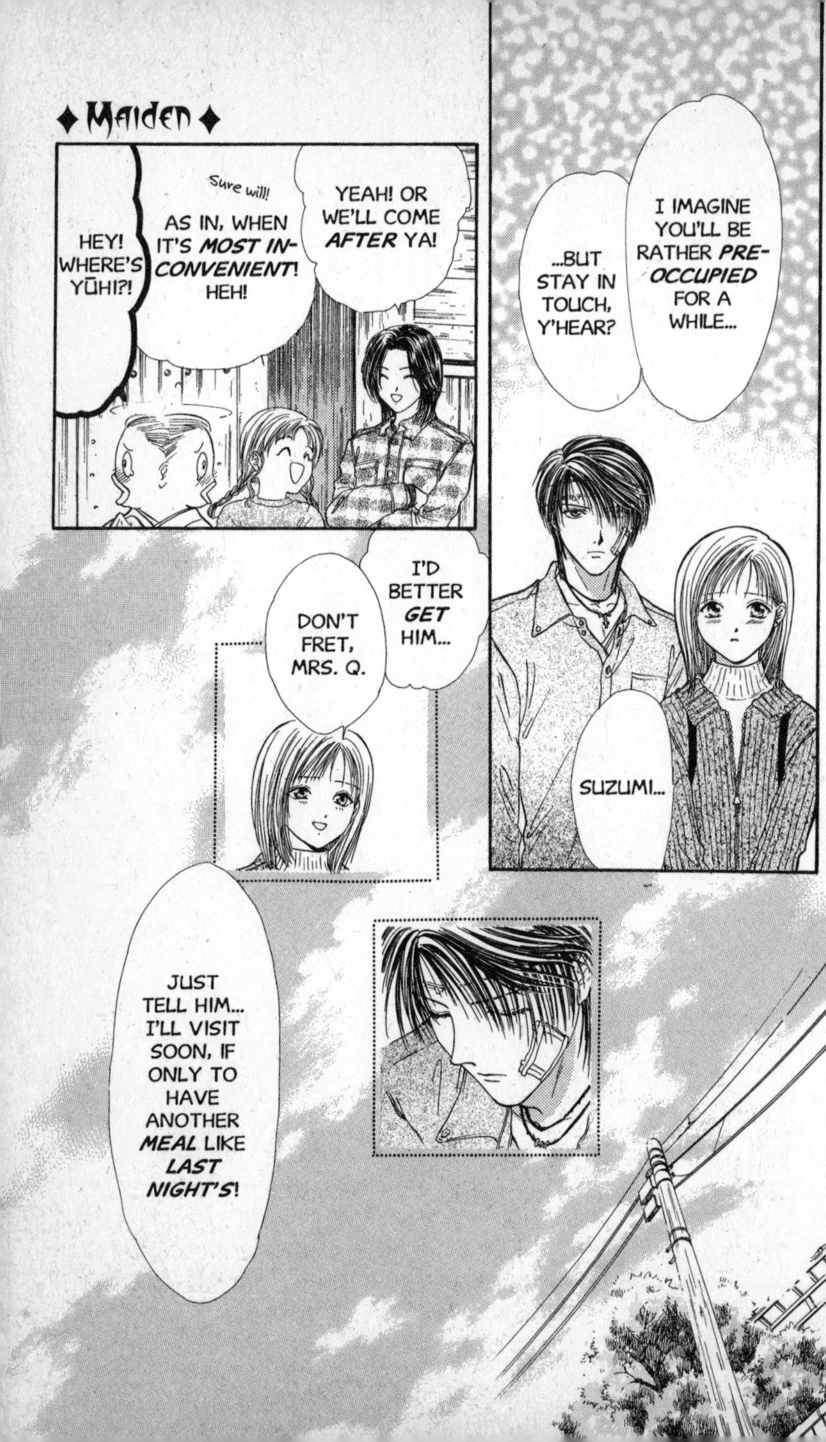
I IMAGINE YOU'LL BE RATHER PRE-OCCUPIED FOR A WHILE...
...BUT STAY IN TOUCH, Y'HEAR?
SUZUMI...
YEAH! OR WE'LL COME AFTER YA!
Sure will!
AS IN, WHEN IT'S MOST IN-CONVENIENT! HEH!
HEY! WHERE'S YŪHI?!
I'D BETTER GET HIM...
DON'T FRET, MRS. Q.
JUST TELL HIM... I'LL VISIT SOON, IF ONLY TO HAVE ANOTHER MEAL LIKE LAST NIGHT'S!

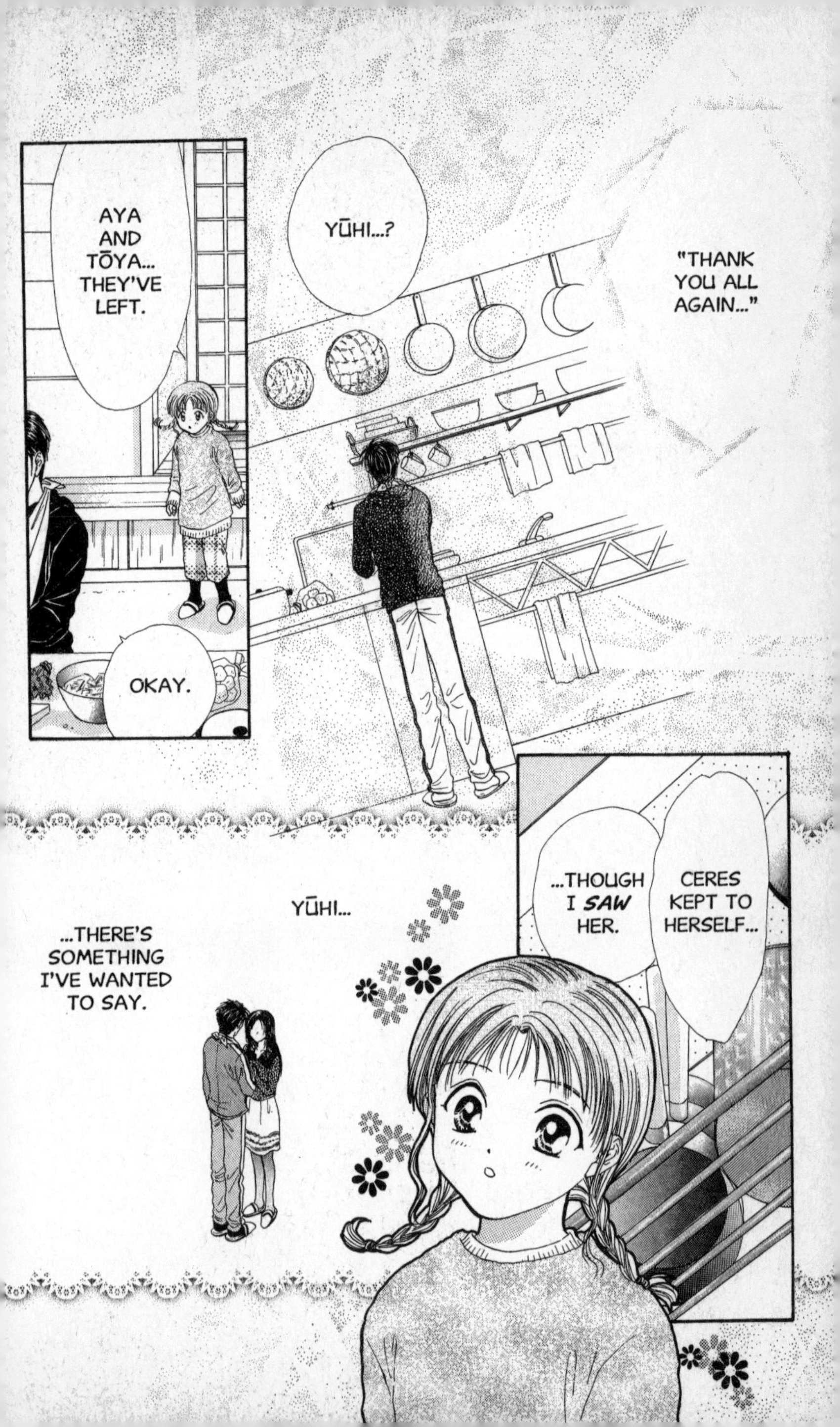
"THANK YOU ALL AGAIN..."
YŪHI...?
AYA AND TŌYA... THEY'VE LEFT.
OKAY.
CERES KEPT TO HERSELF...
...THOUGH I *SAW* HER.
YŪHI...
...THERE'S SOMETHING I'VE WANTED TO SAY.

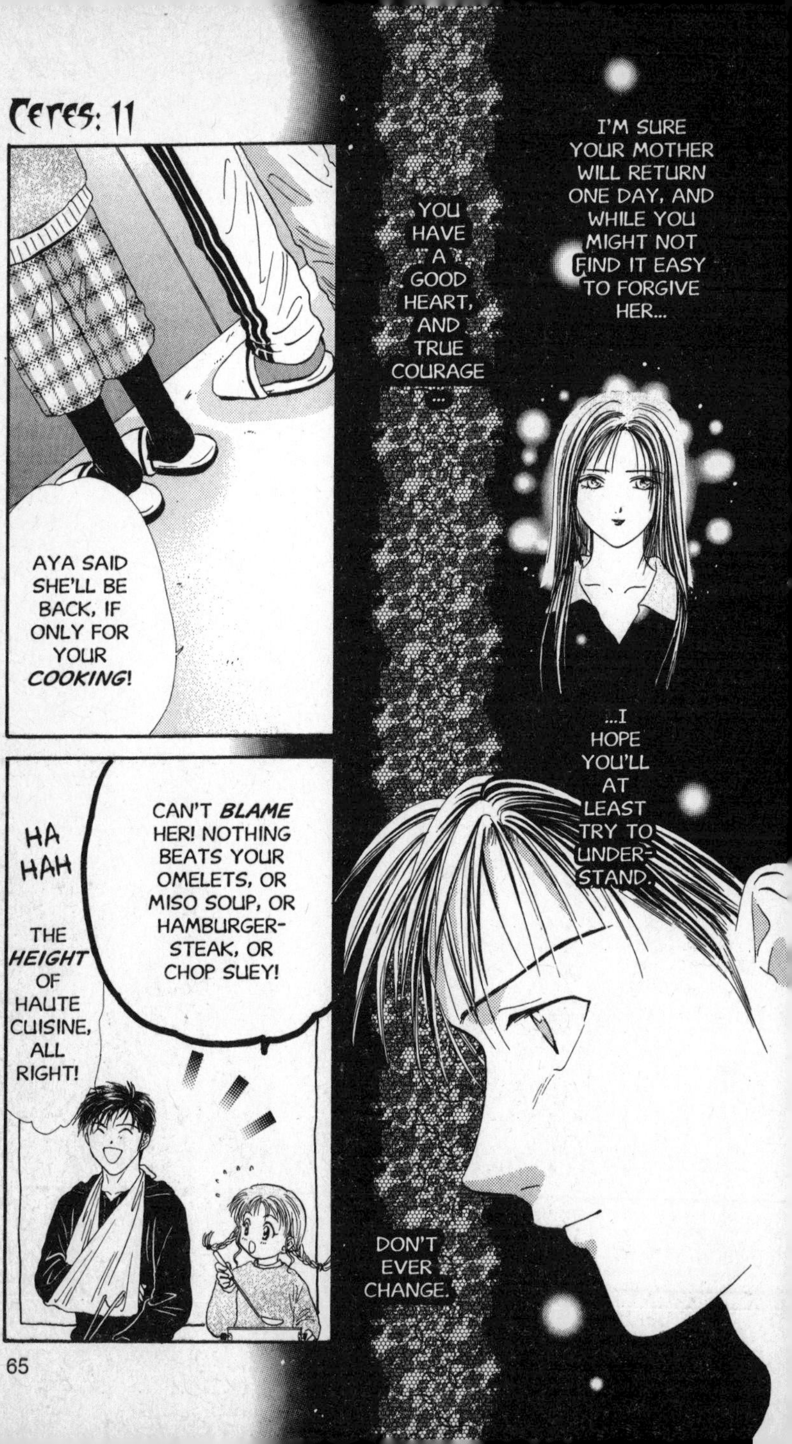
I'M SURE YOUR MOTHER WILL RETURN ONE DAY, AND WHILE YOU MIGHT NOT FIND IT EASY TO FORGIVE HER...
YOU HAVE A GOOD HEART, AND TRUE COURAGE ...
...I HOPE YOU'LL AT LEAST TRY TO UNDER-STAND.
DON'T EVER CHANGE.
AYA SAID SHE'LL BE BACK, IF ONLY FOR YOUR *COOKING*!
CAN'T *BLAME* HER! NOTHING BEATS YOUR OMELETS, OR MISO SOUP, OR HAMBURGER-STEAK, OR CHOP SUEY!
HA HAH
THE *HEIGHT* OF HAUTE CUISINE, ALL RIGHT!

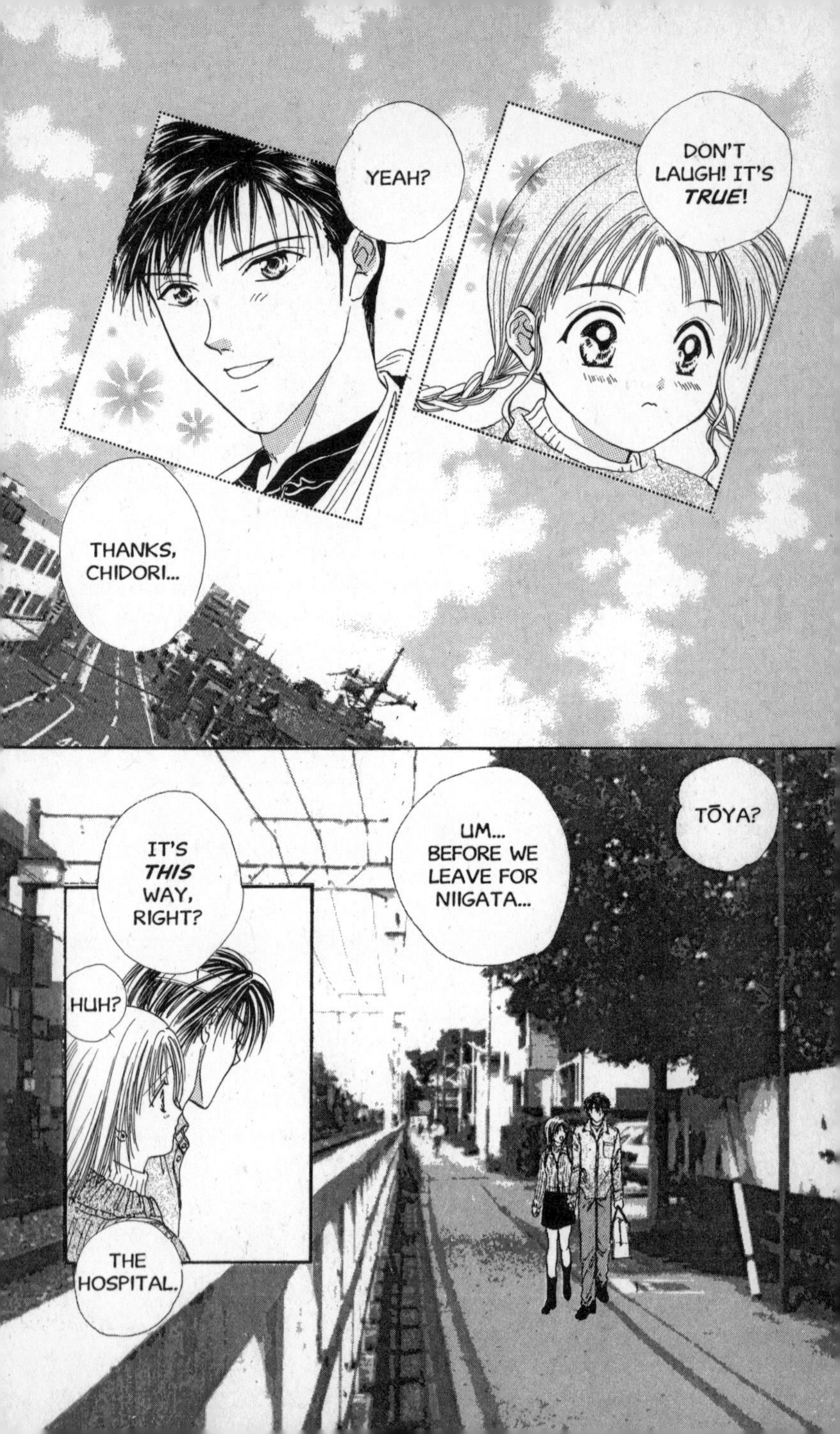
DON'T LAUGH! IT'S *TRUE*!
YEAH?
THANKS, CHIDORI...
TŌYA?
UM... BEFORE WE LEAVE FOR NIIGATA...
IT'S ***THIS*** WAY, RIGHT?
HUH?
THE HOSPITAL.

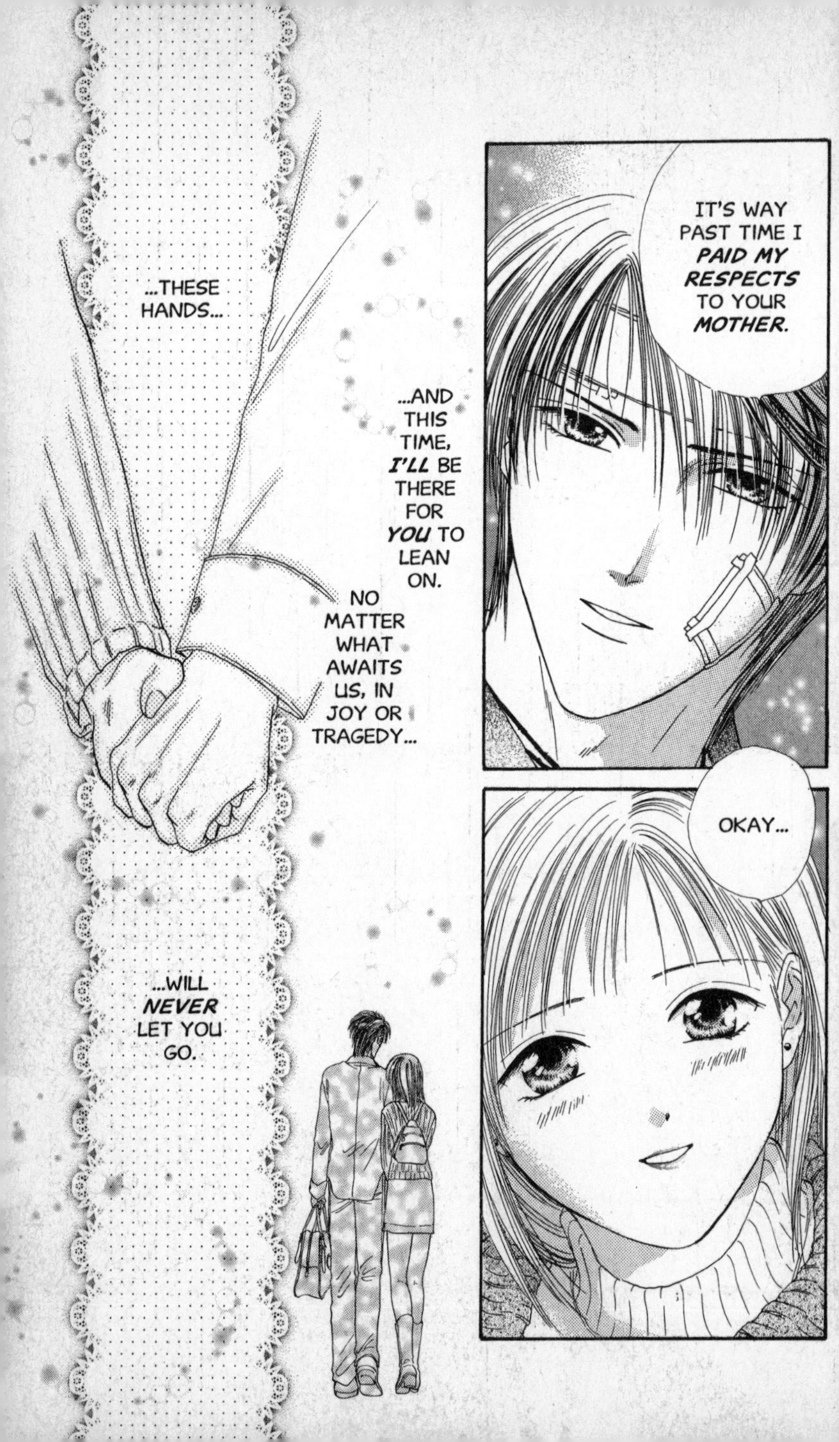
IT'S WAY PAST TIME I PAID MY RESPECTS TO YOUR MOTHER.
OKAY...
...AND THIS TIME, I'LL BE THERE FOR YOU TO LEAN ON.
NO MATTER WHAT AWAITS US, IN JOY OR TRAGEDY...
...THESE HANDS...
...WILL NEVER LET YOU GO.

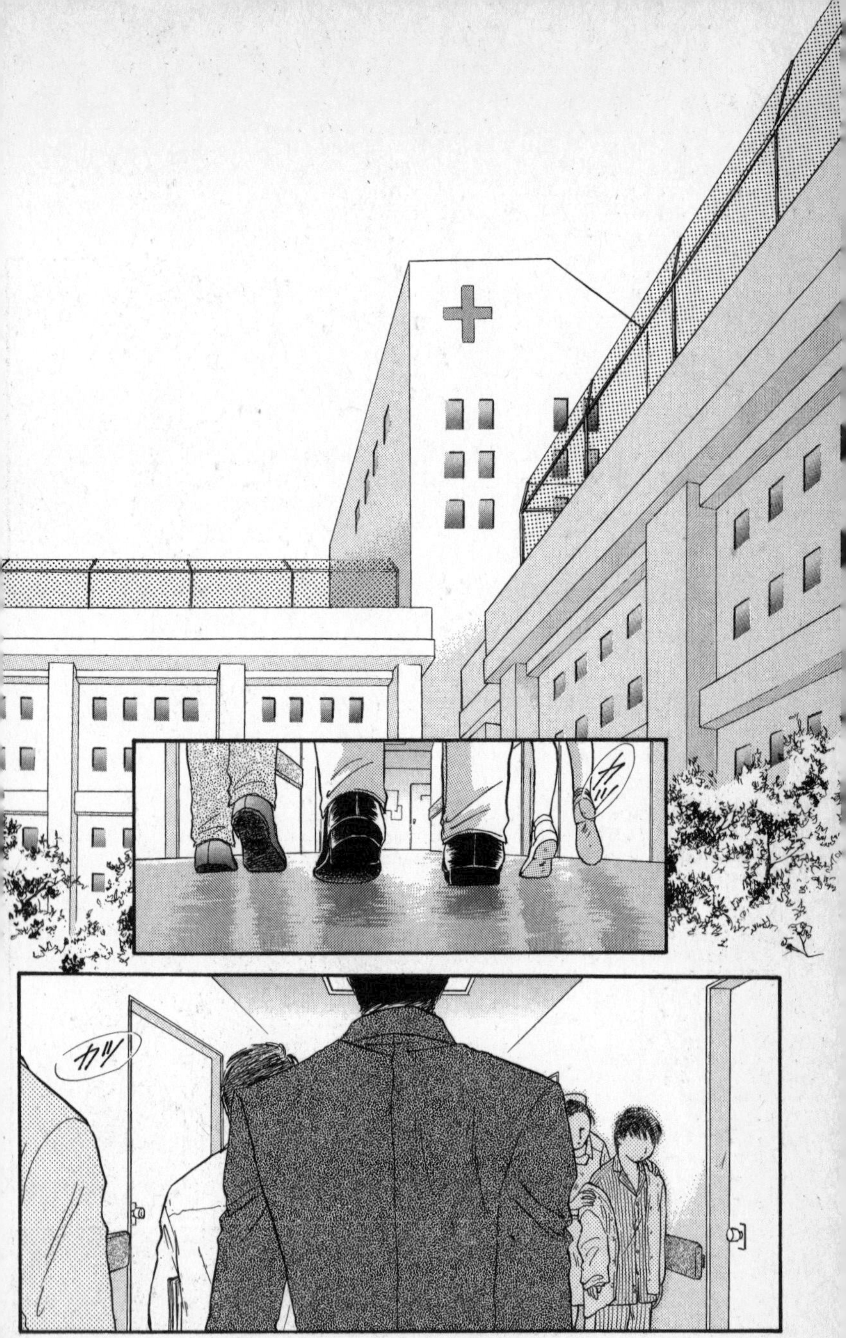
カツ
カツ

◆ Maiden ◆

I met with a professor at a junior college who's also a manga critic, and we talked about sex and violence in manga. He said, "Everyone has violent impulses once in a while, but they **vent** their steam through **reading** such scenes in manga and other media." I totally agree. In an earlier conversation with a friend, we agreed that "if violent movies and manga are to blame, then everyone who sees them must also turn out to become murderers. If children can't distinguish between fantasy and reality, that's more a problem with their upbringing." I support everyone's dreaming and fantasizing about whatever they want to be, but surely people usually do know what's right and wrong! That's not to say that creators are to be held entirely blameless—you can't add violent or sexual scenes just 'cause it sells, or because it attracts an audience. It's a complicated problem, of course. The professor also said, "Everything rides on the aspirations of the creator." Hmm.... Being that I'm the type who insists on bringing things to their logical conclusions, I guess I'd better keep a strong grip on those aspirations! I got a letter that said, "Everyone talks about the dangers of manga, but we kids aren't that dumb!" I was like, "You said it!" Lots of people say that kids these days lack critical/analytical ability, and I can't say that they're totally wrong. I do try to be straightforward. Even so, I get lots of letters from young readers who try to analyze the characters' innermost emotions, and it's that kind of thinking that will lead to better interpersonal relations. Try not to be anti-social, huh?

When people go on and on about the sex scenes, though, I sometimes wonder why they're so obsessed. ◡̈ There was an article in the paper...

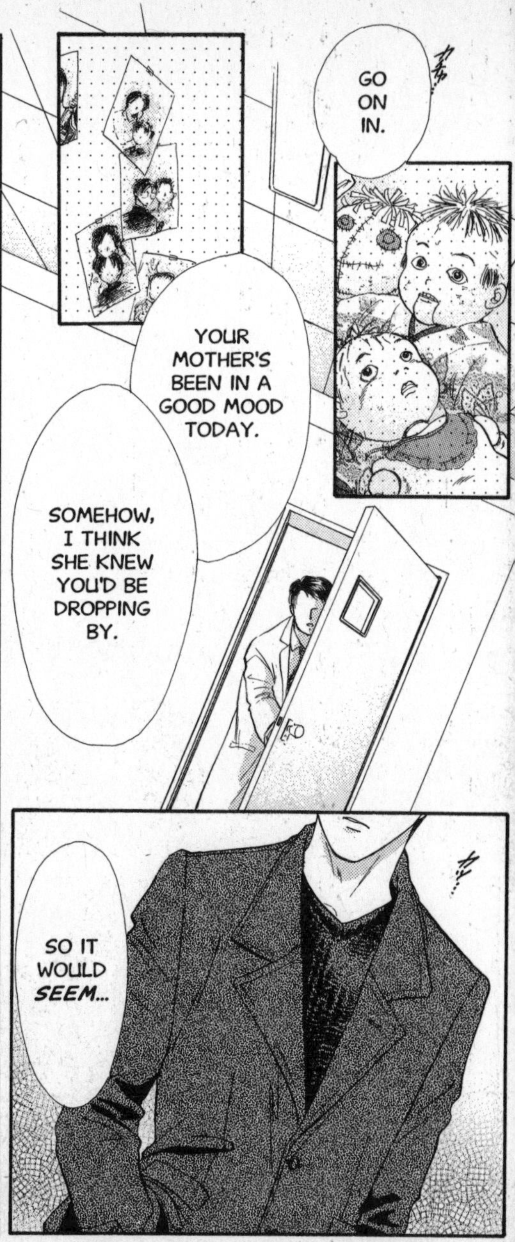
GO ON IN.
YOUR MOTHER'S BEEN IN A GOOD MOOD TODAY.
SOMEHOW, I THINK SHE KNEW YOU'D BE DROPPING BY.
SO IT WOULD *SEEM*...

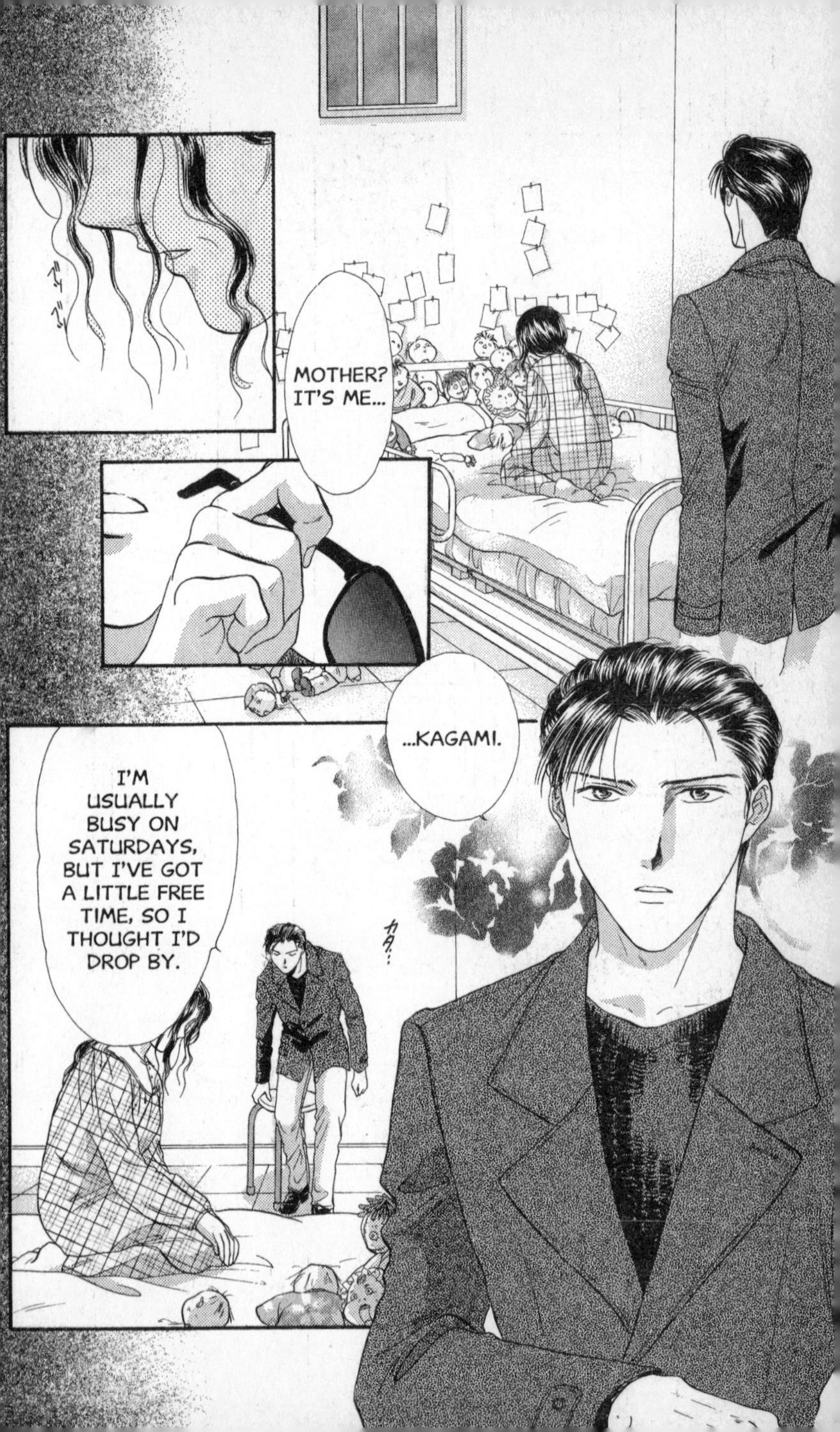
MOTHER? IT'S ME...
...KAGAMI.
I'M USUALLY BUSY ON SATURDAYS, BUT I'VE GOT A LITTLE FREE TIME, SO I THOUGHT I'D DROP BY.

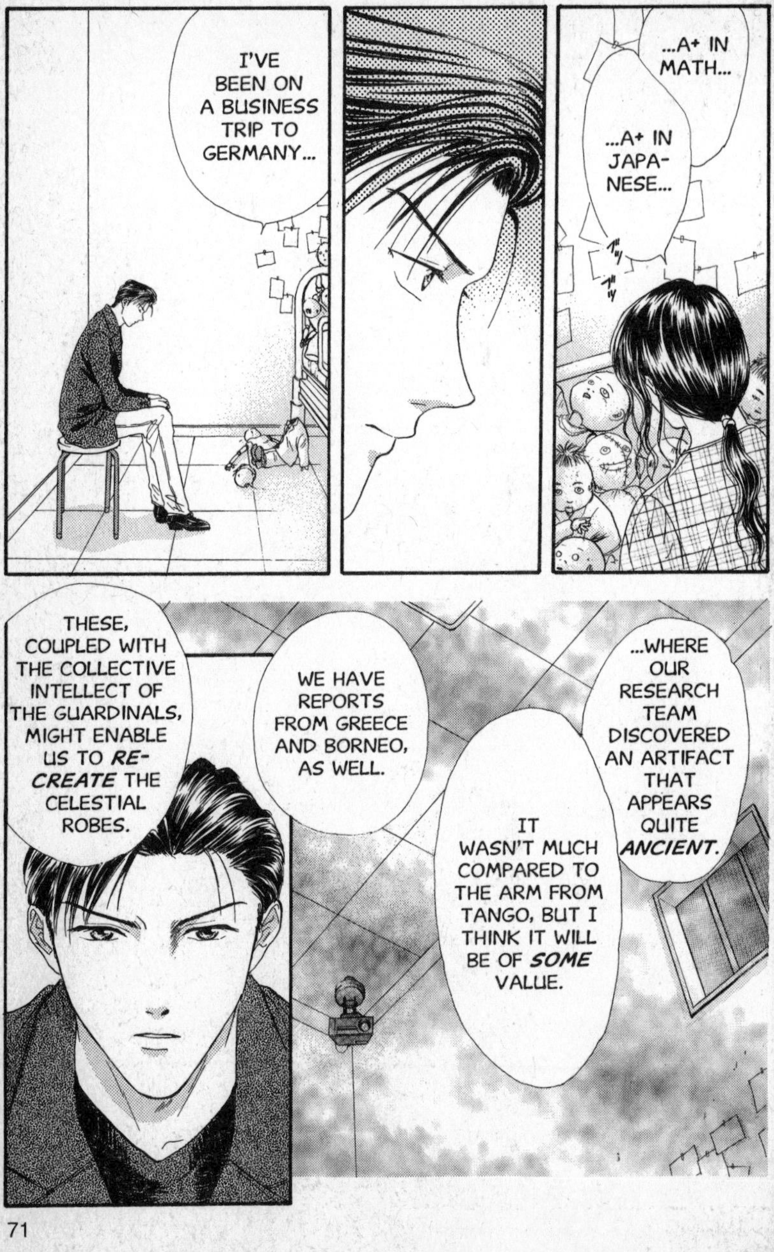
...A+ IN MATH...
...A+ IN JAPANESE...
I'VE BEEN ON A BUSINESS TRIP TO GERMANY...
...WHERE OUR RESEARCH TEAM DISCOVERED AN ARTIFACT THAT APPEARS QUITE *ANCIENT*.
IT WASN'T MUCH COMPARED TO THE ARM FROM TANGO, BUT I THINK IT WILL BE OF *SOME* VALUE.
WE HAVE REPORTS FROM GREECE AND BORNEO, AS WELL.
THESE, COUPLED WITH THE COLLECTIVE INTELLECT OF THE GUARDINALS, MIGHT ENABLE US TO *RE-CREATE* THE CELESTIAL ROBES.

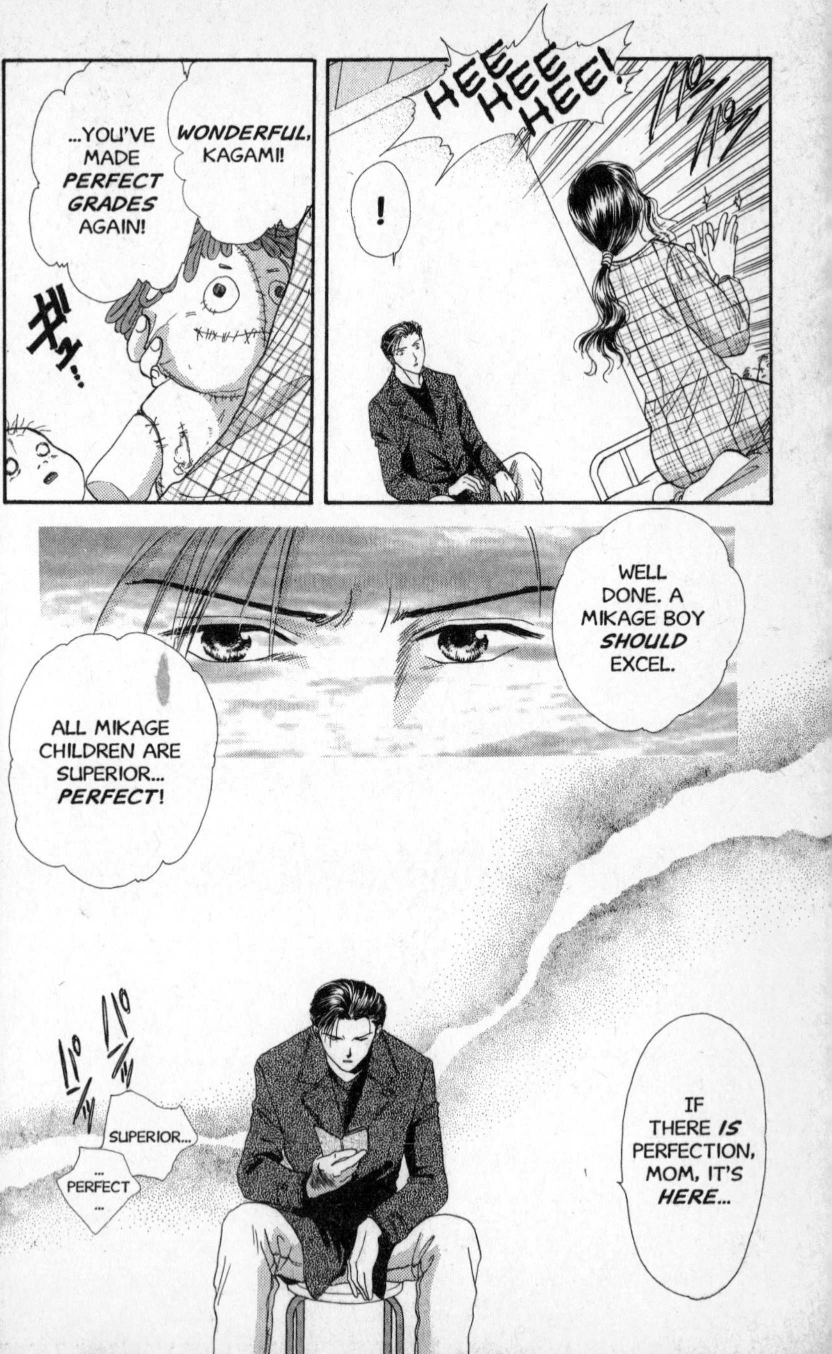
HEE HEE HEE!
!
WONDERFUL, KAGAMI!
...YOU'VE MADE PERFECT GRADES AGAIN!
WELL DONE. A MIKAGE BOY SHOULD EXCEL.
ALL MIKAGE CHILDREN ARE SUPERIOR... PERFECT!
IF THERE IS PERFECTION, MOM, IT'S HERE...
SUPERIOR...
...PERFECT...

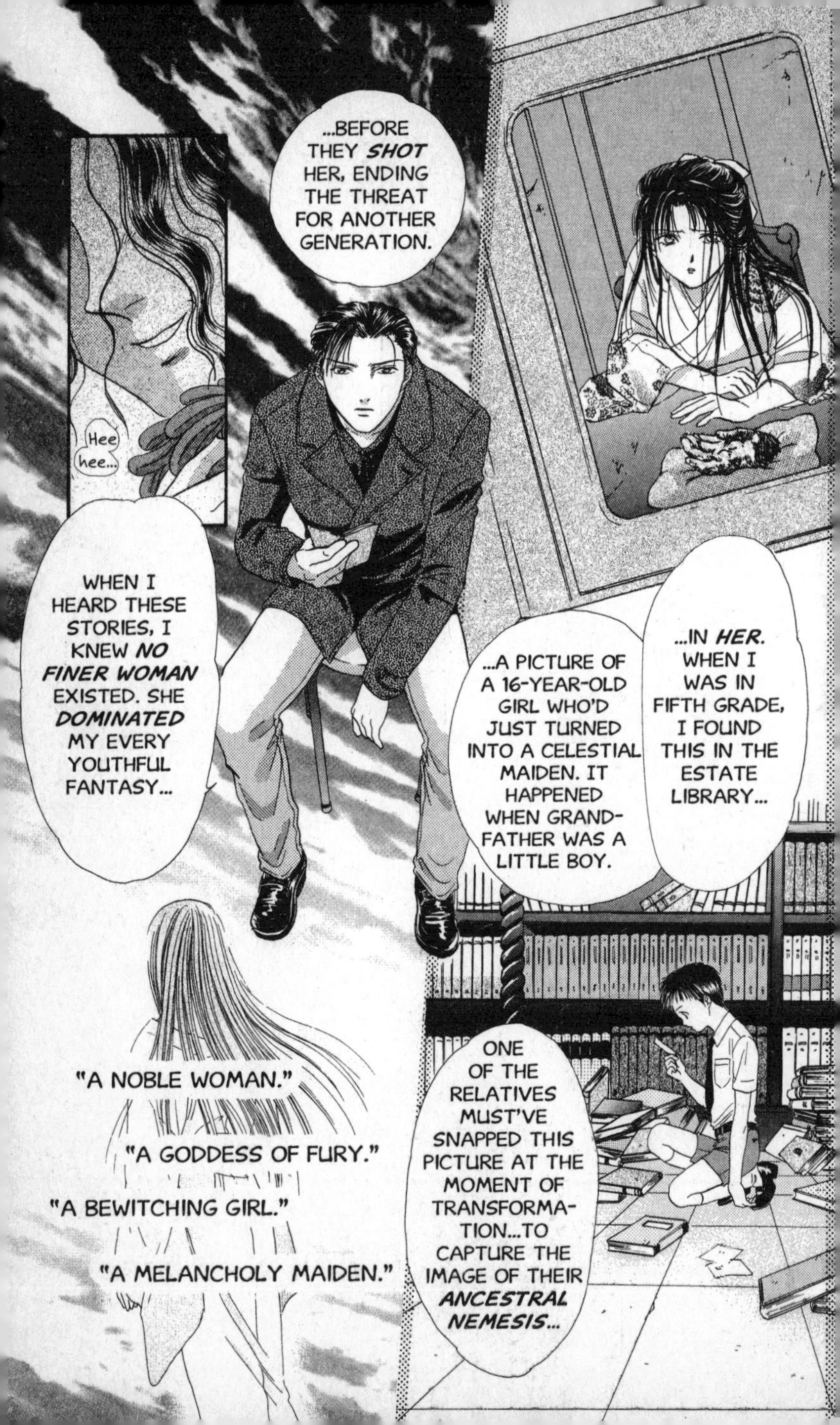
...BEFORE THEY *SHOT* HER, ENDING THE THREAT FOR ANOTHER GENERATION.
Hee hee...
WHEN I HEARD THESE STORIES, I KNEW *NO FINER WOMAN* EXISTED. SHE *DOMINATED* MY EVERY YOUTHFUL FANTASY...
"A NOBLE WOMAN."
"A GODDESS OF FURY."
"A BEWITCHING GIRL."
"A MELANCHOLY MAIDEN."
...IN *HER*. WHEN I WAS IN FIFTH GRADE, I FOUND THIS IN THE ESTATE LIBRARY...
...A PICTURE OF A 16-YEAR-OLD GIRL WHO'D JUST TURNED INTO A CELESTIAL MAIDEN. IT HAPPENED WHEN GRAND-FATHER WAS A LITTLE BOY.
ONE OF THE RELATIVES MUST'VE SNAPPED THIS PICTURE AT THE MOMENT OF TRANSFORMA-TION...TO CAPTURE THE IMAGE OF THEIR *ANCESTRAL NEMESIS*...

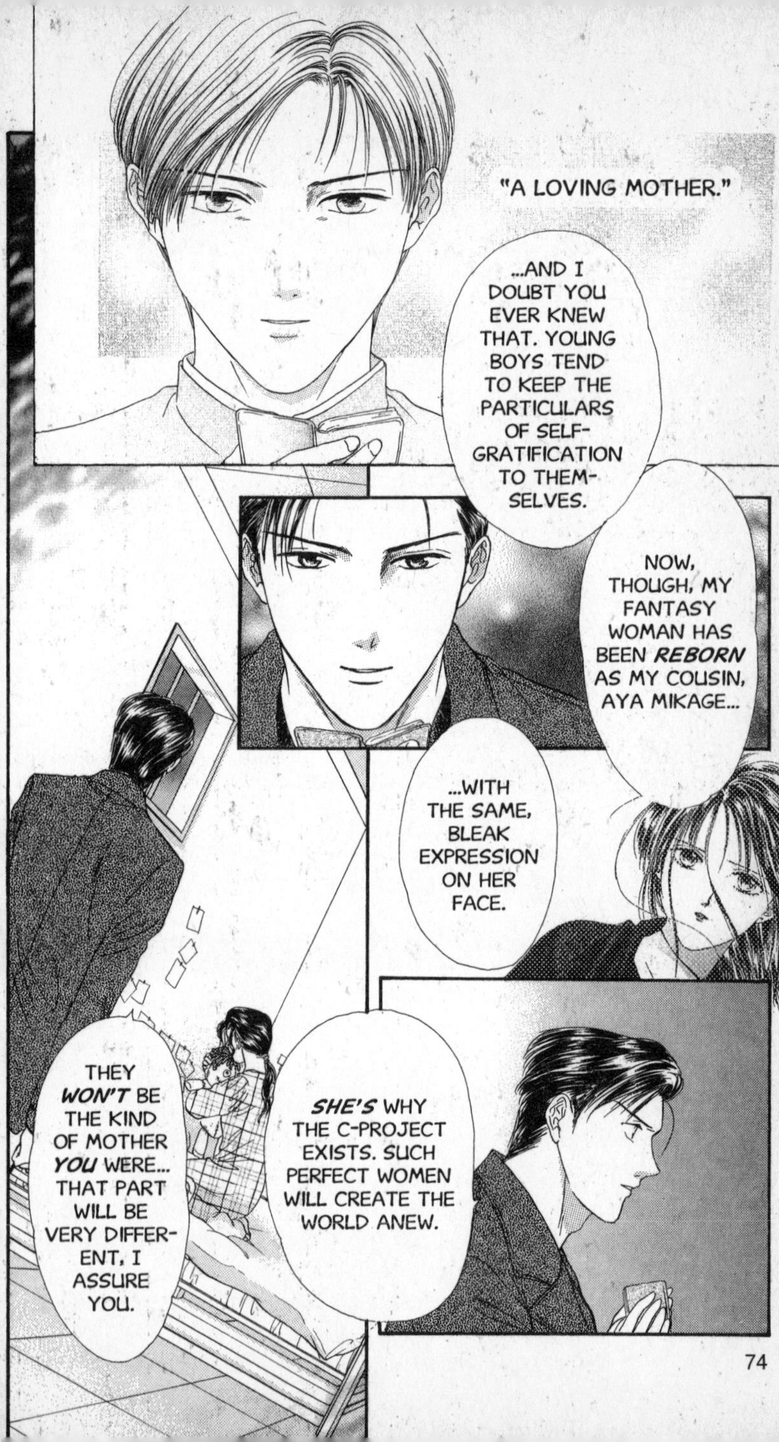
"A LOVING MOTHER."
...AND I DOUBT YOU EVER KNEW THAT. YOUNG BOYS TEND TO KEEP THE PARTICULARS OF SELF-GRATIFICATION TO THEM-SELVES.
NOW, THOUGH, MY FANTASY WOMAN HAS BEEN REBORN AS MY COUSIN, AYA MIKAGE...
...WITH THE SAME, BLEAK EXPRESSION ON HER FACE.
SHE'S WHY THE C-PROJECT EXISTS. SUCH PERFECT WOMEN WILL CREATE THE WORLD ANEW.
THEY WON'T BE THE KIND OF MOTHER YOU WERE... THAT PART WILL BE VERY DIFFER-ENT, I ASSURE YOU.

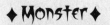

THINK OF IT... A *SUPERIOR HUMAN RACE*, FREE OF DEFECTS.

I'LL SEE YOU LATER, MOTHER...

...!

.....

WHO...

...*ARE* YOU?

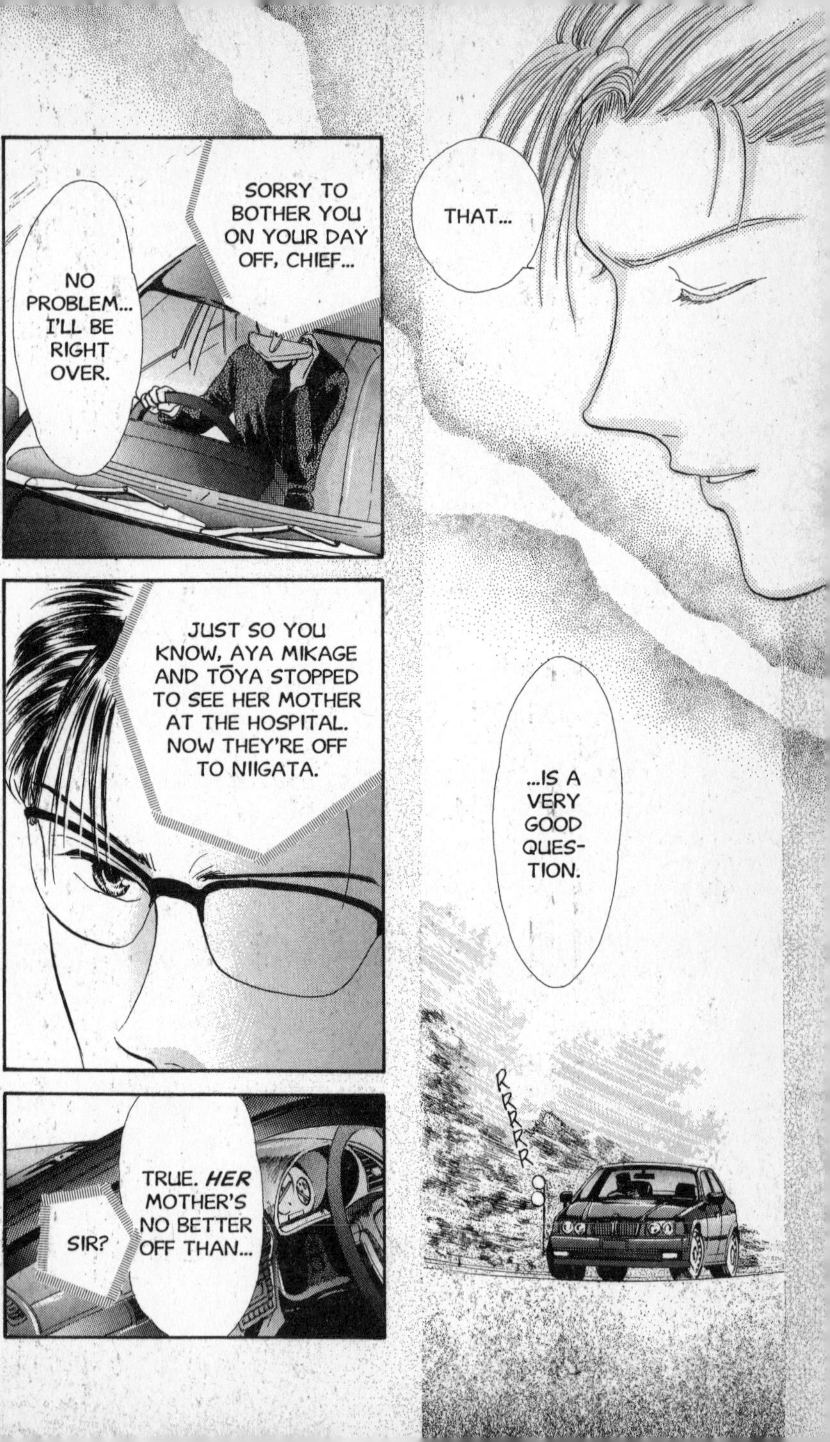
SORRY TO BOTHER YOU ON YOUR DAY OFF, CHIEF...
NO PROBLEM... I'LL BE RIGHT OVER.
JUST SO YOU KNOW, AYA MIKAGE AND TŌYA STOPPED TO SEE HER MOTHER AT THE HOSPITAL. NOW THEY'RE OFF TO NIIGATA.
TRUE. *HER* MOTHER'S NO BETTER OFF THAN...
SIR?
THAT...
...IS A VERY GOOD QUES-TION.
RRRRR

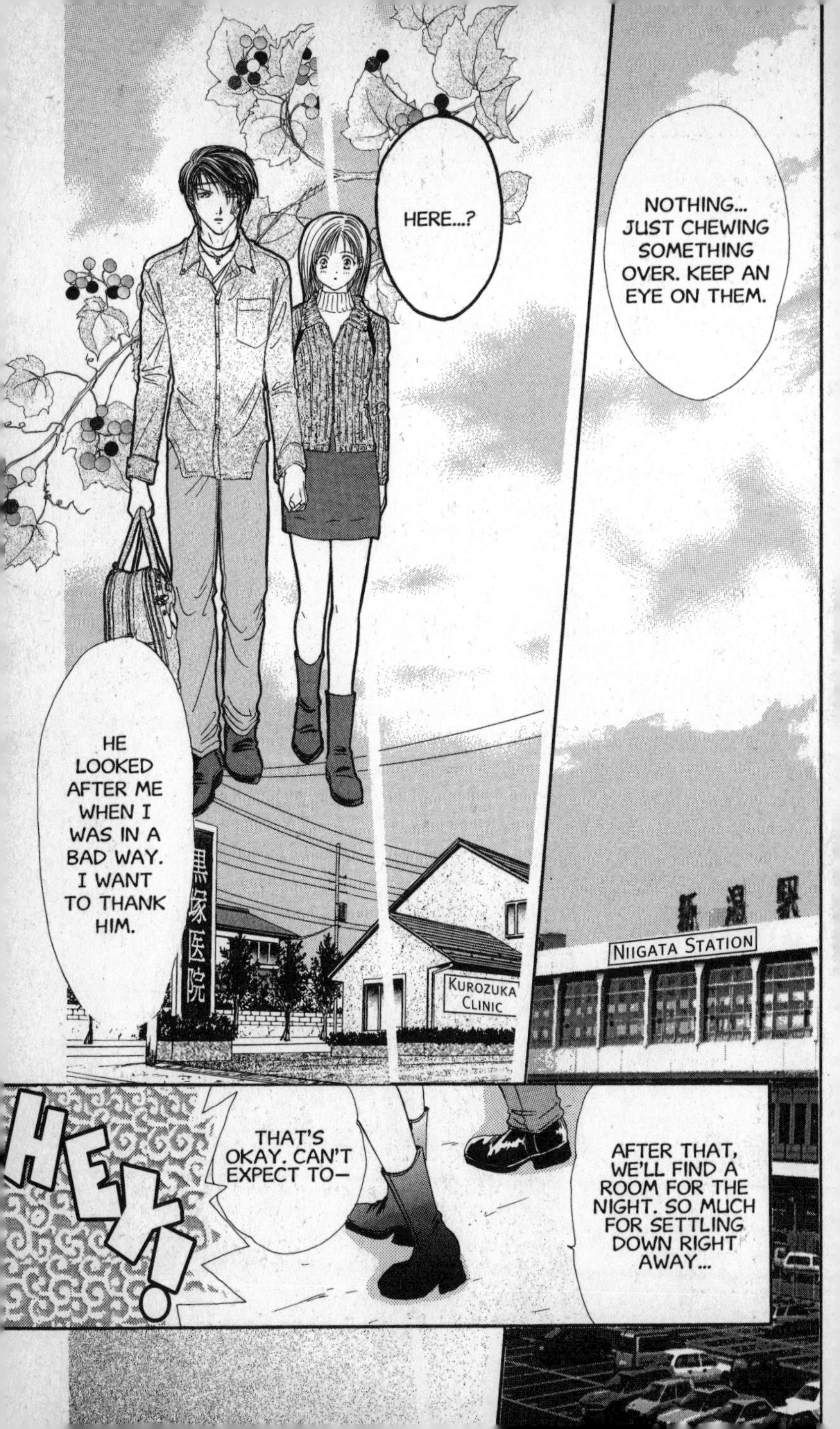
NOTHING... JUST CHEWING SOMETHING OVER. KEEP AN EYE ON THEM.
新潟駅
NIIGATA STATION
HERE...?
HE LOOKED AFTER ME WHEN I WAS IN A BAD WAY. I WANT TO THANK HIM.
黒塚医院
KUROZUKA CLINIC
AFTER THAT, WE'LL FIND A ROOM FOR THE NIGHT. SO MUCH FOR SETTLING DOWN RIGHT AWAY...
THAT'S OKAY. CAN'T EXPECT TO—
HEY!

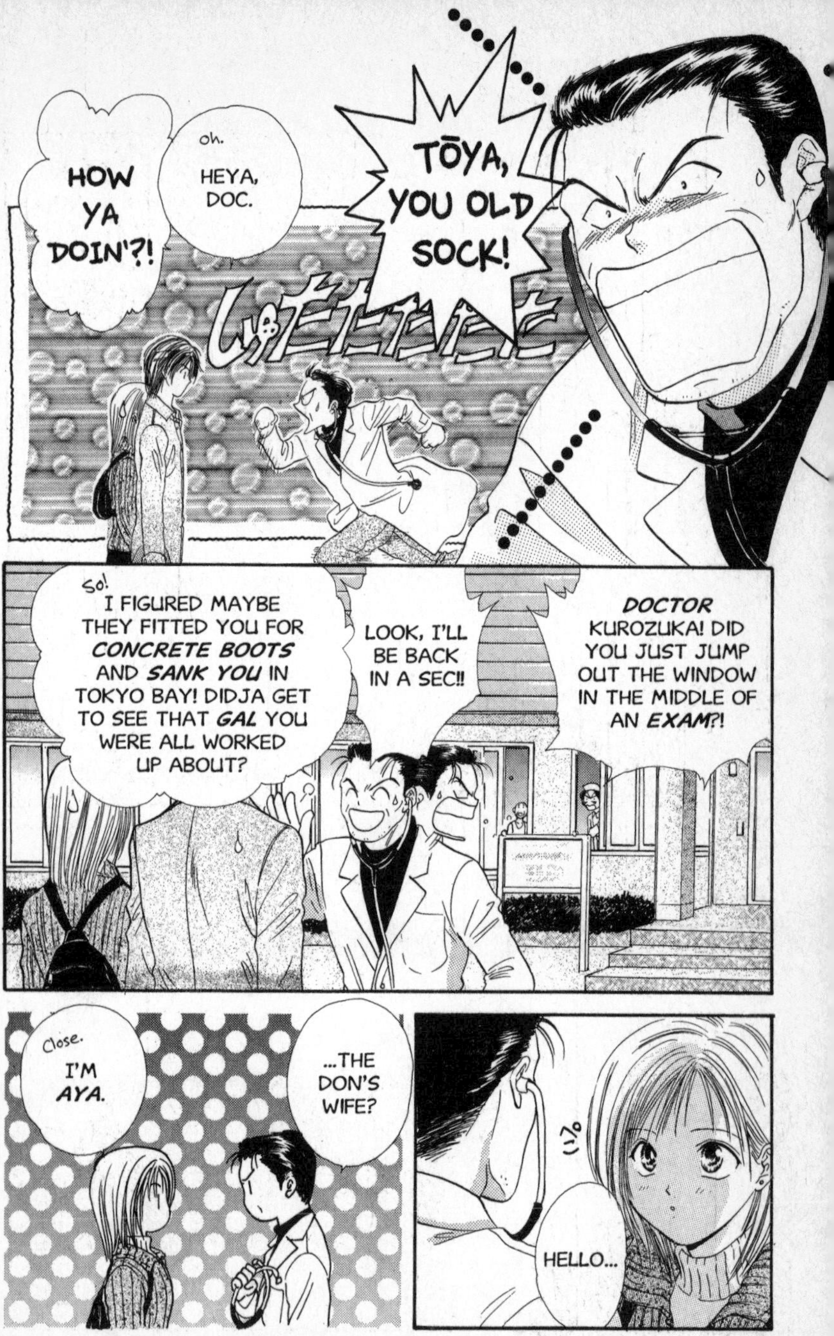
TŌYA, YOU OLD SOCK!
oh.
HEYA, DOC.
HOW YA DOIN'?!
DOCTOR KUROZUKA! DID YOU JUST JUMP OUT THE WINDOW IN THE MIDDLE OF AN EXAM?!
LOOK, I'LL BE BACK IN A SEC!!
So!
I FIGURED MAYBE THEY FITTED YOU FOR CONCRETE BOOTS AND SANK YOU IN TOKYO BAY! DIDJA GET TO SEE THAT GAL YOU WERE ALL WORKED UP ABOUT?
HELLO...
...THE DON'S WIFE?
Close.
I'M AYA.

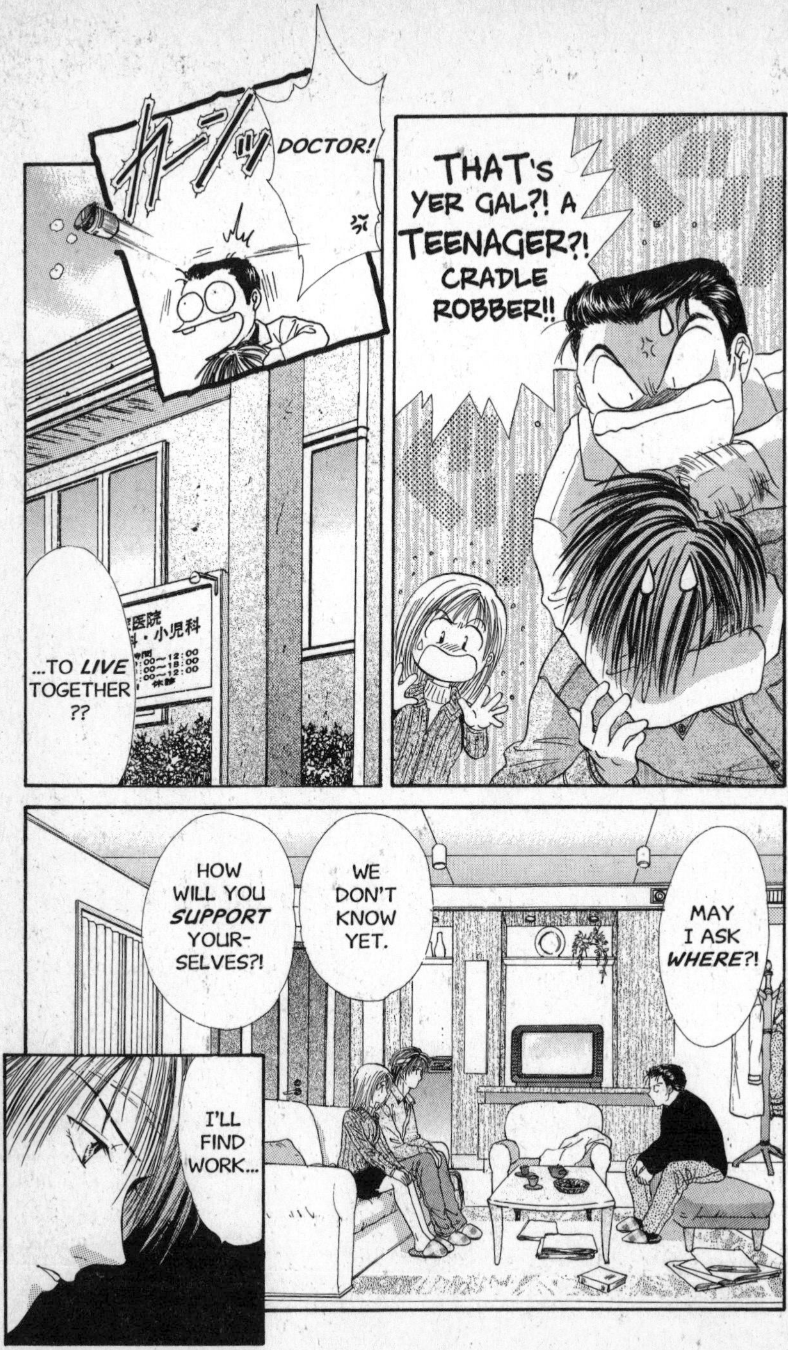
THAT's YER GAL?! A TEENAGER?! CRADLE ROBBER!!
DOCTOR!
...TO LIVE TOGETHER??
MAY I ASK WHERE?!
WE DON'T KNOW YET.
HOW WILL YOU SUPPORT YOUR-SELVES?!
I'LL FIND WORK...

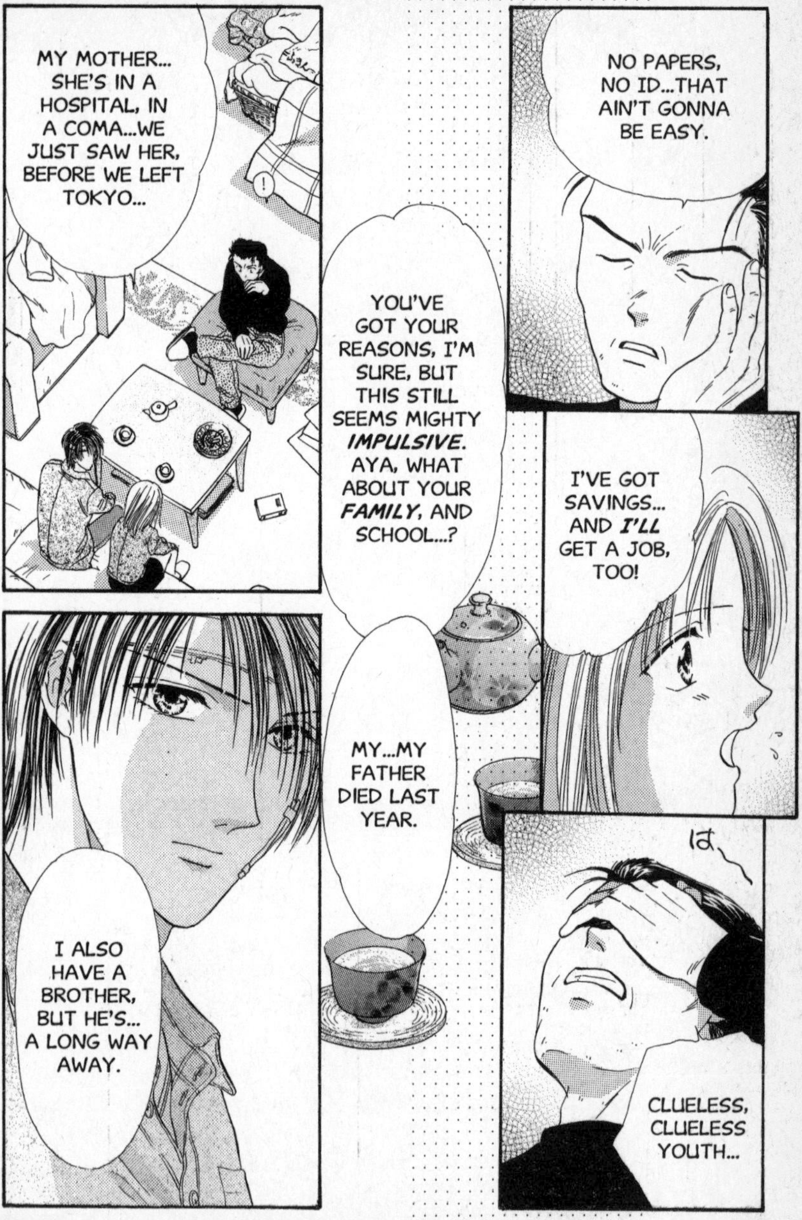
NO PAPERS, NO ID...THAT AIN'T GONNA BE EASY.
I'VE GOT SAVINGS... AND *I'LL* GET A JOB, TOO!
は〜
CLUELESS, CLUELESS YOUTH...
YOU'VE GOT YOUR REASONS, I'M SURE, BUT THIS STILL SEEMS MIGHTY ***IMPULSIVE***. AYA, WHAT ABOUT YOUR ***FAMILY***, AND SCHOOL...?
MY...MY FATHER DIED LAST YEAR.
MY MOTHER... SHE'S IN A HOSPITAL, IN A COMA...WE JUST SAW HER, BEFORE WE LEFT TOKYO...
!
I ALSO HAVE A BROTHER, BUT HE'S... A LONG WAY AWAY.

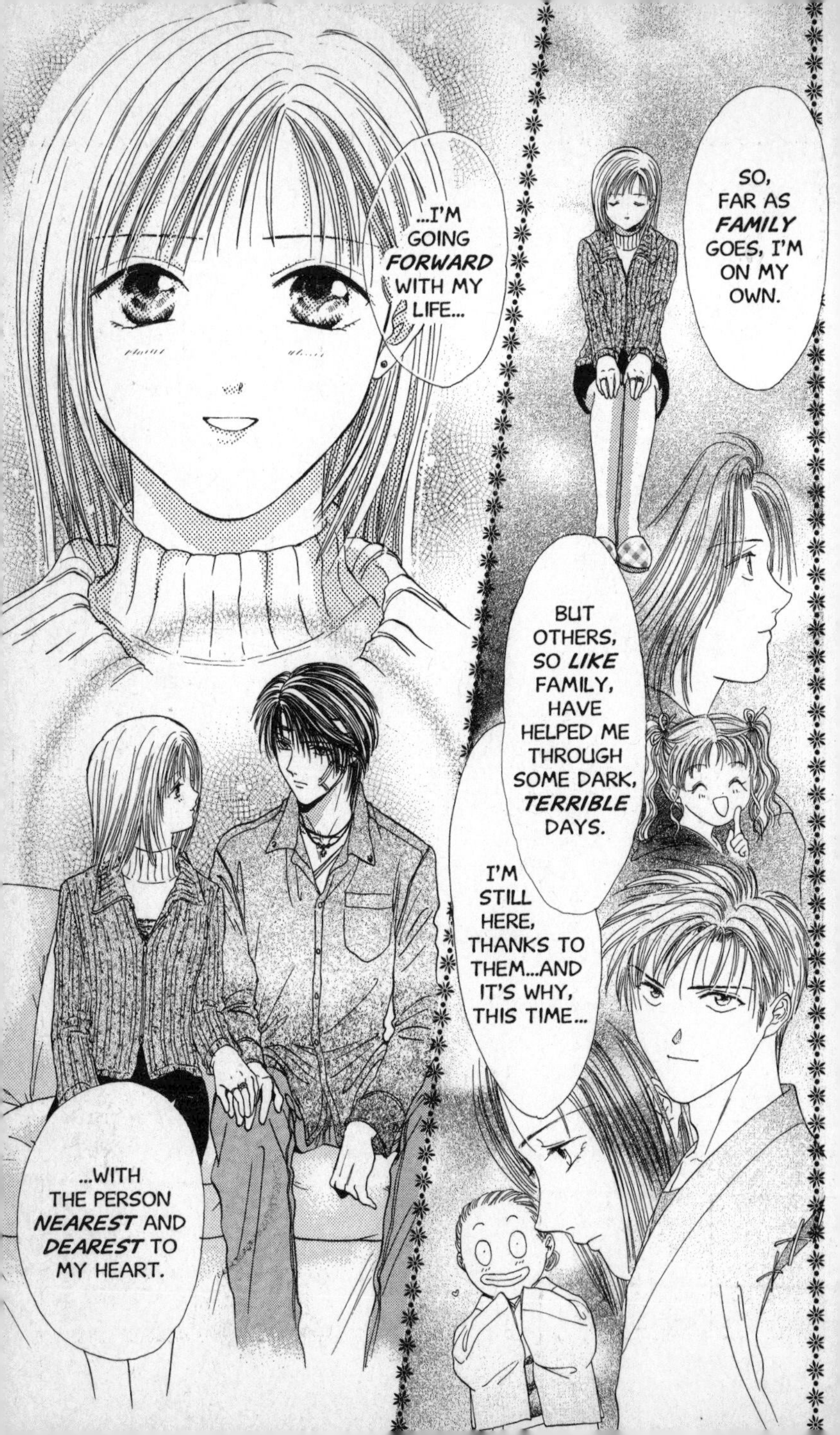
SO, FAR AS *FAMILY* GOES, I'M ON MY OWN.
BUT OTHERS, SO *LIKE* FAMILY, HAVE HELPED ME THROUGH SOME DARK, *TERRIBLE* DAYS.
I'M STILL HERE, THANKS TO THEM...AND IT'S WHY, THIS TIME...
...I'M GOING *FORWARD* WITH MY LIFE...
...WITH THE PERSON *NEAREST* AND *DEAREST* TO MY HEART.

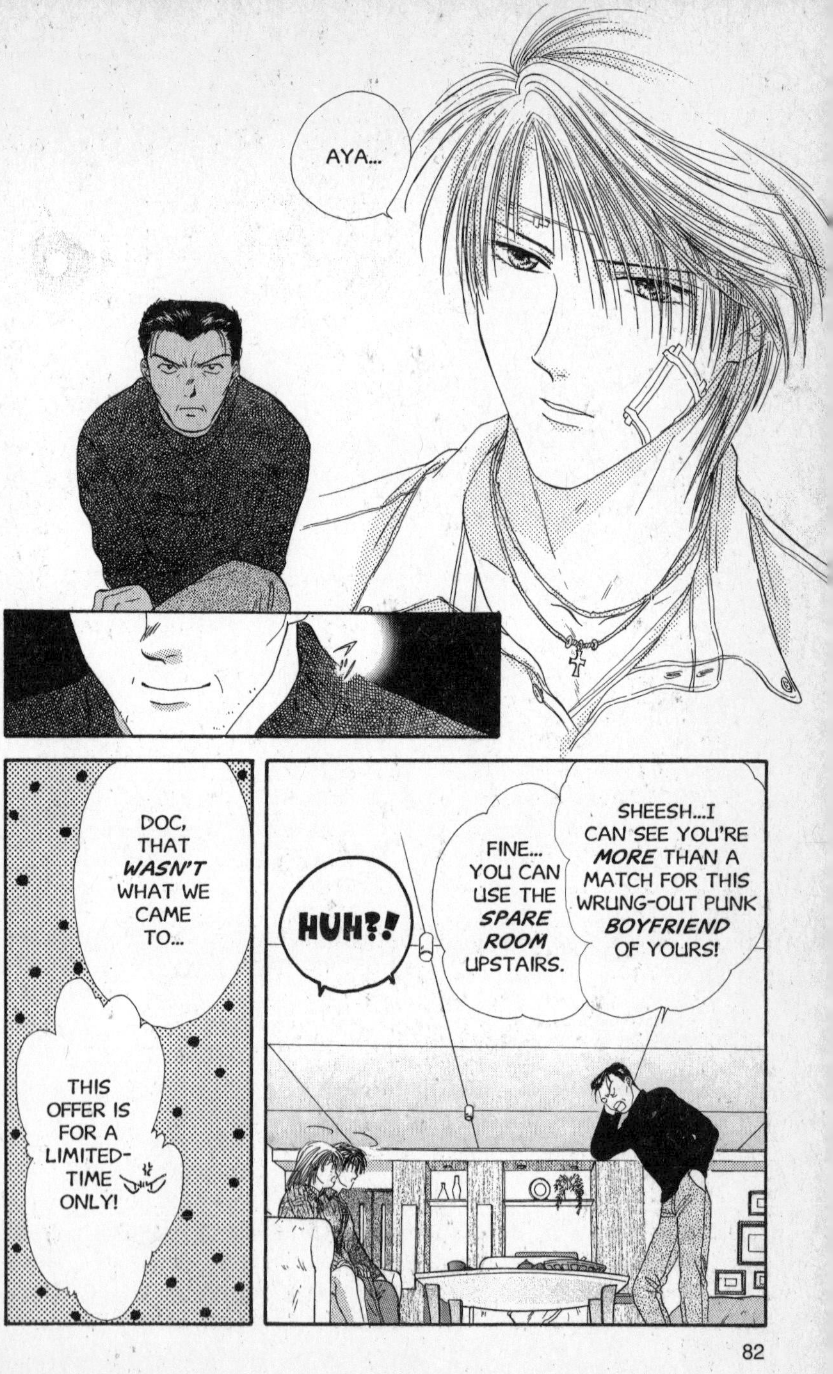
AYA...
SHEESH...I CAN SEE YOU'RE MORE THAN A MATCH FOR THIS WRUNG-OUT PUNK BOYFRIEND OF YOURS!
FINE... YOU CAN USE THE SPARE ROOM UPSTAIRS.
HUH?!
DOC, THAT WASN'T WHAT WE CAME TO...
THIS OFFER IS FOR A LIMITED-TIME ONLY!

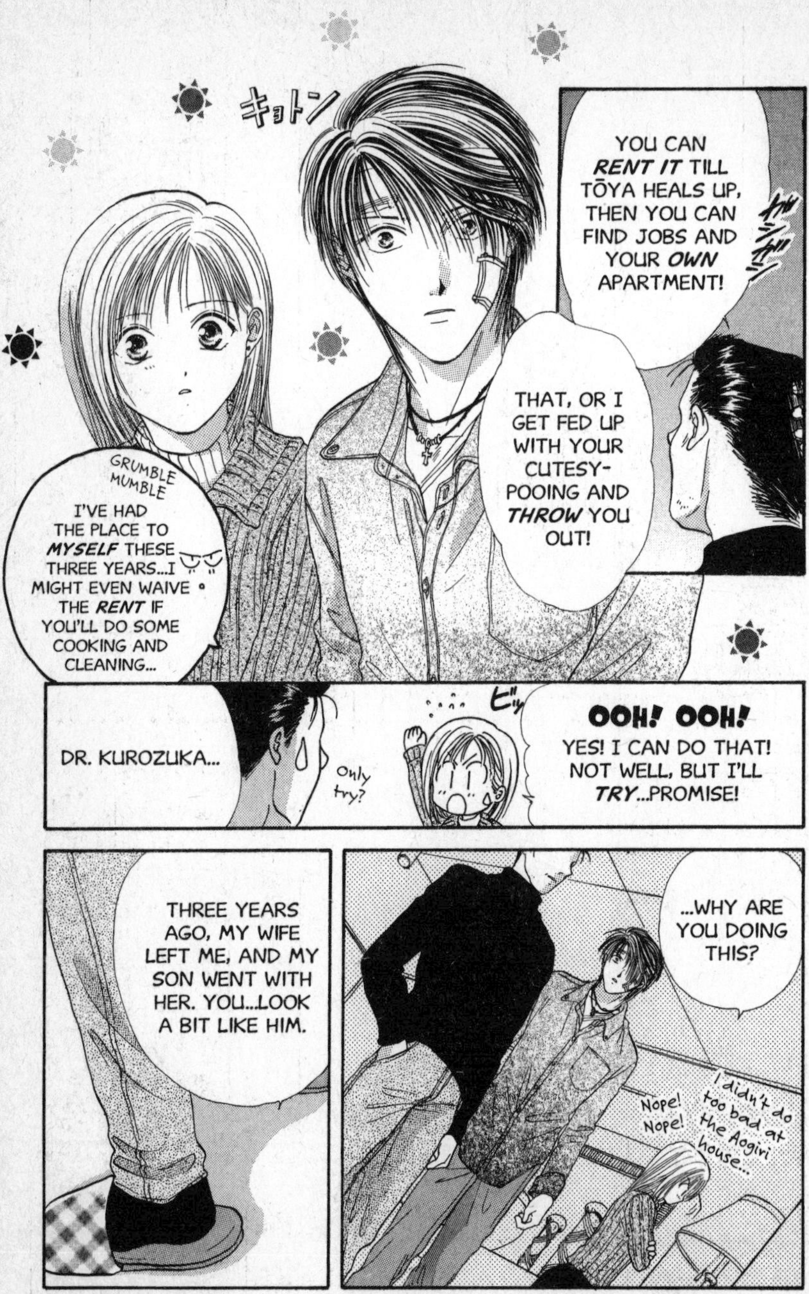
キョトン
YOU CAN RENT IT TILL TŌYA HEALS UP, THEN YOU CAN FIND JOBS AND YOUR OWN APARTMENT!
THAT, OR I GET FED UP WITH YOUR CUTESY-POOING AND THROW YOU OUT!
GRUMBLE MUMBLE
I'VE HAD THE PLACE TO MYSELF THESE THREE YEARS...I MIGHT EVEN WAIVE THE RENT IF YOU'LL DO SOME COOKING AND CLEANING...
OOH! OOH!
YES! I CAN DO THAT! NOT WELL, BUT I'LL TRY...PROMISE!
Only try?
DR. KUROZUKA...
...WHY ARE YOU DOING THIS?
I didn't do too bad at the Aogiri house...
Nope! Nope!
THREE YEARS AGO, MY WIFE LEFT ME, AND MY SON WENT WITH HER. YOU...LOOK A BIT LIKE HIM.

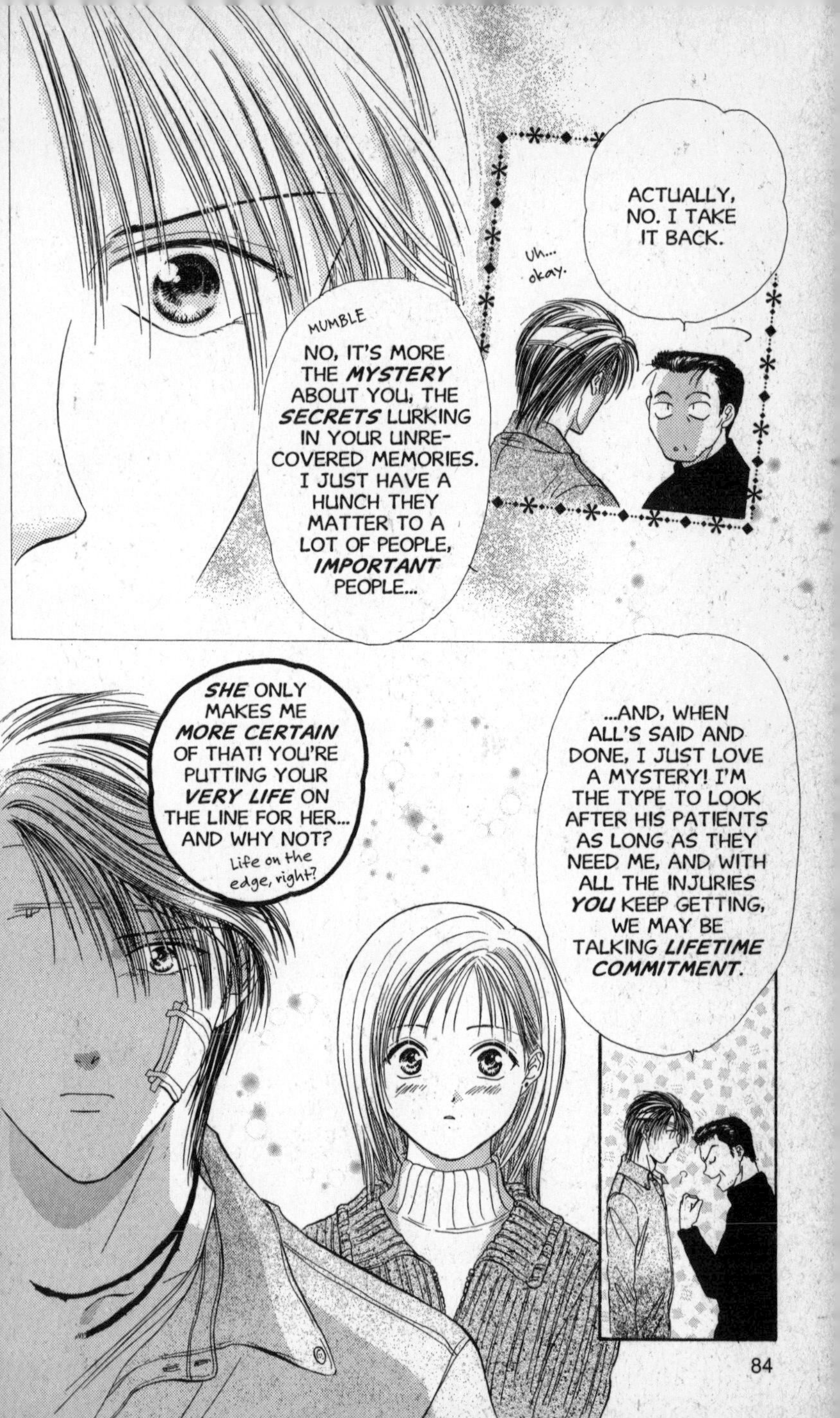
ACTUALLY, NO. I TAKE IT BACK.
Uh... okay.
MUMBLE
NO, IT'S MORE THE ***MYSTERY*** ABOUT YOU, THE ***SECRETS*** LURKING IN YOUR UNRE-COVERED MEMORIES. I JUST HAVE A HUNCH THEY MATTER TO A LOT OF PEOPLE, ***IMPORTANT*** PEOPLE...
SHE ONLY MAKES ME ***MORE CERTAIN*** OF THAT! YOU'RE PUTTING YOUR ***VERY LIFE*** ON THE LINE FOR HER... AND WHY NOT?
Life on the edge, right?
...AND, WHEN ALL'S SAID AND DONE, I JUST LOVE A MYSTERY! I'M THE TYPE TO LOOK AFTER HIS PATIENTS AS LONG AS THEY NEED ME, AND WITH ALL THE INJURIES ***YOU*** KEEP GETTING, WE MAY BE TALKING ***LIFETIME COMMITMENT***.

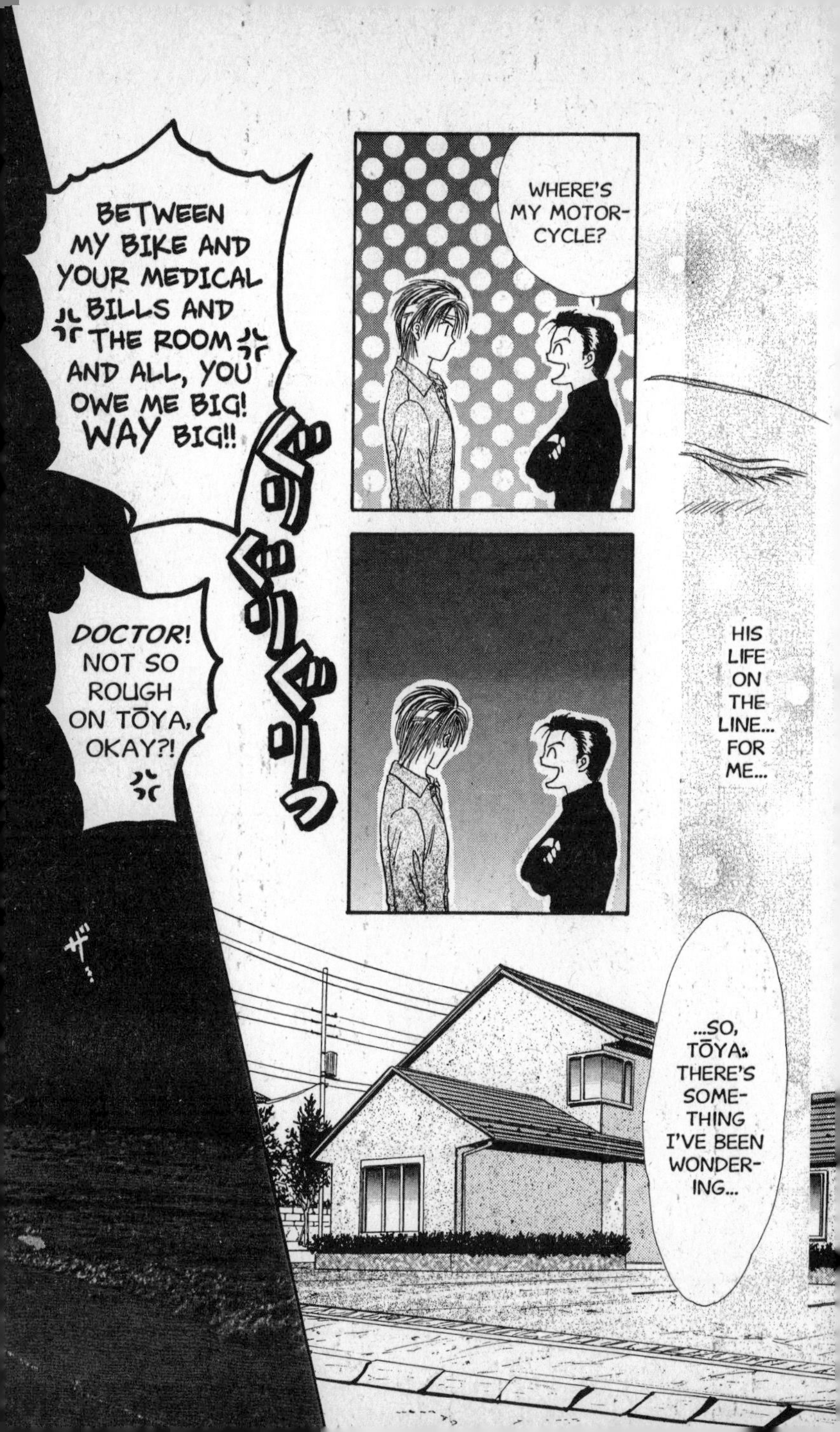
HIS LIFE ON THE LINE... FOR ME...
WHERE'S MY MOTOR-CYCLE?
BETWEEN MY BIKE AND YOUR MEDICAL BILLS AND THE ROOM AND ALL, YOU OWE ME BIG! WAY BIG!!
DOCTOR! NOT SO ROUGH ON TŌYA, OKAY?!
...SO, TŌYA: THERE'S SOME-THING I'VE BEEN WONDER-ING...

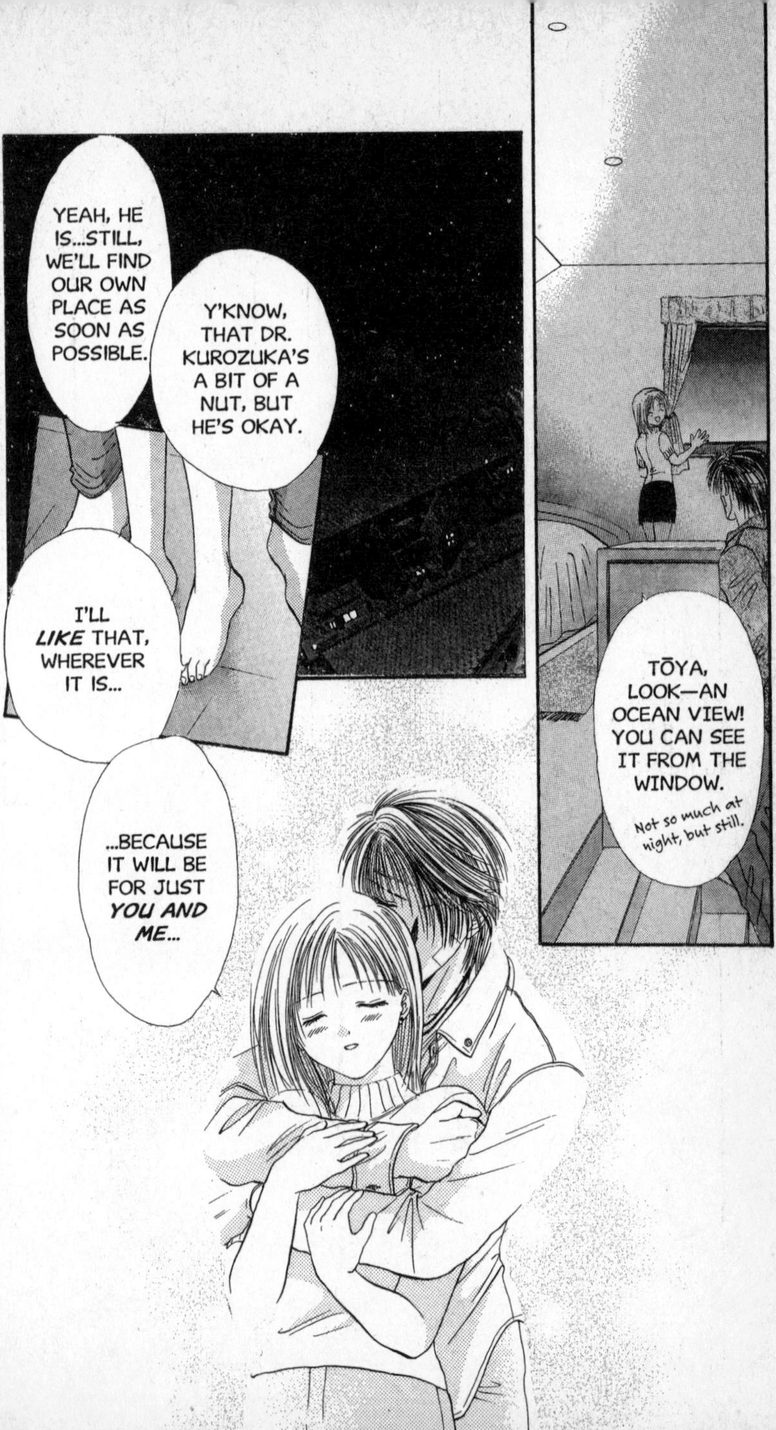
TŌYA, LOOK—AN OCEAN VIEW! YOU CAN SEE IT FROM THE WINDOW.
Not so much at night, but still.
Y'KNOW, THAT DR. KUROZUKA'S A BIT OF A NUT, BUT HE'S OKAY.
YEAH, HE IS...STILL, WE'LL FIND OUR OWN PLACE AS SOON AS POSSIBLE.
I'LL *LIKE* THAT, WHEREVER IT IS...
...BECAUSE IT WILL BE FOR JUST *YOU AND ME*...

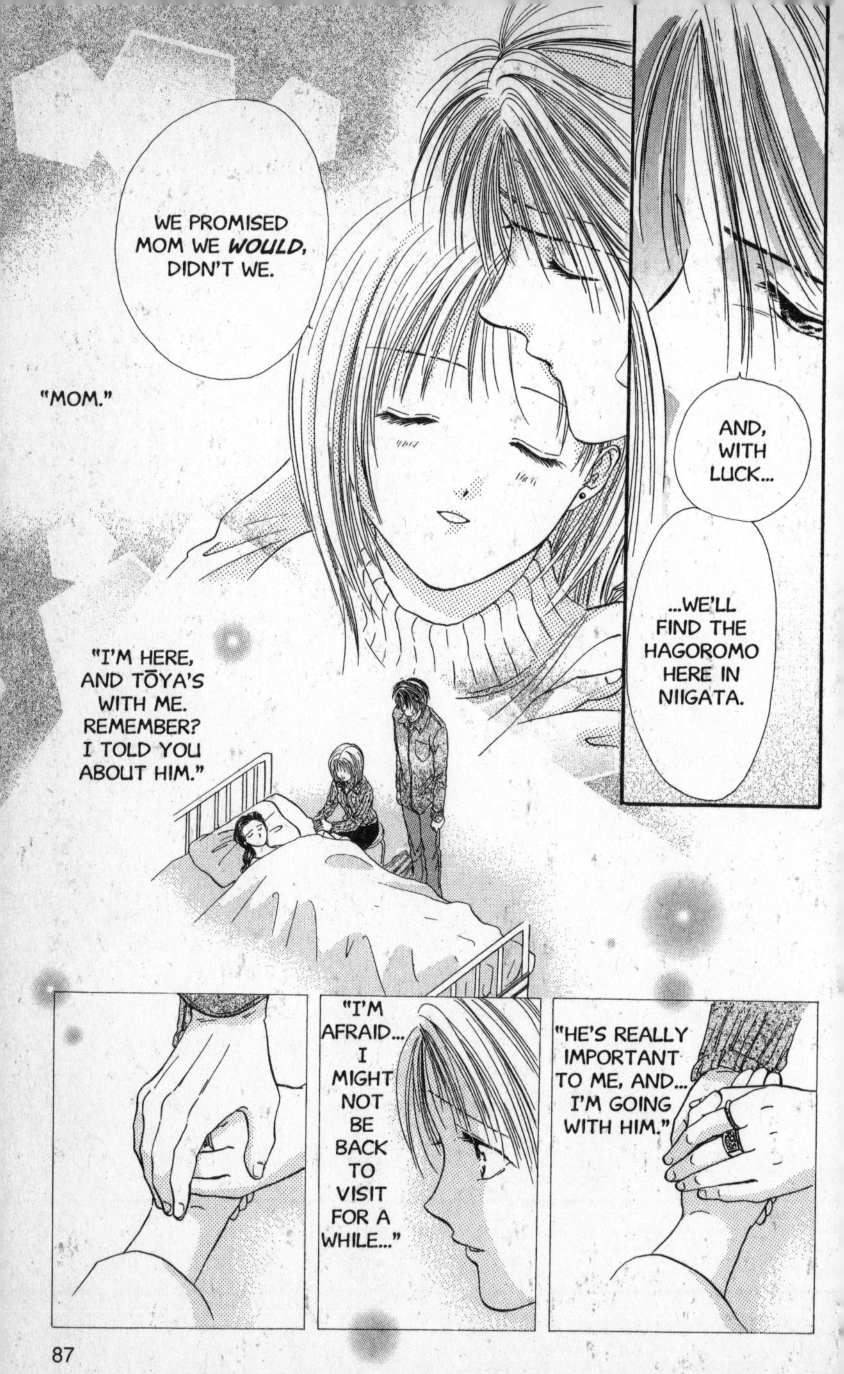
AND, WITH LUCK...
...WE'LL FIND THE HAGOROMO HERE IN NIIGATA.
WE PROMISED MOM WE *WOULD*, DIDN'T WE.
"MOM."
"I'M HERE, AND TŌYA'S WITH ME. REMEMBER? I TOLD YOU ABOUT HIM."
"HE'S REALLY IMPORTANT TO ME, AND... I'M GOING WITH HIM."
"I'M AFRAID... I MIGHT NOT BE BACK TO VISIT FOR A WHILE..."

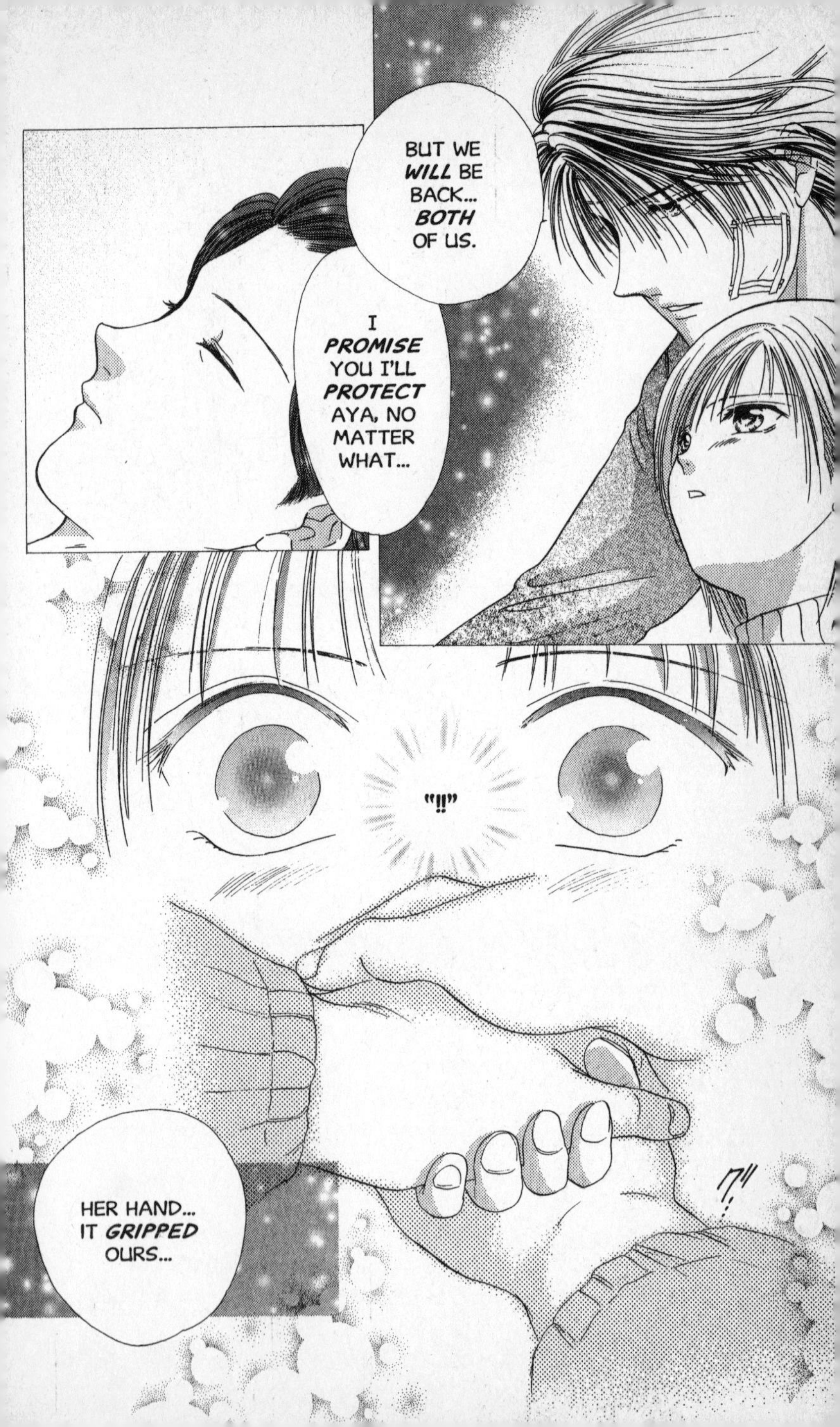
BUT WE *WILL* BE BACK... *BOTH* OF US.
I *PROMISE* YOU I'LL *PROTECT* AYA, NO MATTER WHAT...
"!!"
HER HAND... IT *GRIPPED* OURS...

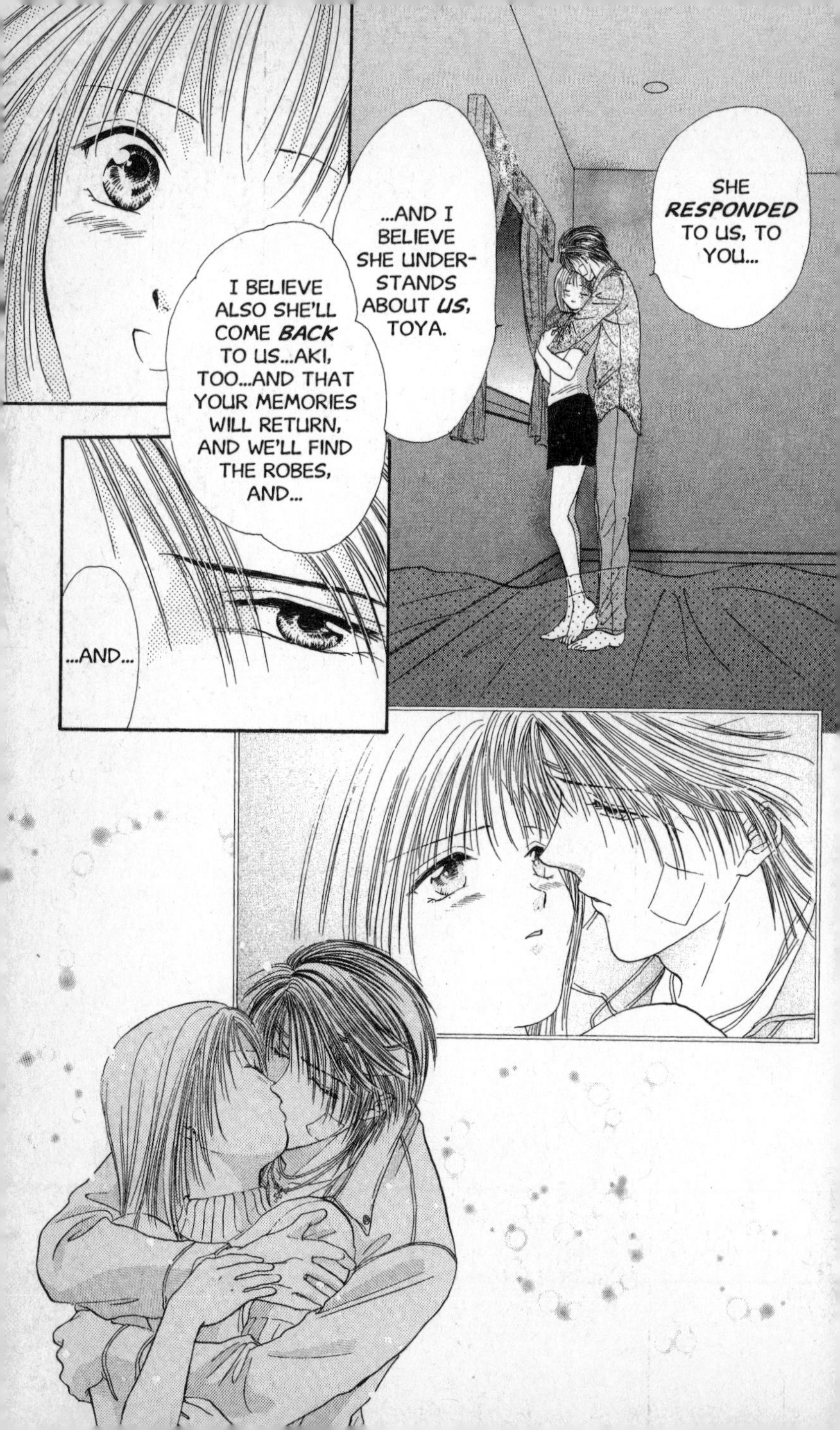
SHE *RESPONDED* TO US, TO YOU...
...AND I BELIEVE SHE UNDER-STANDS ABOUT *US*, TOYA.
I BELIEVE ALSO SHE'LL COME *BACK* TO US...AKI, TOO...AND THAT YOUR MEMORIES WILL RETURN, AND WE'LL FIND THE ROBES, AND...
...AND...

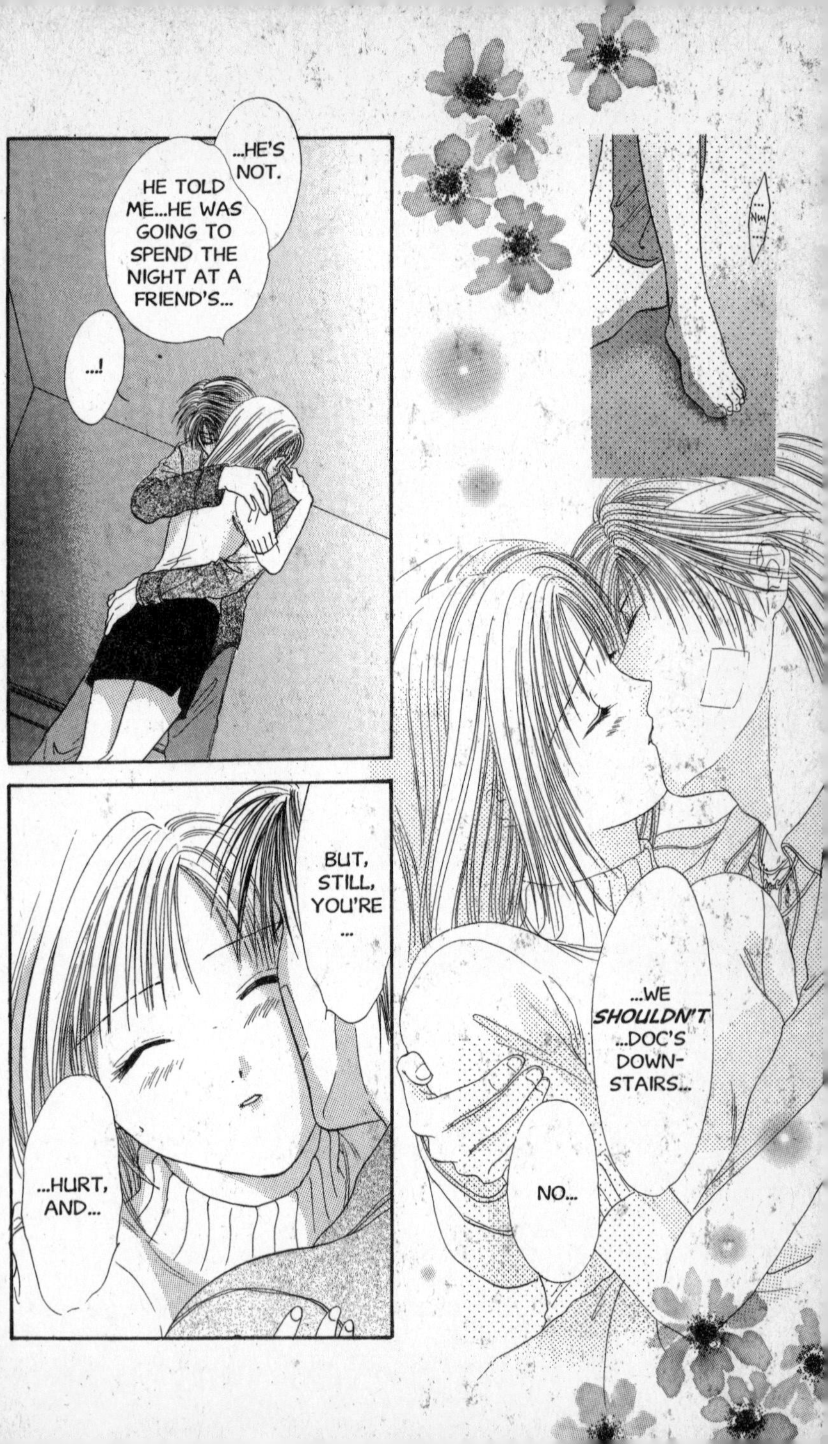
...HE'S NOT.
HE TOLD ME...HE WAS GOING TO SPEND THE NIGHT AT A FRIEND'S...
...!
BUT, STILL, YOU'RE ...
...HURT, AND...
...Nm...
...WE *SHOULDN'T* ...DOC'S DOWN-STAIRS...
NO...

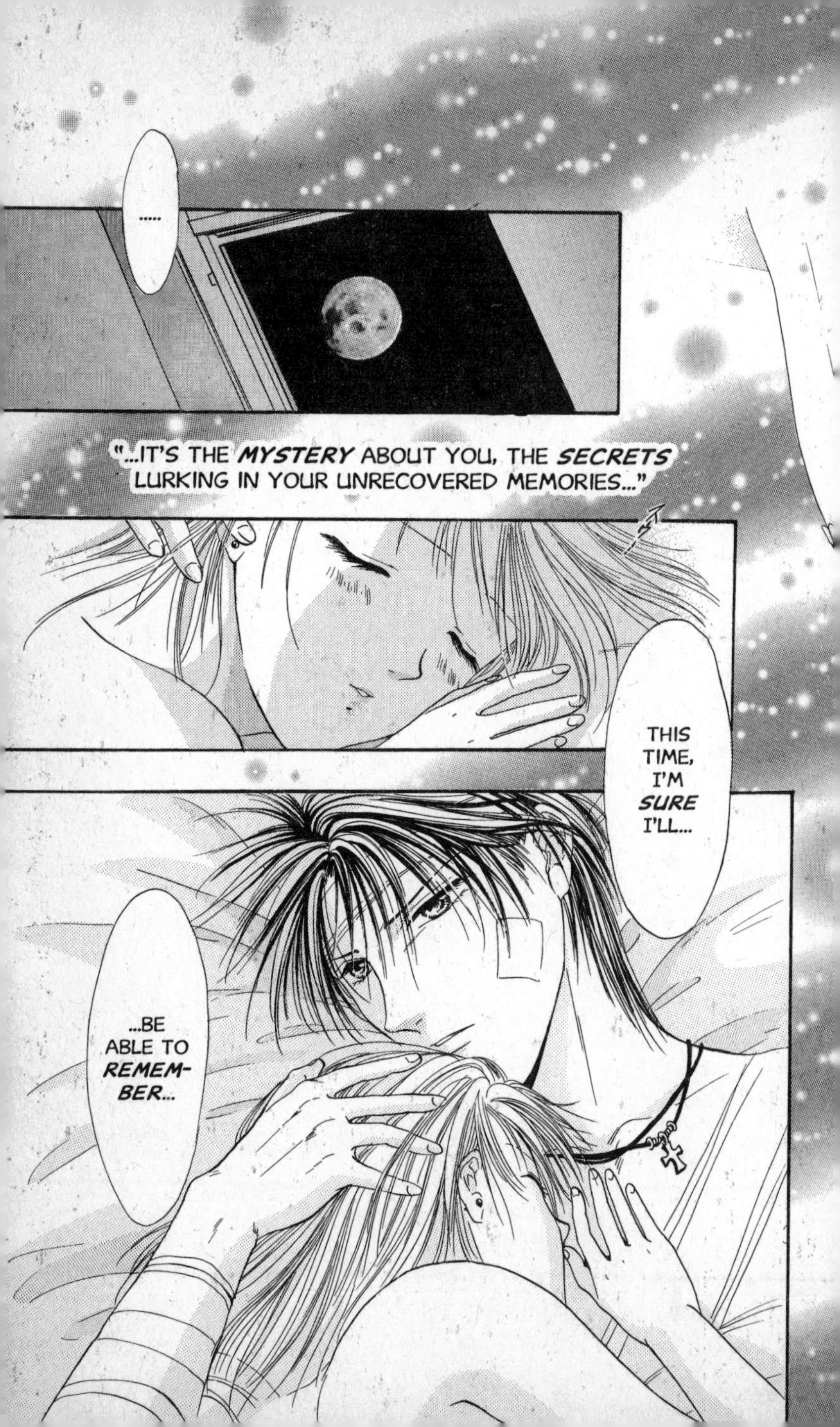
......
"...IT'S THE *MYSTERY* ABOUT YOU, THE *SECRETS* LURKING IN YOUR UNRECOVERED MEMORIES..."
THIS TIME, I'M *SURE* I'LL...
...BE ABLE TO *REMEMBER*...

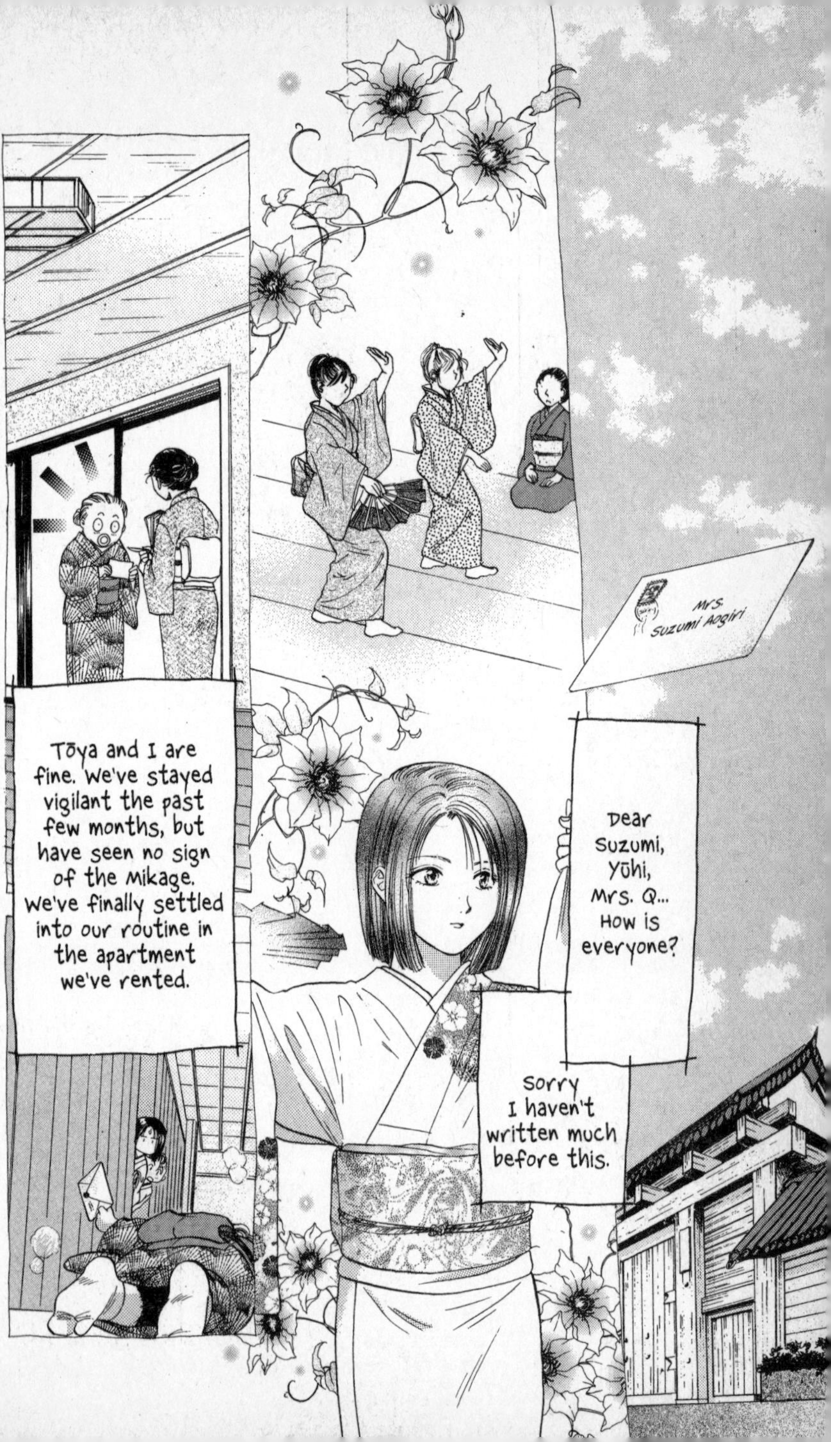
Mrs. Suzumi Aogiri
Dear Suzumi, Yūhi, Mrs. Q... How is everyone?
Sorry I haven't written much before this.
Tōya and I are fine. We've stayed vigilant the past few months, but have seen no sign of the Mikage. We've finally settled into our routine in the apartment we've rented.

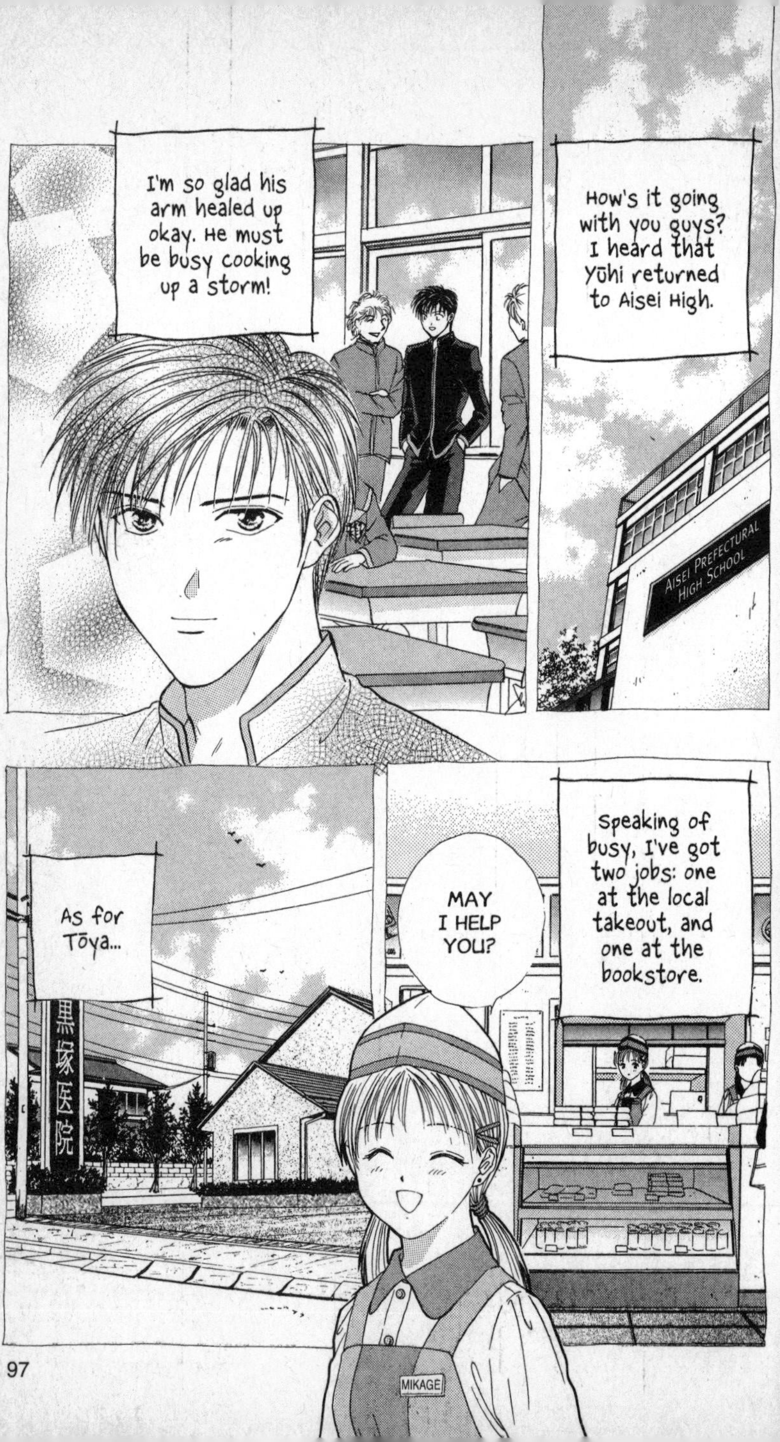
How's it going with you guys? I heard that Yūhi returned to Aisei High.
AISEI PREFECTURAL HIGH SCHOOL
I'm so glad his arm healed up okay. He must be busy cooking up a storm!
Speaking of busy, I've got two jobs: one at the local takeout, and one at the bookstore.
MAY I HELP YOU?
MIKAGE
As for Tōya...
黒塚医院

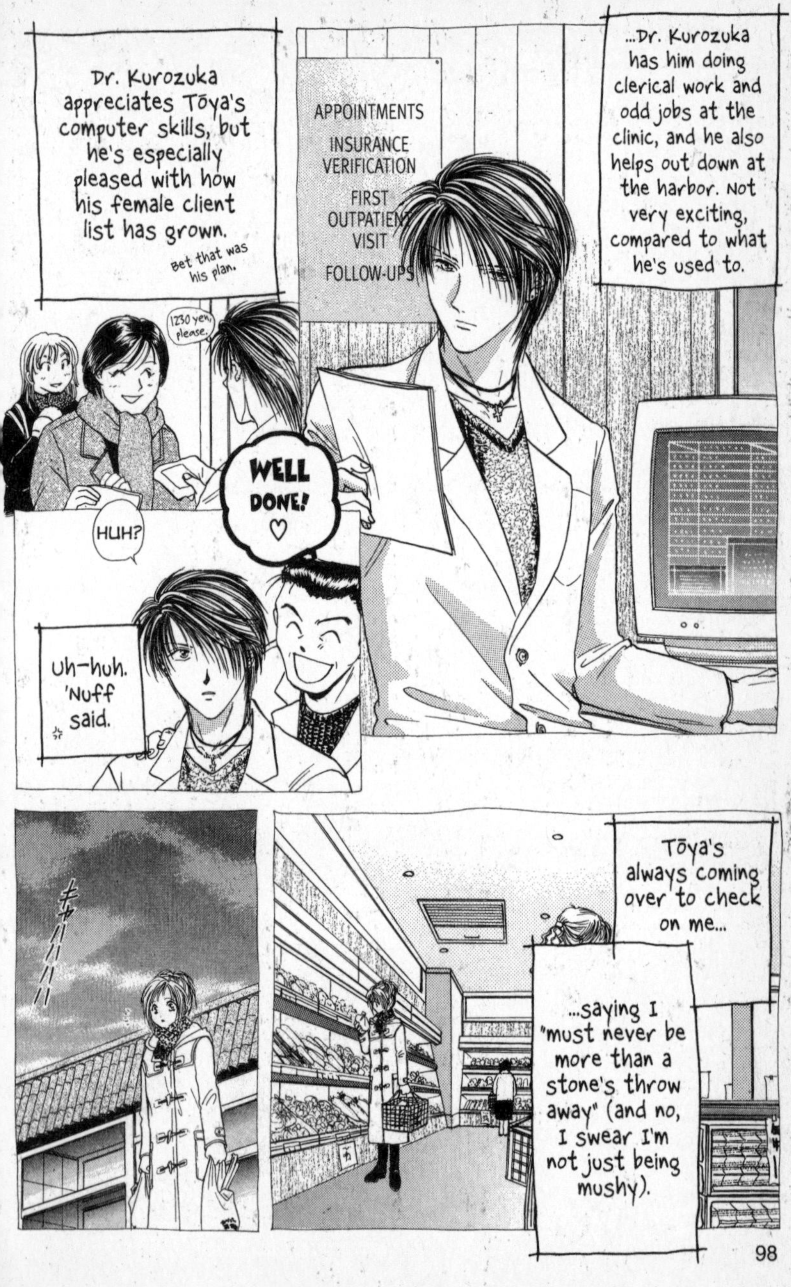

...Dr. Kurozuka has him doing clerical work and odd jobs at the clinic, and he also helps out down at the harbor. Not very exciting, compared to what he's used to.
APPOINTMENTS
INSURANCE VERIFICATION
FIRST OUTPATIENT VISIT
FOLLOW-UPS
Dr. Kurozuka appreciates Tōya's computer skills, but he's especially pleased with how his female client list has grown.
Bet that was his plan.
1230 yen, please.
WELL DONE! ♡
HUH?
Uh-huh. 'Nuff said.
Tōya's always coming over to check on me...
...saying I "must never be more than a stone's throw away" (and no, I swear I'm not just being mushy).

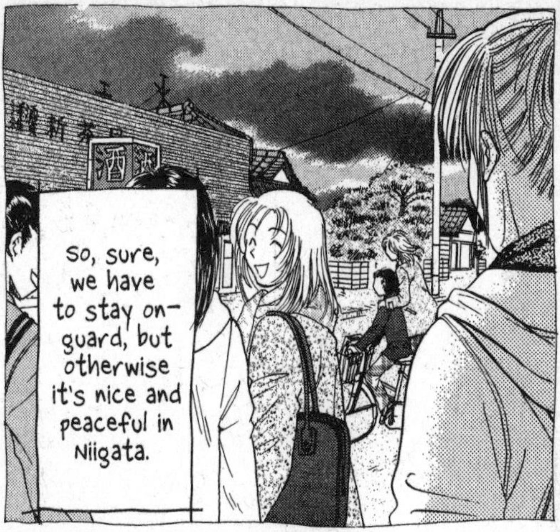
So, sure, we have to stay on-guard, but otherwise it's nice and peaceful in Niigata.
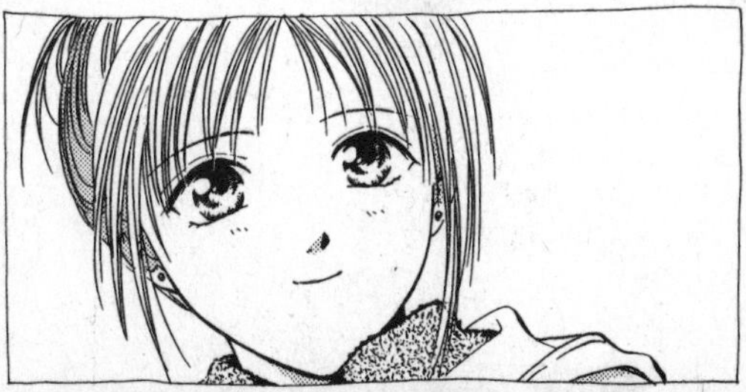
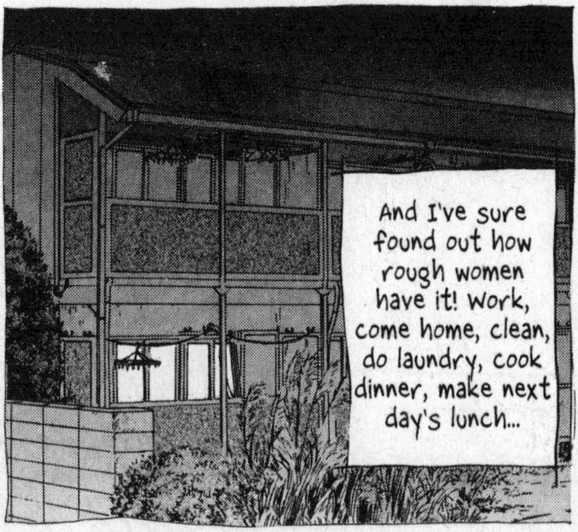
And I've sure found out how rough women have it! Work, come home, clean, do laundry, cook dinner, make next day's lunch...

...about an organization that had been protesting the poster of an actress because it suggested rape. I was all like, "What?! **You're** the ones with dirty minds, thinking **that's** what it suggests!" ◡

A female editor I worked with some years ago once said something intriguing: "People who are offended or whatnot get obsessed because, deep down inside, they're really **curious** about the things that offend them." It's true—people wouldn't even **broach** the topic if they had no thoughts about it. This falls into the same category as those who write nasty letters: If they **really** hated you, they wouldn't even bother. Incidentally, the number of letters I've received about sex—whether they're complaints, or requests for more—is only a tenth of the total volume I've received over these past ten years. Hey, if someone were to tell me that those readers who **don't** write all do have sex on their minds (at least at some point), well, I'd have to agree. ◡ I'm not above giving readers what they want. It made me happy, though, that kids did write in to say that the scene between Aya and Tōya was beautiful. One opinion often heard was, "It was more about them **loving each other** than just about sex, and that's why the love scenes you draw, Sensei, aren't objectionable at all." It all also depends on whatever personal issues the reader brings into it, and I'm sure someone with nothing **but** sex on the brain **will** see it as such. At least, with me, it's treated as something sacred. ◡ (Not that you'd know it from Volume 10, huh?) Hey, I can't be responsible for people's own, personal interpretations. ◡ Still, so what? Love scenes in my stories are only **one** part, unlike titles that sandwich the plot **in-between** the sex. (Not counting genres where sex is the plot, of course.)

Even so, I **have** done titles without any sex at all, you know. Ho ho ho. ...Though when it is there, I guess it does stand out. We're all living beings, though—it wouldn't be normal if we were **totally** uninterested—'cause then we'd never procreate, and humanity would die out. It all comes down to biology, these days, for me.

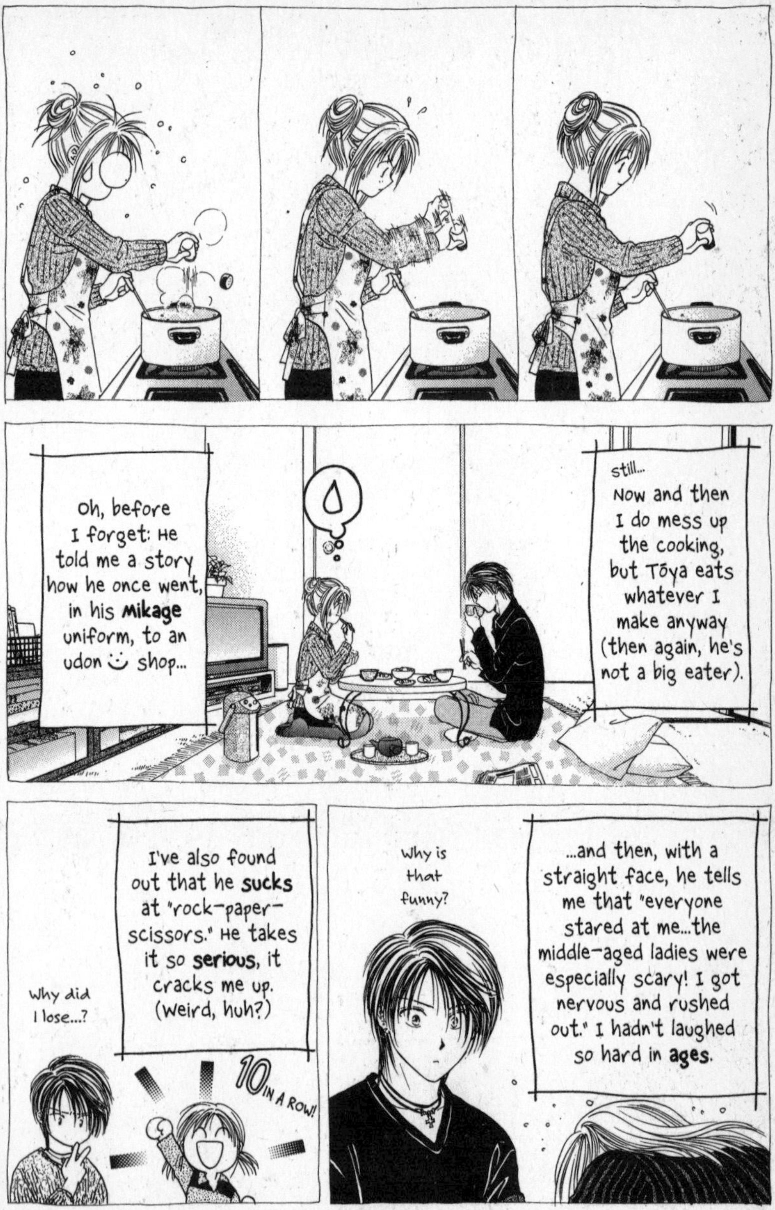
still...
Now and then I do mess up the cooking, but Tōya eats whatever I make anyway (then again, he's not a big eater).
Oh, before I forget: He told me a story how he once went, in his Mikage uniform, to an udon shop...
...and then, with a straight face, he tells me that "everyone stared at me...the middle-aged ladies were especially scary! I got nervous and rushed out." I hadn't laughed so hard in ages.
Why is that funny?
I've also found out that he sucks at "rock-paper-scissors." He takes it so serious, it cracks me up. (Weird, huh?)
10 IN A ROW!
Why did I lose...?

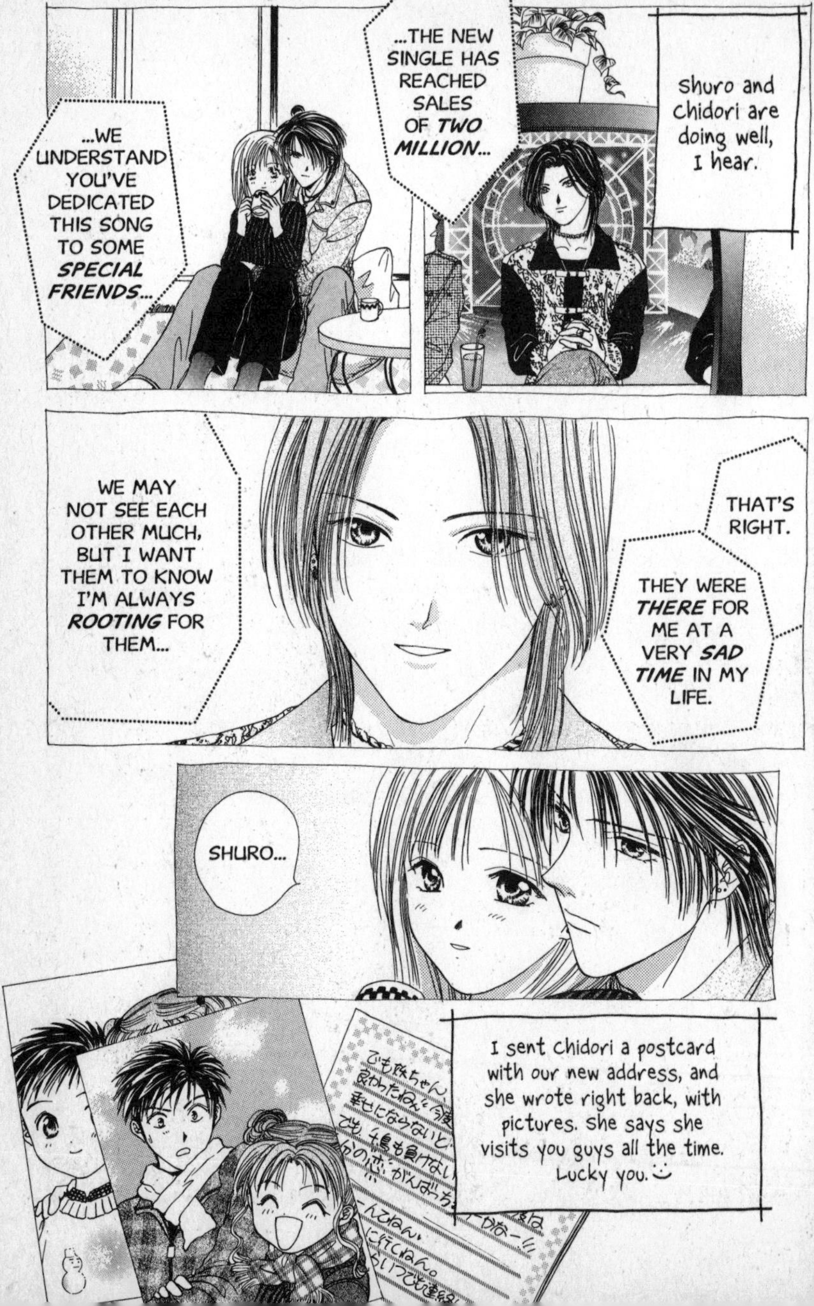
Shuro and Chidori are doing well, I hear.
...THE NEW SINGLE HAS REACHED SALES OF *TWO MILLION*...
...WE UNDERSTAND YOU'VE DEDICATED THIS SONG TO SOME *SPECIAL FRIENDS*...
THAT'S RIGHT.
THEY WERE *THERE* FOR ME AT A VERY *SAD TIME* IN MY LIFE.
WE MAY NOT SEE EACH OTHER MUCH, BUT I WANT THEM TO KNOW I'M ALWAYS *ROOTING* FOR THEM...
SHURO...
I sent Chidori a postcard with our new address, and she wrote right back, with pictures. She says she visits you guys all the time. Lucky you. :)

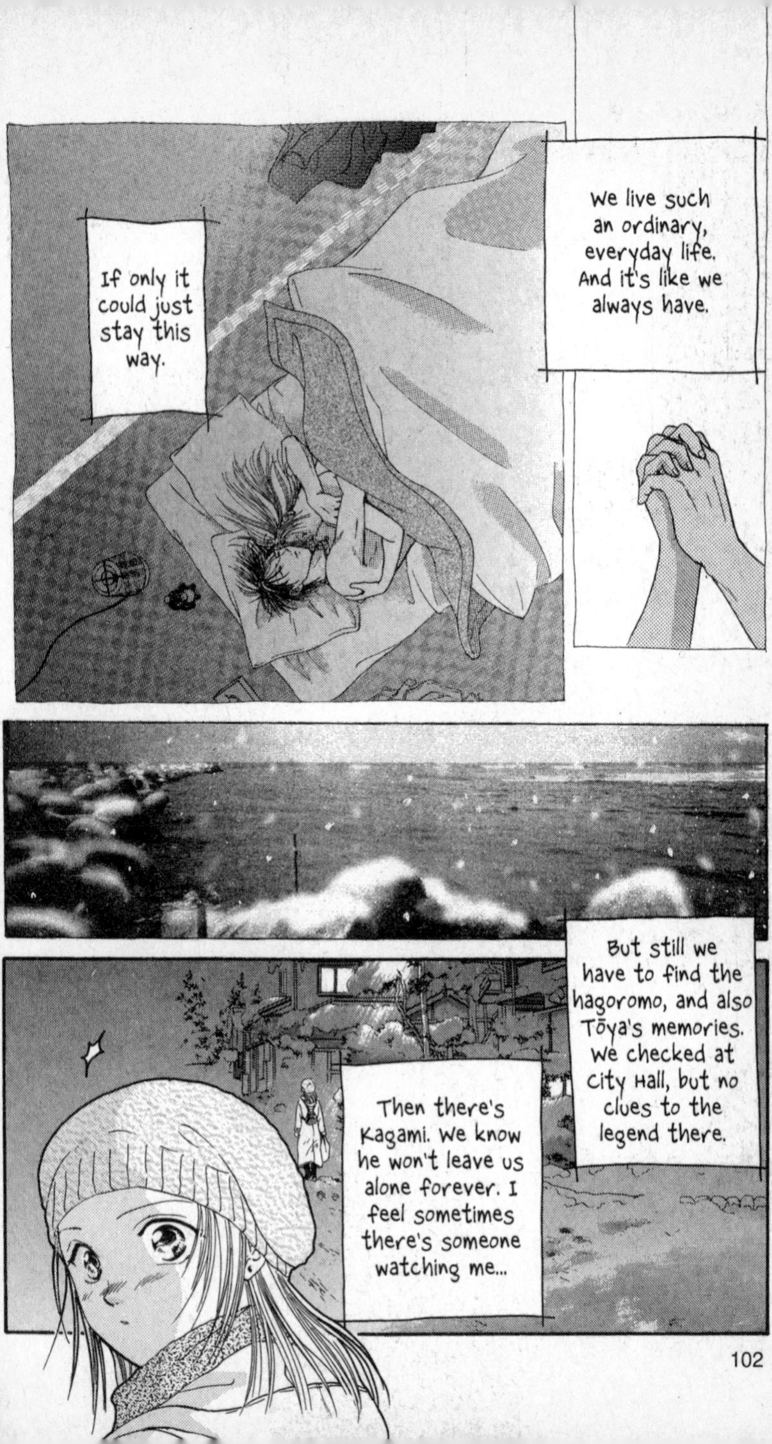
We live such an ordinary, everyday life. And it's like we always have.
If only it could just stay this way.
But still we have to find the hagoromo, and also Tōya's memories. We checked at City Hall, but no clues to the legend there.
Then there's Kagami. We know he won't leave us alone forever. I feel sometimes there's someone watching me...

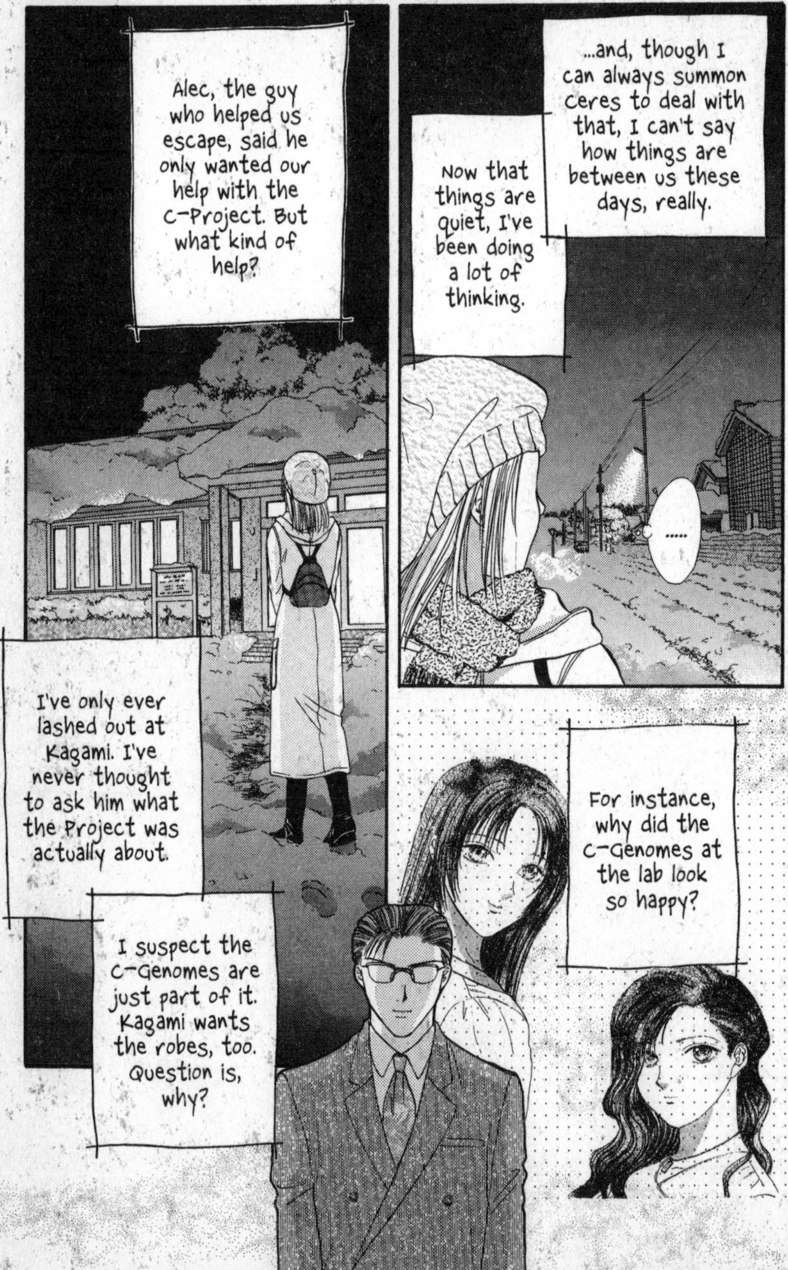
...and, though I can always summon Ceres to deal with that, I can't say how things are between us these days, really.
Now that things are quiet, I've been doing a lot of thinking.
......
Alec, the guy who helped us escape, said he only wanted our help with the C-Project. But what kind of help?
For instance, why did the C-Genomes at the lab look so happy?
I've only ever lashed out at Kagami. I've never thought to ask him what the Project was actually about.
I suspect the C-Genomes are just part of it. Kagami wants the robes, too. Question is, why?

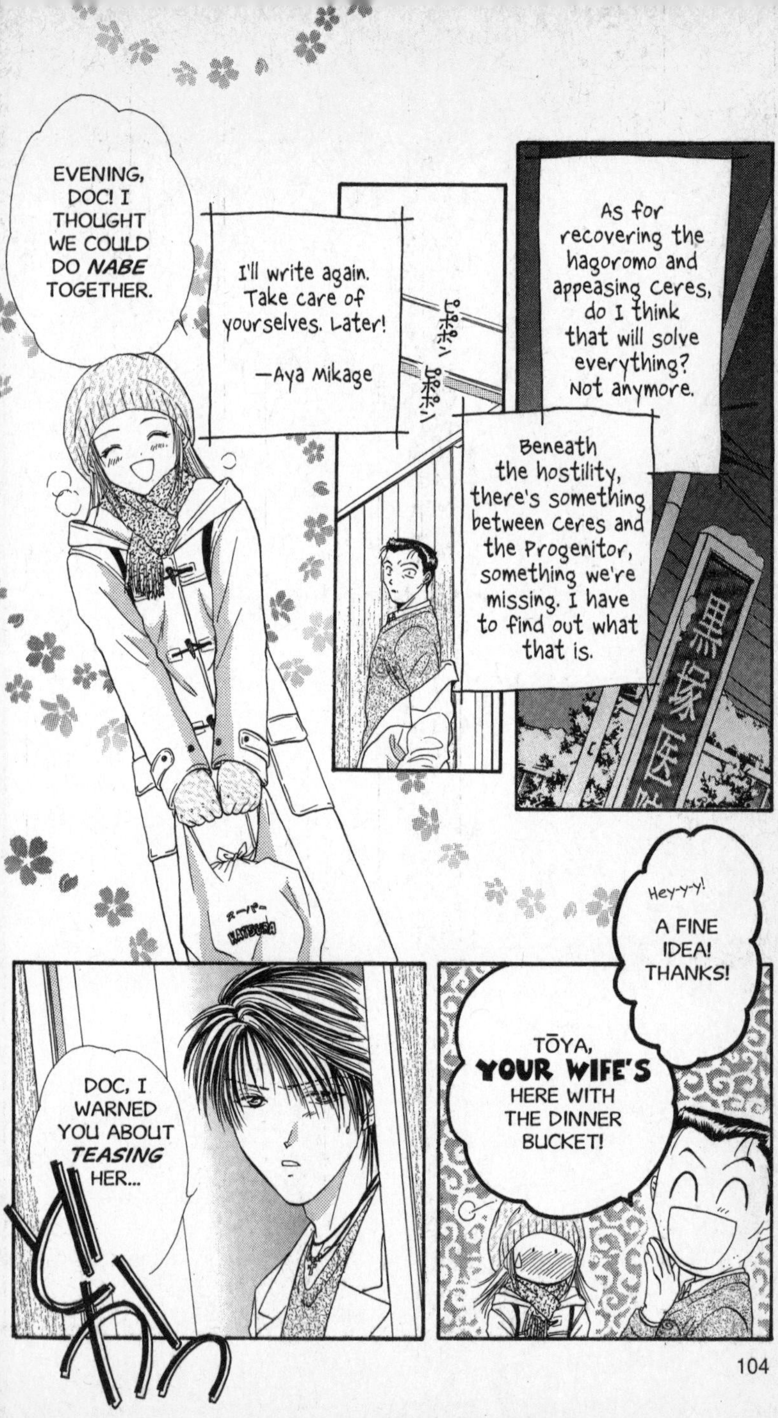
As for recovering the hagoromo and appeasing Ceres, do I think that will solve everything? Not anymore.
Beneath the hostility, there's something between Ceres and the Progenitor, something we're missing. I have to find out what that is.
I'll write again. Take care of yourselves. Later!
—Aya Mikage
EVENING, DOC! I THOUGHT WE COULD DO ***NABE*** TOGETHER.
Hey-y-y!
A FINE IDEA! THANKS!
TŌYA, **YOUR WIFE'S** HERE WITH THE DINNER BUCKET!
DOC, I WARNED YOU ABOUT ***TEASING*** HER...

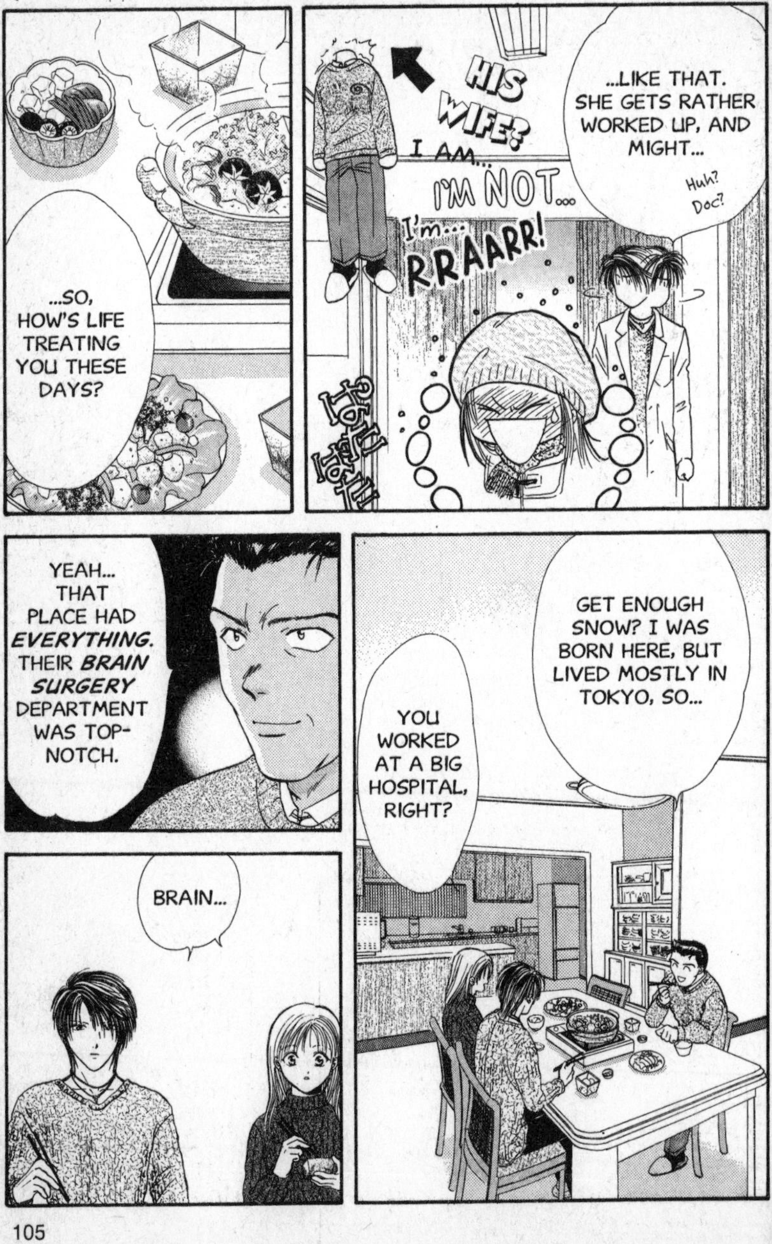
...LIKE THAT. SHE GETS RATHER WORKED UP, AND MIGHT...
Huh? Doc?
HIS WIFE?
I AM...
I'M NOT...
I'm...
RRAARR!
...SO, HOW'S LIFE TREATING YOU THESE DAYS?
GET ENOUGH SNOW? I WAS BORN HERE, BUT LIVED MOSTLY IN TOKYO, SO...
YOU WORKED AT A BIG HOSPITAL, RIGHT?
YEAH... THAT PLACE HAD EVERYTHING. THEIR BRAIN SURGERY DEPARTMENT WAS TOP-NOTCH.
BRAIN...

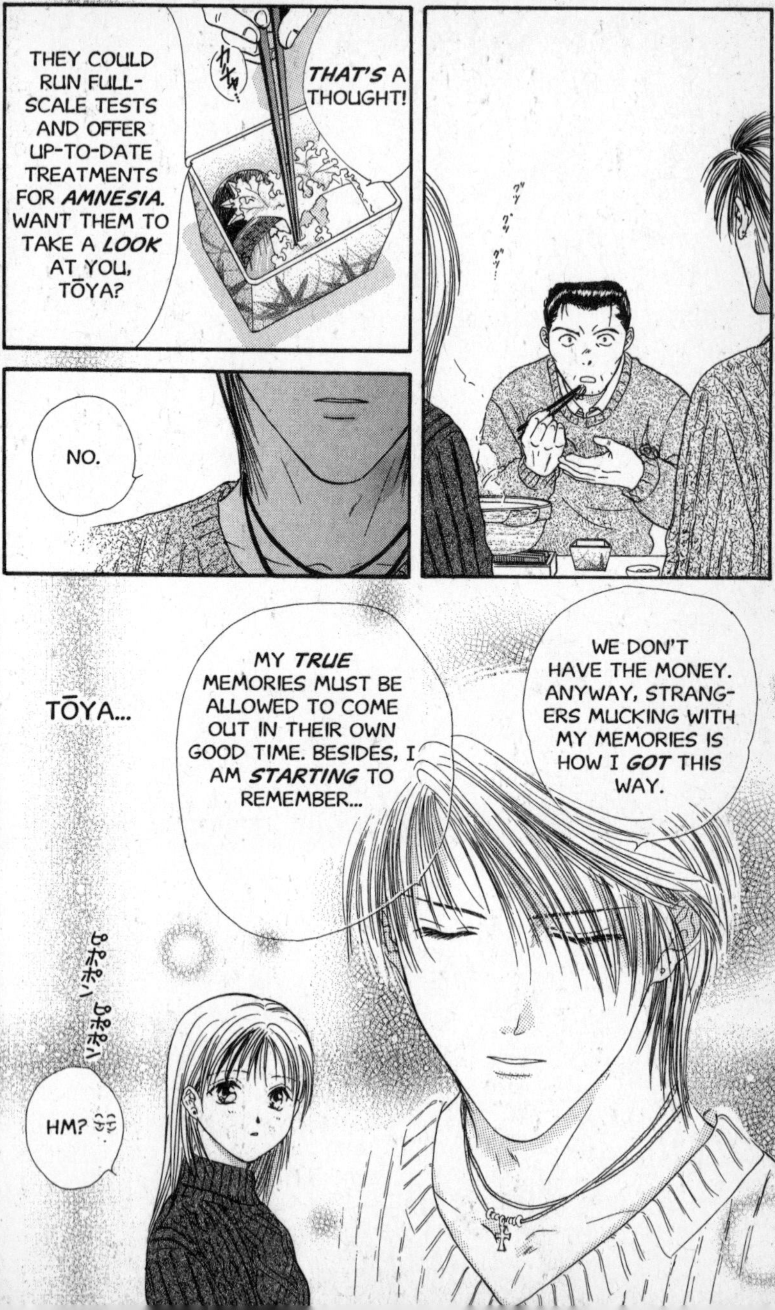
THAT'S A THOUGHT!
THEY COULD RUN FULL-SCALE TESTS AND OFFER UP-TO-DATE TREATMENTS FOR AMNESIA. WANT THEM TO TAKE A LOOK AT YOU, TŌYA?
NO.
WE DON'T HAVE THE MONEY. ANYWAY, STRANGERS MUCKING WITH MY MEMORIES IS HOW I GOT THIS WAY.
MY TRUE MEMORIES MUST BE ALLOWED TO COME OUT IN THEIR OWN GOOD TIME. BESIDES, I AM STARTING TO REMEMBER...
TŌYA...
HM?

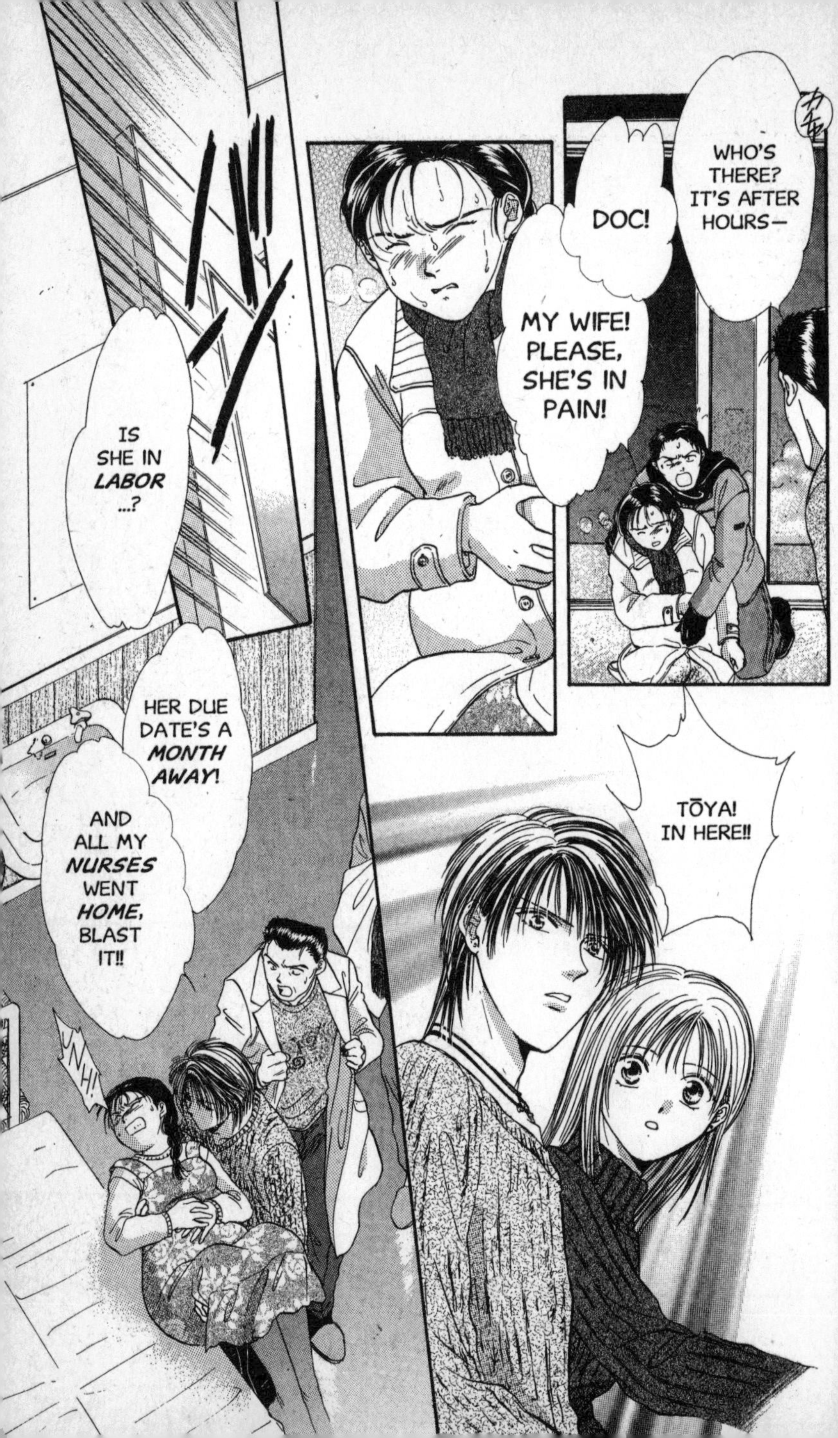
WHO'S THERE? IT'S AFTER HOURS—
DOC!
MY WIFE! PLEASE, SHE'S IN PAIN!
TŌYA! IN HERE!!
IS SHE IN *LABOR* ...?
HER DUE DATE'S A *MONTH AWAY*!
AND ALL MY *NURSES* WENT *HOME*, BLAST IT!!
UNH!

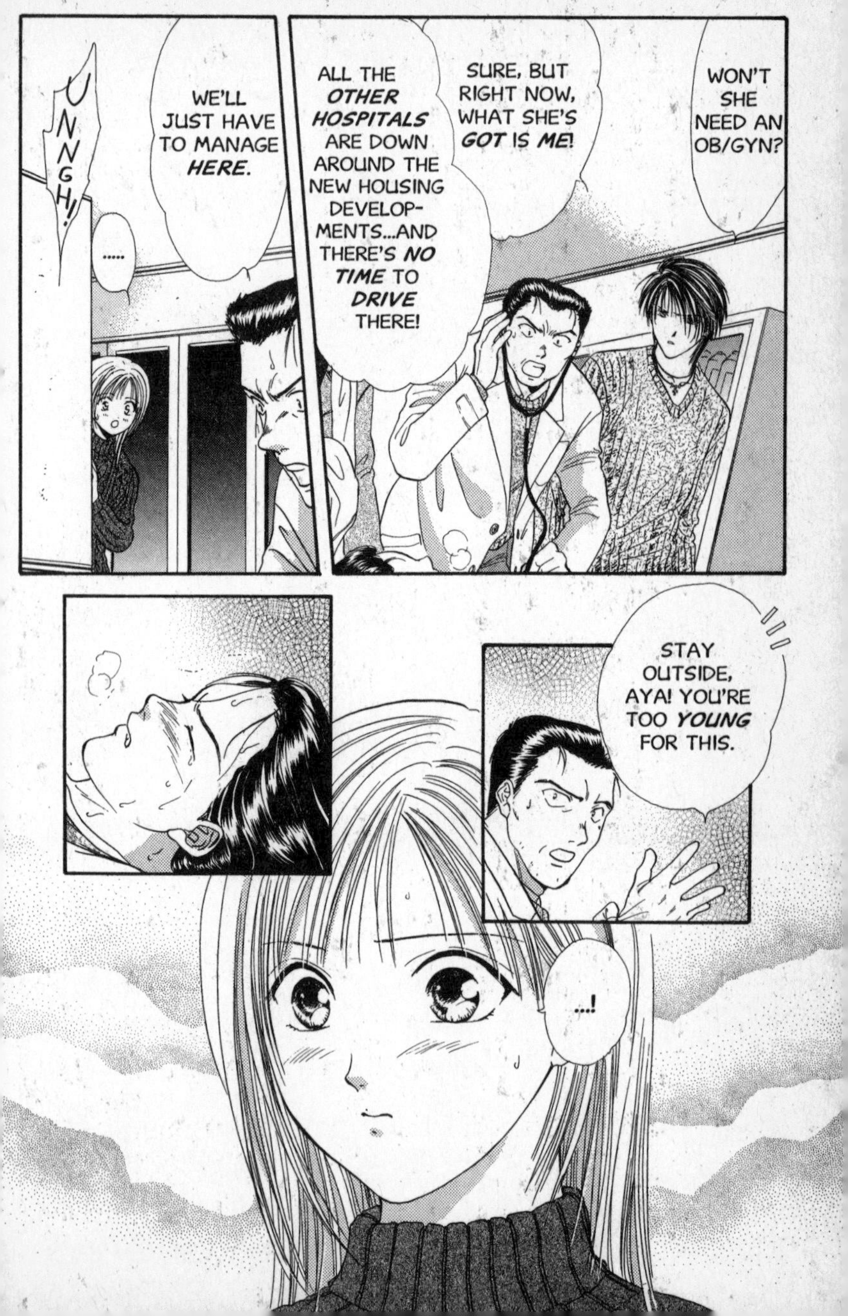
WON'T SHE NEED AN OB/GYN?
SURE, BUT RIGHT NOW, WHAT SHE'S *GOT* IS *ME*!
ALL THE *OTHER HOSPITALS* ARE DOWN AROUND THE NEW HOUSING DEVELOP-MENTS...AND THERE'S *NO TIME* TO *DRIVE* THERE!
WE'LL JUST HAVE TO MANAGE *HERE.*
UNNGH!
......
STAY OUTSIDE, AYA! YOU'RE TOO *YOUNG* FOR THIS.
...!

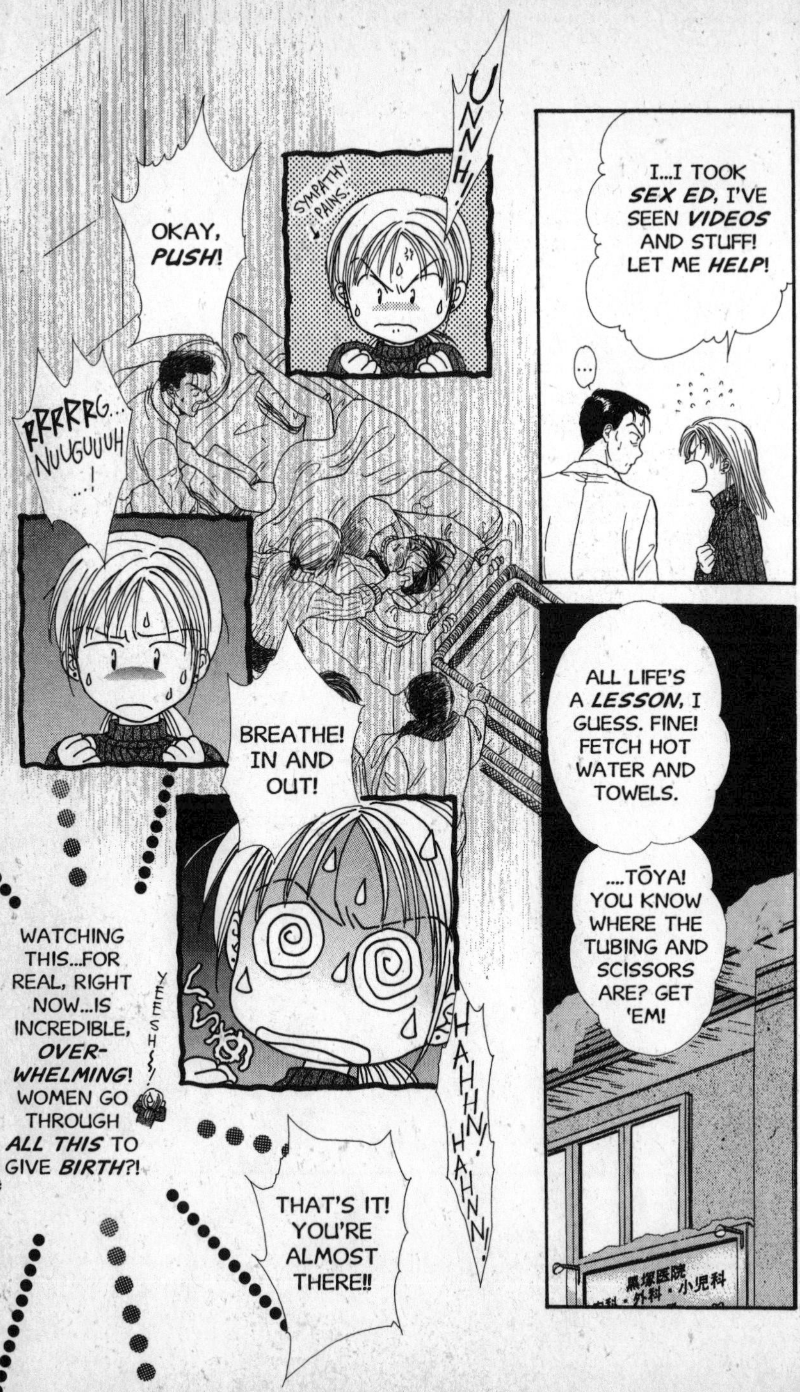
I...I TOOK SEX ED, I'VE SEEN VIDEOS AND STUFF! LET ME HELP!
...
ALL LIFE'S A LESSON, I GUESS. FINE! FETCH HOT WATER AND TOWELS.
....TŌYA! YOU KNOW WHERE THE TUBING AND SCISSORS ARE? GET 'EM!
黒塚医院
外科・小児科
UNNH!
SYMPATHY PAINS.
OKAY, PUSH!
RRRRG... NUUGUUUH ...!
BREATHE! IN AND OUT!
HAHHN! HAHNN!
YEESH!
WATCHING THIS...FOR REAL, RIGHT NOW...IS INCREDIBLE, OVER-WHELMING! WOMEN GO THROUGH ALL THIS TO GIVE BIRTH?!
THAT'S IT! YOU'RE ALMOST THERE!!

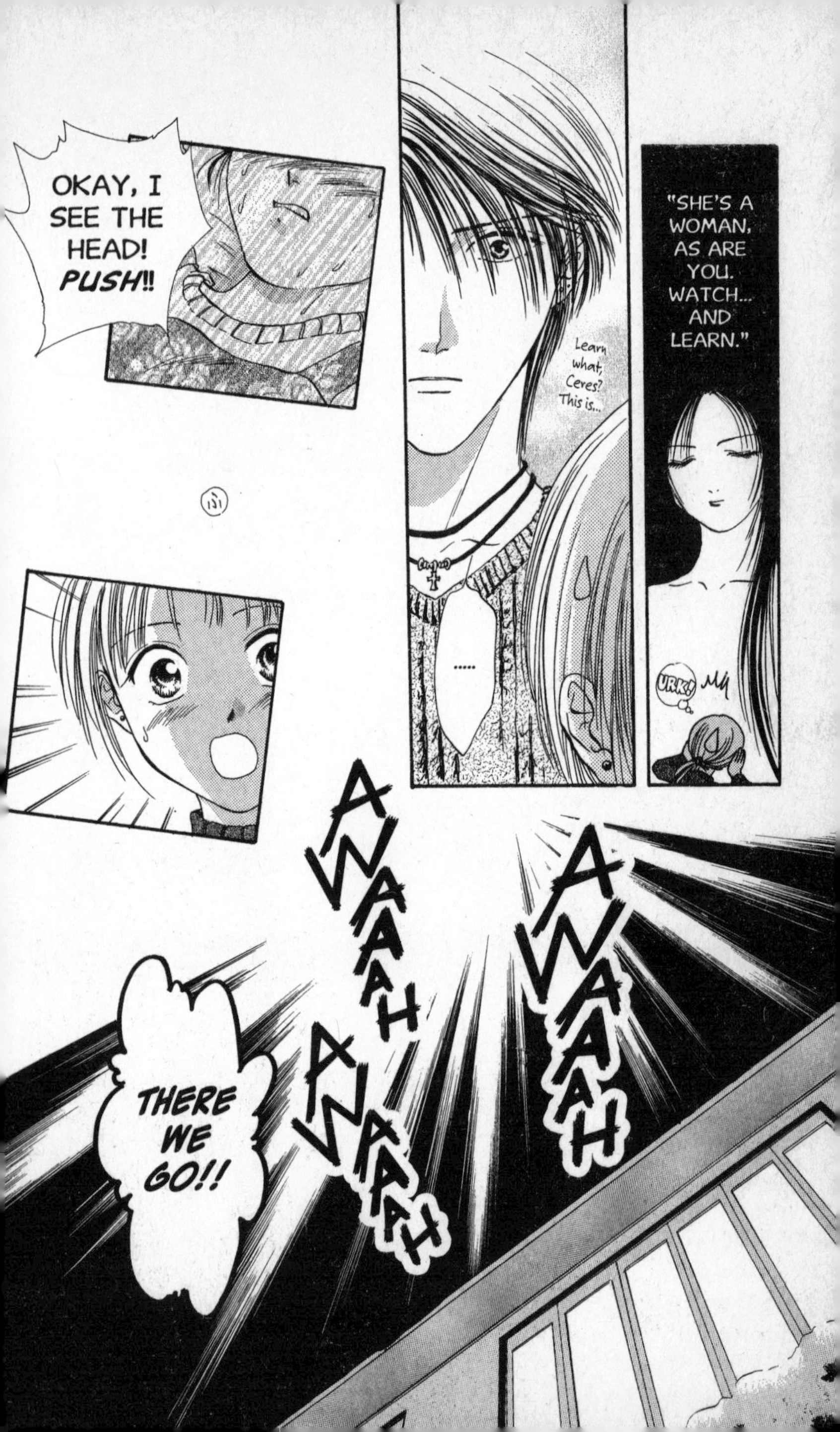
"SHE'S A WOMAN, AS ARE YOU. WATCH... AND LEARN."
URK!
Learn what, Ceres? This is...
.....
OKAY, I SEE THE HEAD! PUSH!!
AWAAAH
AWAAAH AWAAAH
THERE WE GO!!

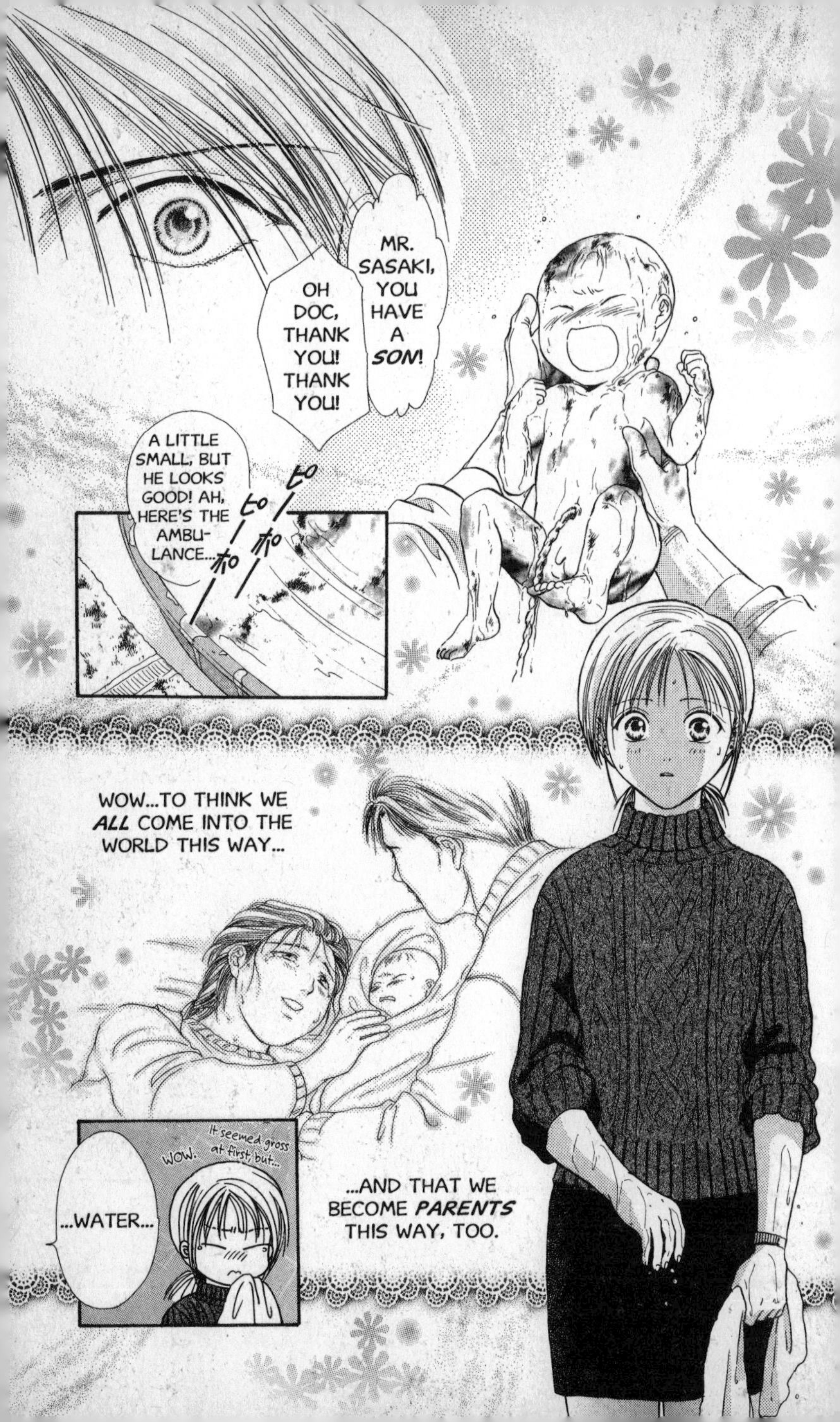
MR. SASAKI, YOU HAVE A *SON*!
OH DOC, THANK YOU! THANK YOU!
A LITTLE SMALL, BUT HE LOOKS GOOD! AH, HERE'S THE AMBU-LANCE...
ピーポーピーポー
WOW...TO THINK WE *ALL* COME INTO THE WORLD THIS WAY...
...AND THAT WE BECOME *PARENTS* THIS WAY, TOO.
It seemed gross at first, but...
WOW.
...WATER...

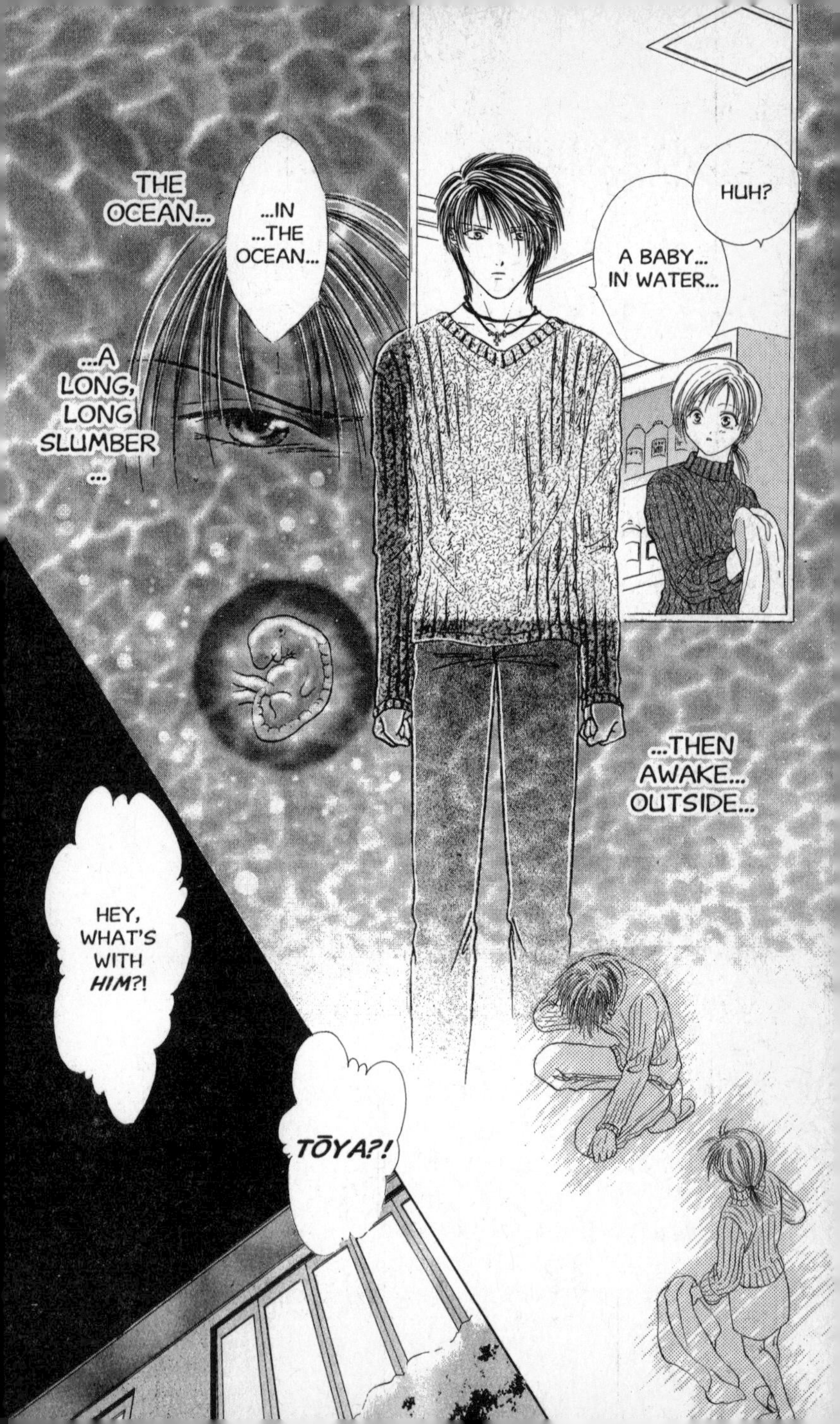
HUH?
A BABY... IN WATER...
...IN ...THE OCEAN...
THE OCEAN...
...A LONG, LONG SLUMBER ...
...THEN AWAKE... OUTSIDE...
TŌYA?!
HEY, WHAT'S WITH *HIM*?!

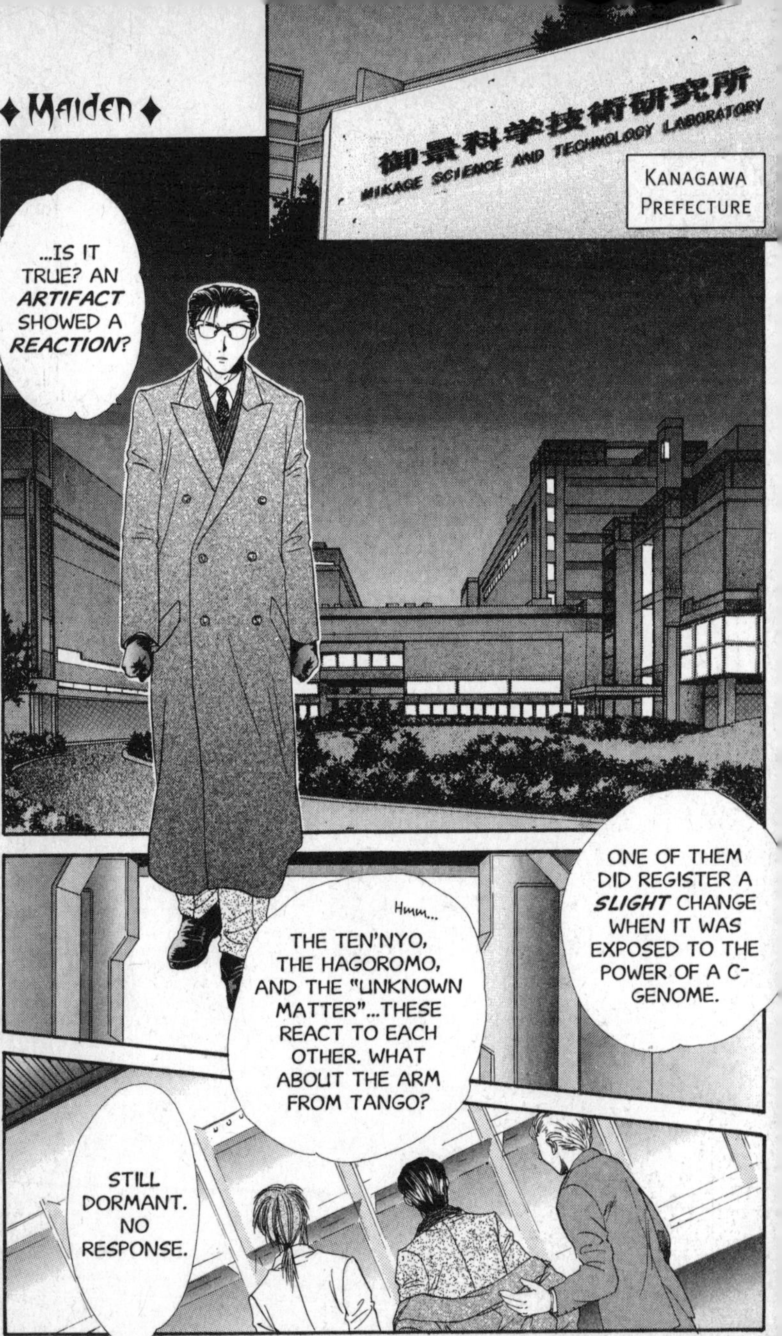
御景科学技術研究所
MIKAGE SCIENCE AND TECHNOLOGY LABORATORY
KANAGAWA PREFECTURE
...IS IT TRUE? AN *ARTIFACT* SHOWED A *REACTION*?
ONE OF THEM DID REGISTER A *SLIGHT* CHANGE WHEN IT WAS EXPOSED TO THE POWER OF A C-GENOME.
Hmm...
THE TEN'NYO, THE HAGOROMO, AND THE "UNKNOWN MATTER"...THESE REACT TO EACH OTHER. WHAT ABOUT THE ARM FROM TANGO?
STILL DORMANT. NO RESPONSE.

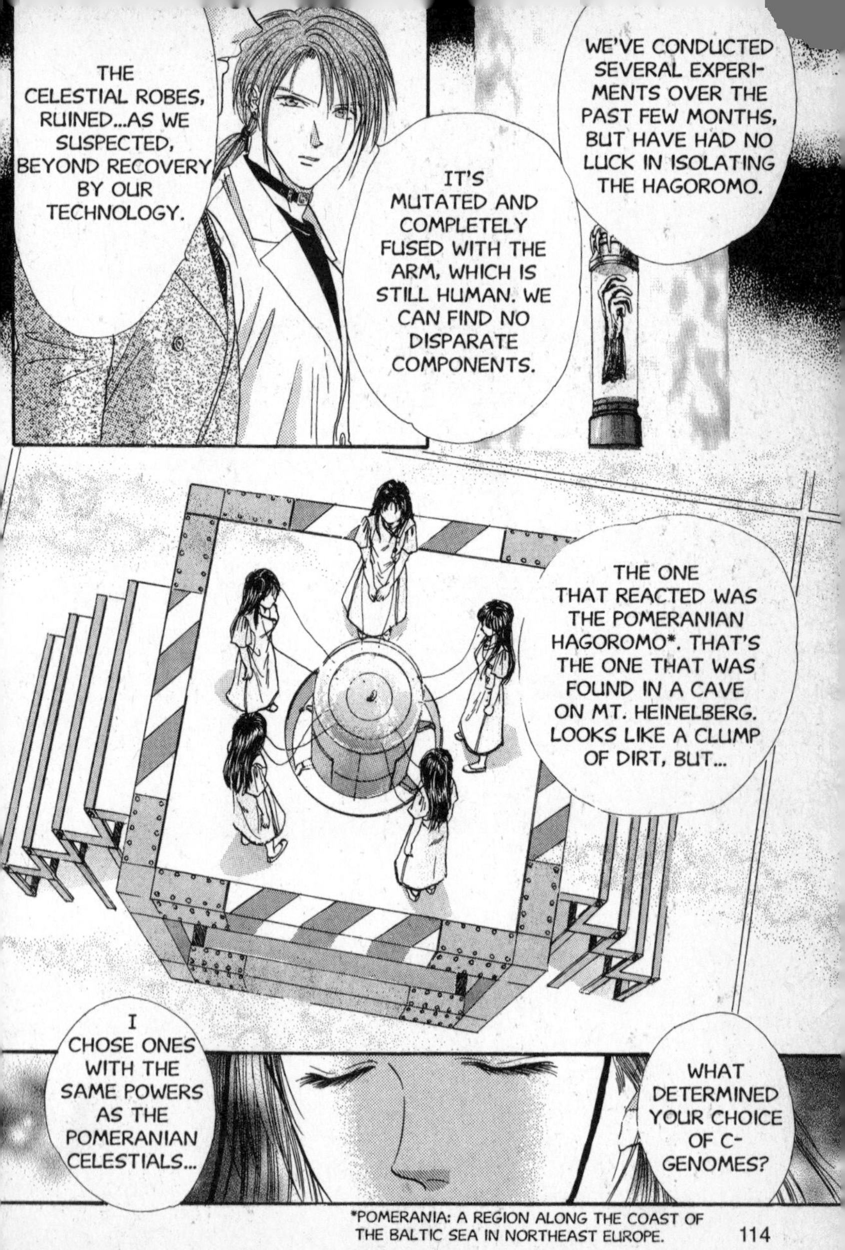
WE'VE CONDUCTED SEVERAL EXPERI- MENTS OVER THE PAST FEW MONTHS, BUT HAVE HAD NO LUCK IN ISOLATING THE HAGOROMO.
IT'S MUTATED AND COMPLETELY FUSED WITH THE ARM, WHICH IS STILL HUMAN. WE CAN FIND NO DISPARATE COMPONENTS.
THE CELESTIAL ROBES, RUINED...AS WE SUSPECTED, BEYOND RECOVERY BY OUR TECHNOLOGY.
THE ONE THAT REACTED WAS THE POMERANIAN HAGOROMO*. THAT'S THE ONE THAT WAS FOUND IN A CAVE ON MT. HEINELBERG. LOOKS LIKE A CLUMP OF DIRT, BUT...
WHAT DETERMINED YOUR CHOICE OF C- GENOMES?
I CHOSE ONES WITH THE SAME POWERS AS THE POMERANIAN CELESTIALS...

*POMERANIA: A REGION ALONG THE COAST OF THE BALTIC SEA IN NORTHEAST EUROPE.

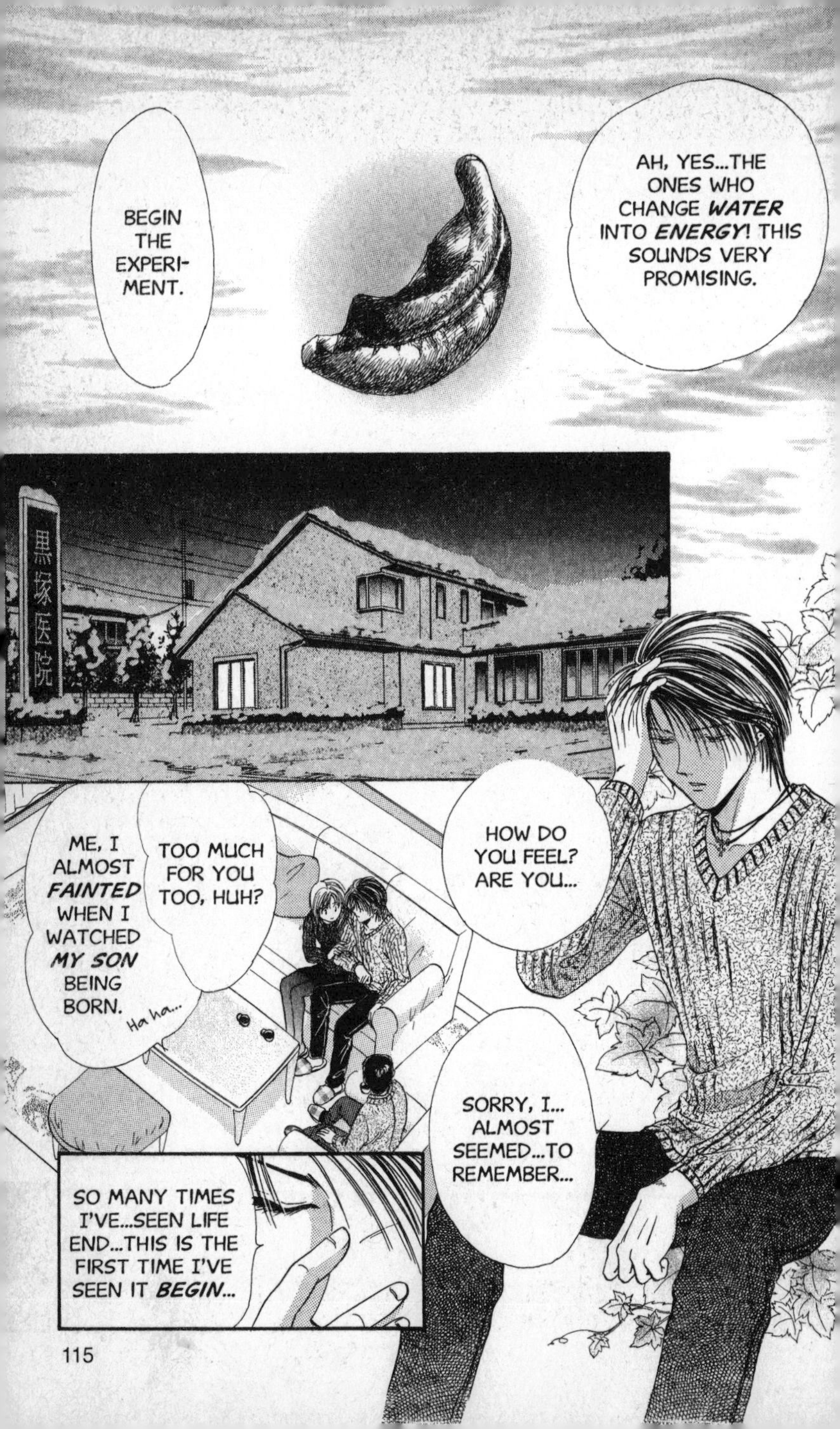
AH, YES...THE ONES WHO CHANGE WATER INTO ENERGY! THIS SOUNDS VERY PROMISING.
BEGIN THE EXPERI-MENT.
黒塚医院
HOW DO YOU FEEL? ARE YOU...
TOO MUCH FOR YOU TOO, HUH?
ME, I ALMOST FAINTED WHEN I WATCHED MY SON BEING BORN.
Ha ha...
SORRY, I... ALMOST SEEMED...TO REMEMBER...
SO MANY TIMES I'VE...SEEN LIFE END...THIS IS THE FIRST TIME I'VE SEEN IT BEGIN...

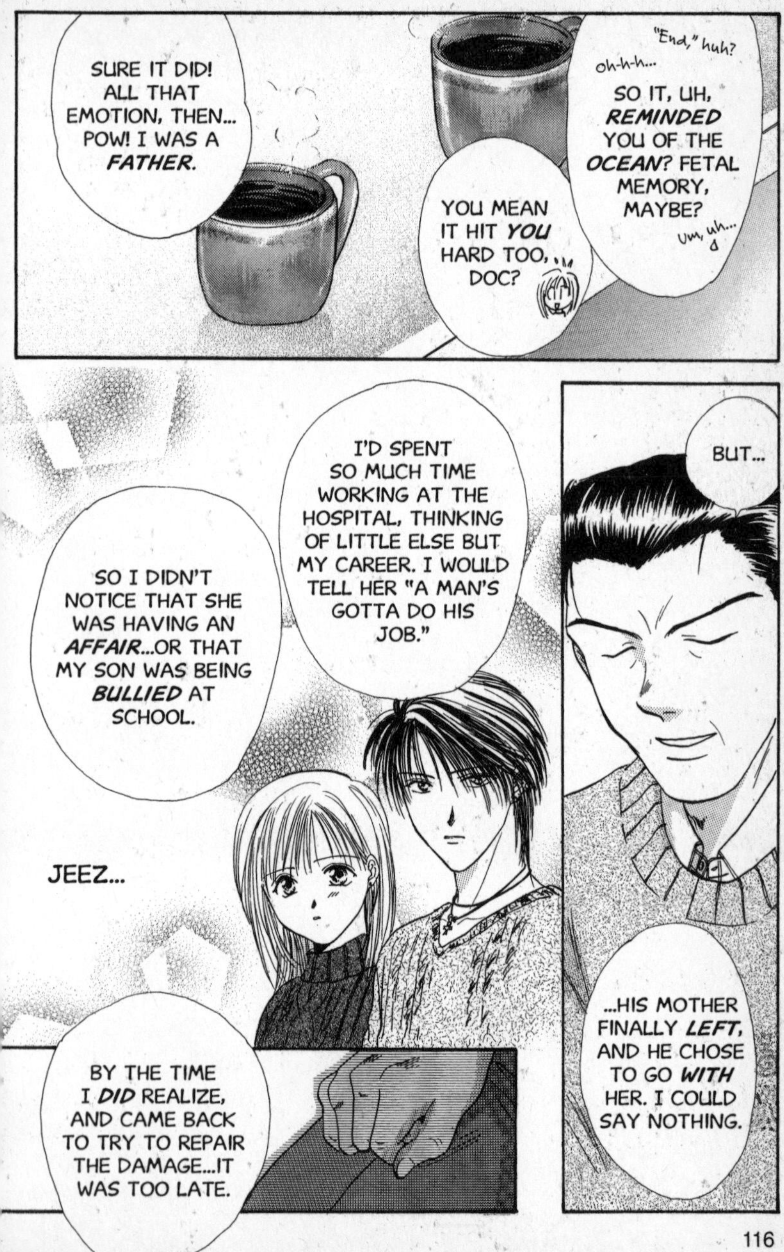
"End," huh?
oh-h-h...
SO IT, UH, *REMINDED* YOU OF THE *OCEAN*? FETAL MEMORY, MAYBE?
Um, uh...
YOU MEAN IT HIT *YOU* HARD TOO, DOC?
SURE IT DID! ALL THAT EMOTION, THEN... POW! I WAS A *FATHER*.
BUT...
I'D SPENT SO MUCH TIME WORKING AT THE HOSPITAL, THINKING OF LITTLE ELSE BUT MY CAREER. I WOULD TELL HER "A MAN'S GOTTA DO HIS JOB."
SO I DIDN'T NOTICE THAT SHE WAS HAVING AN *AFFAIR*...OR THAT MY SON WAS BEING *BULLIED* AT SCHOOL.
JEEZ...
BY THE TIME I *DID* REALIZE, AND CAME BACK TO TRY TO REPAIR THE DAMAGE...IT WAS TOO LATE.
...HIS MOTHER FINALLY *LEFT*, AND HE CHOSE TO GO *WITH* HER. I COULD SAY NOTHING.

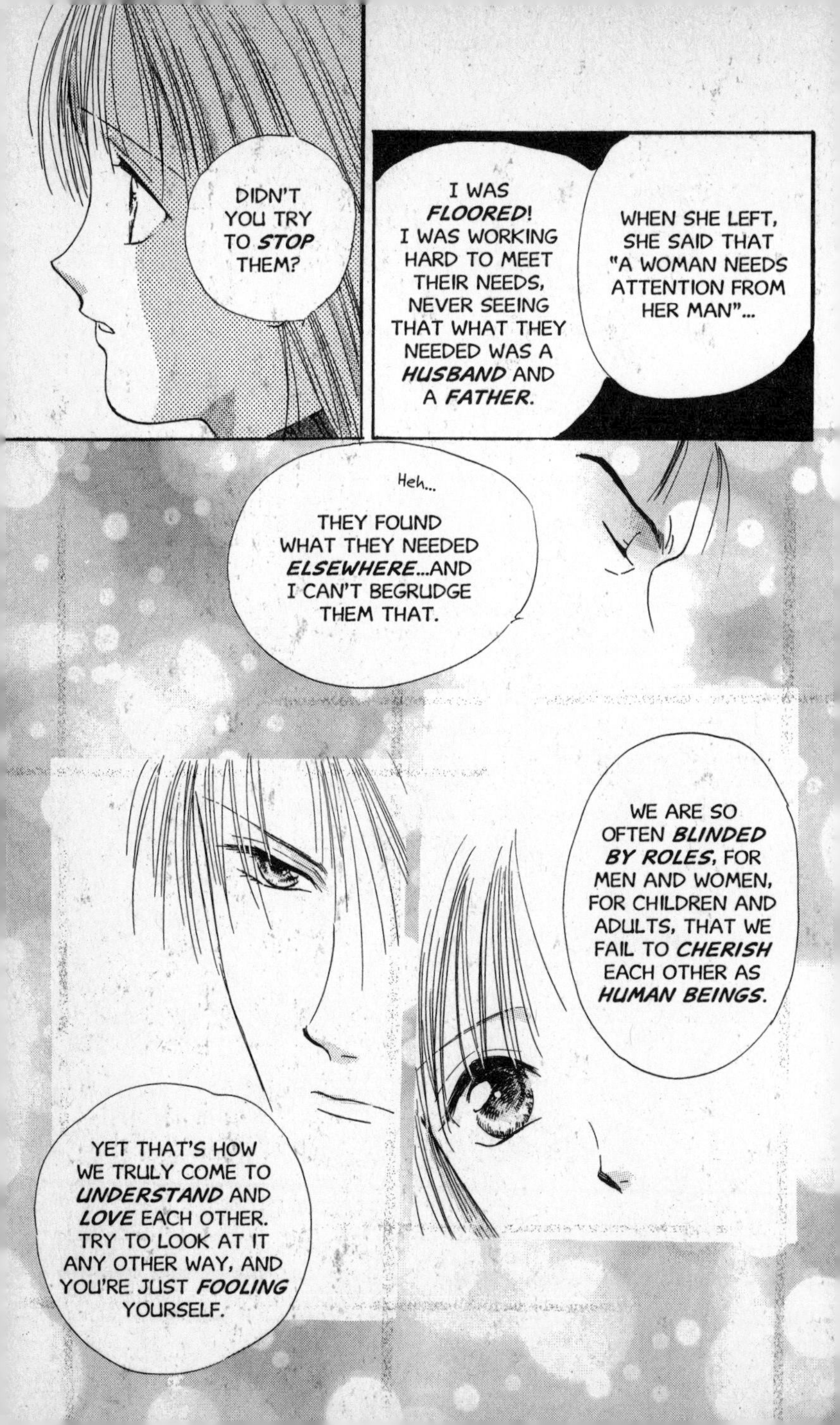
WHEN SHE LEFT, SHE SAID THAT "A WOMAN NEEDS ATTENTION FROM HER MAN"...
I WAS FLOORED! I WAS WORKING HARD TO MEET THEIR NEEDS, NEVER SEEING THAT WHAT THEY NEEDED WAS A HUSBAND AND A FATHER.
DIDN'T YOU TRY TO STOP THEM?
Heh...
THEY FOUND WHAT THEY NEEDED ELSEWHERE...AND I CAN'T BEGRUDGE THEM THAT.
WE ARE SO OFTEN BLINDED BY ROLES, FOR MEN AND WOMEN, FOR CHILDREN AND ADULTS, THAT WE FAIL TO CHERISH EACH OTHER AS HUMAN BEINGS.
YET THAT'S HOW WE TRULY COME TO UNDERSTAND AND LOVE EACH OTHER. TRY TO LOOK AT IT ANY OTHER WAY, AND YOU'RE JUST FOOLING YOURSELF.

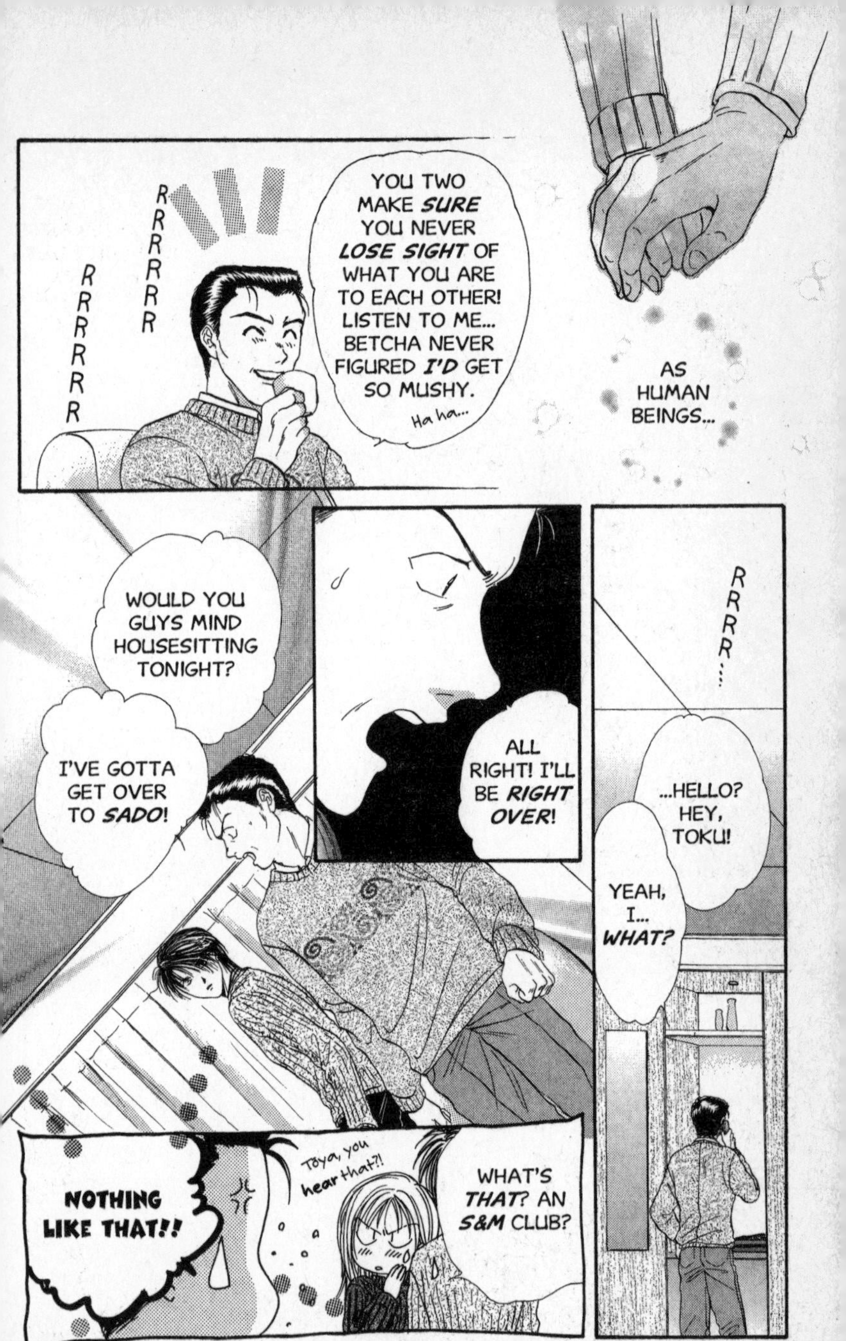
AS HUMAN BEINGS...
RRRRRR
RRRRRR
YOU TWO MAKE SURE YOU NEVER LOSE SIGHT OF WHAT YOU ARE TO EACH OTHER! LISTEN TO ME... BETCHA NEVER FIGURED I'D GET SO MUSHY.
Ha ha...
RRRR...
...HELLO? HEY, TOKU!
YEAH, I... WHAT?
ALL RIGHT! I'LL BE RIGHT OVER!
WOULD YOU GUYS MIND HOUSESITTING TONIGHT?
I'VE GOTTA GET OVER TO SADO!
WHAT'S THAT? AN S&M CLUB?
Tōya, you hear that?!
NOTHING LIKE THAT!!

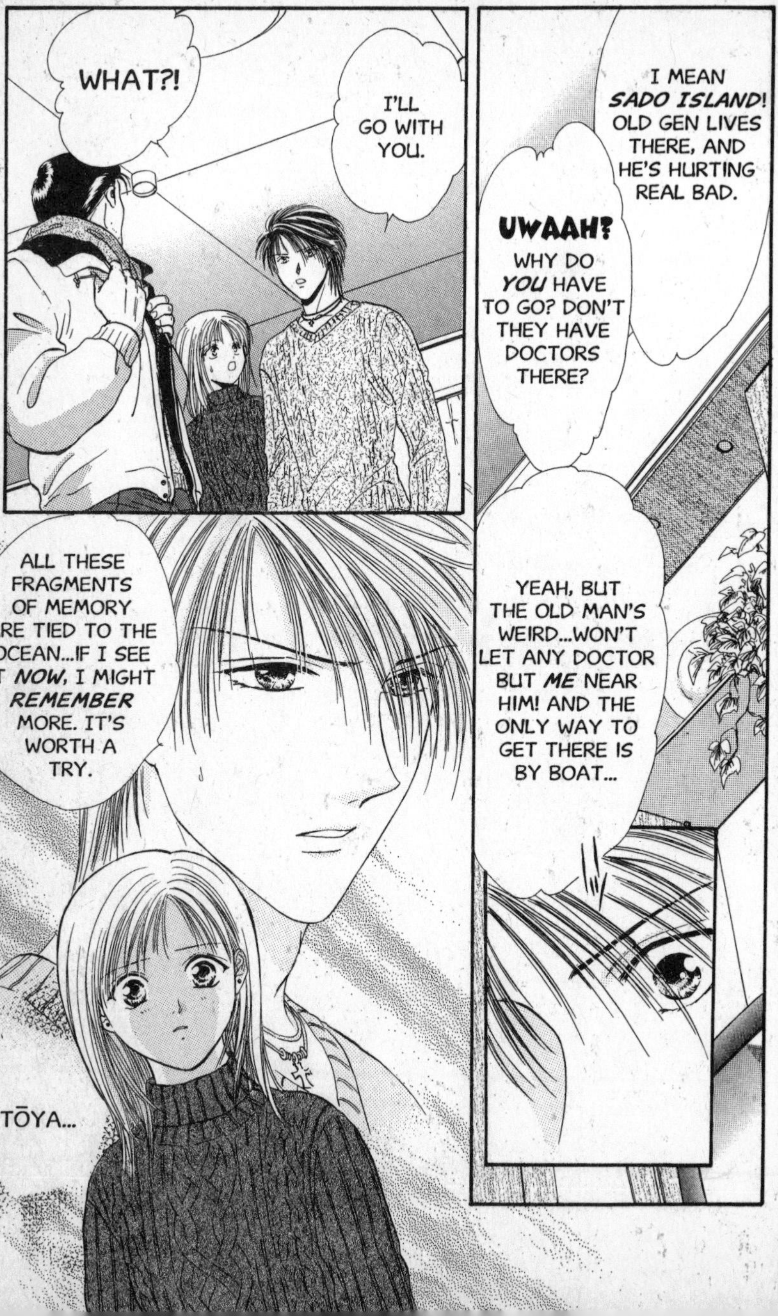
I MEAN *SADO ISLAND*! OLD GEN LIVES THERE, AND HE'S HURTING REAL BAD.
UWAAH? WHY DO *YOU* HAVE TO GO? DON'T THEY HAVE DOCTORS THERE?
YEAH, BUT THE OLD MAN'S WEIRD...WON'T LET ANY DOCTOR BUT *ME* NEAR HIM! AND THE ONLY WAY TO GET THERE IS BY BOAT...
I'LL GO WITH YOU.
WHAT?!
ALL THESE FRAGMENTS OF MEMORY ARE TIED TO THE OCEAN...IF I SEE IT *NOW*, I MIGHT *REMEMBER* MORE. IT'S WORTH A TRY.
TŌYA...

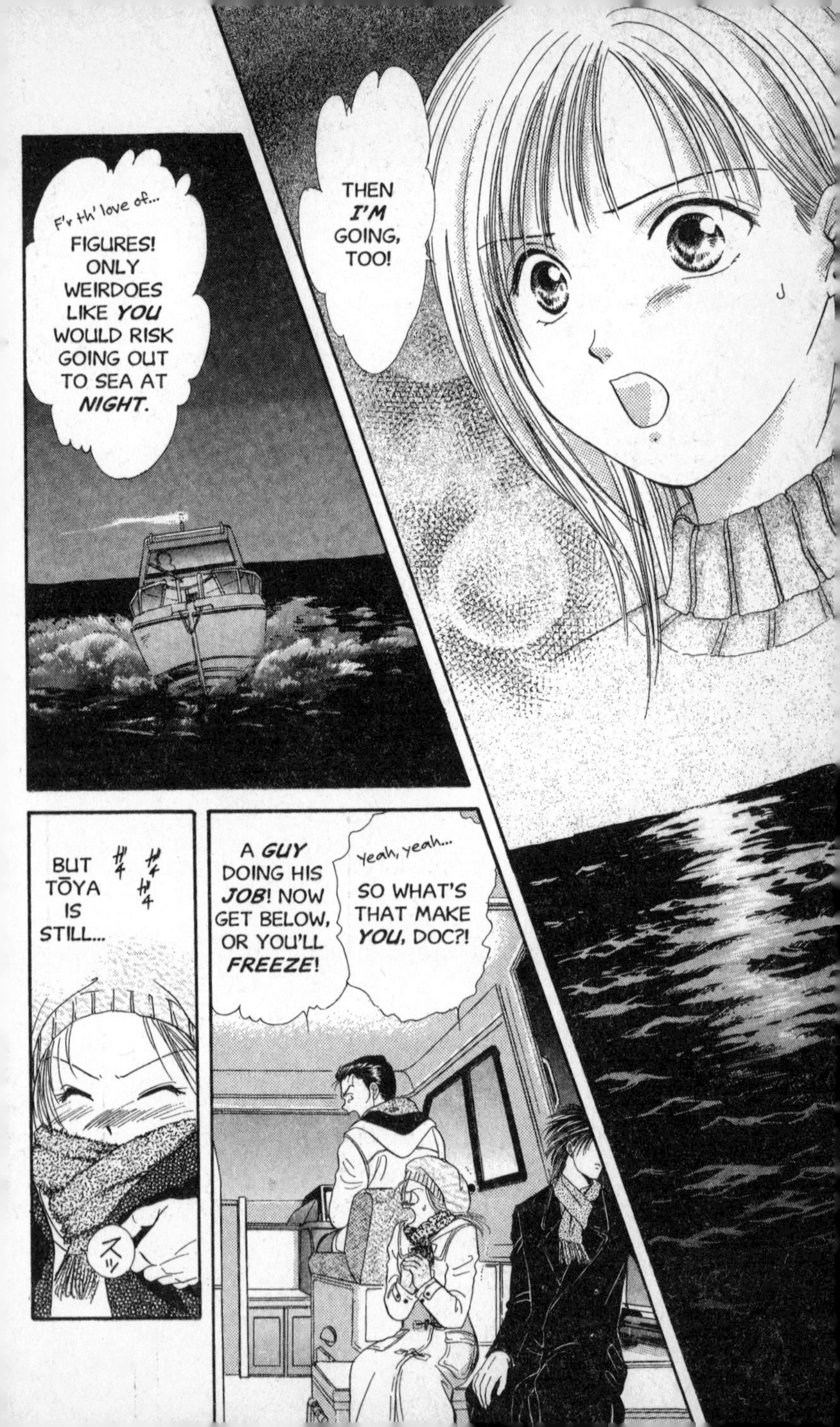
THEN *I'M* GOING, TOO!
F'r th' love of...
FIGURES! ONLY WEIRDOES LIKE *YOU* WOULD RISK GOING OUT TO SEA AT *NIGHT*.
Yeah, yeah...
SO WHAT'S THAT MAKE *YOU*, DOC?!
A *GUY* DOING HIS *JOB*! NOW GET BELOW, OR YOU'LL *FREEZE*!
BUT TŌYA IS STILL...
スッ

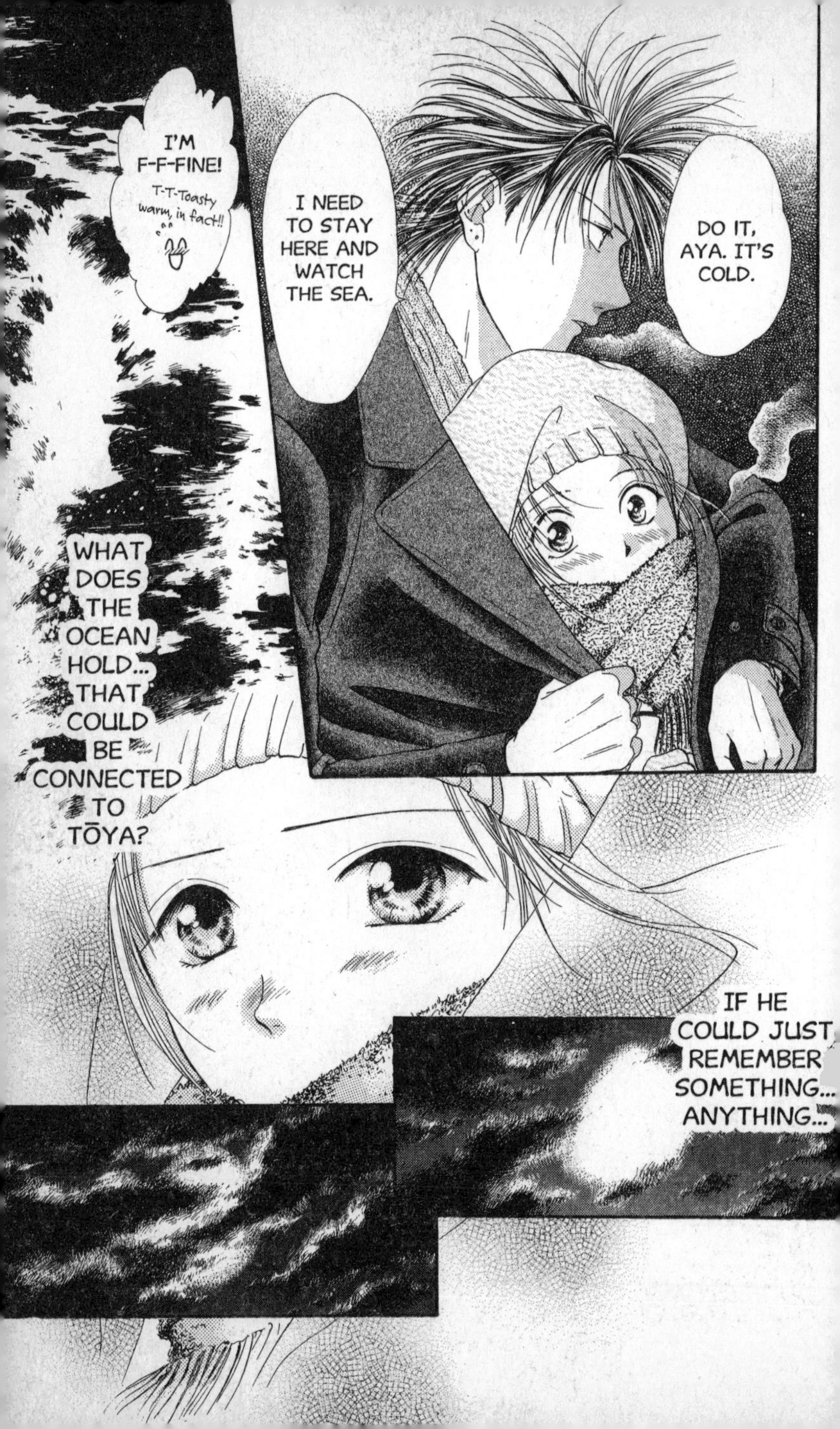
DO IT, AYA. IT'S COLD.
I NEED TO STAY HERE AND WATCH THE SEA.
I'M F-F-FINE!
T-T-Toasty warm, in fact!!
WHAT DOES THE OCEAN HOLD... THAT COULD BE CONNECTED TO TŌYA?
IF HE COULD JUST REMEMBER SOMETHING... ANYTHING...

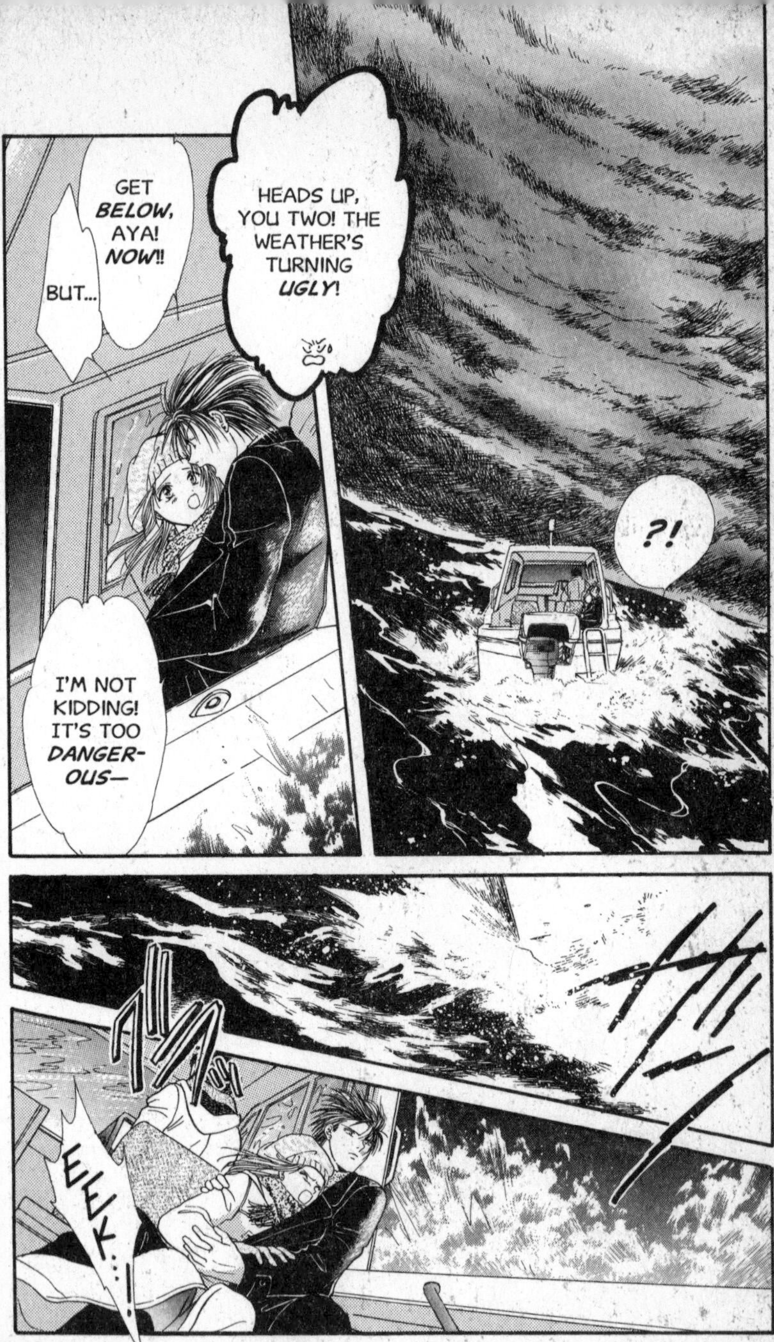
HEADS UP, YOU TWO! THE WEATHER'S TURNING *UGLY*!
?!
GET *BELOW*, AYA! *NOW*!!
BUT...
I'M NOT KIDDING! IT'S TOO *DANGER-OUS*—
EEK...!

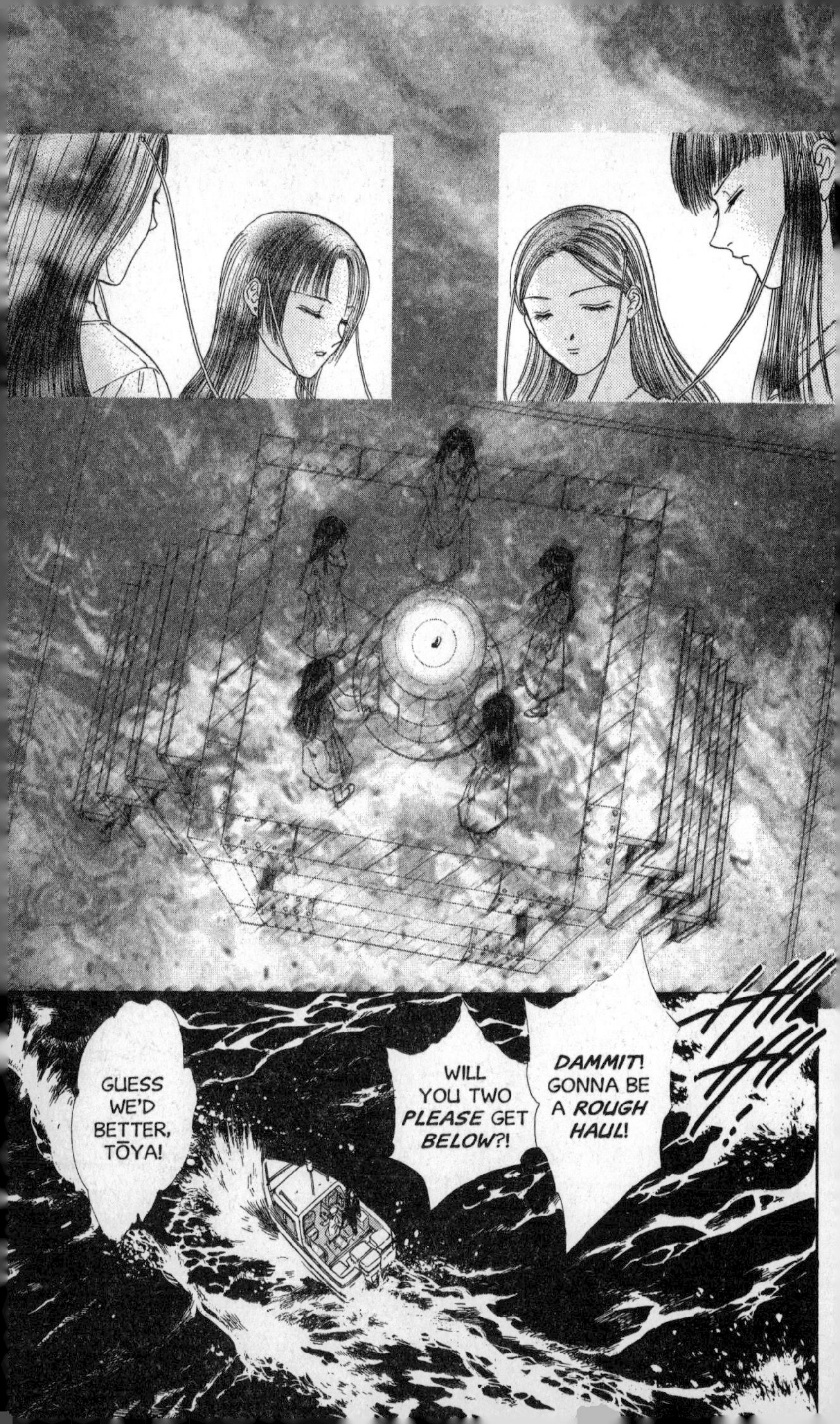
DAMMIT! GONNA BE A ROUGH HAUL!
WILL YOU TWO PLEASE GET BELOW?!
GUESS WE'D BETTER, TŌYA!

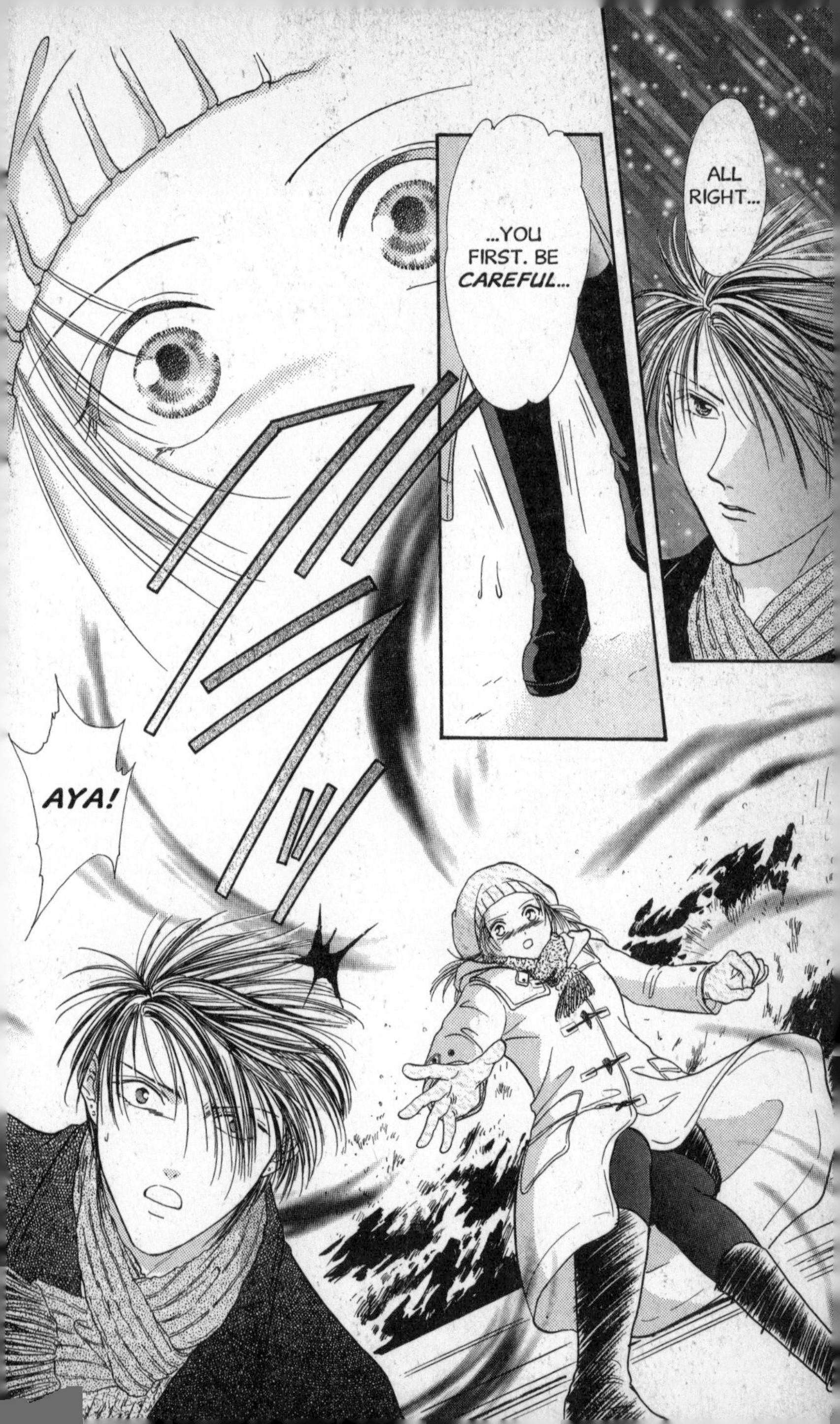
ALL RIGHT...
...YOU FIRST. BE *CAREFUL*...
AYA!

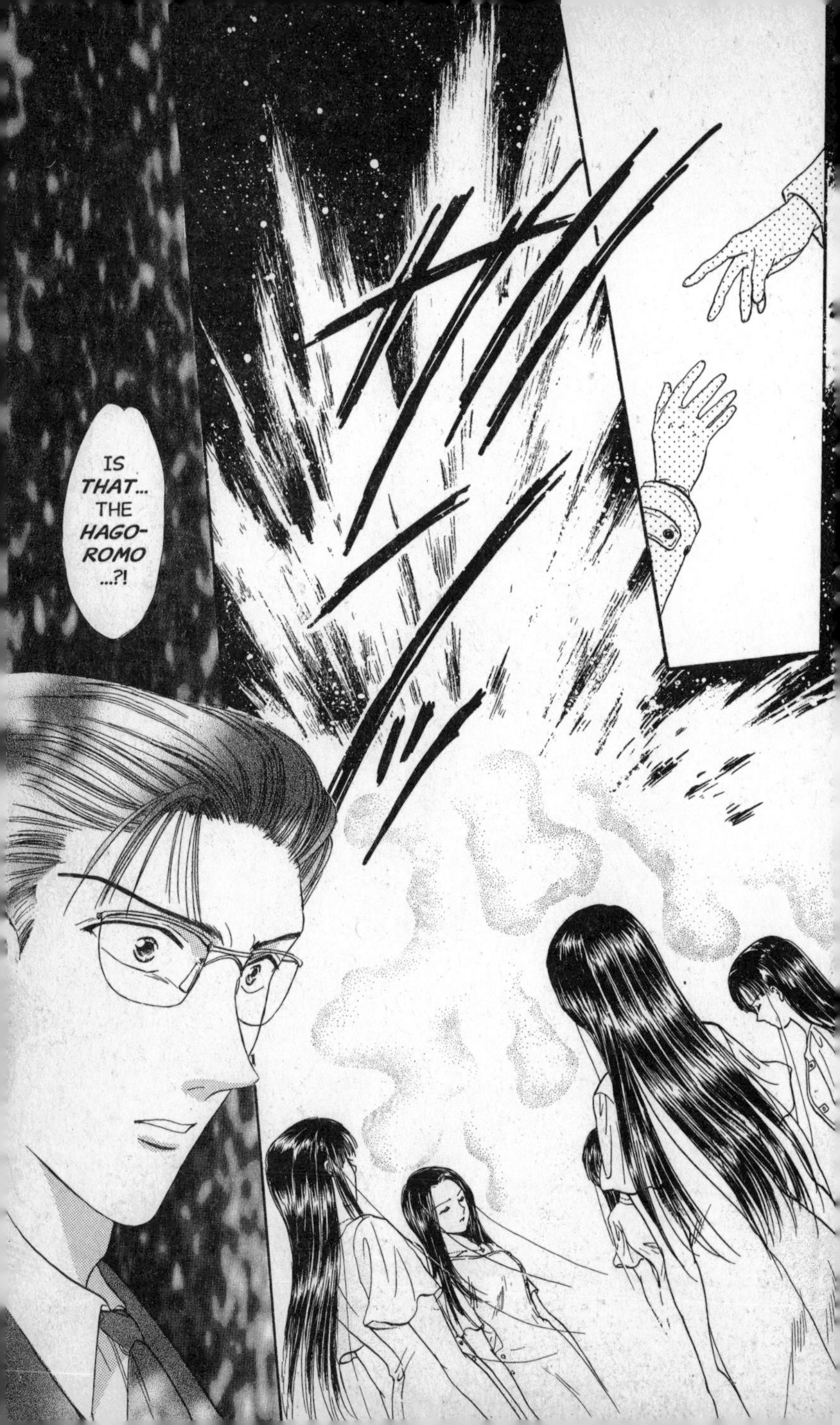
IS THAT... THE HAGO-ROMO ...?!

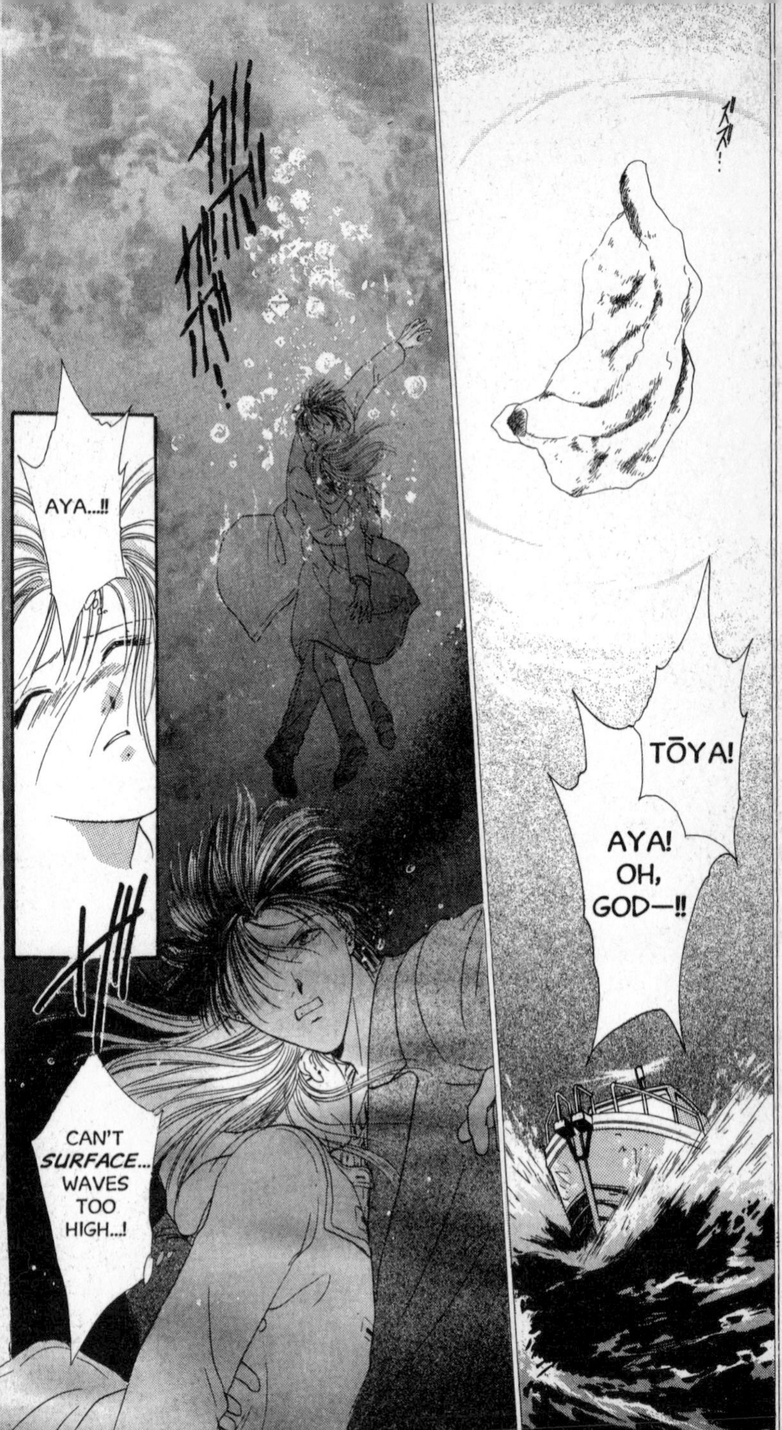
TŌYA!
AYA! OH, GOD—!!
AYA...!!
CAN'T *SURFACE*... WAVES TOO HIGH...!

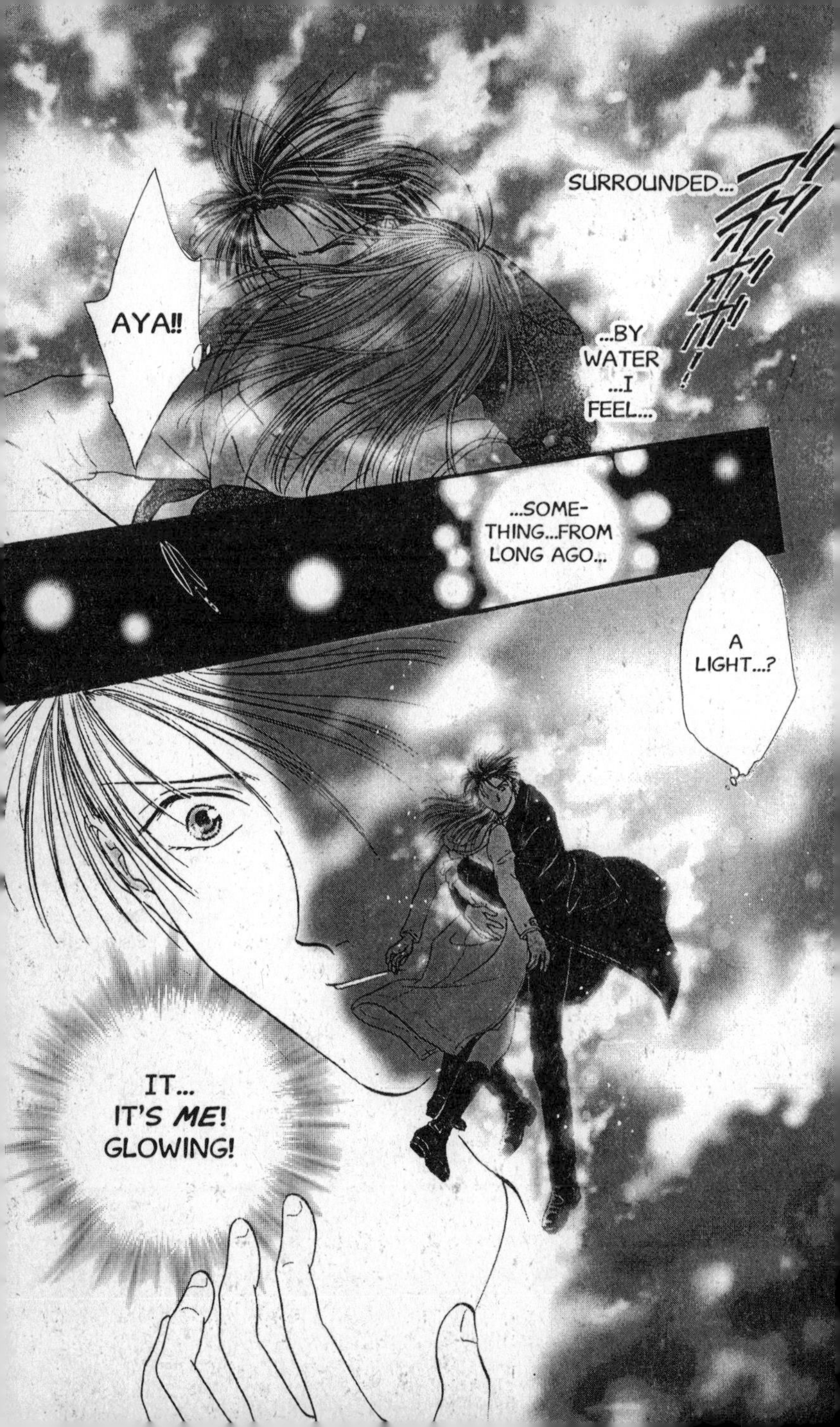
SURROUNDED...
...BY WATER ...I FEEL...
AYA!!
...SOME-THING...FROM LONG AGO...
A LIGHT...?
IT... IT'S *ME*! GLOWING!

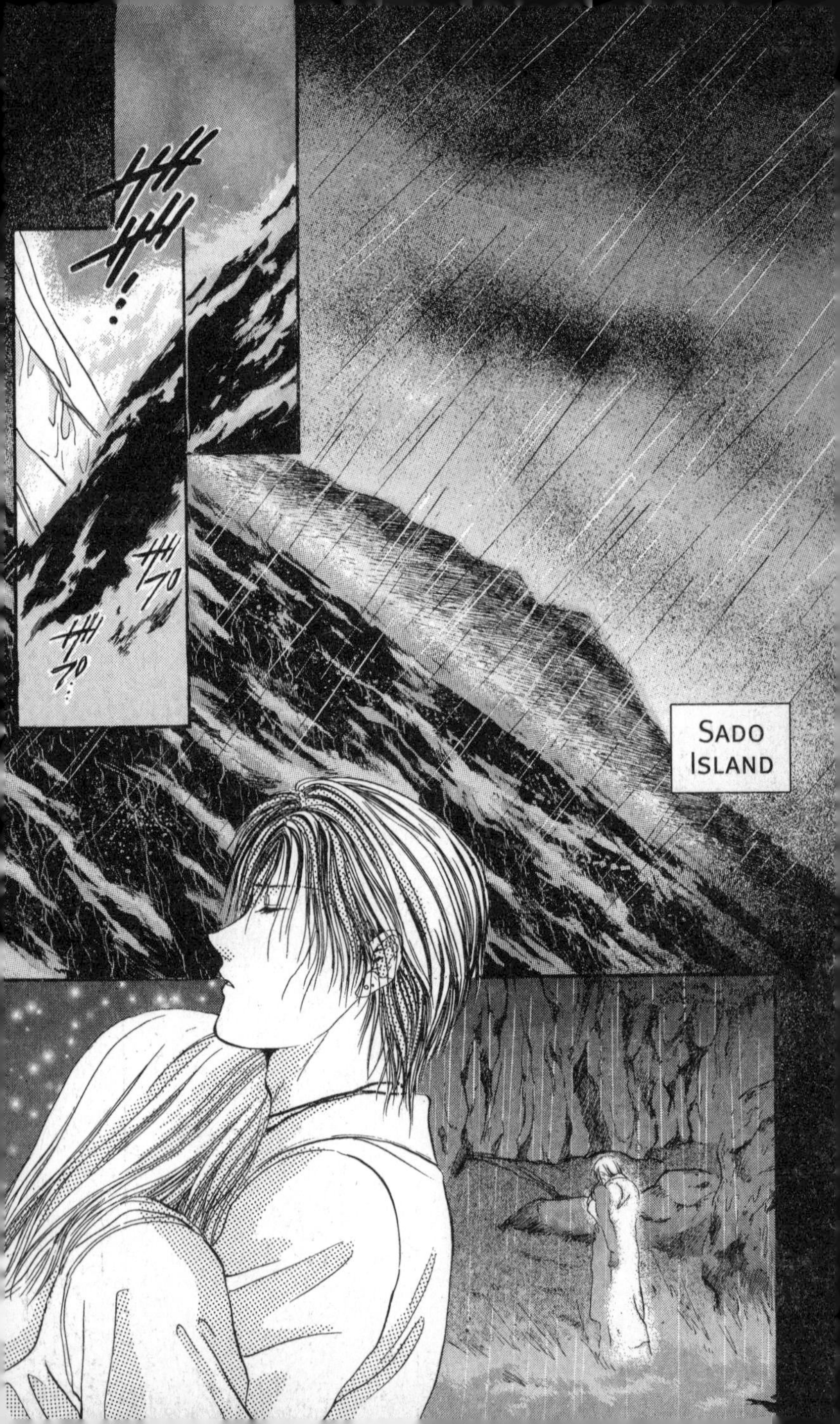
SADO ISLAND

◆ Maiden ◆

I got this one letter that said, "You don't **hate** kogal girls, do you? Sob!" (Wonder if she's even reading this...) I wrote in an earlier column that Aya wasn't immediately popular because she acted like a "kogal." What this girl wrote was, "I may look like a 'kogal' on the outside, but inside, Aya and I think the same way. It made me sad to think I'm not worthy of reading this manga." That's not true, though! Sure, people do tend to frown upon **stereotypical** "kogal" behavior (including "paid dating"), so they assume all girls who **look** that way, **act** that way. You might think looks don't matter...but it's from looks that people get their first impressions. They make assumptions about your personality, based on your appearance. You may say it's the inside that counts...but, in the end, that kind of thinking will do you in. Is it wrong for people to judge others this way? Sure. But still, they do.

Anyway, far be it from me to discriminate among my readers. I was happy to hear from her! I've said before that Aya's a type I wouldn't have been friends with in high school, because I was shy (and still am, in fact).

...Speaking of outward appearances, Japan sure is into herd behavior. I went to an anime convention in North Carolina again (in March '99), and Americans sure do have a sense of individuality. Even in fashion—no two people were dressed alike. One reader argued against (?) Aya's lines in Volume 2, page 173, but it was exactly what the assistants—and, of course, I--all thought when **we** were back in high school. Everyone's made differently, so no one should think the same thing is cute or good, so why...? When I was in school, it was the way we wore our school uniforms, and what we did to our bags (we used to squash them flat). I thought it was so cool, at first....

To be continued!

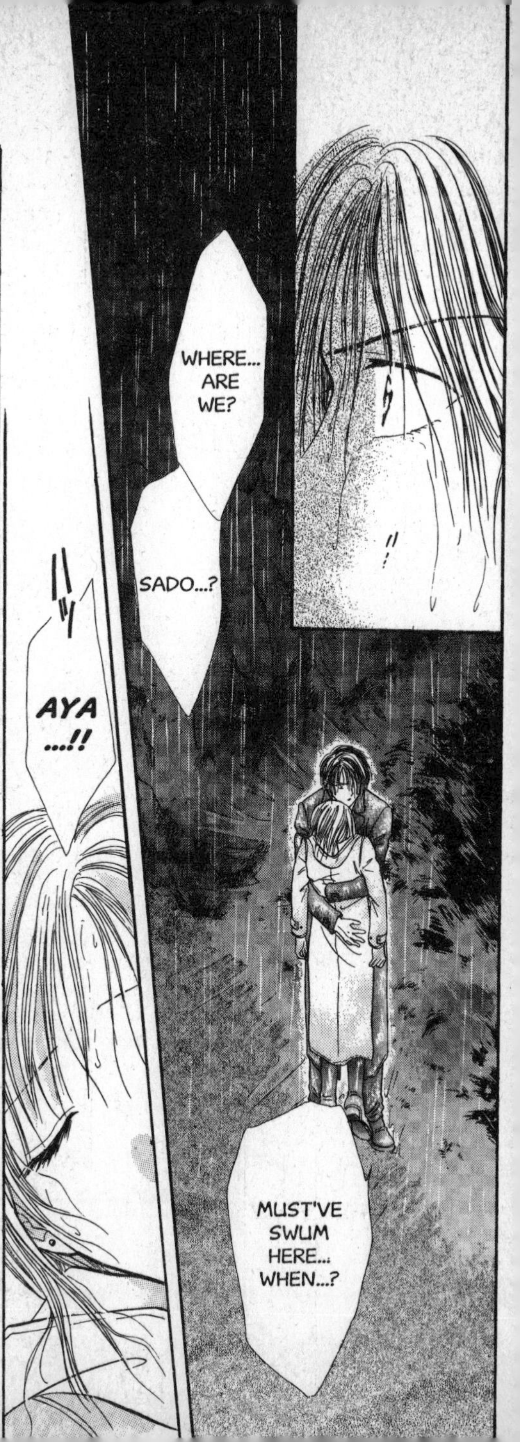
WHERE... ARE WE?
SADO...?
AYA ...!!
MUST'VE SWUM HERE... WHEN...?

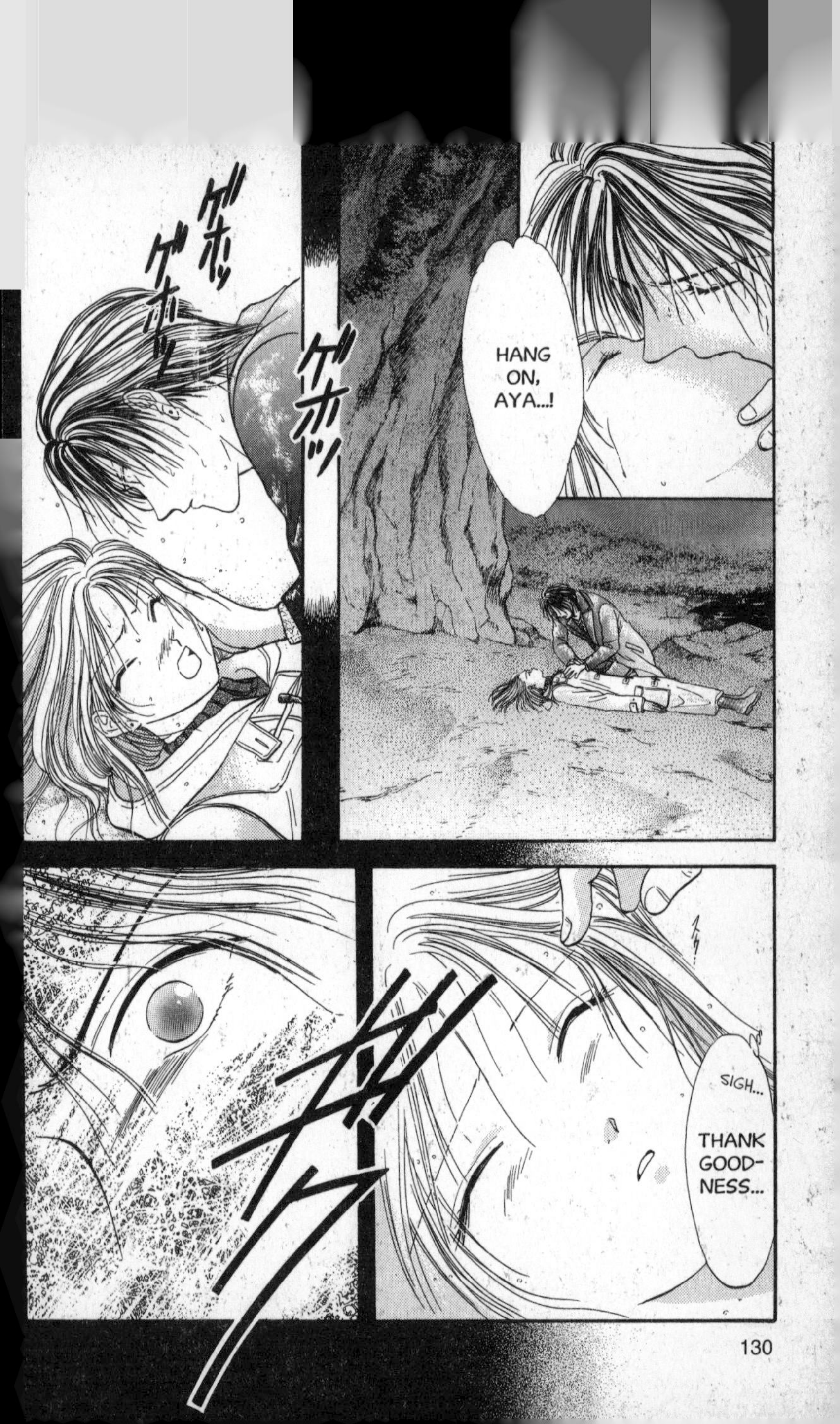
HANG ON, AYA...!
ゲホッ
ゲホッ
ゲホッ
SIGH...
THANK GOOD-NESS...

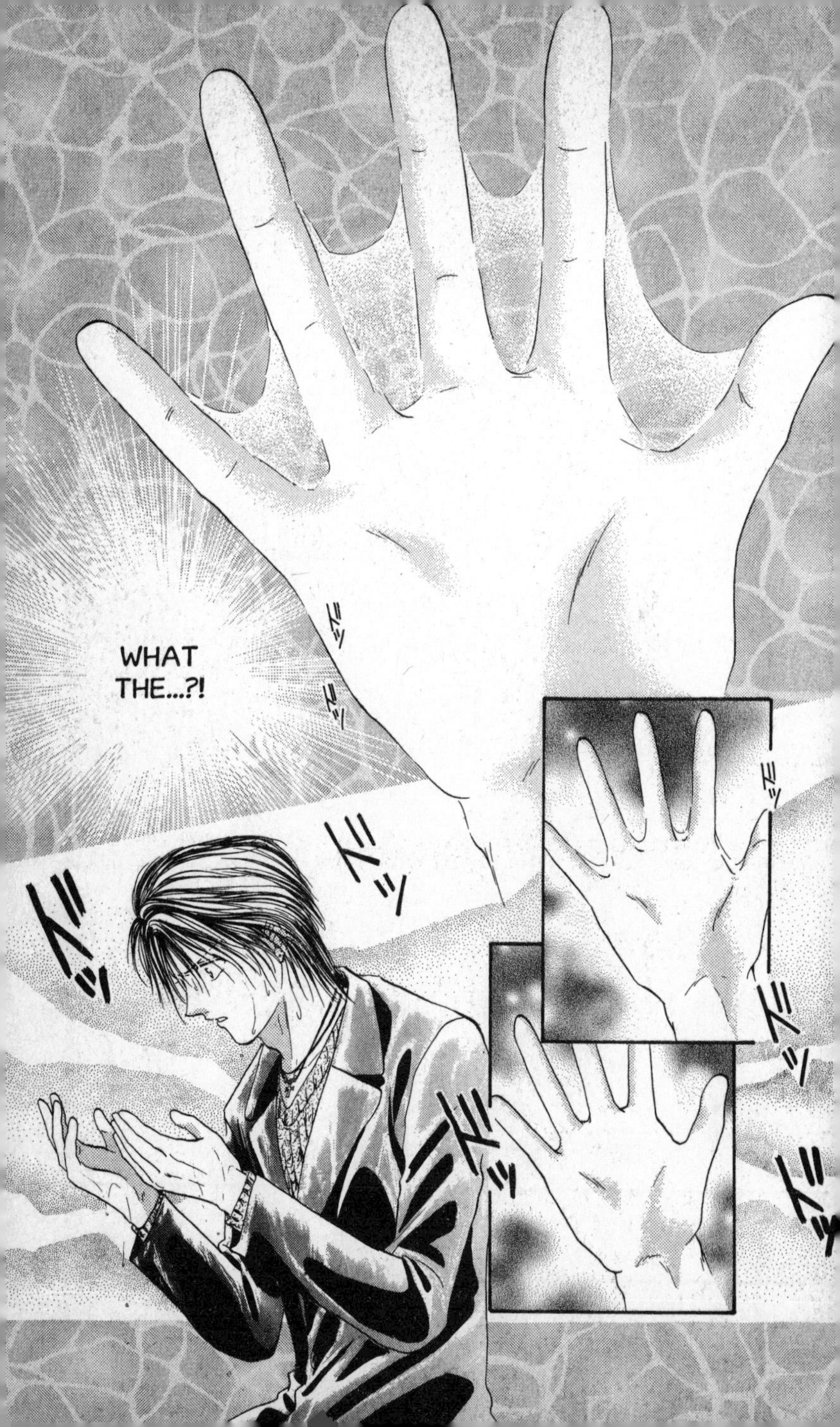
WHAT THE...?!
ズッ
ズッ
ズッ
ズッ
ズッ
ズッ
ズッ
ズッ

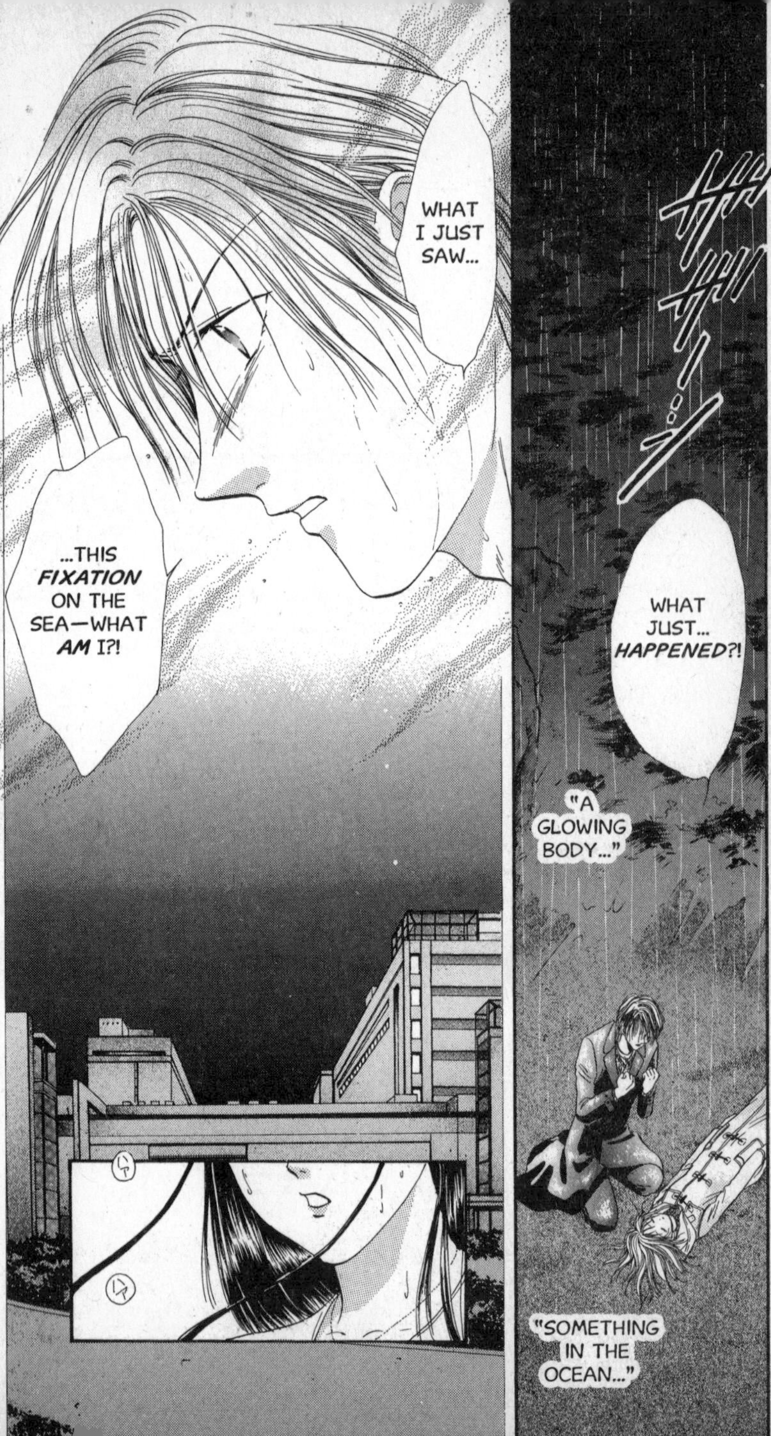
WHAT JUST... HAPPENED?!
"A GLOWING BODY..."
"SOMETHING IN THE OCEAN..."
WHAT I JUST SAW...
...THIS FIXATION ON THE SEA—WHAT AM I?!

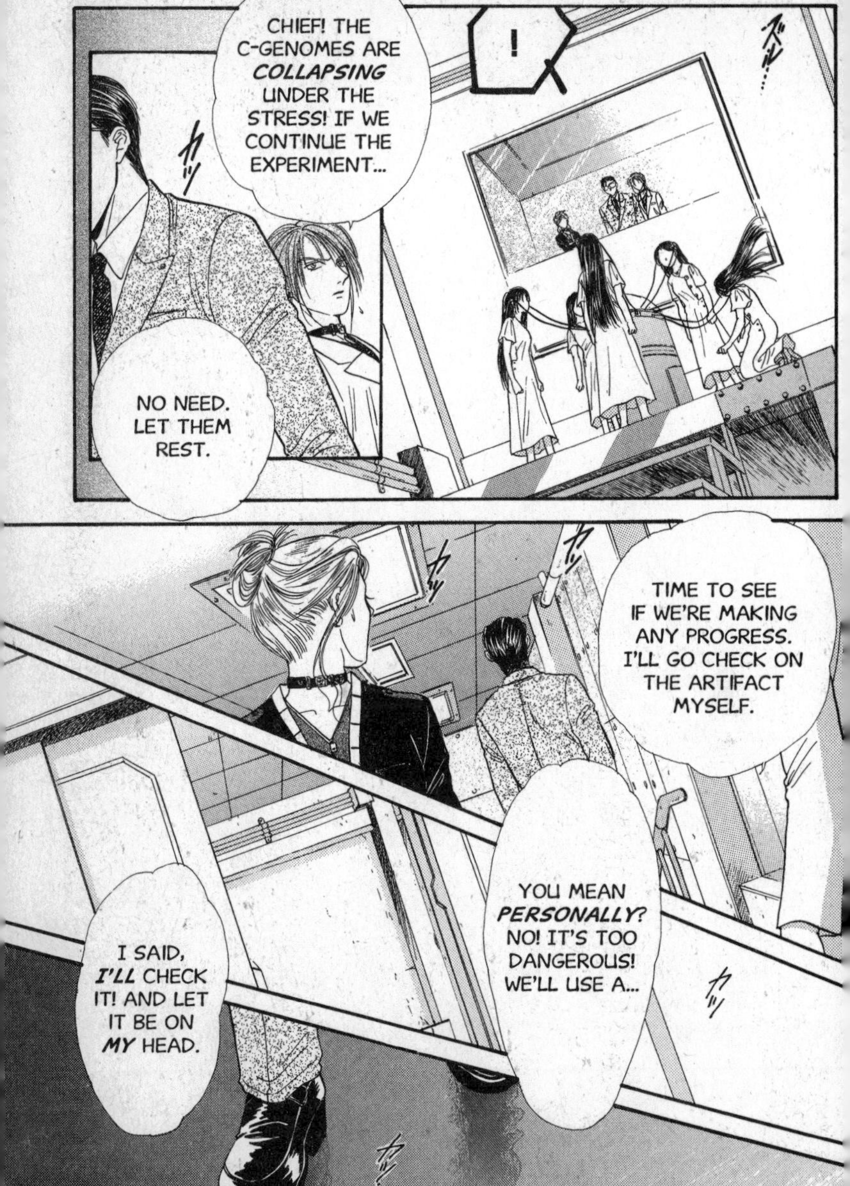
!
CHIEF! THE C-GENOMES ARE *COLLAPSING* UNDER THE STRESS! IF WE CONTINUE THE EXPERIMENT...
NO NEED. LET THEM REST.
TIME TO SEE IF WE'RE MAKING ANY PROGRESS. I'LL GO CHECK ON THE ARTIFACT MYSELF.
YOU MEAN *PERSONALLY*? NO! IT'S TOO DANGEROUS! WE'LL USE A...
I SAID, *I'LL* CHECK IT! AND LET IT BE ON *MY* HEAD.

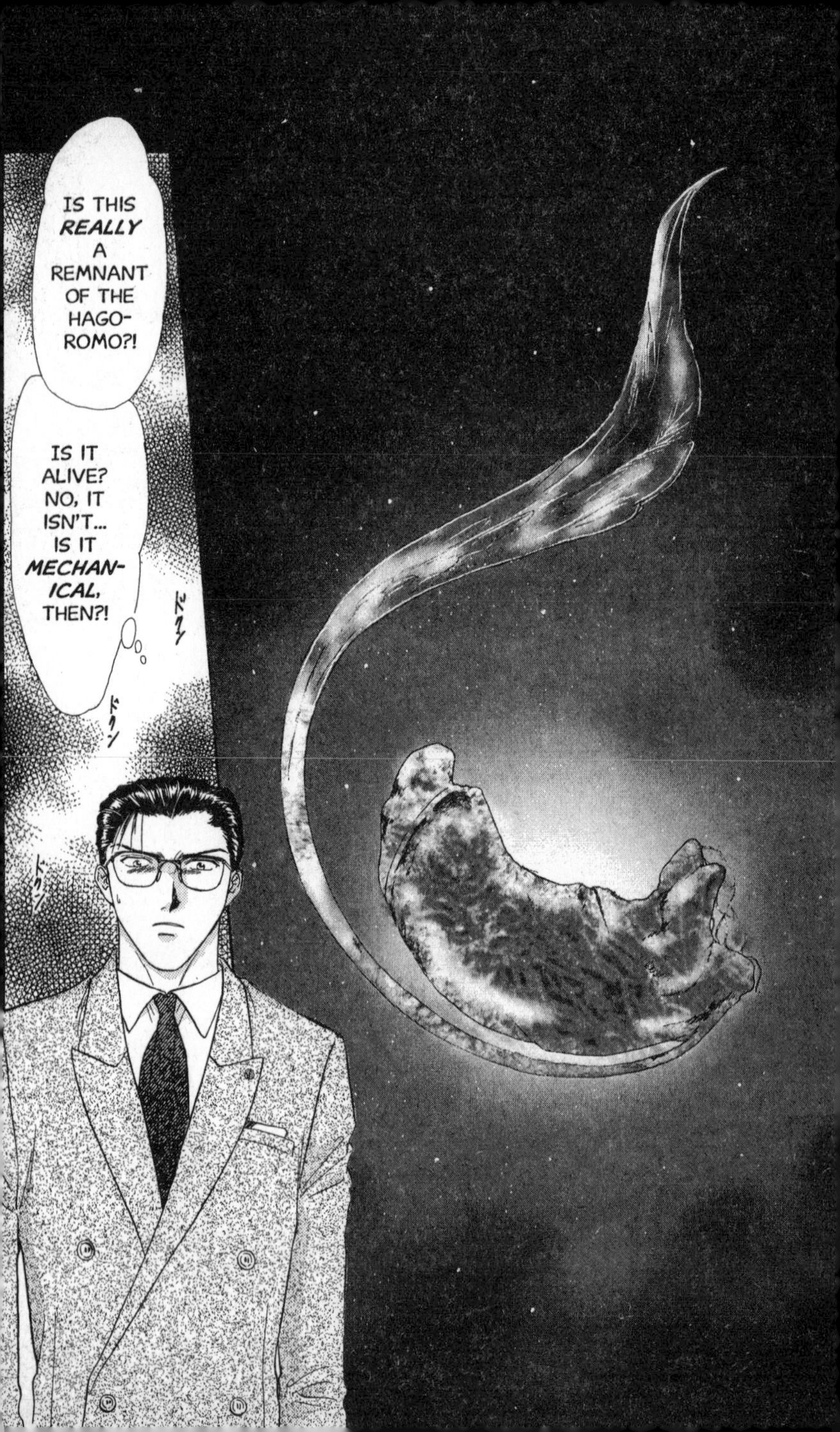
IS THIS *REALLY* A REMNANT OF THE HAGO-ROMO?!
IS IT ALIVE? NO, IT ISN'T... IS IT *MECHAN-ICAL*, THEN?!

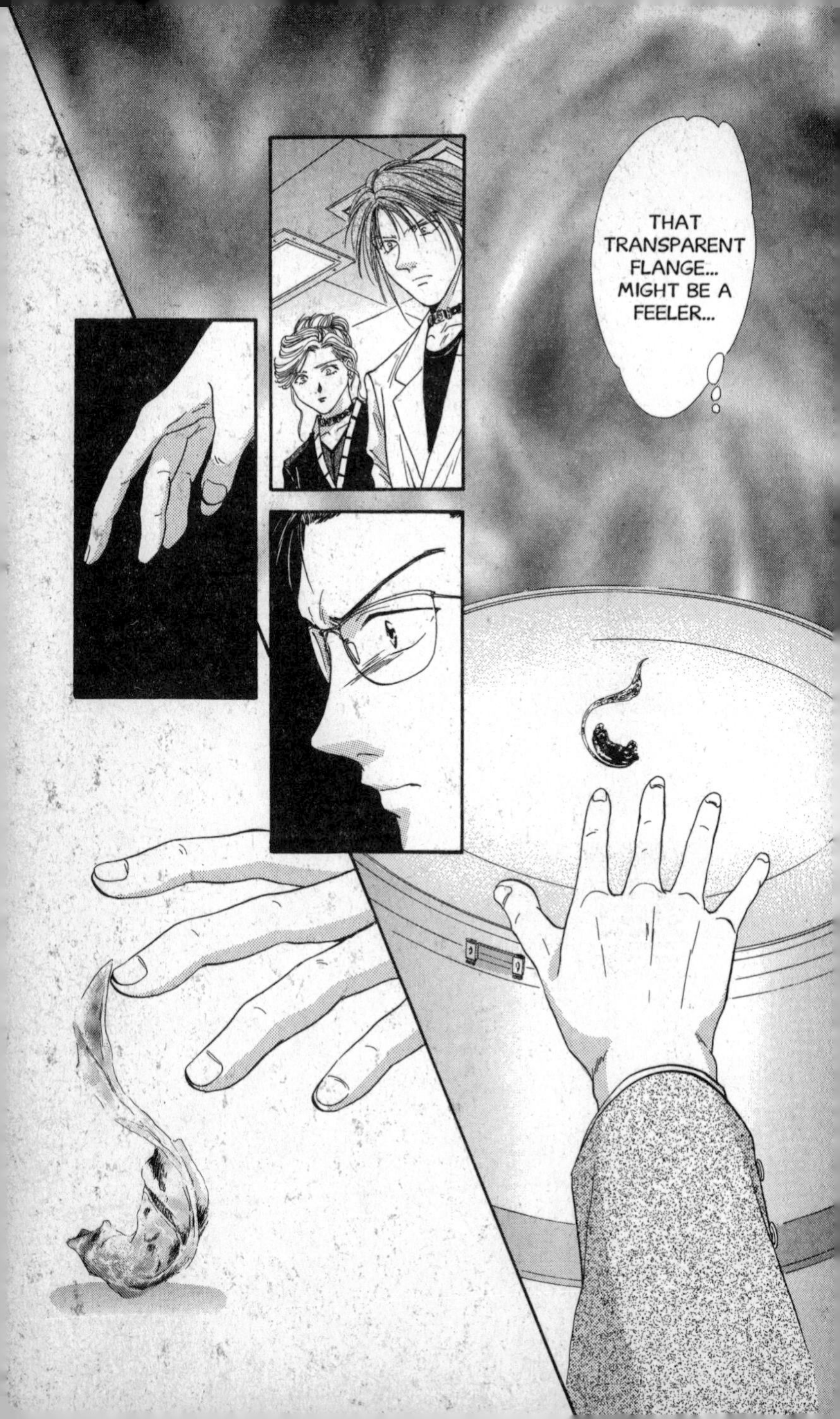
THAT TRANSPARENT FLANGE... MIGHT BE A FEELER...

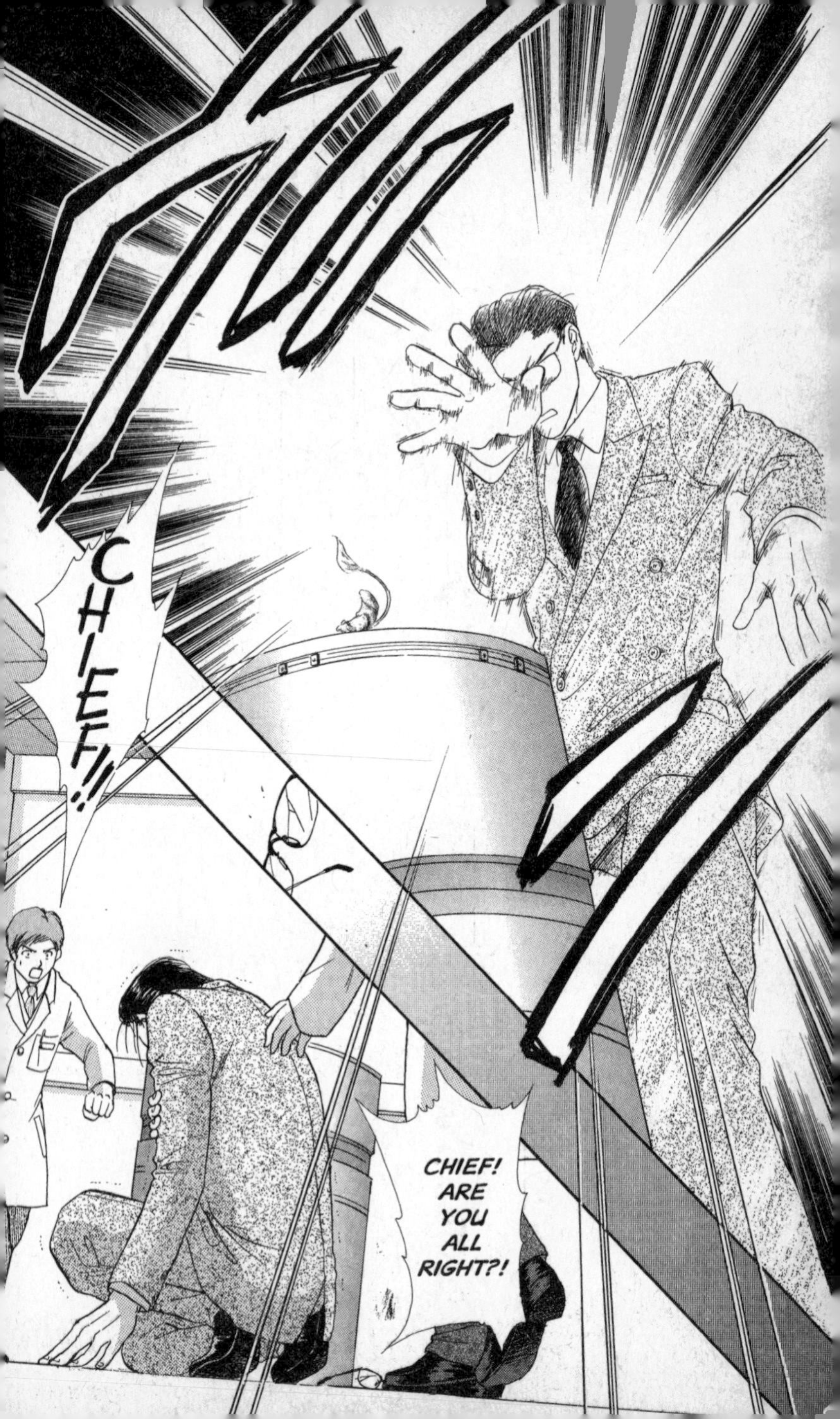
CHIEF!!!
CHIEF! ARE YOU ALL RIGHT?!

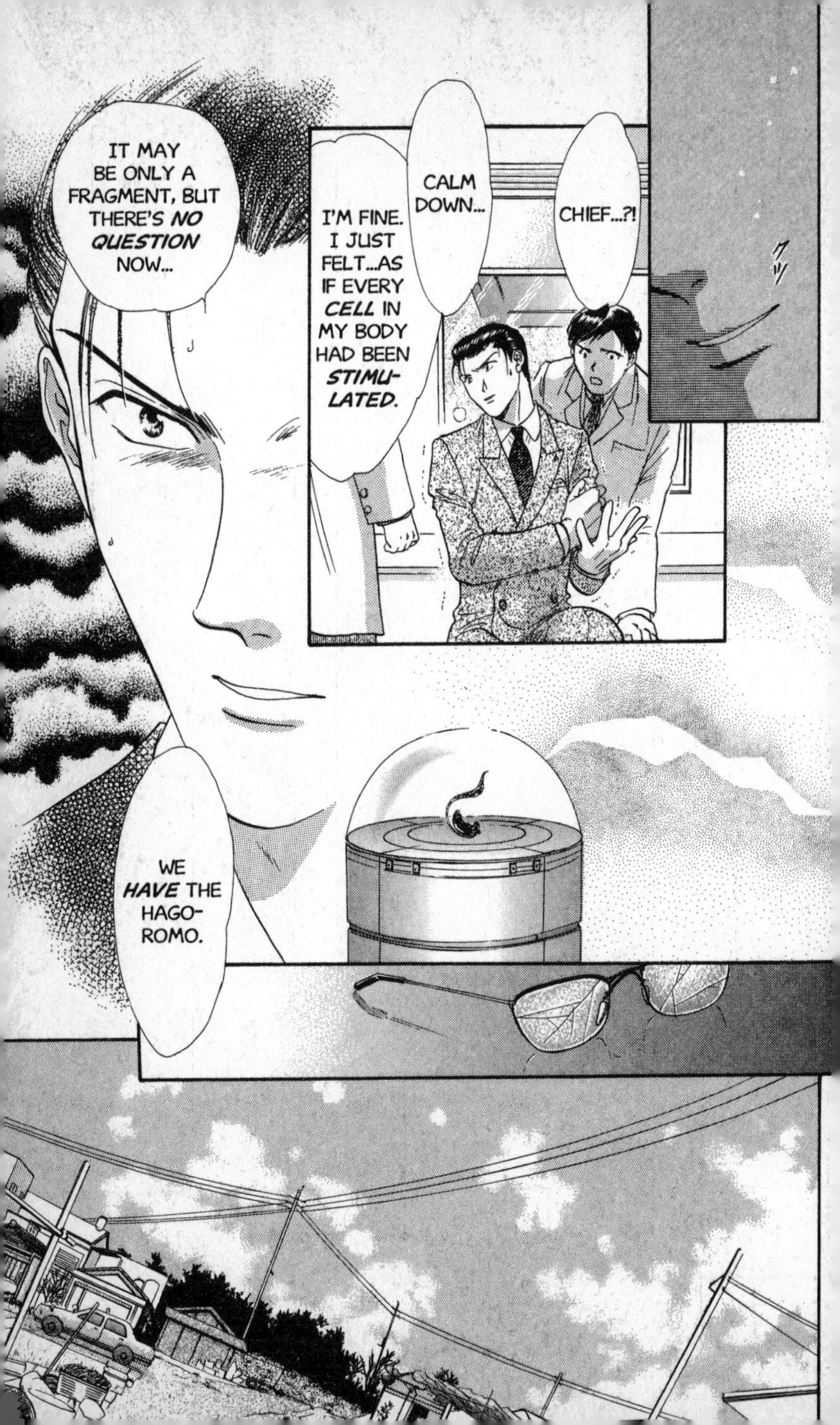

CHIEF...?!
CALM DOWN...
I'M FINE. I JUST FELT...AS IF EVERY *CELL* IN MY BODY HAD BEEN *STIMULATED*.
IT MAY BE ONLY A FRAGMENT, BUT THERE'S *NO QUESTION* NOW...
WE *HAVE* THE HAGOROMO.

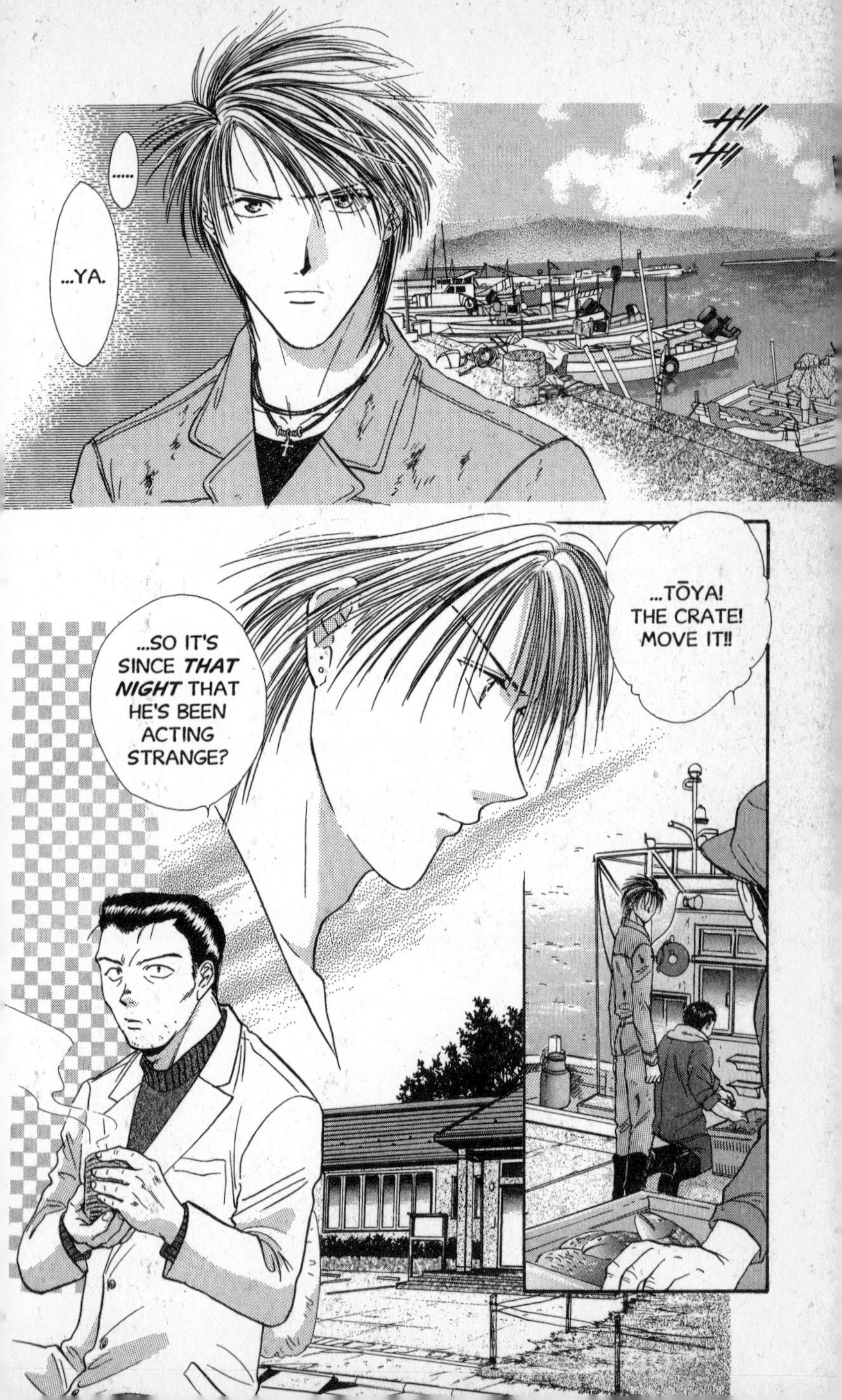

......
...YA.
...TŌYA! THE CRATE! MOVE IT!!
...SO IT'S SINCE ***THAT NIGHT*** THAT HE'S BEEN ACTING STRANGE?

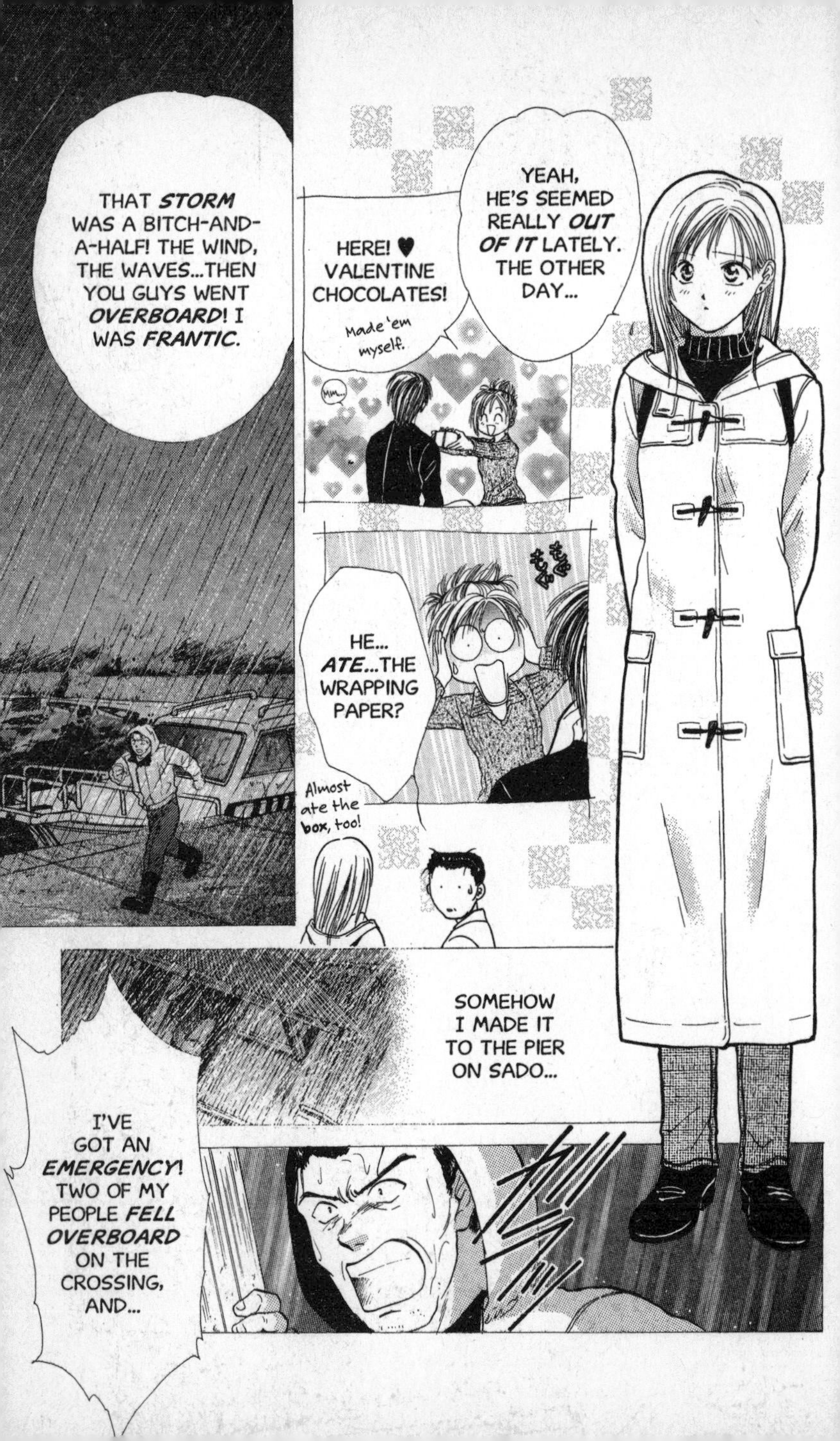
YEAH, HE'S SEEMED REALLY *OUT OF IT* LATELY. THE OTHER DAY...
HERE! ♥ VALENTINE CHOCOLATES!
Made 'em myself.
MM...
HE... *ATE*...THE WRAPPING PAPER?
Almost ate the **box**, too!
THAT *STORM* WAS A BITCH-AND-A-HALF! THE WIND, THE WAVES...THEN YOU GUYS WENT *OVERBOARD*! I WAS *FRANTIC*.
SOMEHOW I MADE IT TO THE PIER ON SADO...
I'VE GOT AN *EMERGENCY*! TWO OF MY PEOPLE *FELL OVERBOARD* ON THE CROSSING, AND...

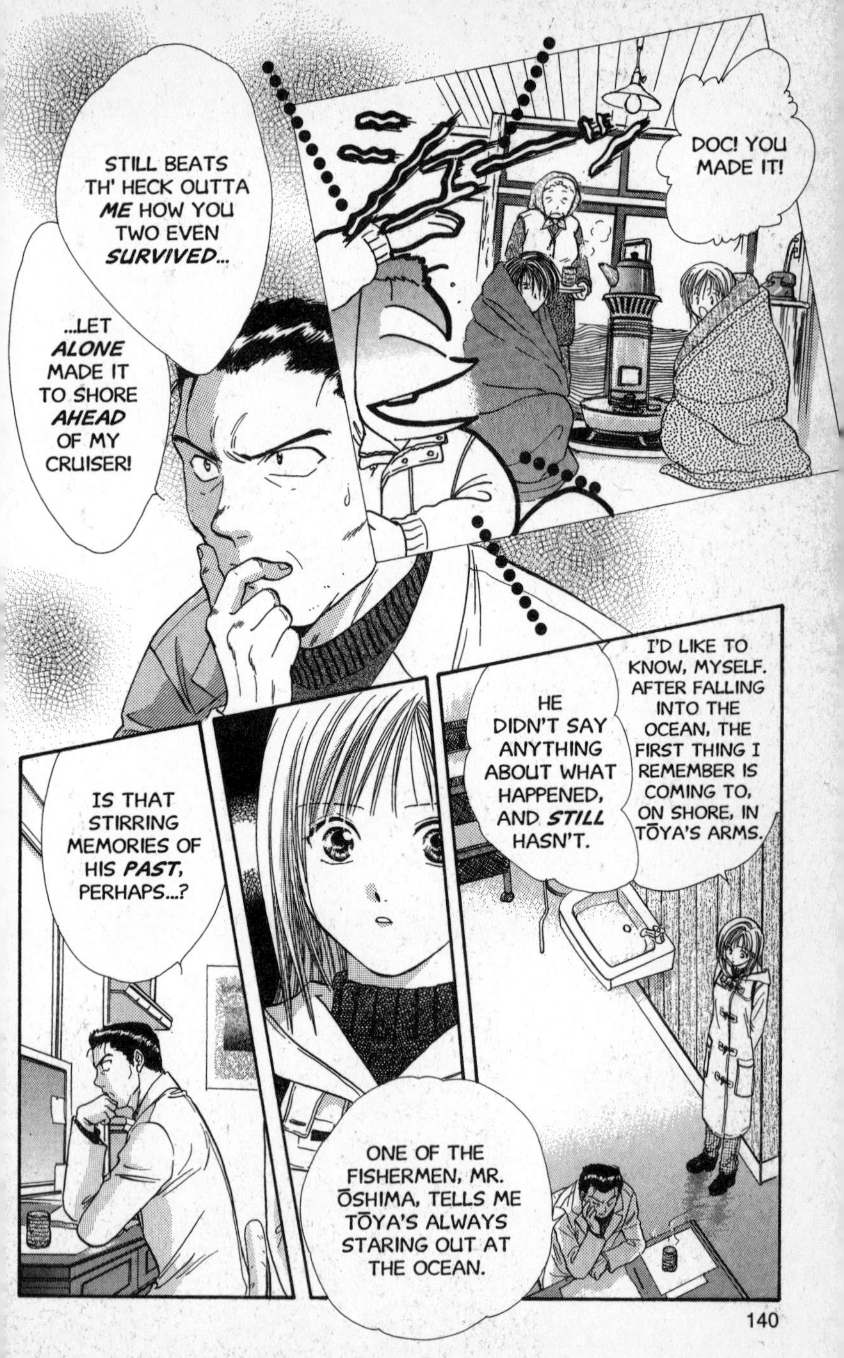
DOC! YOU MADE IT!
STILL BEATS TH' HECK OUTTA *ME* HOW YOU TWO EVEN *SURVIVED*...
...LET *ALONE* MADE IT TO SHORE *AHEAD* OF MY CRUISER!
I'D LIKE TO KNOW, MYSELF. AFTER FALLING INTO THE OCEAN, THE FIRST THING I REMEMBER IS COMING TO, ON SHORE, IN TŌYA'S ARMS.
HE DIDN'T SAY ANYTHING ABOUT WHAT HAPPENED, AND *STILL* HASN'T.
ONE OF THE FISHERMEN, MR. ŌSHIMA, TELLS ME TŌYA'S ALWAYS STARING OUT AT THE OCEAN.
IS THAT STIRRING MEMORIES OF HIS *PAST*, PERHAPS...?

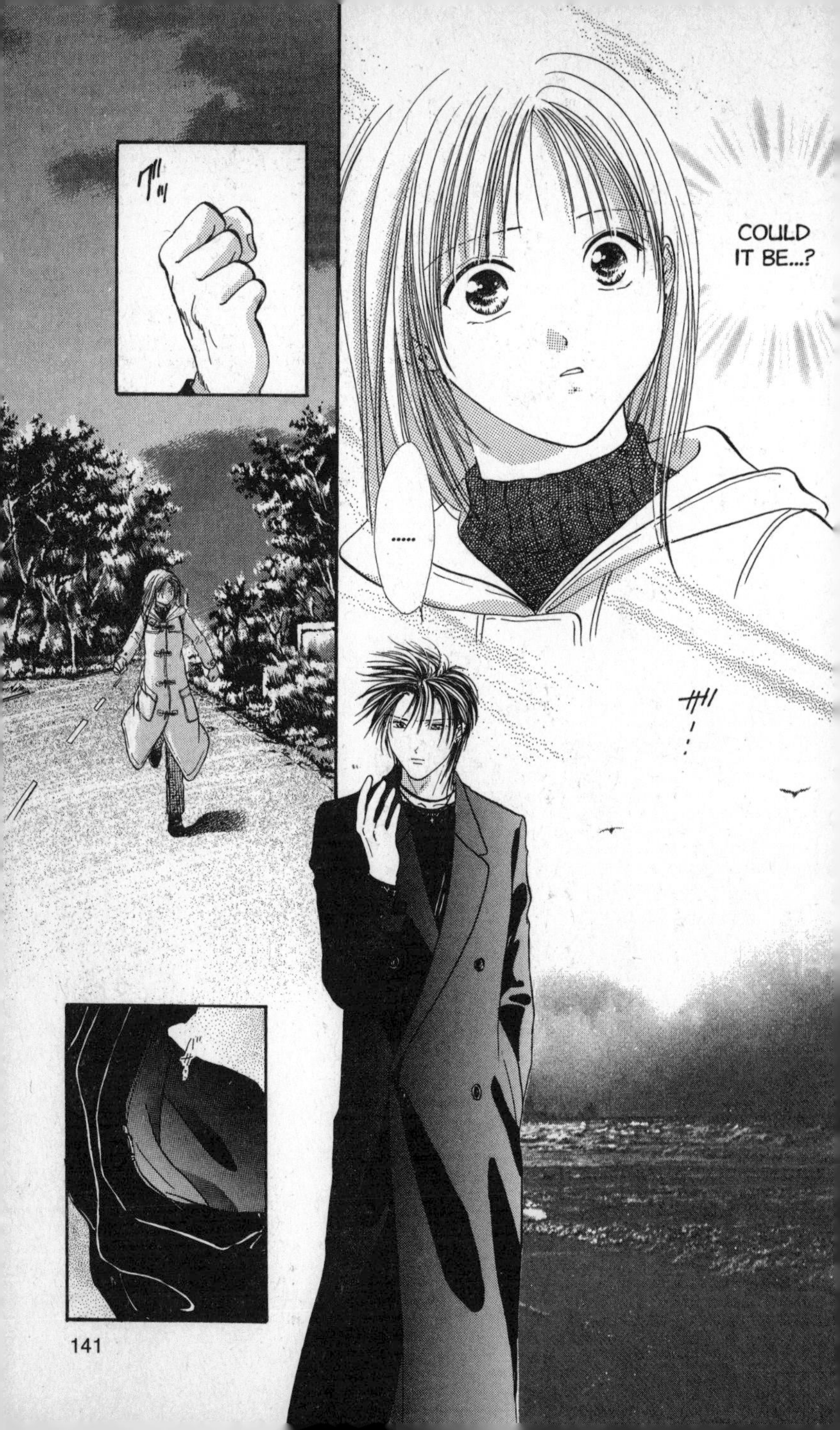
COULD IT BE...?
.....

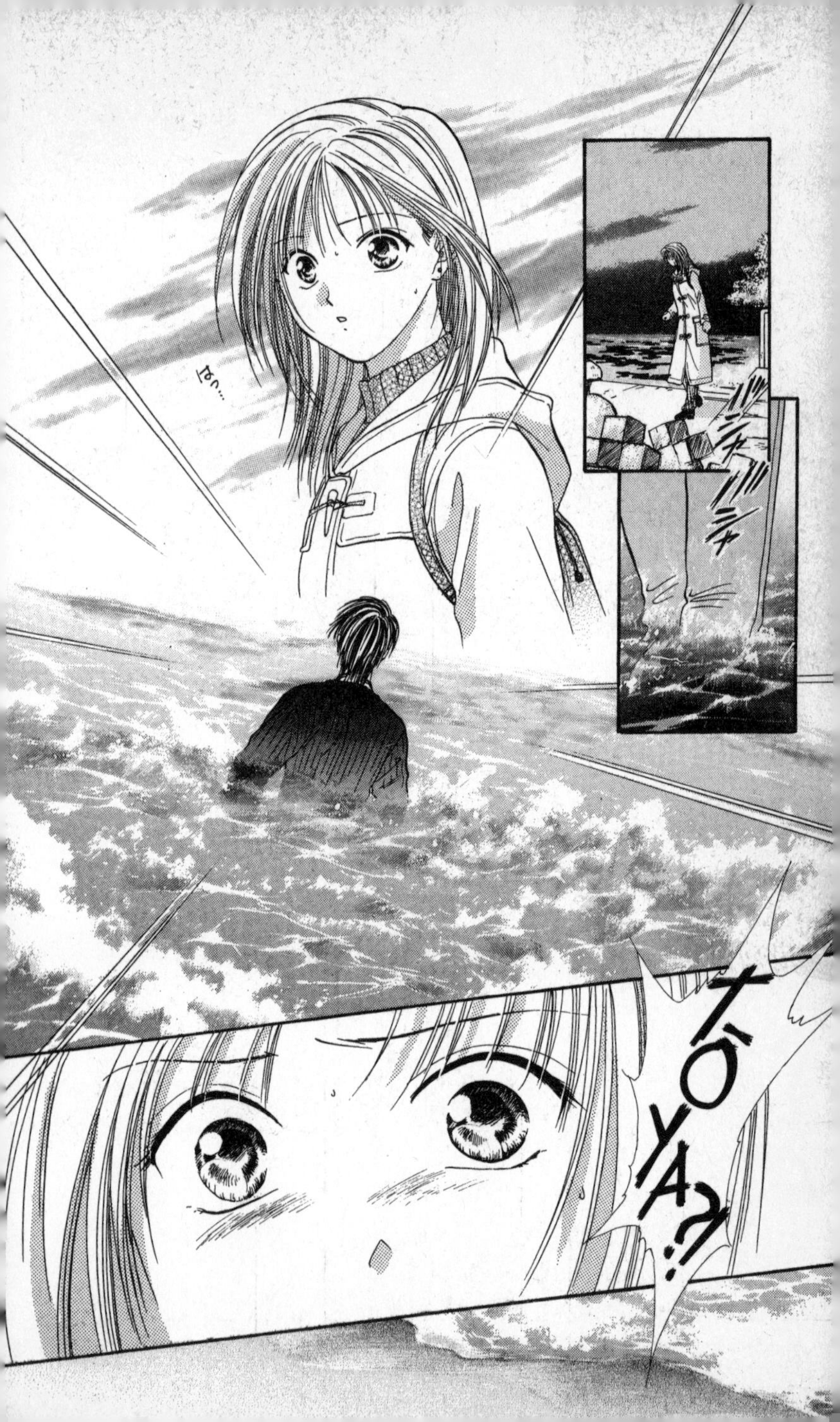
バシャ
バシャ
はっ…
TÔYA?!

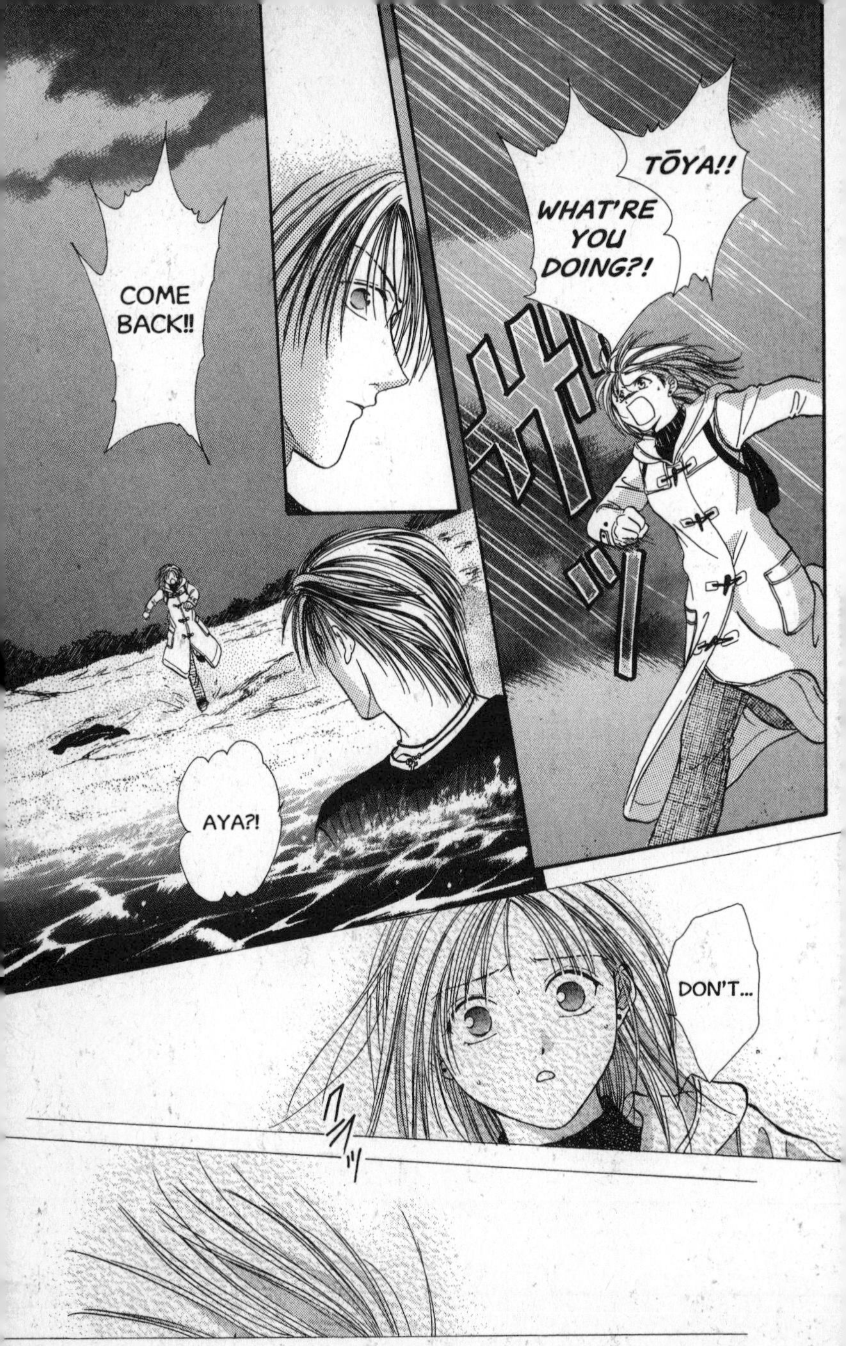
TŌYA!!
WHAT'RE YOU DOING?!
COME BACK!!
AYA?!
DON'T...

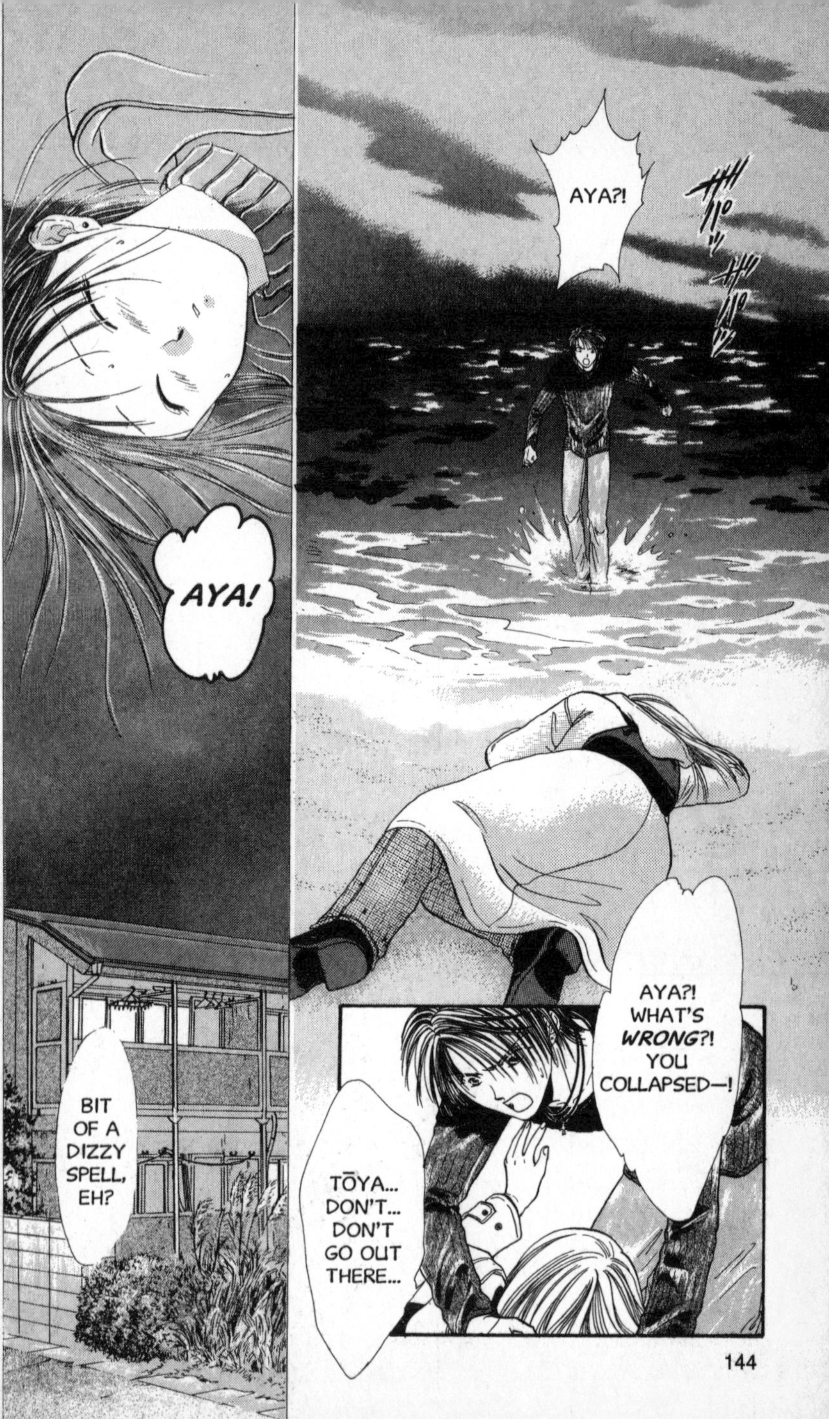
AYA?!
AYA?! WHAT'S **WRONG**?! YOU COLLAPSED—!
TŌYA... DON'T... DON'T GO OUT THERE...
AYA!
BIT OF A DIZZY SPELL, EH?

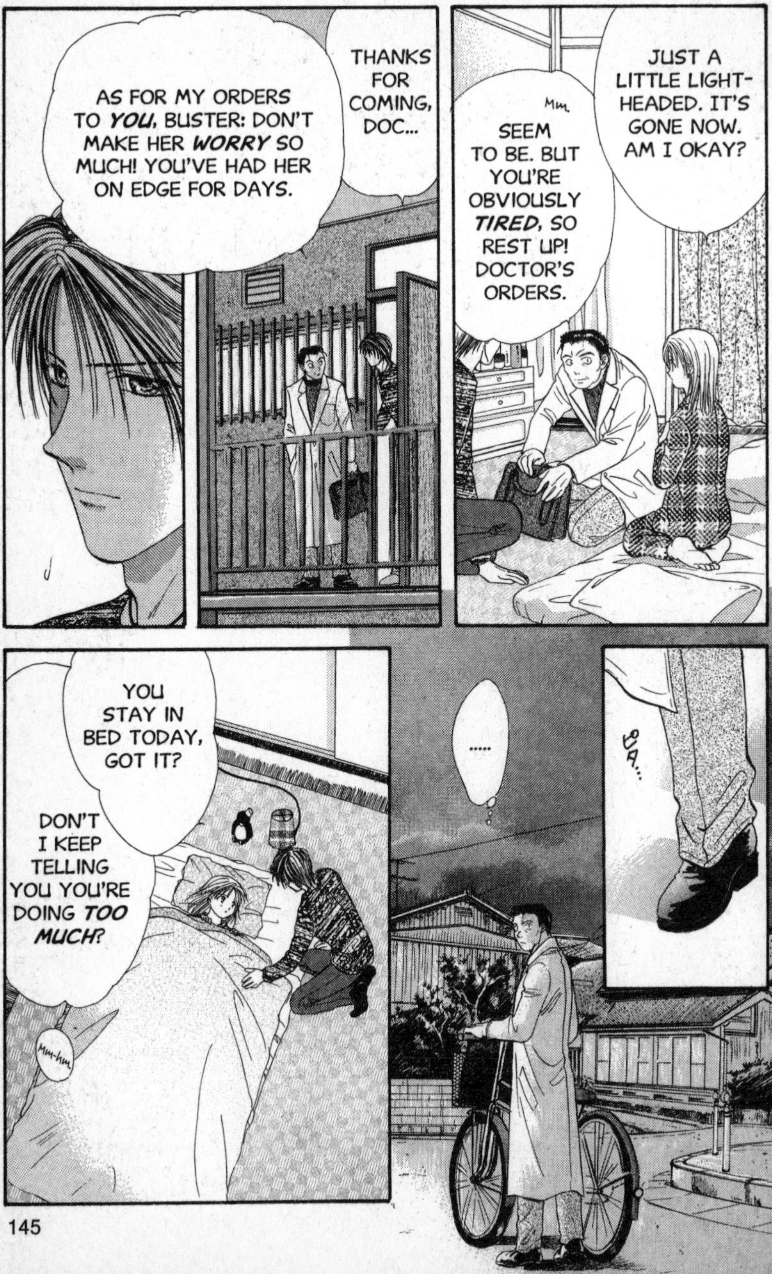
JUST A LITTLE LIGHT-HEADED. IT'S GONE NOW. AM I OKAY?
Mm.
SEEM TO BE. BUT YOU'RE OBVIOUSLY *TIRED*, SO REST UP! DOCTOR'S ORDERS.
THANKS FOR COMING, DOC...
AS FOR MY ORDERS TO *YOU*, BUSTER: DON'T MAKE HER *WORRY* SO MUCH! YOU'VE HAD HER ON EDGE FOR DAYS.
.....
YOU STAY IN BED TODAY, GOT IT?
DON'T I KEEP TELLING YOU YOU'RE DOING *TOO MUCH*?
Mm-hm.

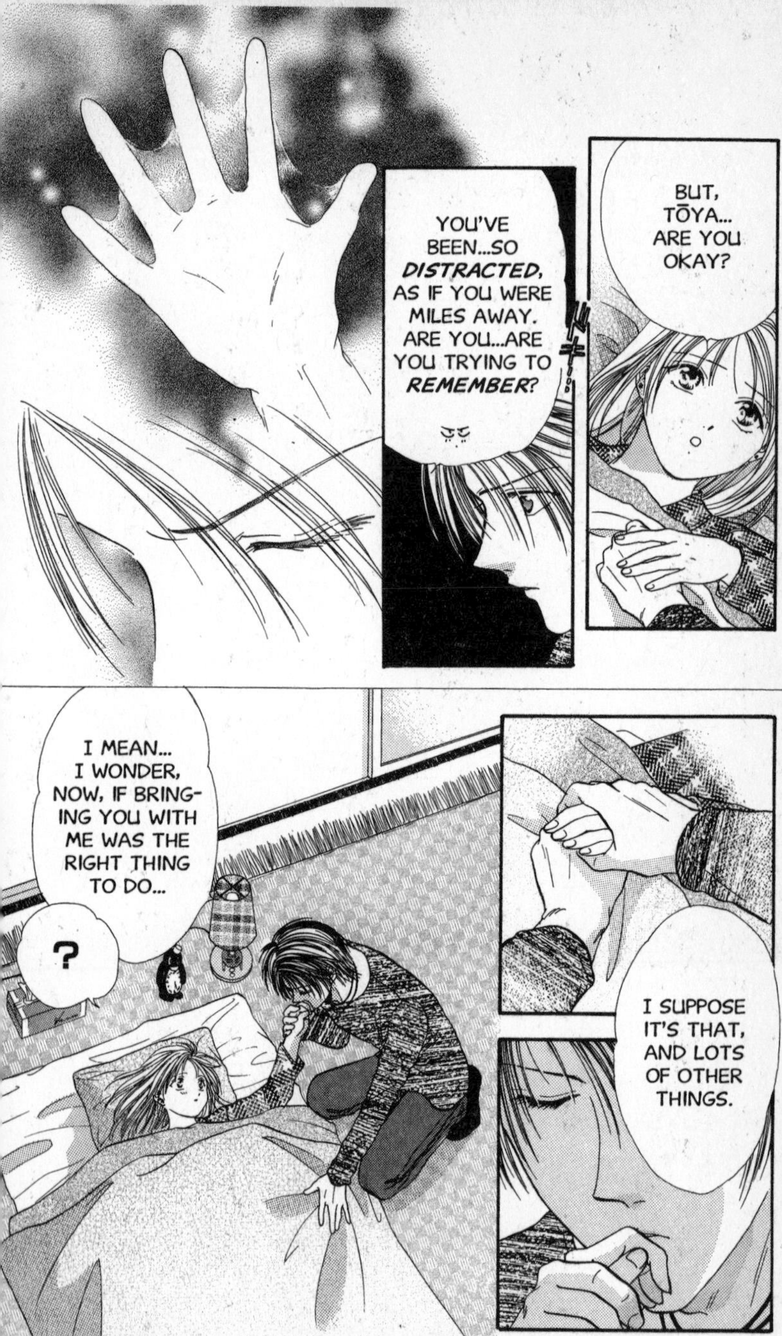
BUT, TŌYA... ARE YOU OKAY?
YOU'VE BEEN...SO ***DISTRACTED***, AS IF YOU WERE MILES AWAY. ARE YOU...ARE YOU TRYING TO ***REMEMBER***?
I SUPPOSE IT'S THAT, AND LOTS OF OTHER THINGS.
I MEAN... I WONDER, NOW, IF BRINGING YOU WITH ME WAS THE RIGHT THING TO DO...
?

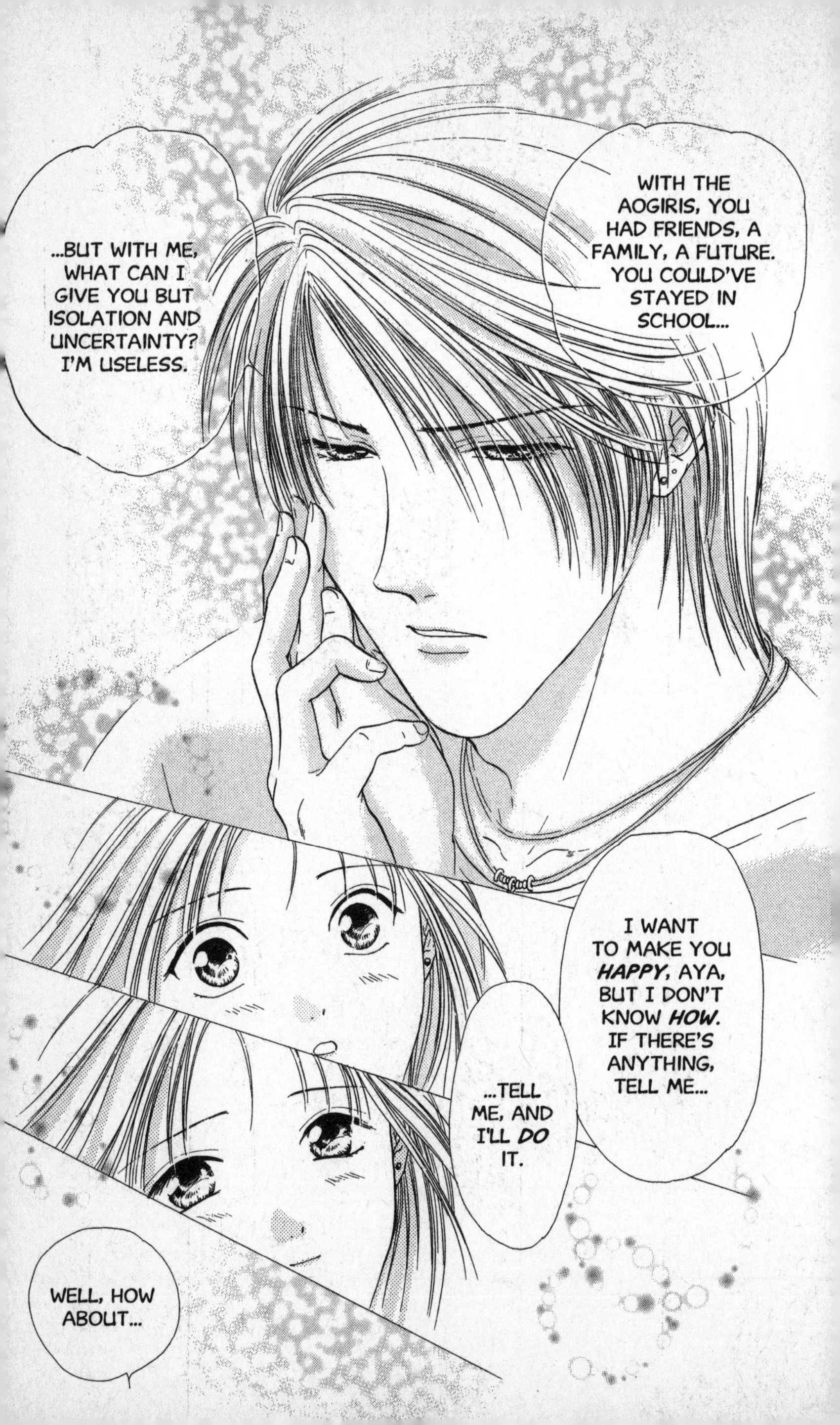
WITH THE AOGIRIS, YOU HAD FRIENDS, A FAMILY, A FUTURE. YOU COULD'VE STAYED IN SCHOOL...
...BUT WITH ME, WHAT CAN I GIVE YOU BUT ISOLATION AND UNCERTAINTY? I'M USELESS.
I WANT TO MAKE YOU *HAPPY*, AYA, BUT I DON'T KNOW *HOW*. IF THERE'S ANYTHING, TELL ME...
...TELL ME, AND I'LL *DO* IT.
WELL, HOW ABOUT...

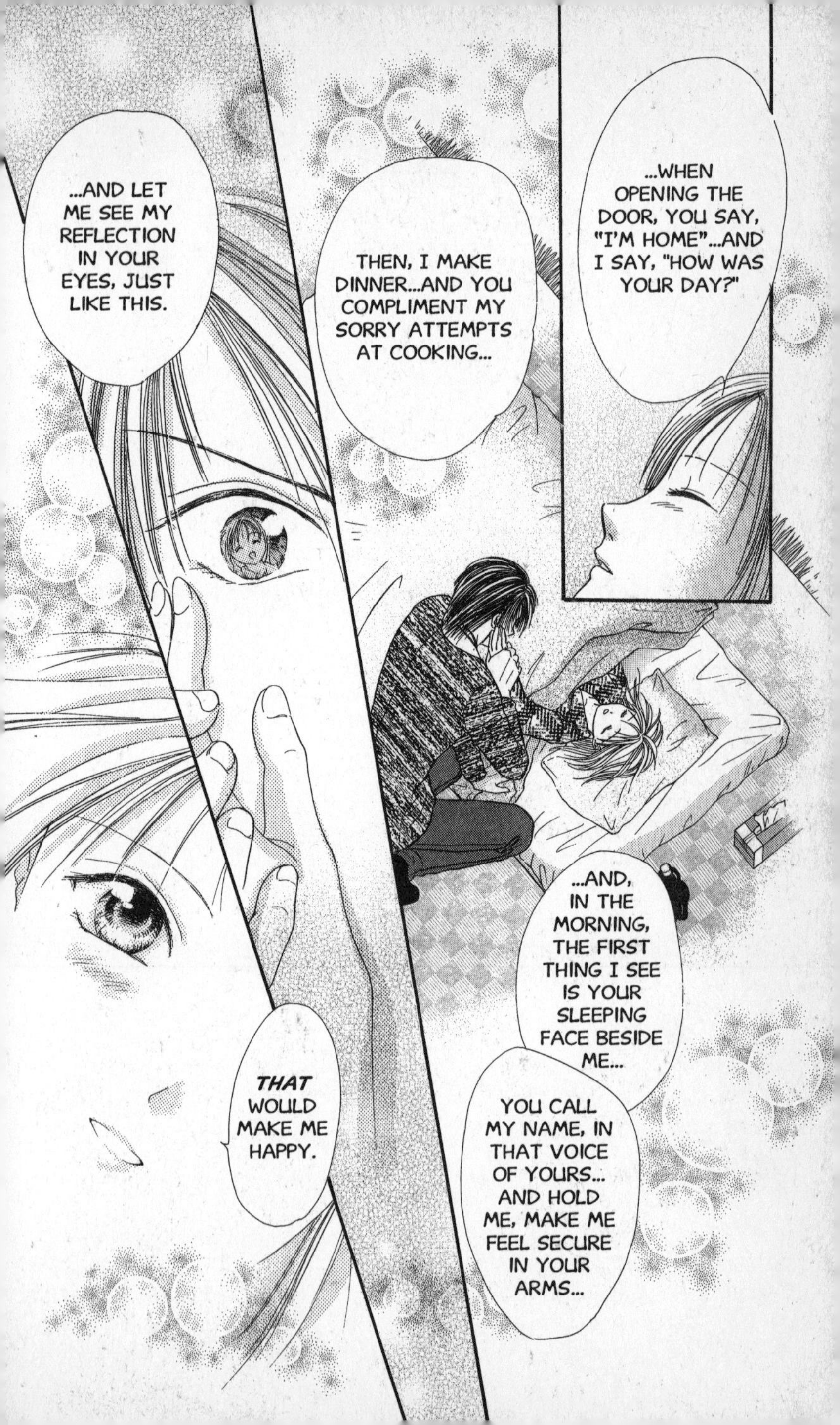
...WHEN OPENING THE DOOR, YOU SAY, "I'M HOME"...AND I SAY, "HOW WAS YOUR DAY?"
THEN, I MAKE DINNER...AND YOU COMPLIMENT MY SORRY ATTEMPTS AT COOKING...
...AND LET ME SEE MY REFLECTION IN YOUR EYES, JUST LIKE THIS.
...AND, IN THE MORNING, THE FIRST THING I SEE IS YOUR SLEEPING FACE BESIDE ME...
YOU CALL MY NAME, IN THAT VOICE OF YOURS... AND HOLD ME, MAKE ME FEEL SECURE IN YOUR ARMS...
THAT WOULD MAKE ME HAPPY.

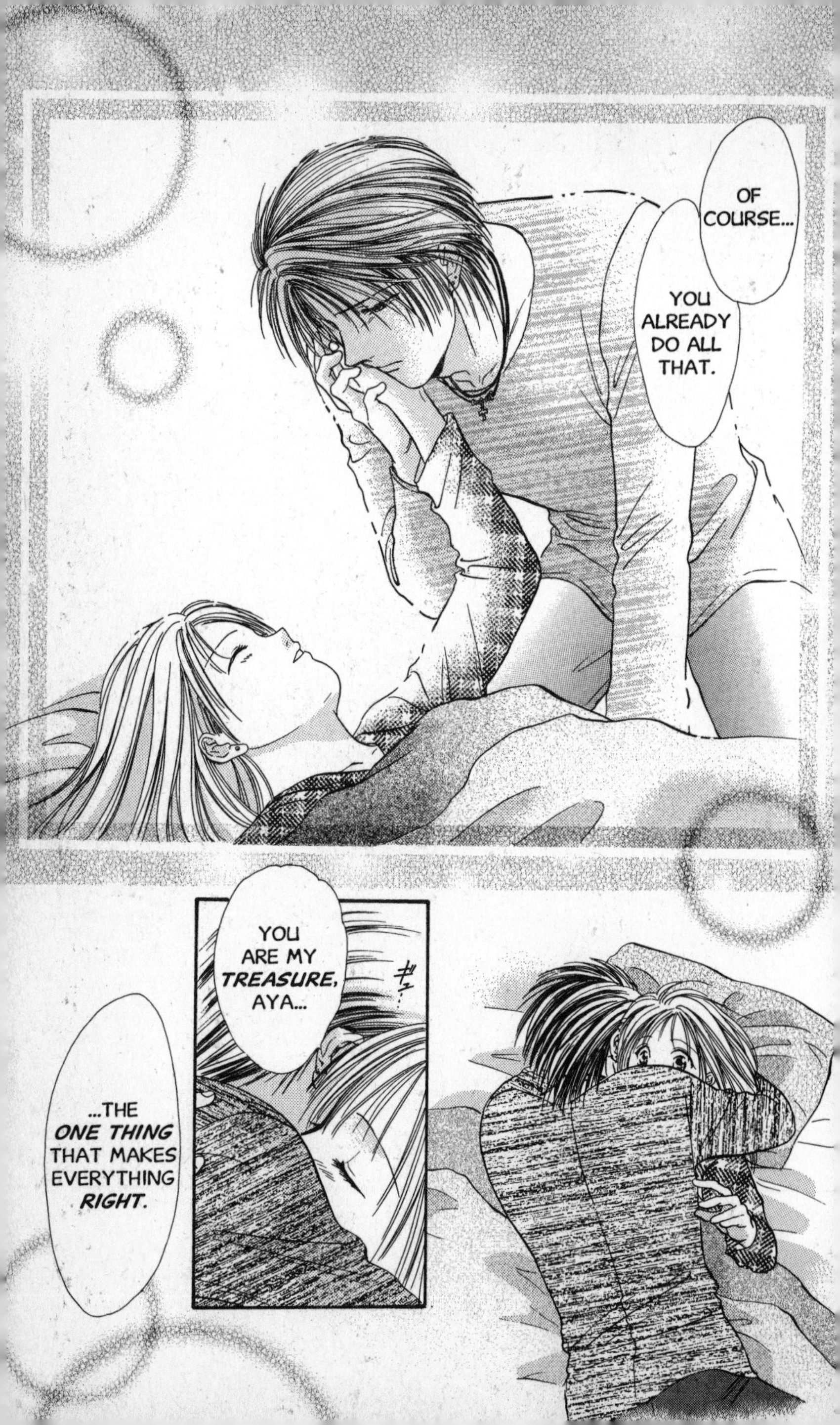
OF COURSE...
YOU ALREADY DO ALL THAT.
YOU ARE MY *TREASURE*, AYA...
...THE *ONE THING* THAT MAKES EVERYTHING *RIGHT*.

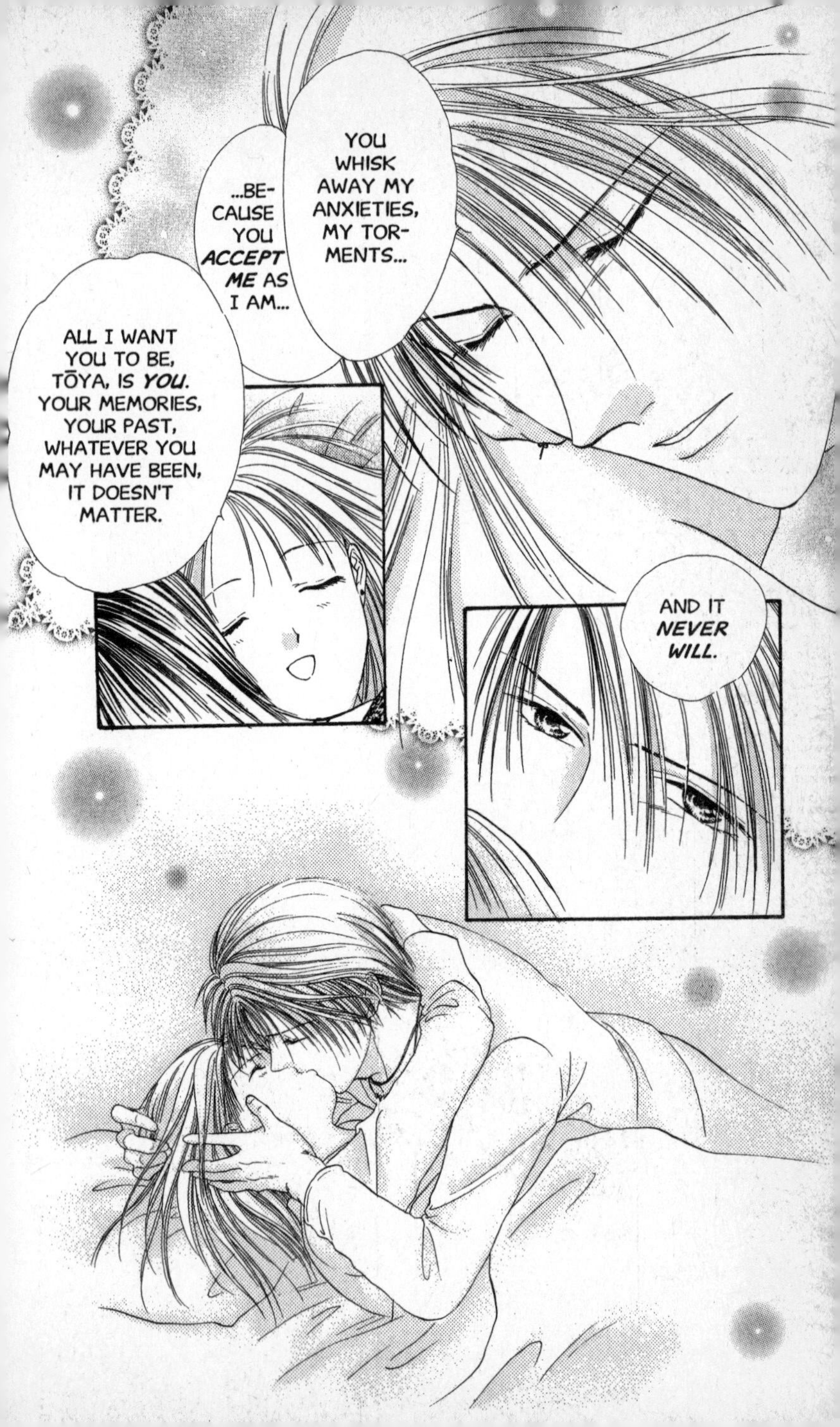
YOU WHISK AWAY MY ANXIETIES, MY TOR-MENTS...
...BE-CAUSE YOU *ACCEPT ME* AS I AM...
ALL I WANT YOU TO BE, TŌYA, IS *YOU*. YOUR MEMORIES, YOUR PAST, WHATEVER YOU MAY HAVE BEEN, IT DOESN'T MATTER.
AND IT *NEVER WILL*.

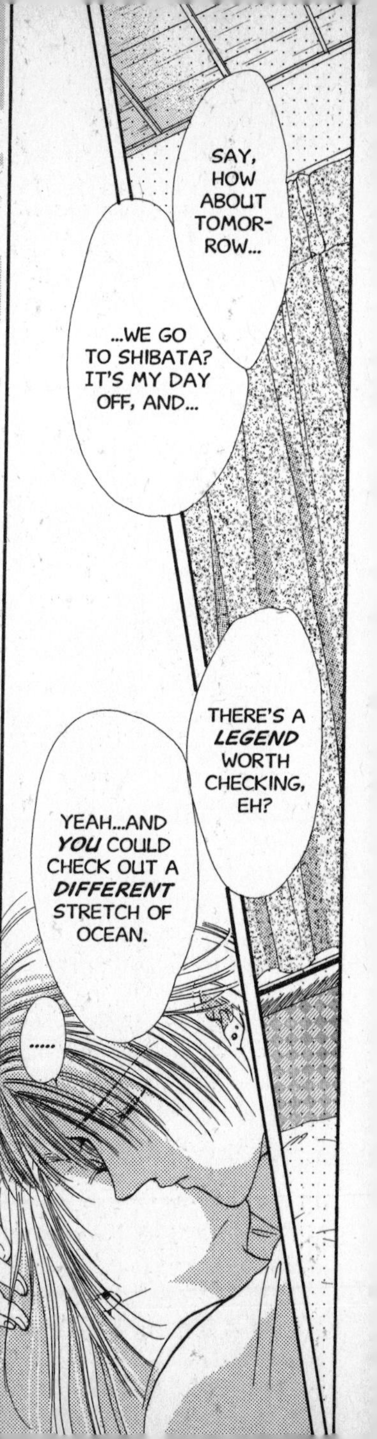
SAY, HOW ABOUT TOMOR-ROW...
...WE GO TO SHIBATA? IT'S MY DAY OFF, AND...
THERE'S A *LEGEND* WORTH CHECKING, EH?
YEAH...AND *YOU* COULD CHECK OUT A *DIFFERENT* STRETCH OF OCEAN.
......

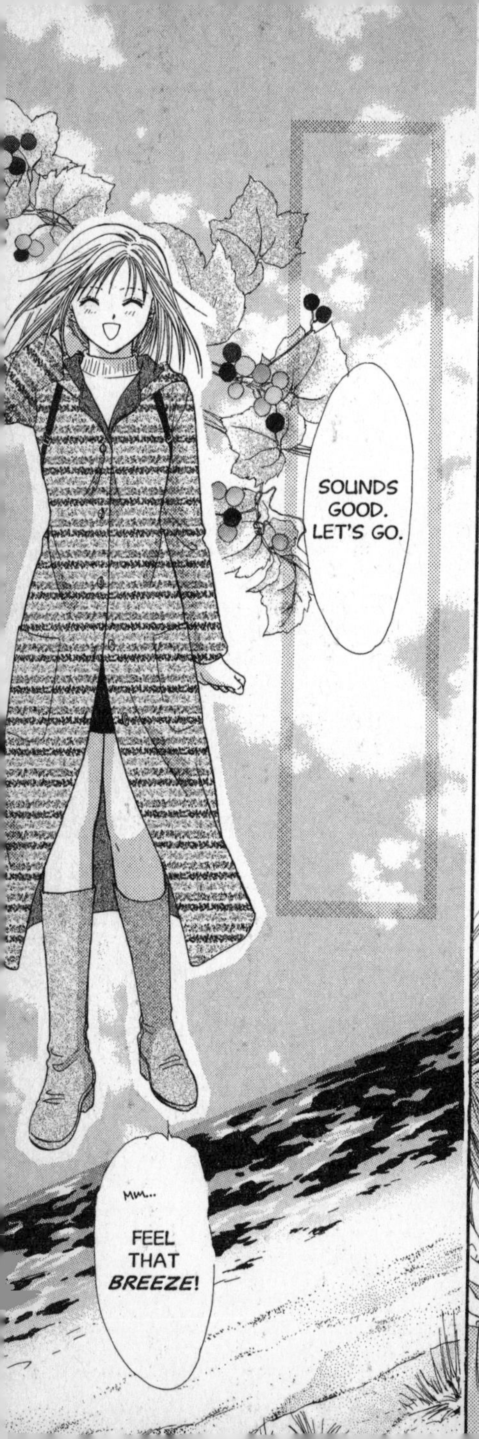
SOUNDS GOOD. LET'S GO.
MM... FEEL THAT *BREEZE*!

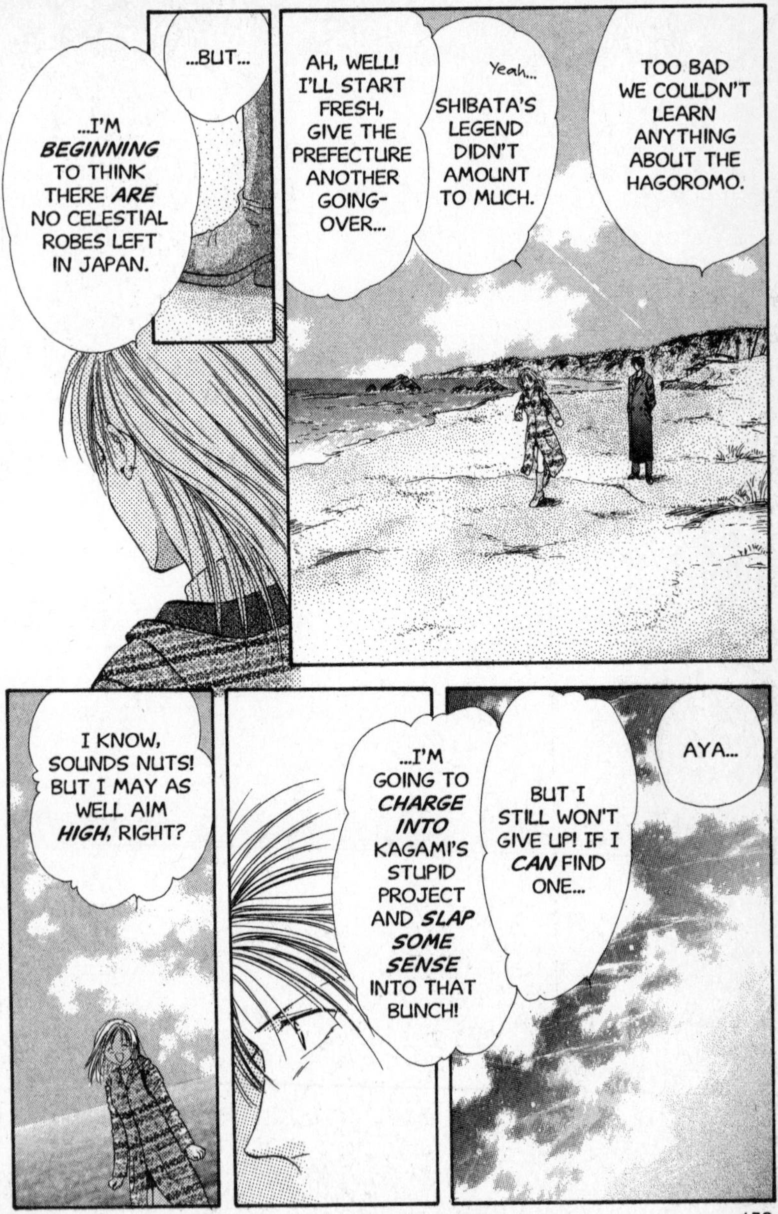
TOO BAD WE COULDN'T LEARN ANYTHING ABOUT THE HAGOROMO.
Yeah...
SHIBATA'S LEGEND DIDN'T AMOUNT TO MUCH.
AH, WELL! I'LL START FRESH, GIVE THE PREFECTURE ANOTHER GOING-OVER...
...BUT...
...I'M BEGINNING TO THINK THERE ARE NO CELESTIAL ROBES LEFT IN JAPAN.
AYA...
BUT I STILL WON'T GIVE UP! IF I CAN FIND ONE...
...I'M GOING TO CHARGE INTO KAGAMI'S STUPID PROJECT AND SLAP SOME SENSE INTO THAT BUNCH!
I KNOW, SOUNDS NUTS! BUT I MAY AS WELL AIM HIGH, RIGHT?

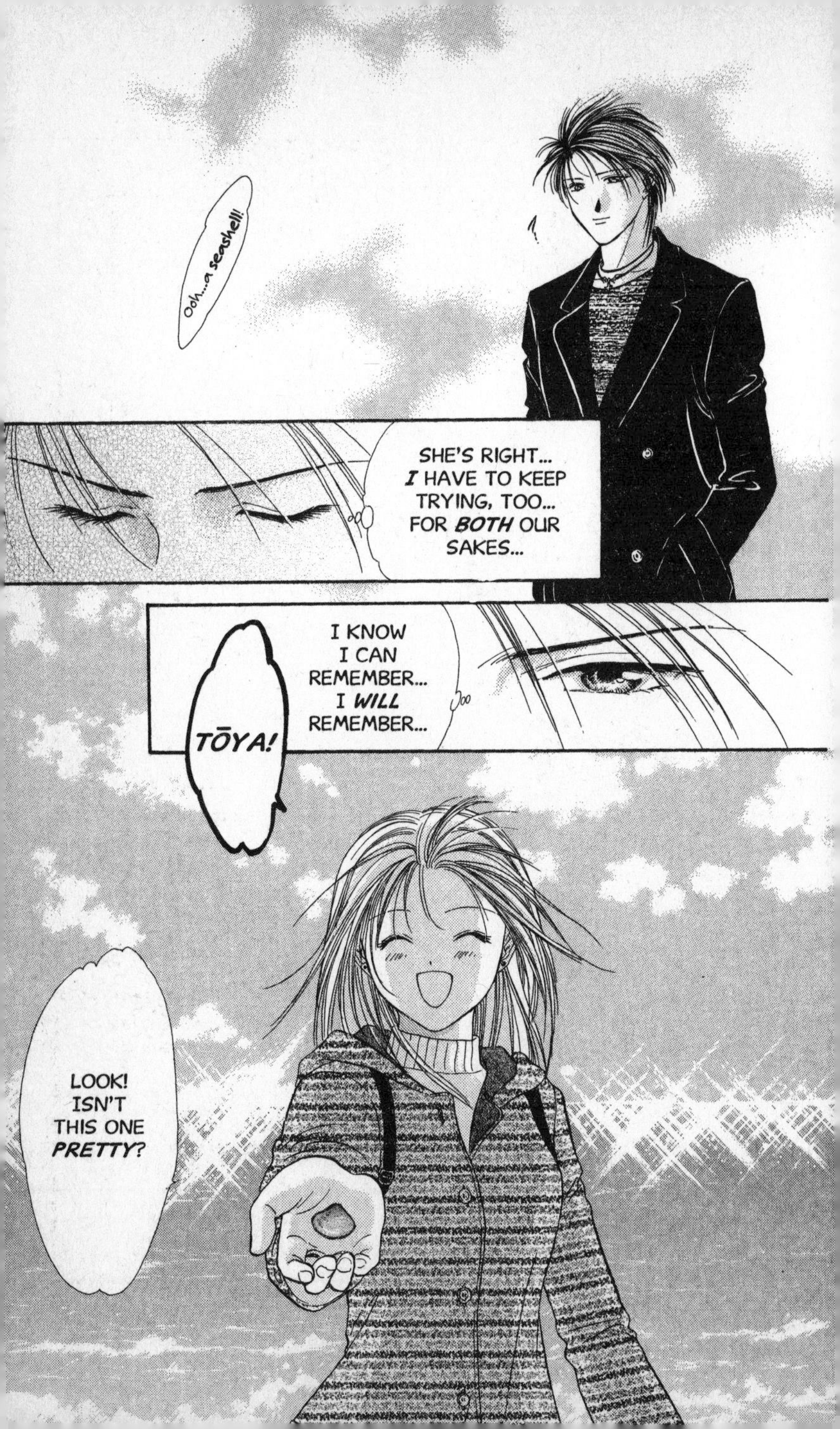
Ooh...a seashell!
?
SHE'S RIGHT... *I* HAVE TO KEEP TRYING, TOO... FOR *BOTH* OUR SAKES...
I KNOW I CAN REMEMBER... I *WILL* REMEMBER...
TŌYA!
LOOK! ISN'T THIS ONE *PRETTY*?

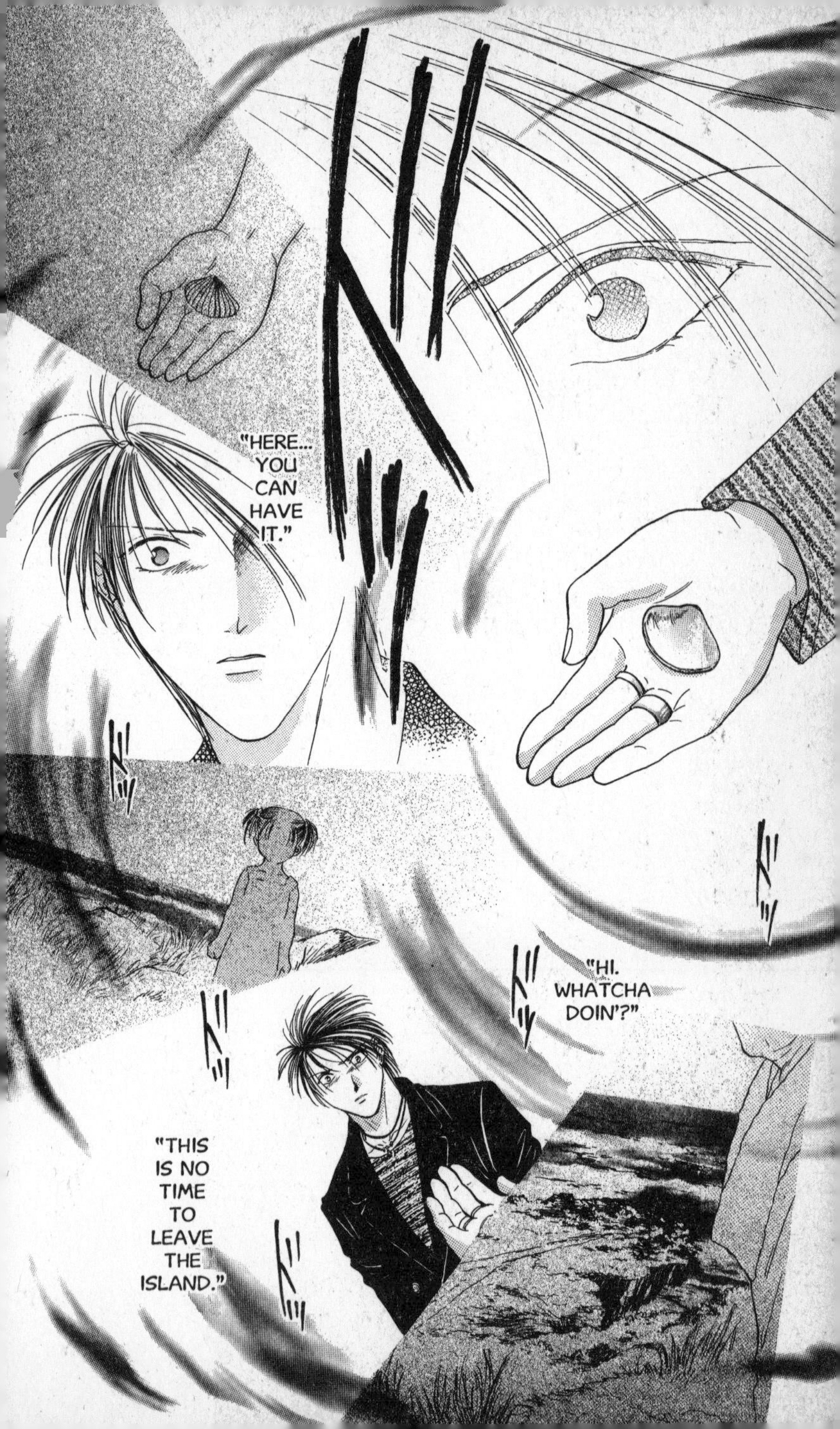
"HERE... YOU CAN HAVE IT."
"HI. WHATCHA DOIN'?"
"THIS IS NO TIME TO LEAVE THE ISLAND."

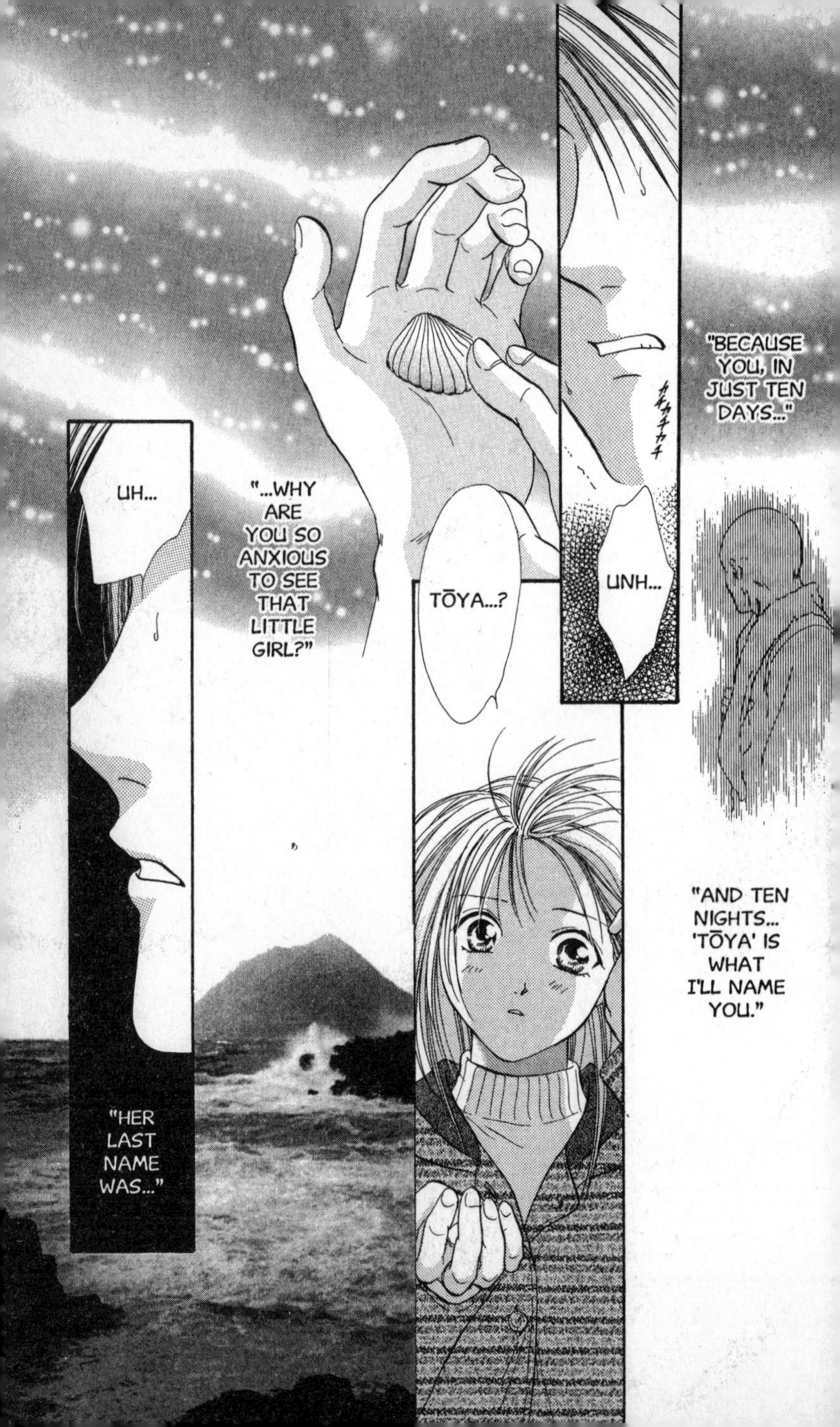
"BECAUSE YOU, IN JUST TEN DAYS..."
UNH...
TŌYA...?
"AND TEN NIGHTS... 'TŌYA' IS WHAT I'LL NAME YOU."
"...WHY ARE YOU SO ANXIOUS TO SEE THAT LITTLE GIRL?"
UH...
"HER LAST NAME WAS..."

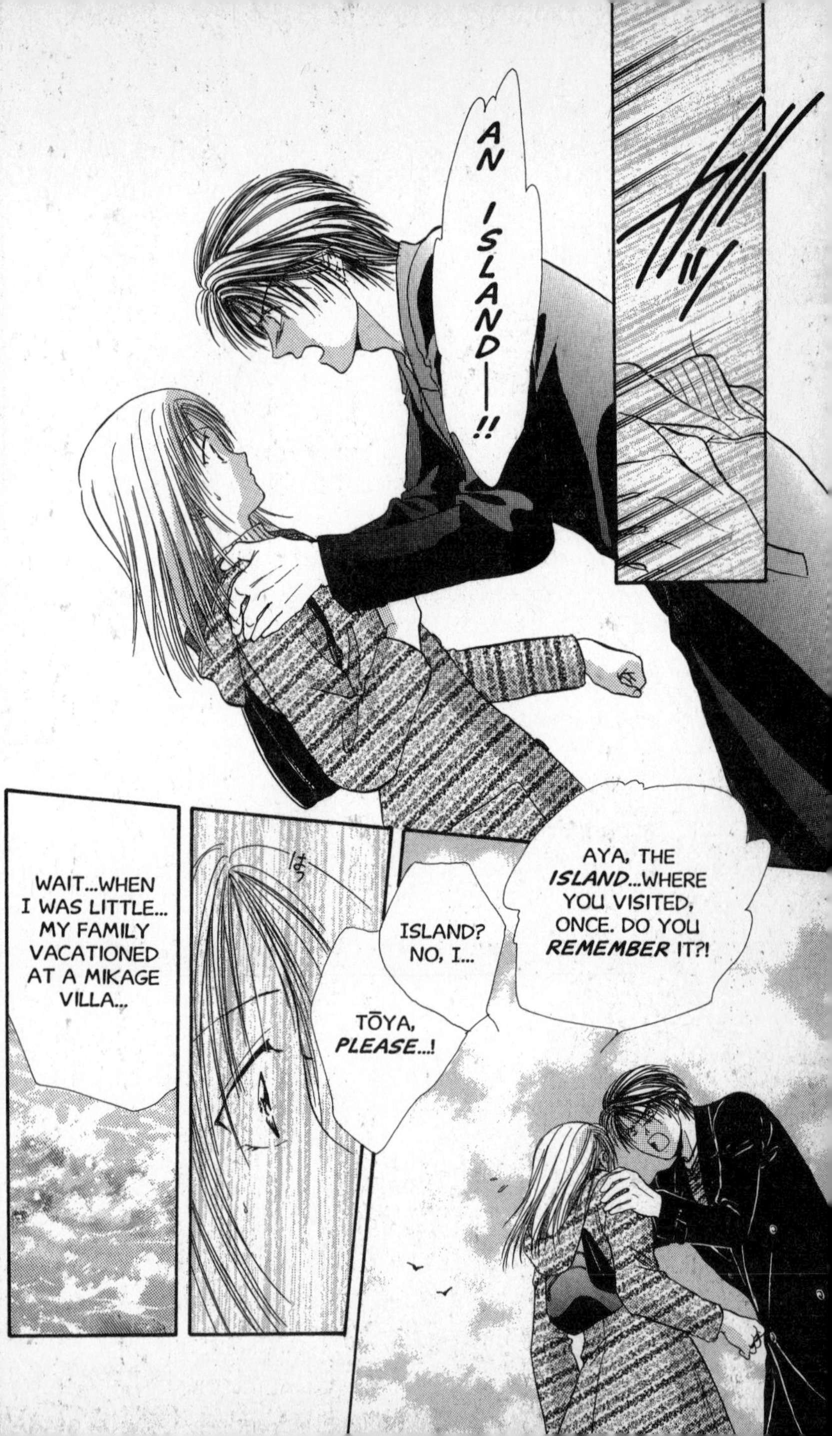
AN ISLAND——!!
AYA, THE *ISLAND*...WHERE YOU VISITED, ONCE. DO YOU *REMEMBER* IT?!
ISLAND? NO, I...
TŌYA, *PLEASE*...!
WAIT...WHEN I WAS LITTLE... MY FAMILY VACATIONED AT A MIKAGE VILLA...

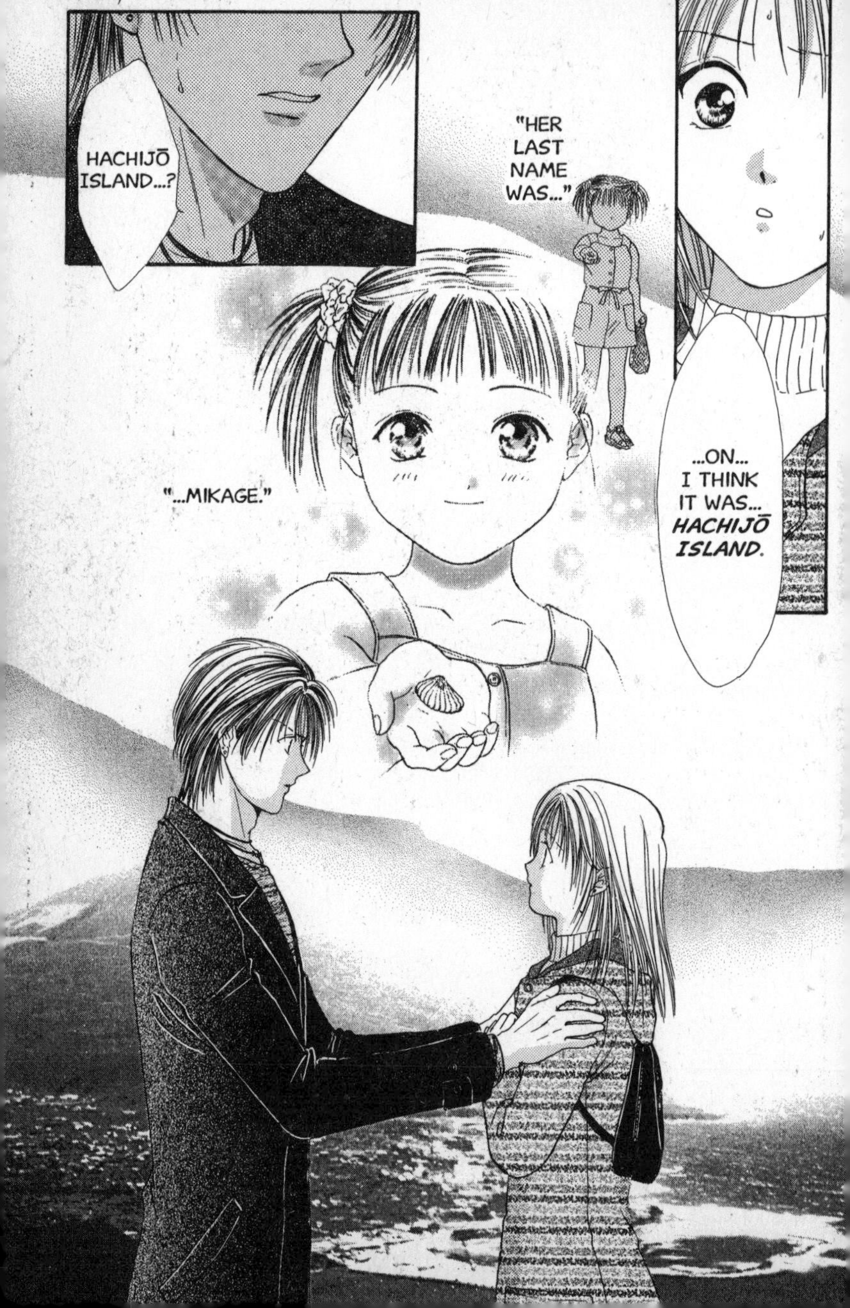
...ON... I THINK IT WAS... HACHIJŌ ISLAND.
HACHIJŌ ISLAND...?
"HER LAST NAME WAS..."
"...MIKAGE."

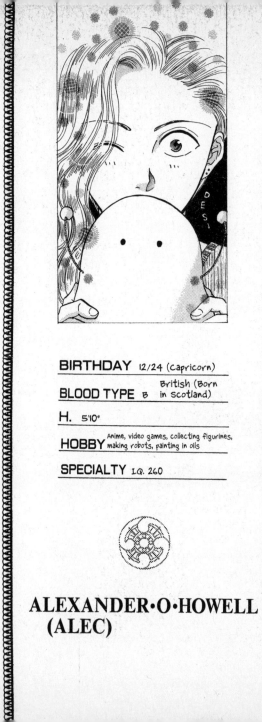

BIRTHDAY 12/24 (capricorn)

BLOOD TYPE B   British (Born in scotland)

H. 5'10"

HOBBY Anime, video games, collecting figurines, making robots, painting in oils

SPECIALTY I.Q. 260

ALEXANDER·O·HOWELL (ALEC)

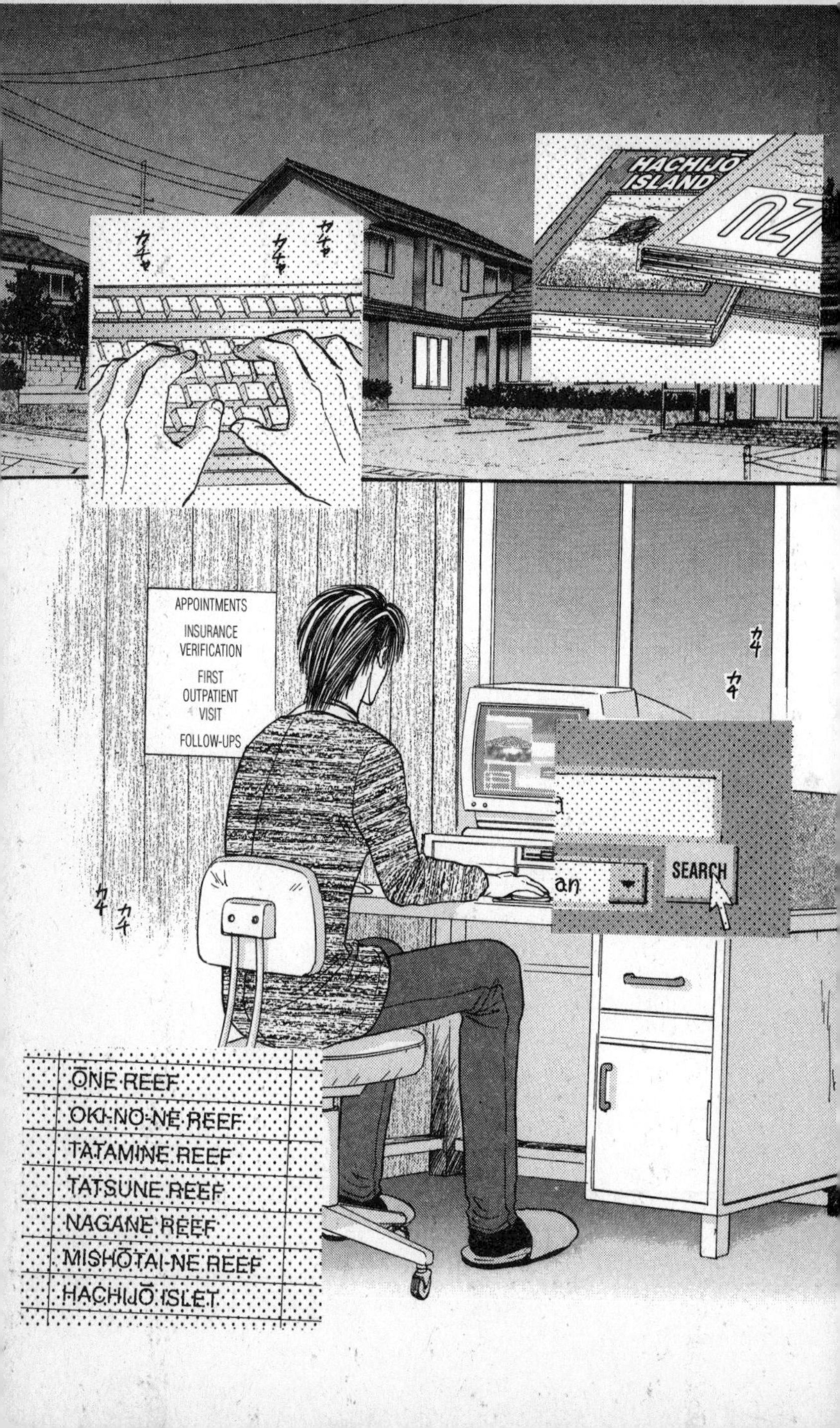
HACHIJO ISLAND
カチャ
カチャ
カチャ
カチ
カチ
APPOINTMENTS
INSURANCE VERIFICATION
FIRST OUTPATIENT VISIT
FOLLOW-UPS
an
SEARCH
カチ
カチ
ONE REEF
OKI-NO-NE REEF
TATAMINE REEF
TATSUNE REEF
NAGANE REEF
MISHŌTAI-NE REEF
HACHIJŌ ISLET

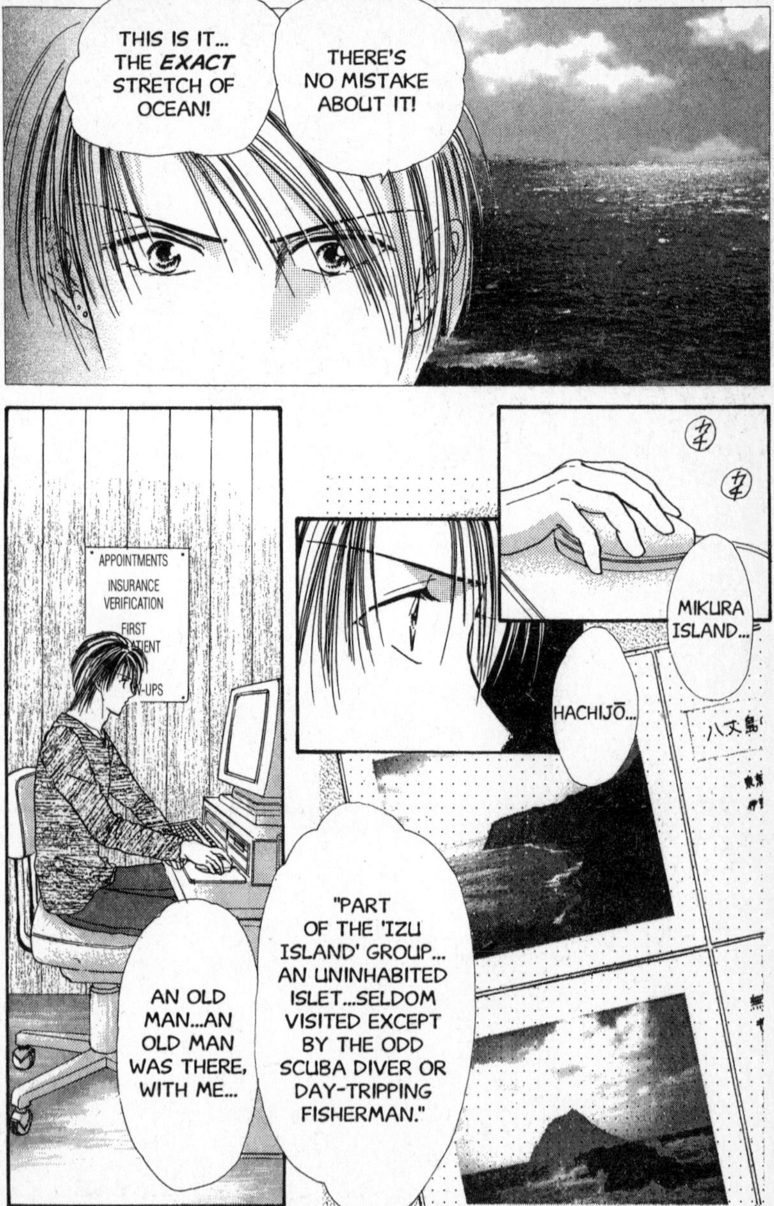
THERE'S NO MISTAKE ABOUT IT!
THIS IS IT... THE *EXACT* STRETCH OF OCEAN!
MIKURA ISLAND...
HACHIJŌ...
八丈島
"PART OF THE 'IZU ISLAND' GROUP... AN UNINHABITED ISLET...SELDOM VISITED EXCEPT BY THE ODD SCUBA DIVER OR DAY-TRIPPING FISHERMAN."
AN OLD MAN...AN OLD MAN WAS THERE, WITH ME...
APPOINTMENTS
INSURANCE VERIFICATION
FIRST

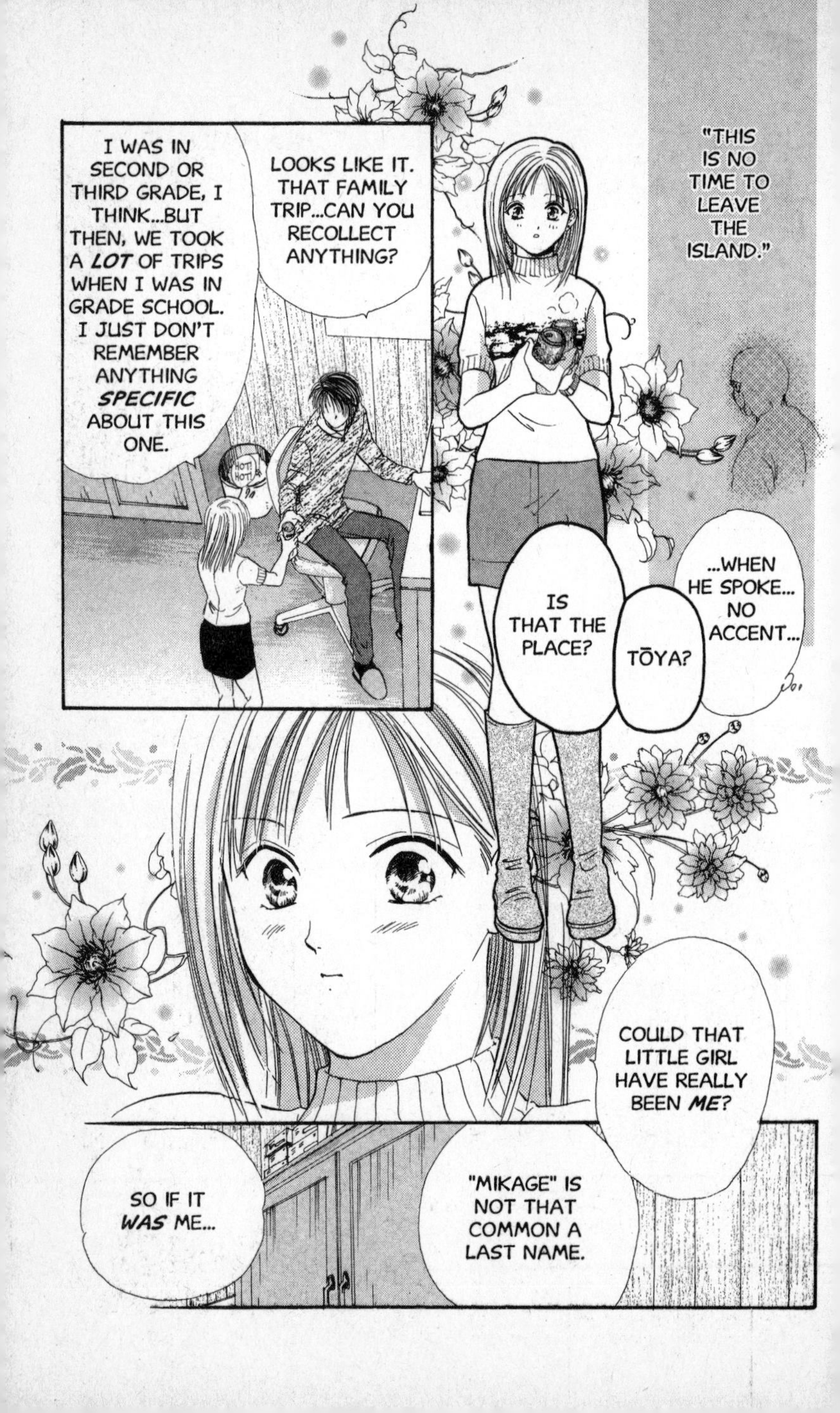
"THIS IS NO TIME TO LEAVE THE ISLAND."
...WHEN HE SPOKE... NO ACCENT...
TŌYA?
IS THAT THE PLACE?
LOOKS LIKE IT. THAT FAMILY TRIP...CAN YOU RECOLLECT ANYTHING?
I WAS IN SECOND OR THIRD GRADE, I THINK...BUT THEN, WE TOOK A *LOT* OF TRIPS WHEN I WAS IN GRADE SCHOOL. I JUST DON'T REMEMBER ANYTHING *SPECIFIC* ABOUT THIS ONE.
COULD THAT LITTLE GIRL HAVE REALLY BEEN *ME*?
"MIKAGE" IS NOT THAT COMMON A LAST NAME.
SO IF IT *WAS* ME...

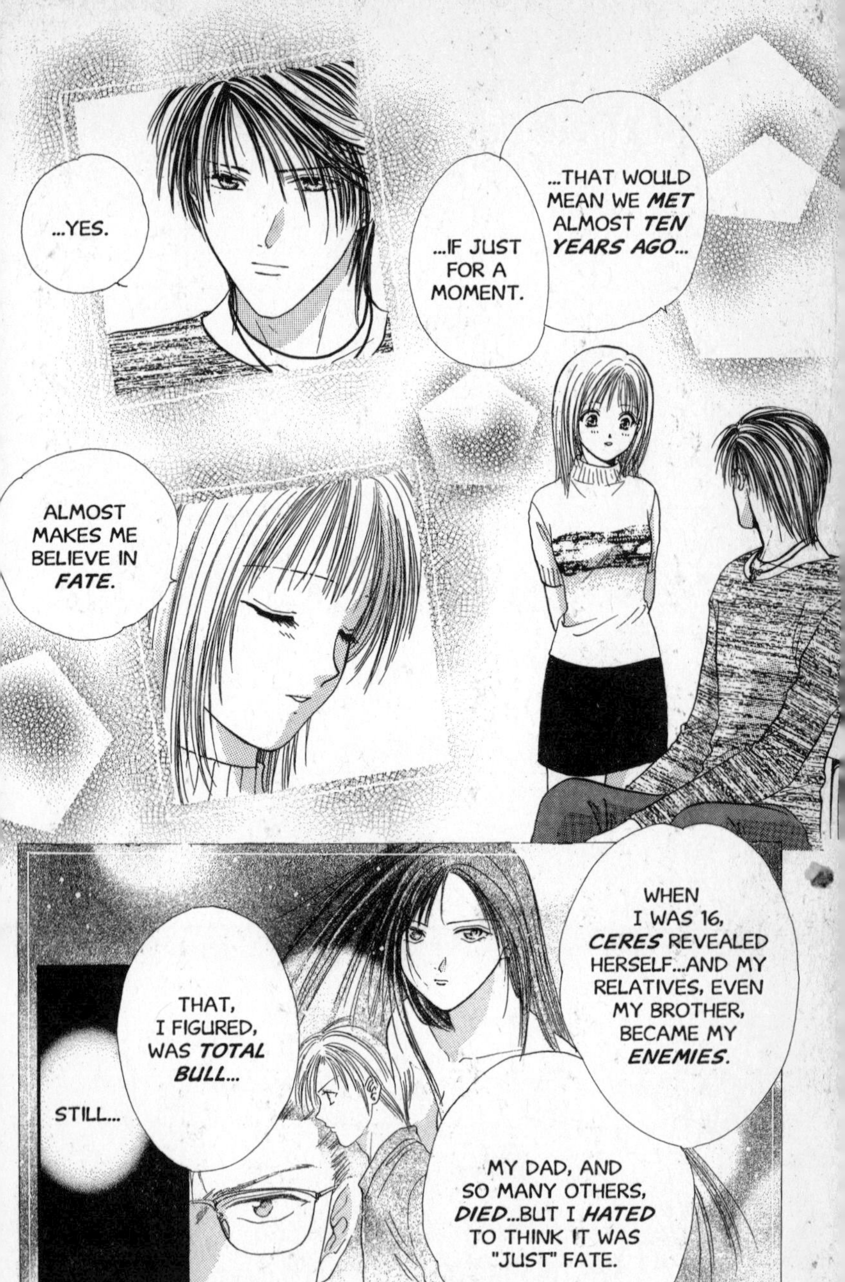
...THAT WOULD MEAN WE MET ALMOST TEN YEARS AGO...
...IF JUST FOR A MOMENT.
...YES.
ALMOST MAKES ME BELIEVE IN FATE.
WHEN I WAS 16, CERES REVEALED HERSELF...AND MY RELATIVES, EVEN MY BROTHER, BECAME MY ENEMIES.
MY DAD, AND SO MANY OTHERS, DIED...BUT I HATED TO THINK IT WAS "JUST" FATE.
THAT, I FIGURED, WAS TOTAL BULL...
STILL...

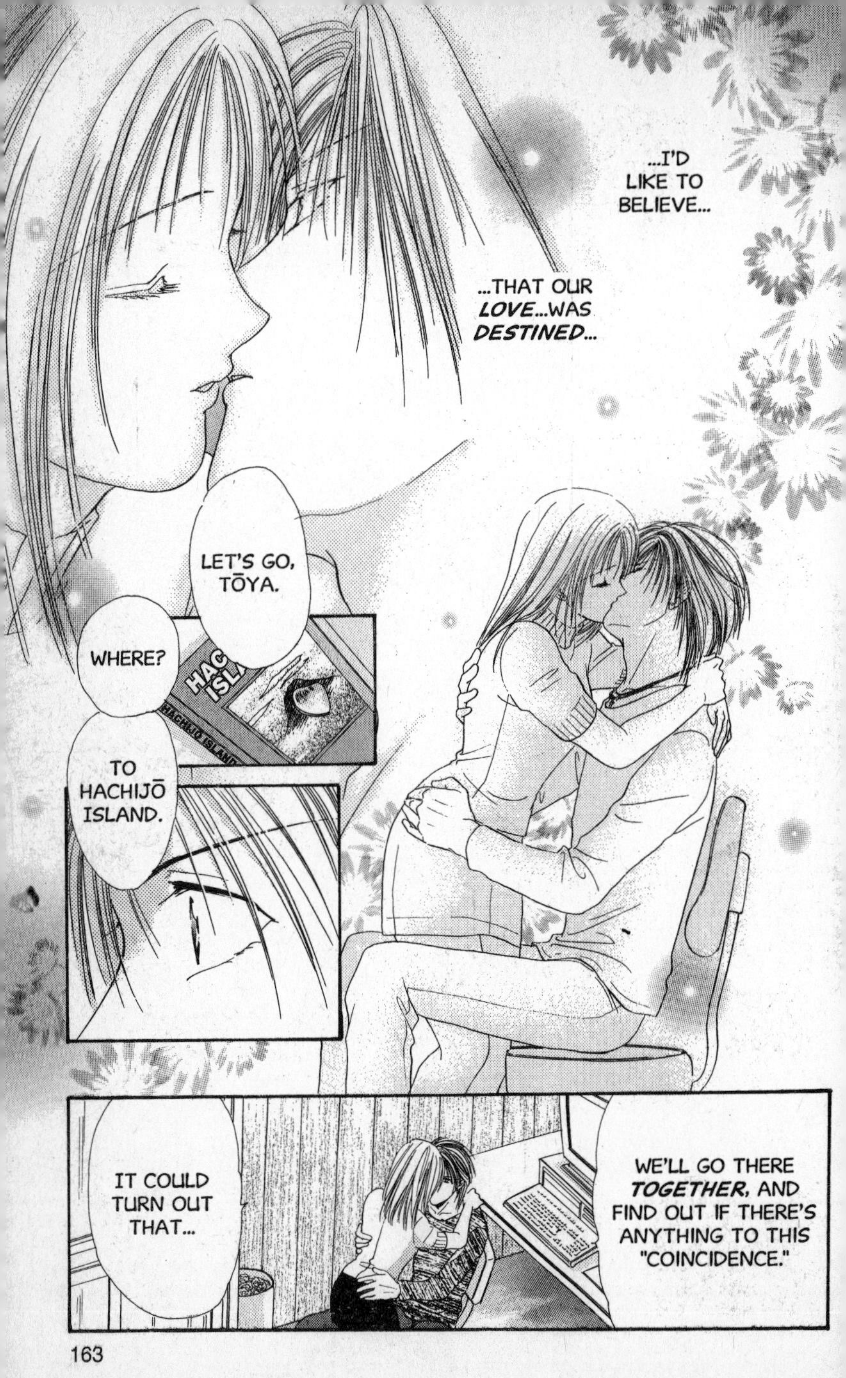
...I'D LIKE TO BELIEVE...
...THAT OUR *LOVE*...WAS ***DESTINED***...
LET'S GO, TŌYA.
WHERE?
TO HACHIJŌ ISLAND.
WE'LL GO THERE ***TOGETHER,*** AND FIND OUT IF THERE'S ANYTHING TO THIS "COINCIDENCE."
IT COULD TURN OUT THAT...

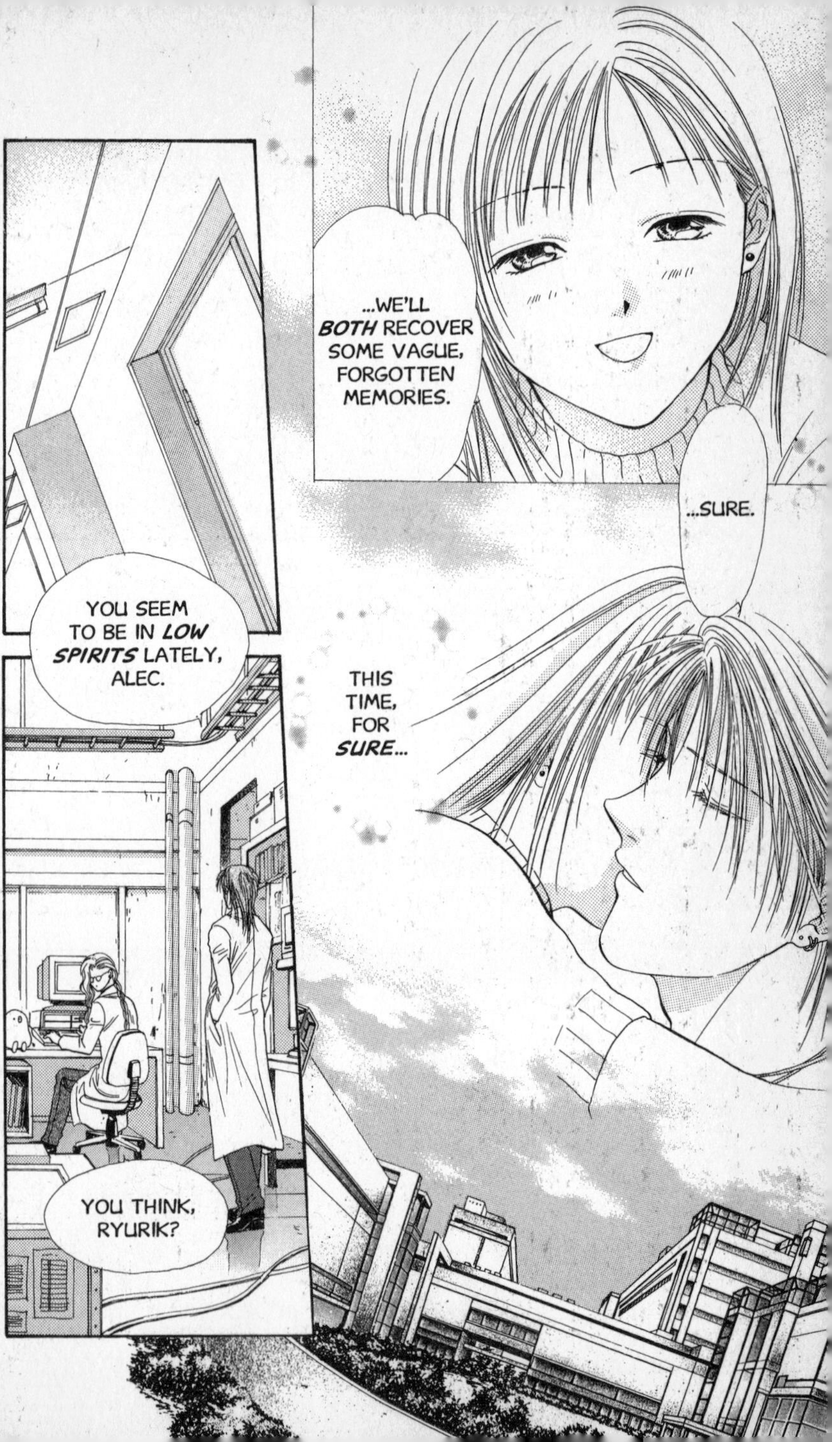
...WE'LL *BOTH* RECOVER SOME VAGUE, FORGOTTEN MEMORIES.
...SURE.
THIS TIME, FOR *SURE*...
YOU SEEM TO BE IN *LOW SPIRITS* LATELY, ALEC.
YOU THINK, RYURIK?

...but, once I got to be a senior, I realized how dumb it was. Looking back, I guess all I'd wanted was to have a squashed book bag, like everyone else. My friend had even said, "Why would you even **want** a bag this ugly?" But wasn't making **any** fuss about something like a bag just as dumb...?

If you really, truly like something, is there anything wrong with that? The book I quoted from last time goes into this...let's just say I consider the author a "life mentor." "Individuality gives each person purpose, and a way of life unique to themselves," he writes. Individuality isn't just about doing something different from others—it's something that shines through when you devote yourself to worthwhile pursuits! People who make too much of appearances or popularity or fads have no real sense of themselves. What matters is how you're individual **inside**, not how you **dress**. "Taking advice and guidance is necessary to the process of building character; refusing to listen is merely being stubborn, not asserting individuality." Exactly right. "Make the effort to live to the utmost of your abilities, and you'll begin to see what only you can do!" "Don't lose faith in yourself." Listen to the opinions of those around you, and then develop whatever it is about you that's unique to **you**. It doesn't have to be anything flashy...! You should live true to yourself, and try your hardest. You'll get a sense of fulfillment—a sense that you're truly **alive**. Slacking off may be fun, sure, but in the end, it's **you** who'll be losing out.

Ooh, almost out of space...
"Appare Zipang! (Bravo! Japan)," Volume 2, will be out in July... be on the lookout for an "FY" novel, too!

Volume 11's been an unusually **peaceful** volume, hasn't it. So lovey-dovey...! The assistants are convinced it won't last. ...They onto something, you think?

See you next time! '99 5/24

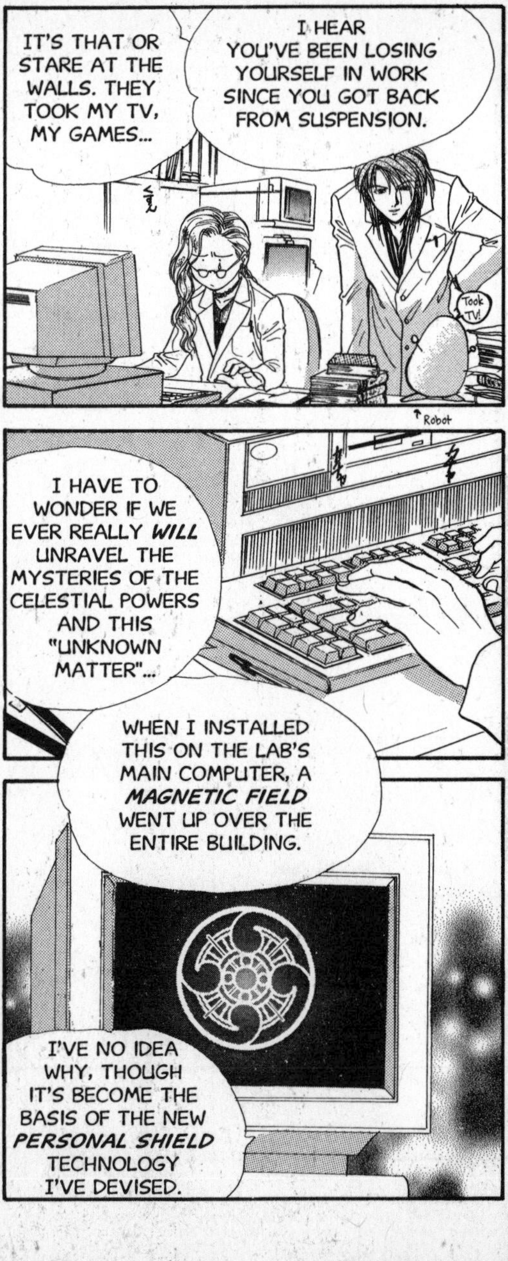
I HEAR YOU'VE BEEN LOSING YOURSELF IN WORK SINCE YOU GOT BACK FROM SUSPENSION.
IT'S THAT OR STARE AT THE WALLS. THEY TOOK MY TV, MY GAMES...
Took TV!
Robot
I HAVE TO WONDER IF WE EVER REALLY *WILL* UNRAVEL THE MYSTERIES OF THE CELESTIAL POWERS AND THIS "UNKNOWN MATTER"...
WHEN I INSTALLED THIS ON THE LAB'S MAIN COMPUTER, A *MAGNETIC FIELD* WENT UP OVER THE ENTIRE BUILDING.
I'VE NO IDEA WHY, THOUGH IT'S BECOME THE BASIS OF THE NEW *PERSONAL SHIELD* TECHNOLOGY I'VE DEVISED.

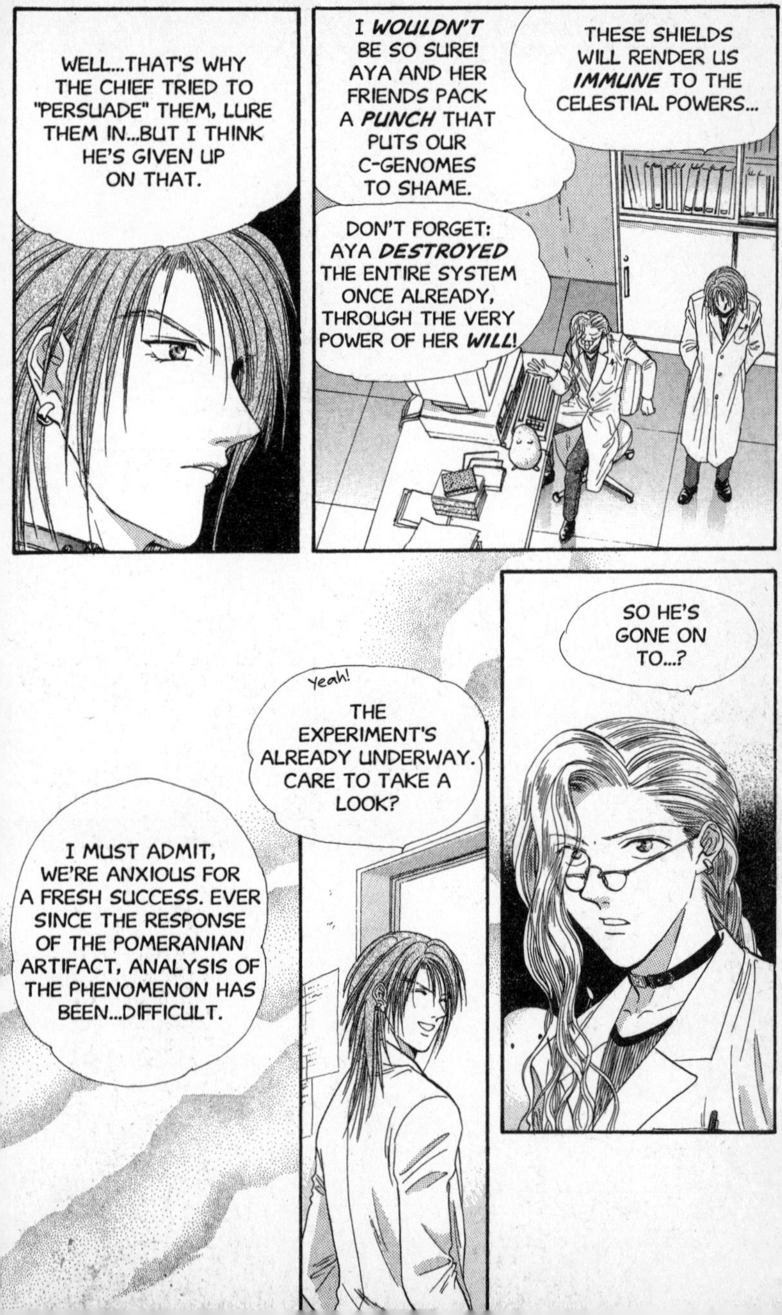
THESE SHIELDS WILL RENDER US IMMUNE TO THE CELESTIAL POWERS...
I WOULDN'T BE SO SURE! AYA AND HER FRIENDS PACK A PUNCH THAT PUTS OUR C-GENOMES TO SHAME.
DON'T FORGET: AYA DESTROYED THE ENTIRE SYSTEM ONCE ALREADY, THROUGH THE VERY POWER OF HER WILL!
WELL...THAT'S WHY THE CHIEF TRIED TO "PERSUADE" THEM, LURE THEM IN...BUT I THINK HE'S GIVEN UP ON THAT.
SO HE'S GONE ON TO...?
Yeah!
THE EXPERIMENT'S ALREADY UNDERWAY. CARE TO TAKE A LOOK?
I MUST ADMIT, WE'RE ANXIOUS FOR A FRESH SUCCESS. EVER SINCE THE RESPONSE OF THE POMERANIAN ARTIFACT, ANALYSIS OF THE PHENOMENON HAS BEEN...DIFFICULT.

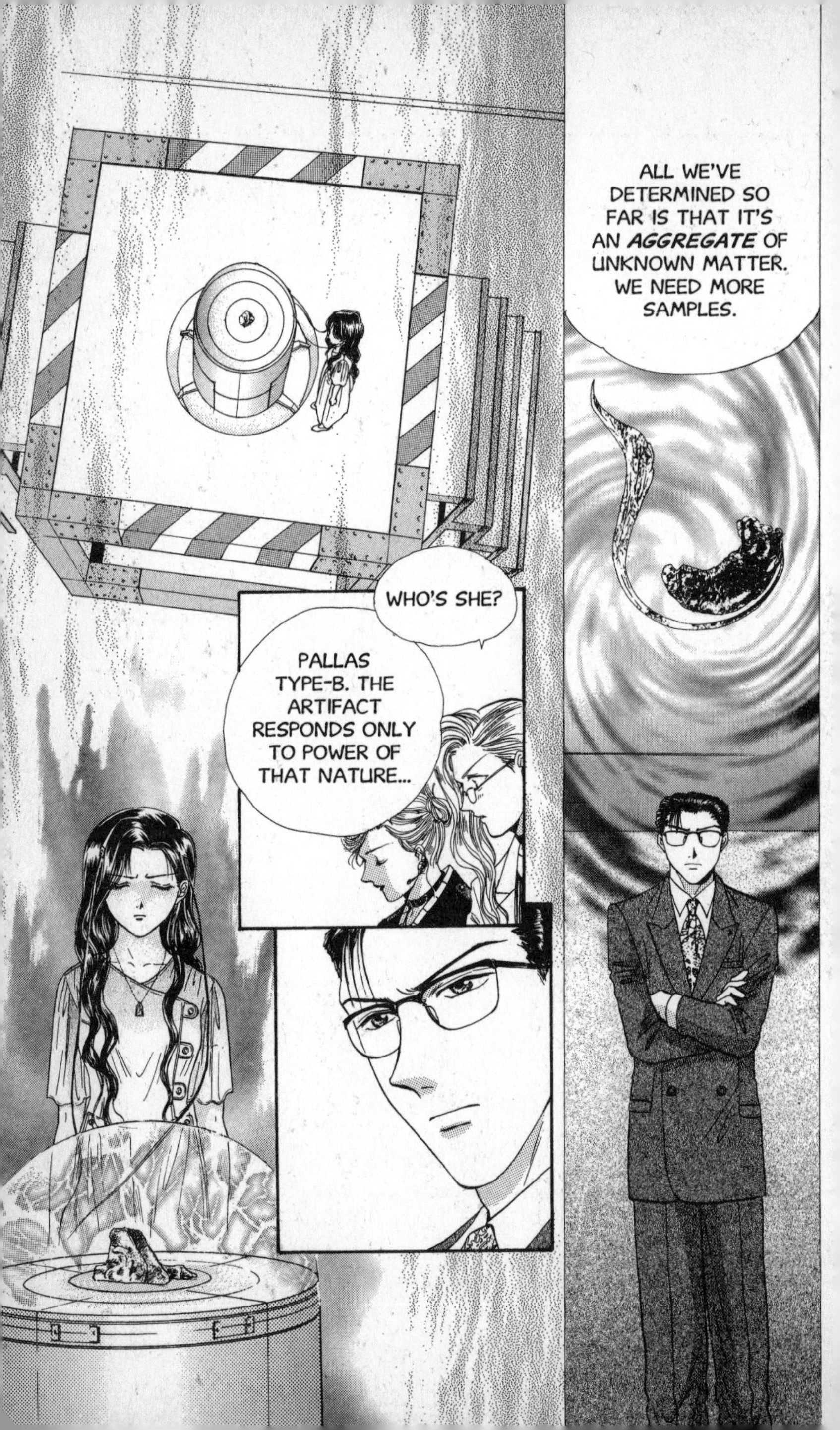
ALL WE'VE DETERMINED SO FAR IS THAT IT'S AN *AGGREGATE* OF UNKNOWN MATTER. WE NEED MORE SAMPLES.
WHO'S SHE?
PALLAS TYPE-B. THE ARTIFACT RESPONDS ONLY TO POWER OF THAT NATURE...

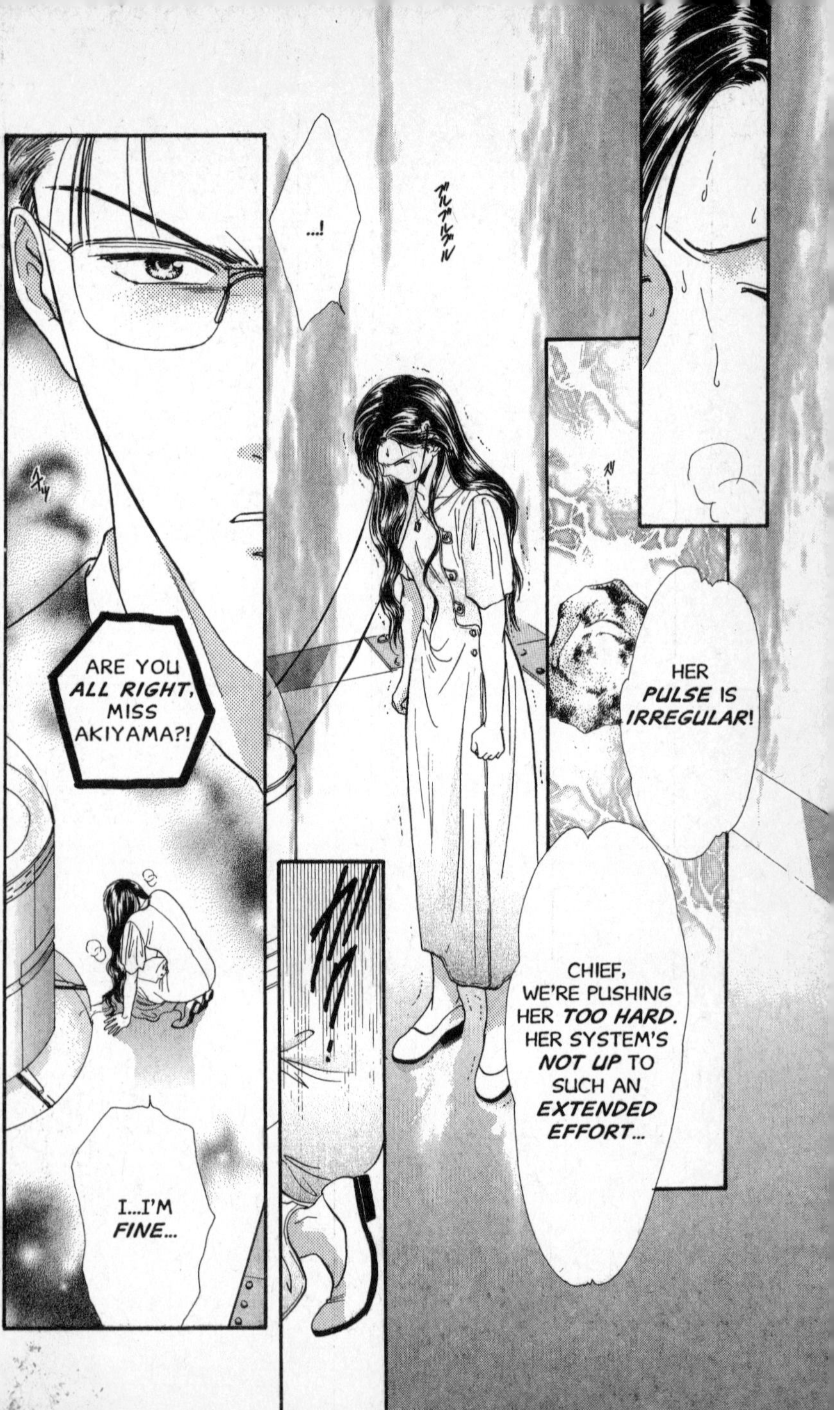
HER PULSE IS IRREGULAR!
CHIEF, WE'RE PUSHING HER TOO HARD. HER SYSTEM'S NOT UP TO SUCH AN EXTENDED EFFORT...
...!
ARE YOU ALL RIGHT, MISS AKIYAMA?!
I...I'M FINE...

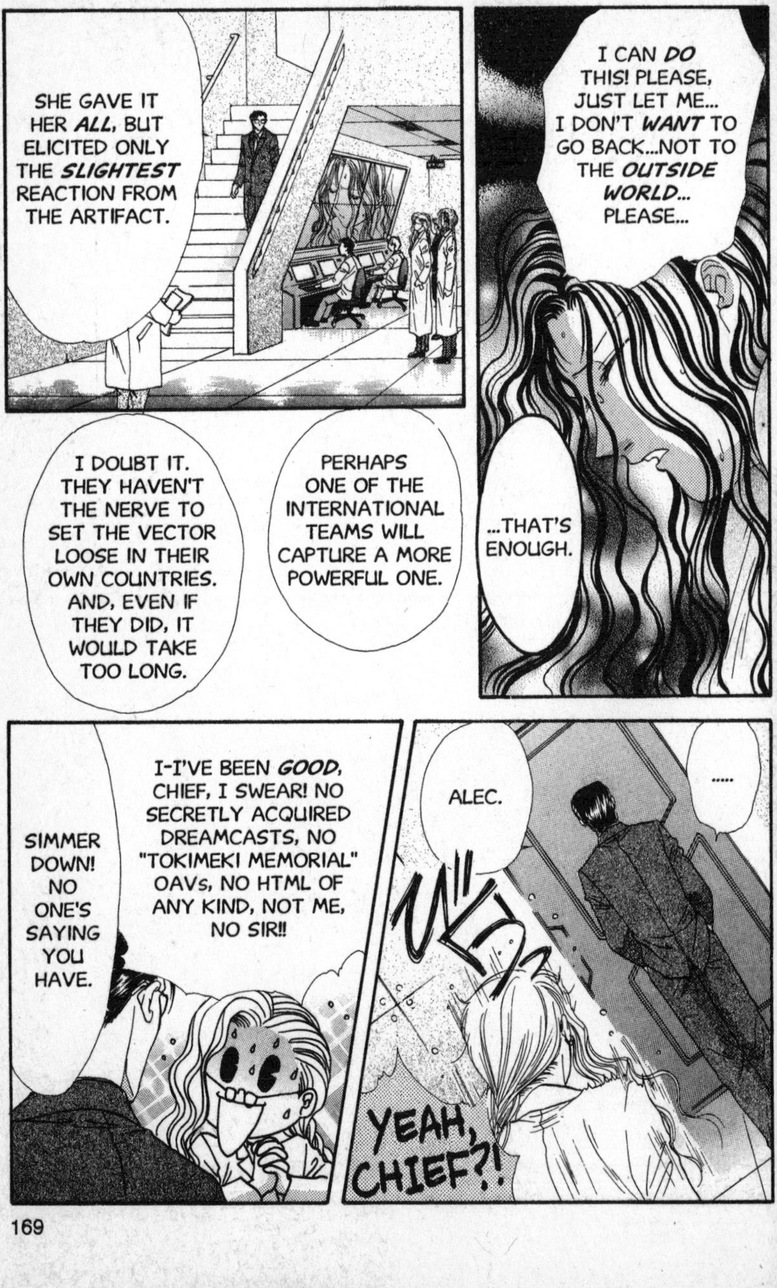
I CAN DO THIS! PLEASE, JUST LET ME... I DON'T WANT TO GO BACK...NOT TO THE OUTSIDE WORLD... PLEASE...
...THAT'S ENOUGH.
SHE GAVE IT HER ALL, BUT ELICITED ONLY THE SLIGHTEST REACTION FROM THE ARTIFACT.
PERHAPS ONE OF THE INTERNATIONAL TEAMS WILL CAPTURE A MORE POWERFUL ONE.
I DOUBT IT. THEY HAVEN'T THE NERVE TO SET THE VECTOR LOOSE IN THEIR OWN COUNTRIES. AND, EVEN IF THEY DID, IT WOULD TAKE TOO LONG.
.....
ALEC.
YEAH, CHIEF?!
I-I'VE BEEN GOOD, CHIEF, I SWEAR! NO SECRETLY ACQUIRED DREAMCASTS, NO "TOKIMEKI MEMORIAL" OAVs, NO HTML OF ANY KIND, NOT ME, NO SIR!!
SIMMER DOWN! NO ONE'S SAYING YOU HAVE.

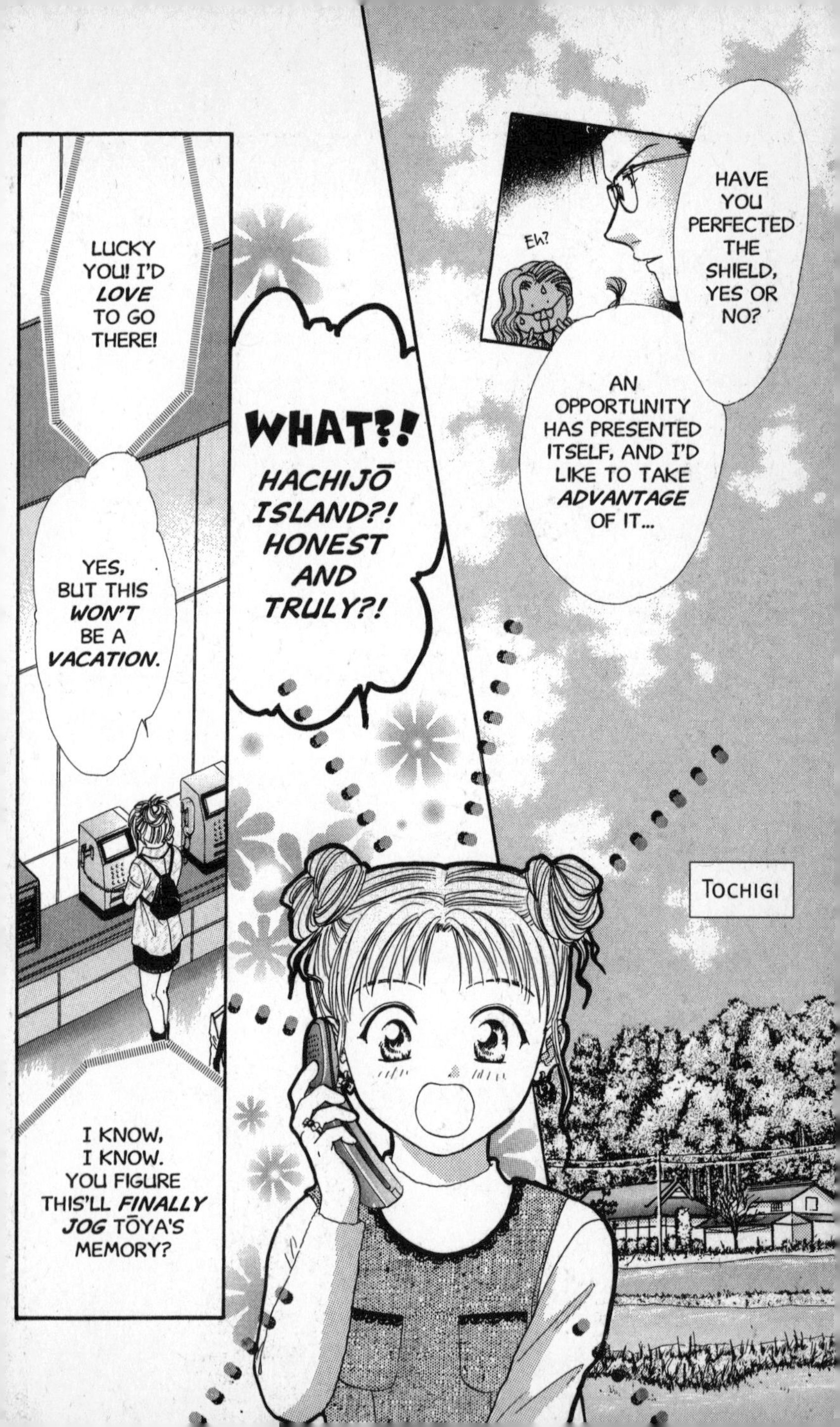
HAVE YOU PERFECTED THE SHIELD, YES OR NO?
Eh?
AN OPPORTUNITY HAS PRESENTED ITSELF, AND I'D LIKE TO TAKE *ADVANTAGE* OF IT...
TOCHIGI
WHAT?! *HACHIJŌ ISLAND?! HONEST AND TRULY?!*
LUCKY YOU! I'D *LOVE* TO GO THERE!
YES, BUT THIS *WON'T* BE A *VACATION*.
I KNOW, I KNOW. YOU FIGURE THIS'LL *FINALLY JOG* TŌYA'S MEMORY?

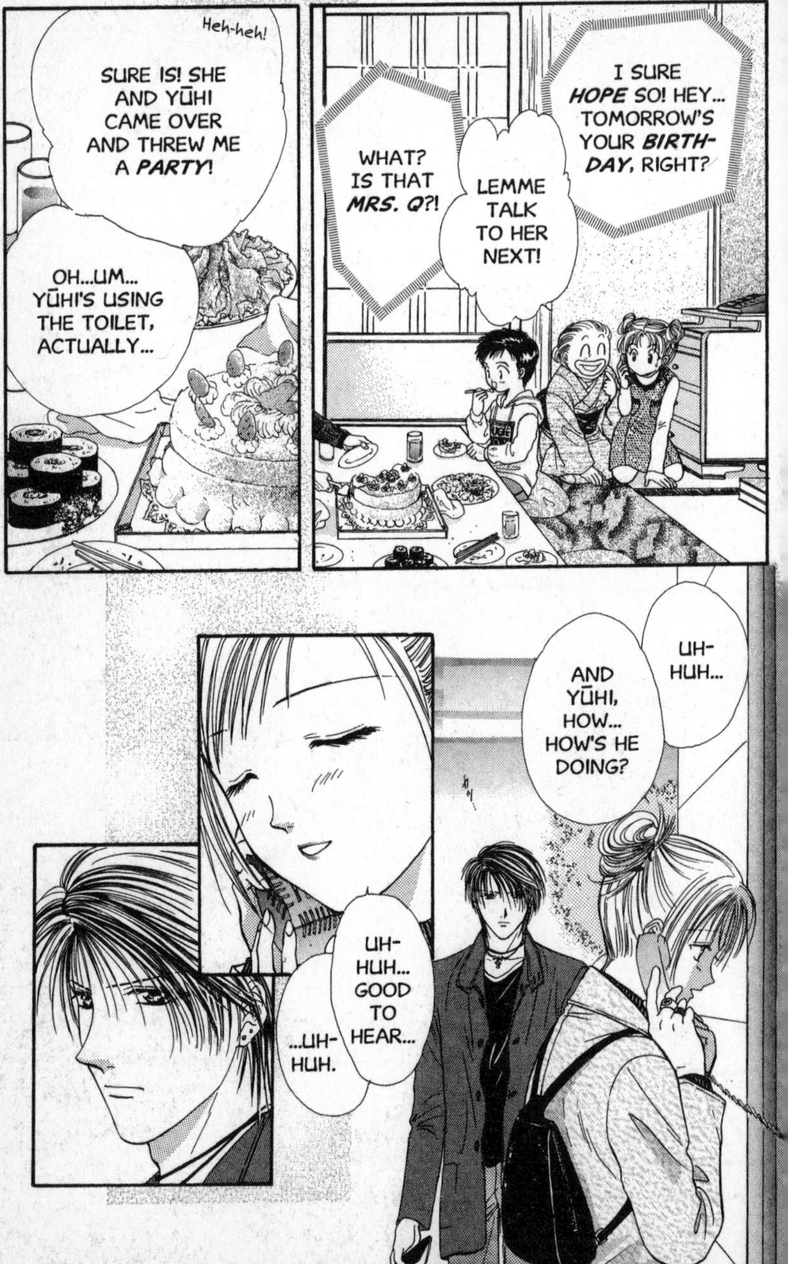
I SURE HOPE SO! HEY... TOMORROW'S YOUR BIRTH-DAY, RIGHT?
LEMME TALK TO HER NEXT!
WHAT? IS THAT MRS. Q?!
Heh-heh!
SURE IS! SHE AND YŪHI CAME OVER AND THREW ME A PARTY!
OH...UM... YŪHI'S USING THE TOILET, ACTUALLY...
UH-HUH...
AND YŪHI, HOW... HOW'S HE DOING?
UH-HUH... GOOD TO HEAR...
...UH-HUH.

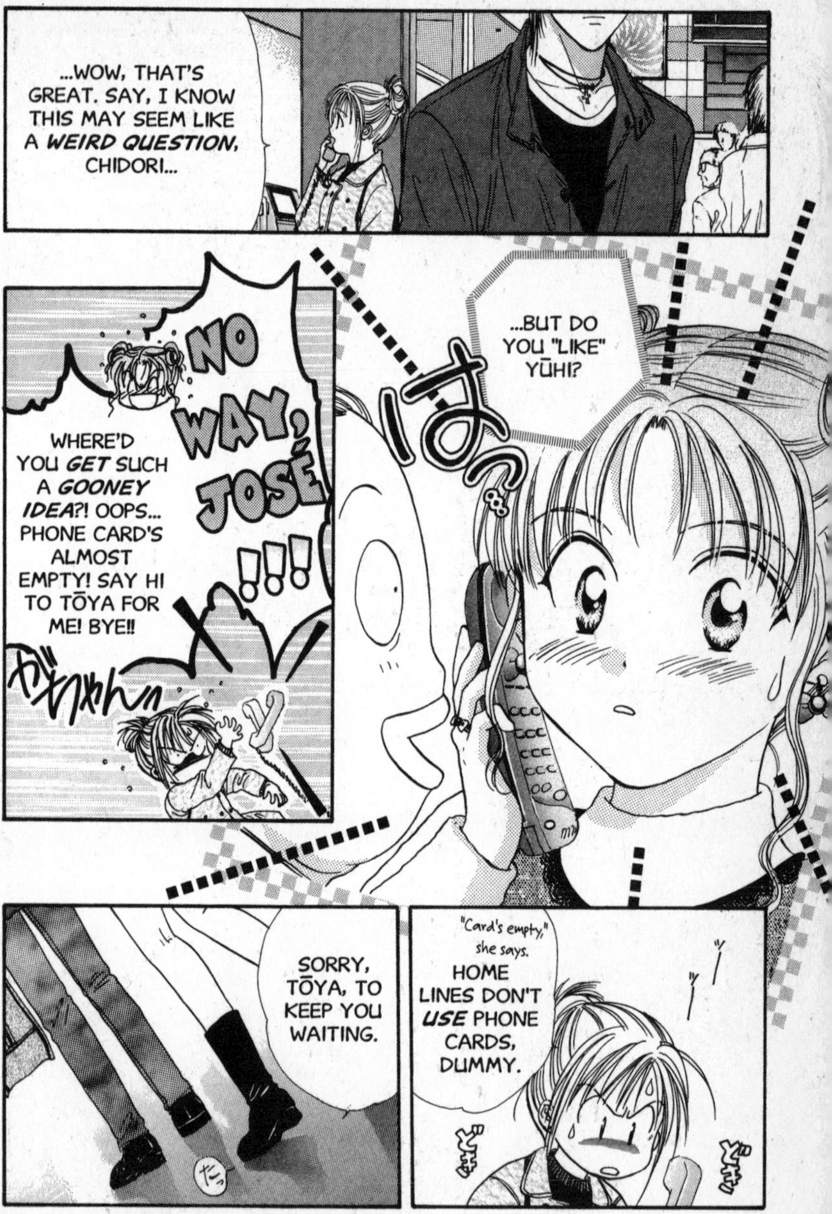
...WOW, THAT'S GREAT. SAY, I KNOW THIS MAY SEEM LIKE A *WEIRD QUESTION,* CHIDORI...
...BUT DO YOU "LIKE" YŪHI?
はっ
NO WAY, JOSÉ!!!
WHERE'D YOU *GET* SUCH A *GOONEY IDEA*?! OOPS... PHONE CARD'S ALMOST EMPTY! SAY HI TO TŌYA FOR ME! BYE!!
"Card's empty," she says.
HOME LINES DON'T *USE* PHONE CARDS, DUMMY.
SORRY, TŌYA, TO KEEP YOU WAITING.

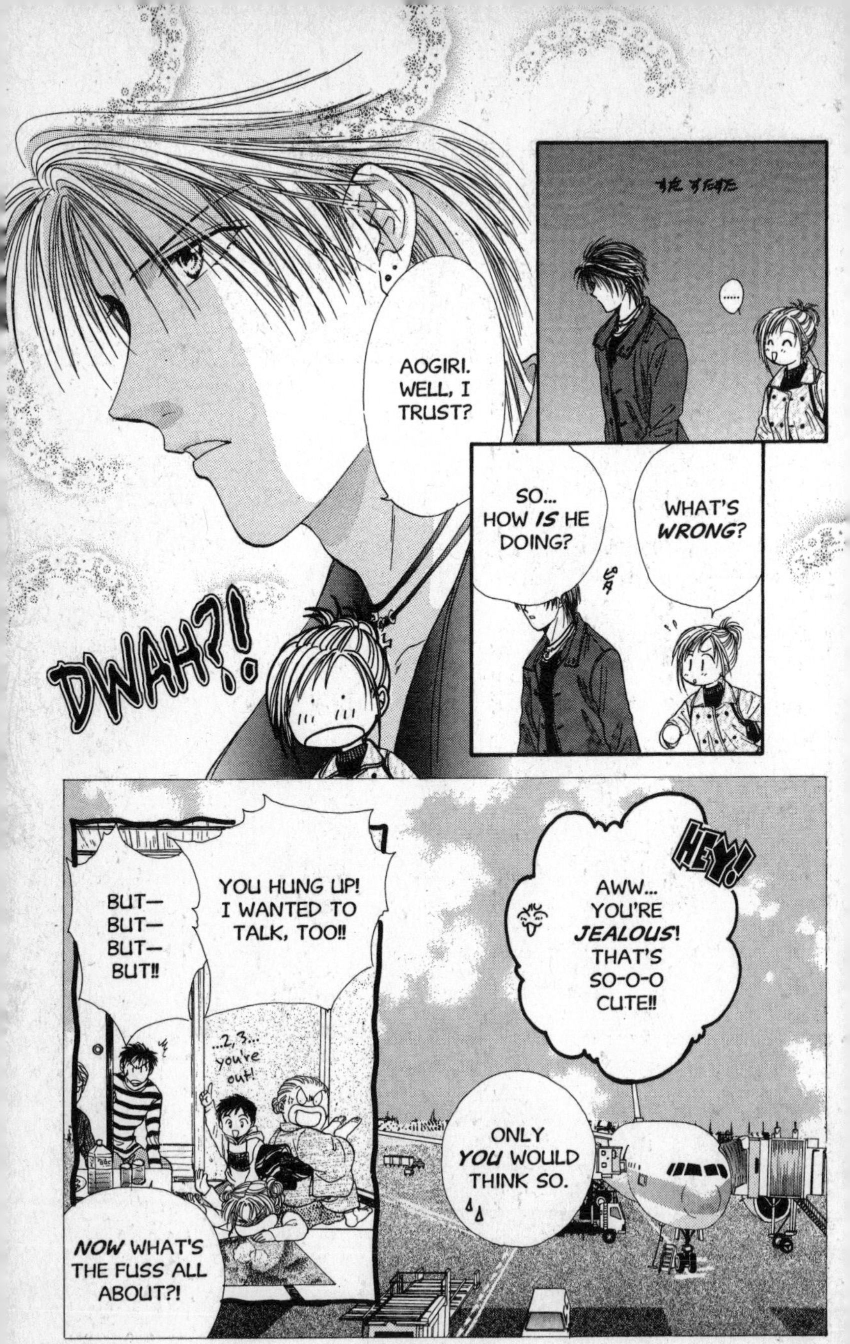
......
WHAT'S WRONG?
SO... HOW IS HE DOING?
AOGIRI. WELL, I TRUST?
DWAH?!
HEY!
AWW... YOU'RE JEALOUS! THAT'S SO-O-O CUTE!!
ONLY YOU WOULD THINK SO.
YOU HUNG UP! I WANTED TO TALK, TOO!!
BUT— BUT— BUT— BUT!!
...2, 3... you're out!
NOW WHAT'S THE FUSS ALL ABOUT?!

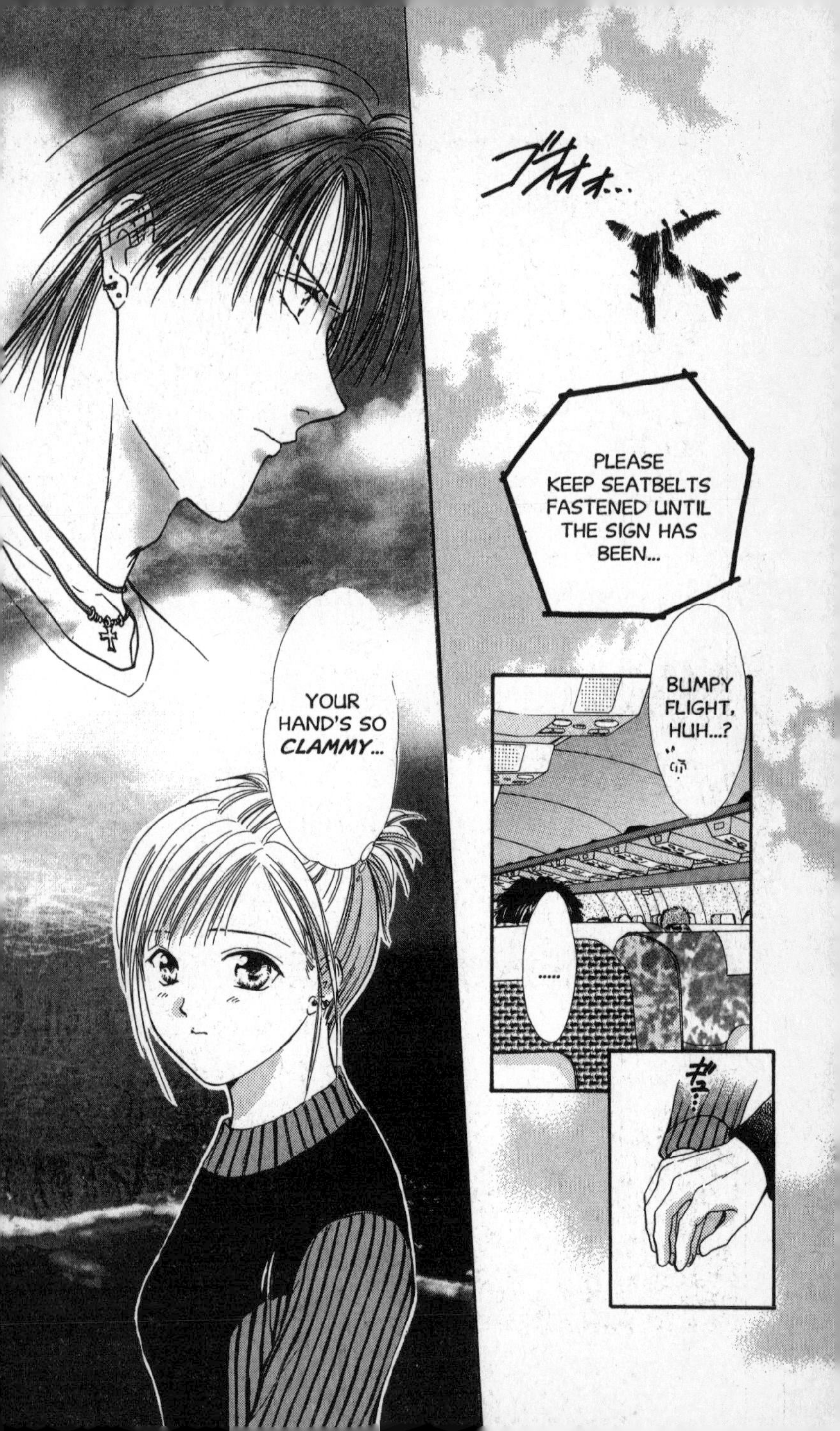
PLEASE KEEP SEATBELTS FASTENED UNTIL THE SIGN HAS BEEN...
BUMPY FLIGHT, HUH...?
......
YOUR HAND'S SO *CLAMMY*...

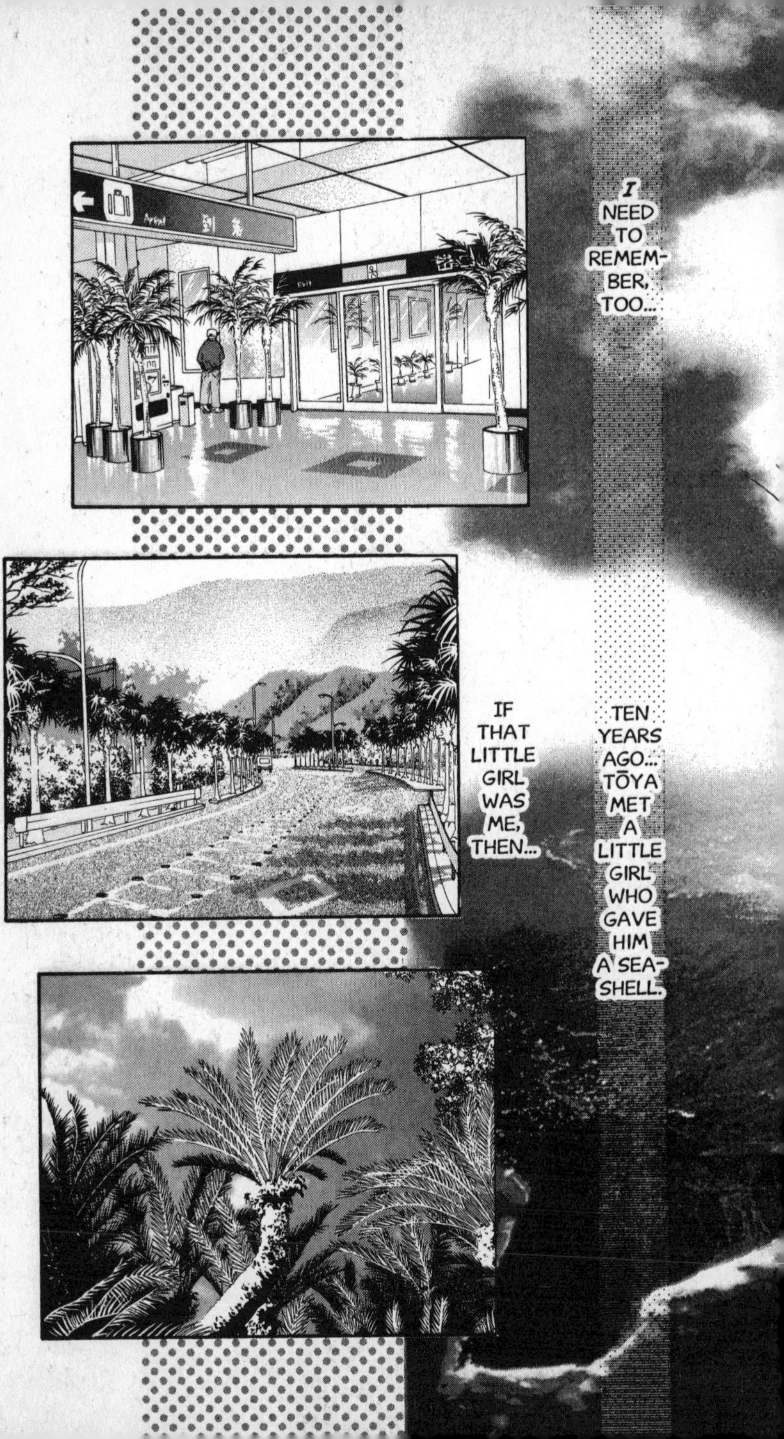
I NEED TO REMEMBER, TOO...
TEN YEARS AGO... TŌYA MET A LITTLE GIRL WHO GAVE HIM A SEASHELL.
IF THAT LITTLE GIRL WAS ME, THEN...

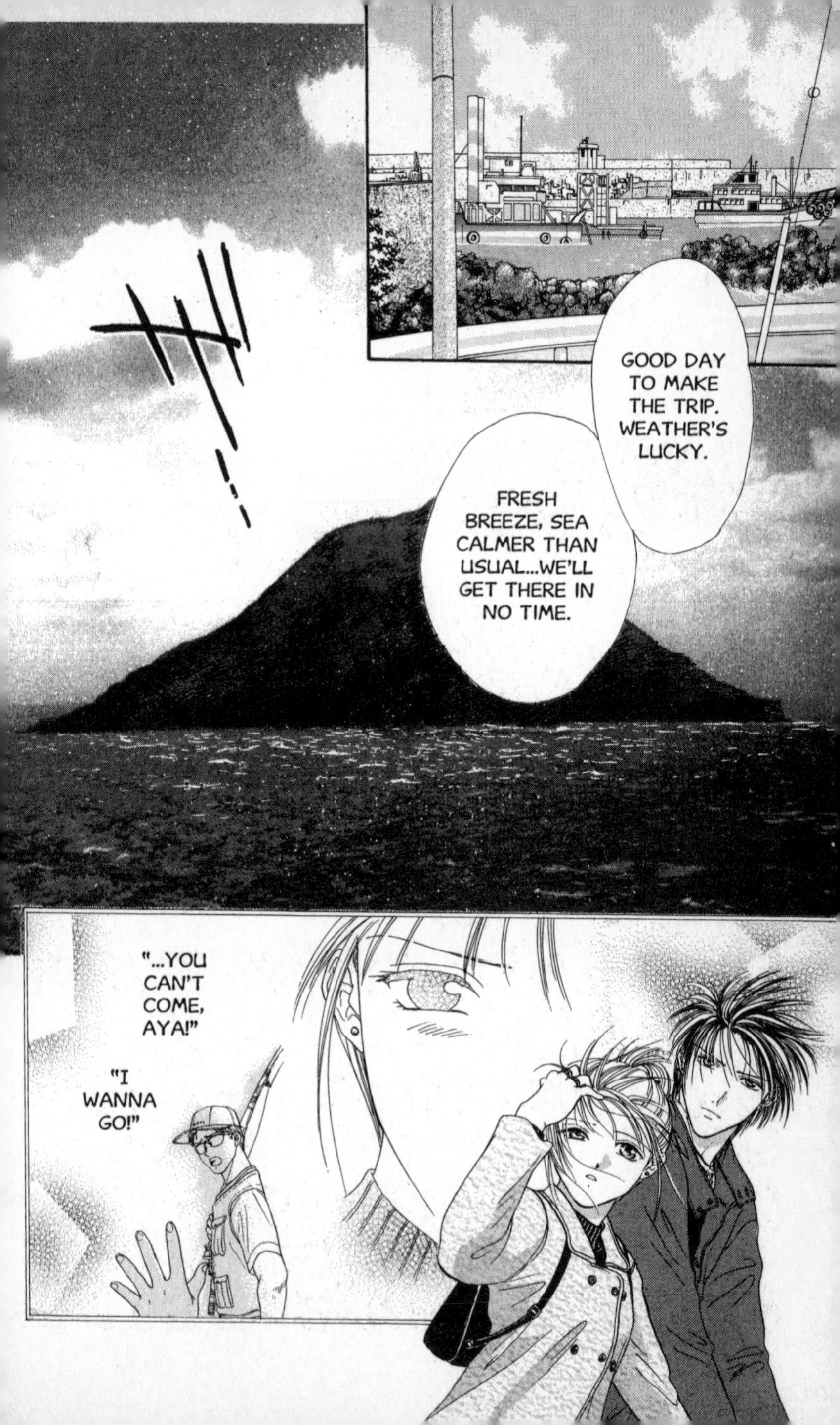
GOOD DAY TO MAKE THE TRIP. WEATHER'S LUCKY.
FRESH BREEZE, SEA CALMER THAN USUAL...WE'LL GET THERE IN NO TIME.
"...YOU CAN'T COME, AYA!"
"I WANNA GO!"

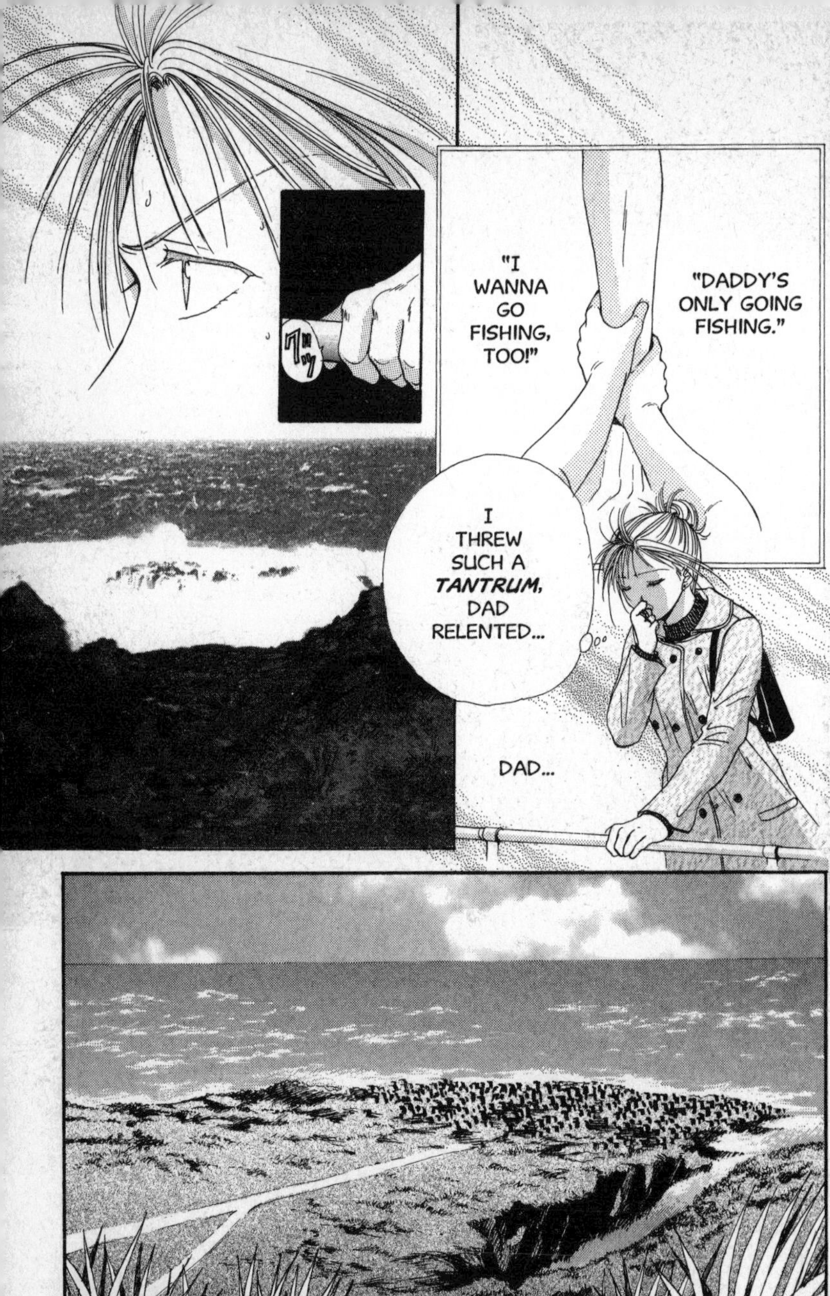
"DADDY'S ONLY GOING FISHING."
"I WANNA GO FISHING, TOO!"
I THREW SUCH A *TANTRUM,* DAD RELENTED...
DAD...

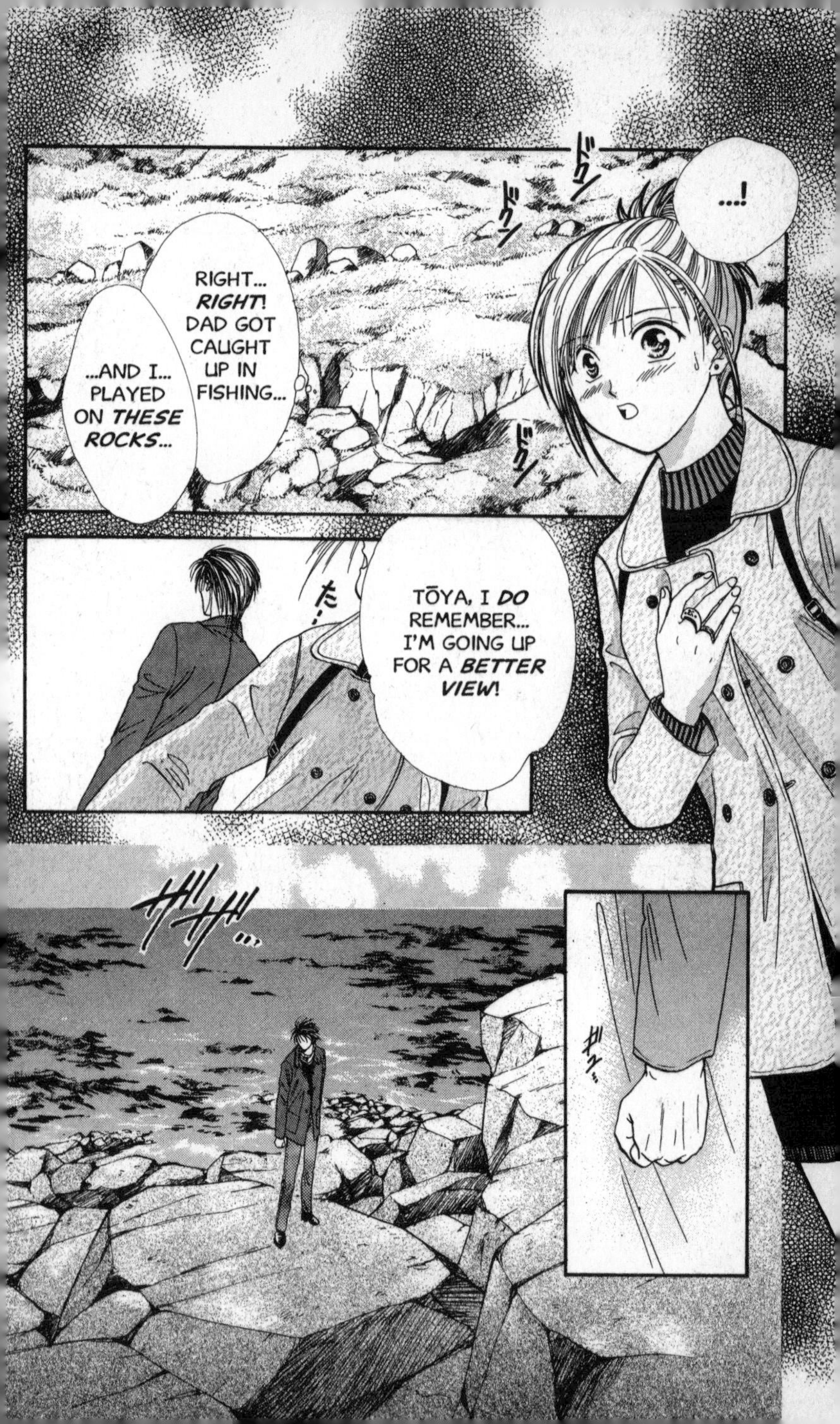
...!
ドクン
ドクン
RIGHT... *RIGHT*! DAD GOT CAUGHT UP IN FISHING...
...AND I... PLAYED ON *THESE ROCKS*...
ドクン
TŌYA, I *DO* REMEMBER... I'M GOING UP FOR A *BETTER VIEW*!
た…
ザザ…

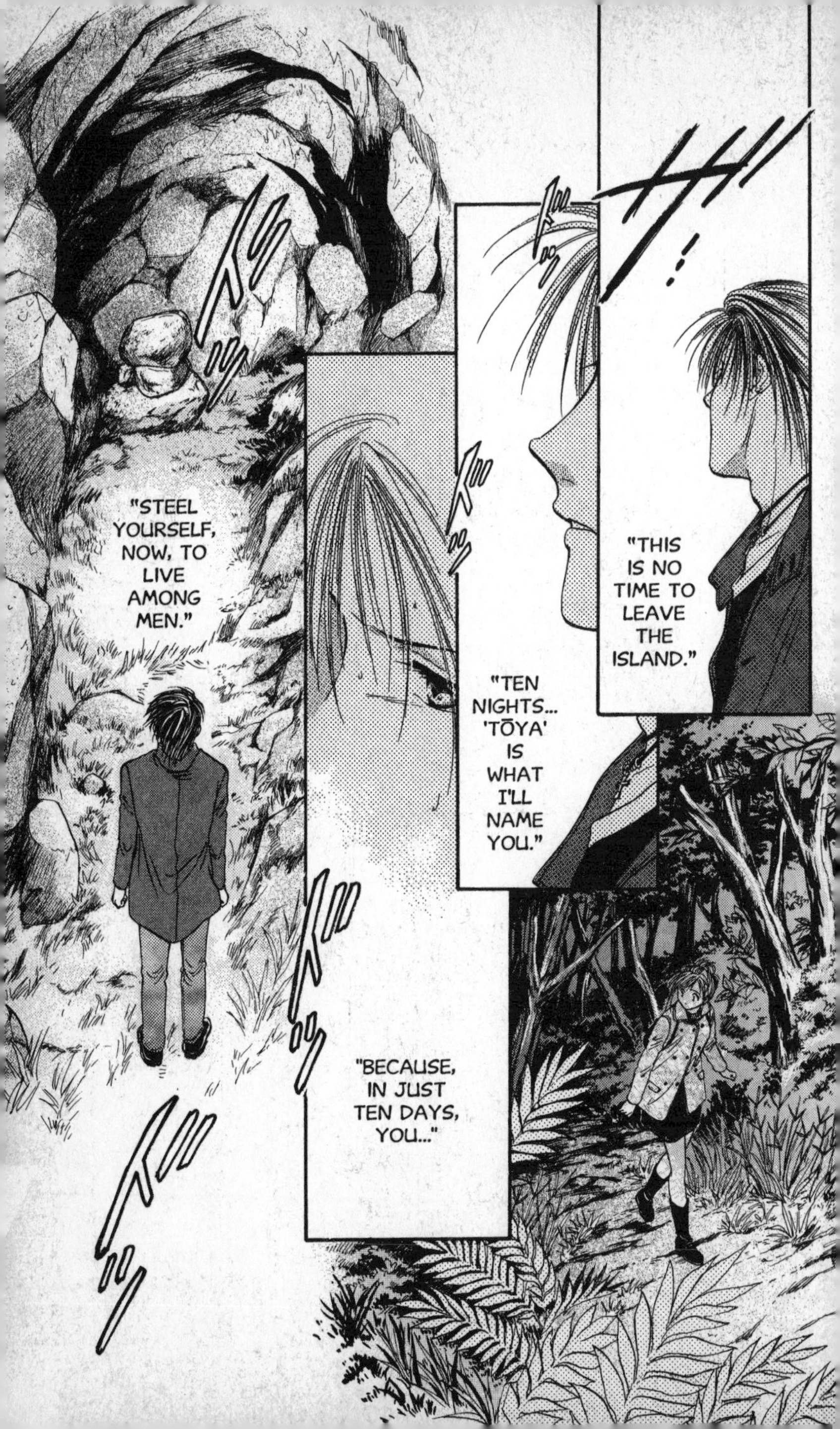
"THIS IS NO TIME TO LEAVE THE ISLAND."
"TEN NIGHTS... 'TŌYA' IS WHAT I'LL NAME YOU."
"BECAUSE, IN JUST TEN DAYS, YOU..."
"STEEL YOURSELF, NOW, TO LIVE AMONG MEN."

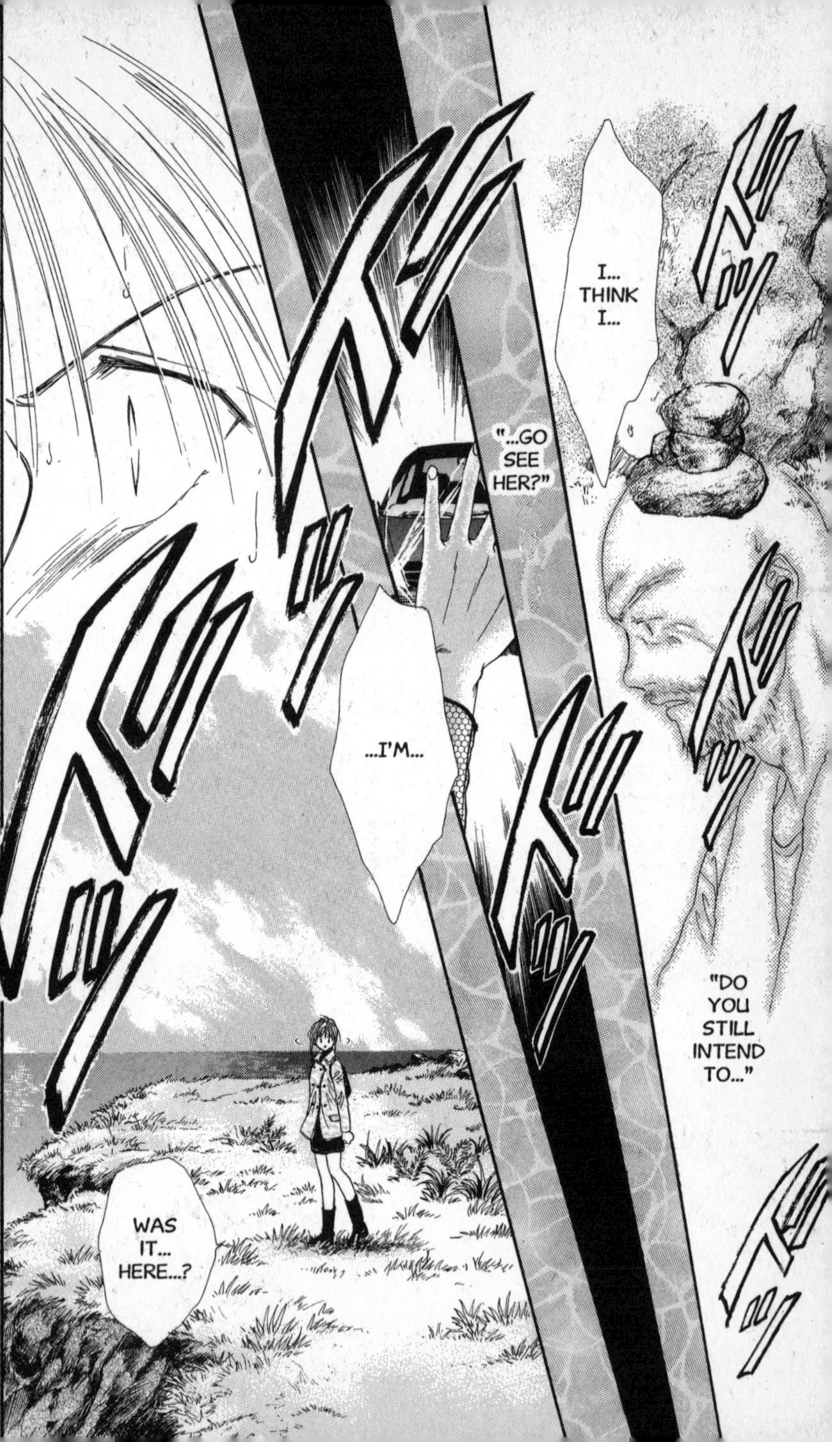
I... THINK I...
"...GO SEE HER?"
"DO YOU STILL INTEND TO..."
...I'M...
WAS IT... HERE...?

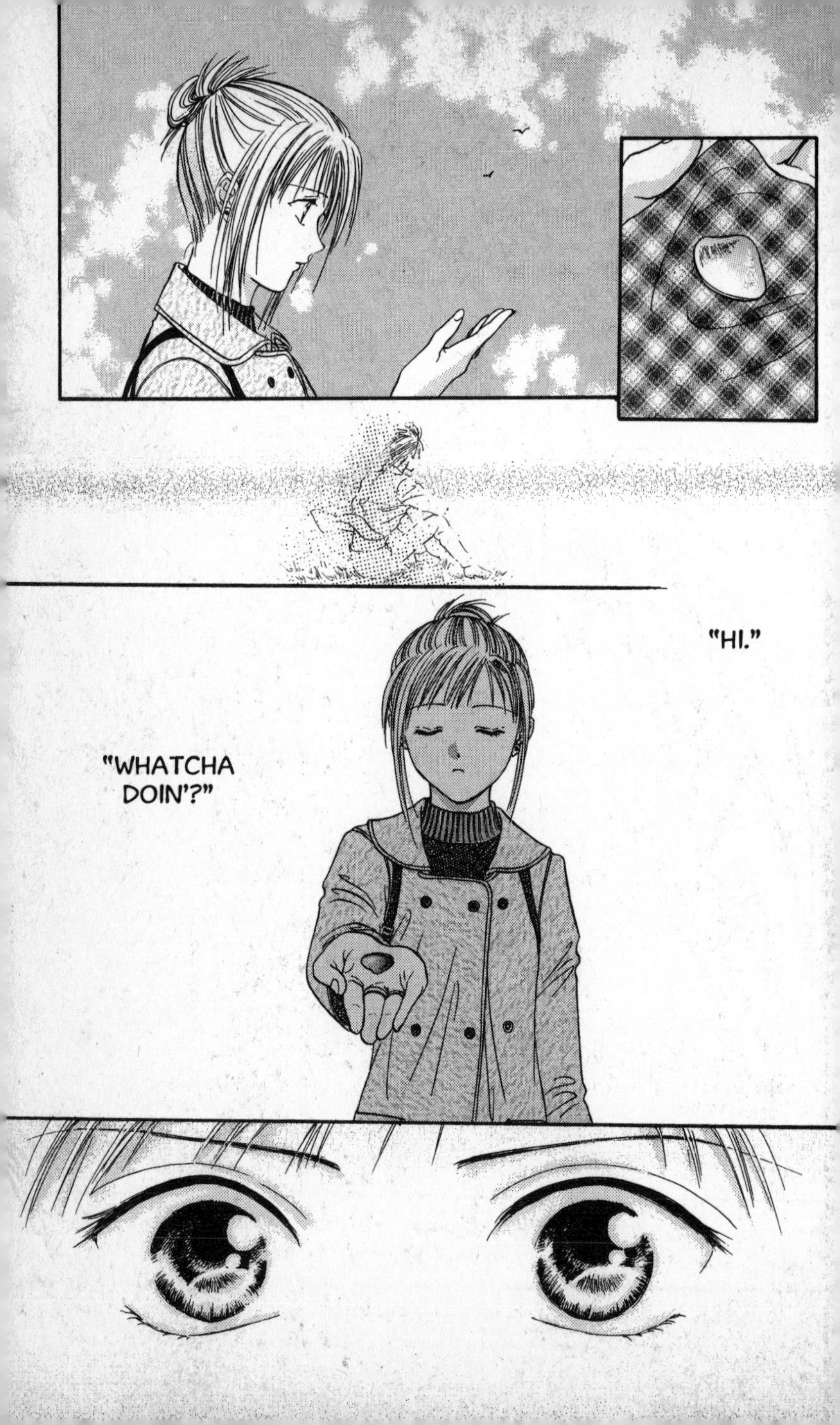
"HI."
"WHATCHA DOIN'?"

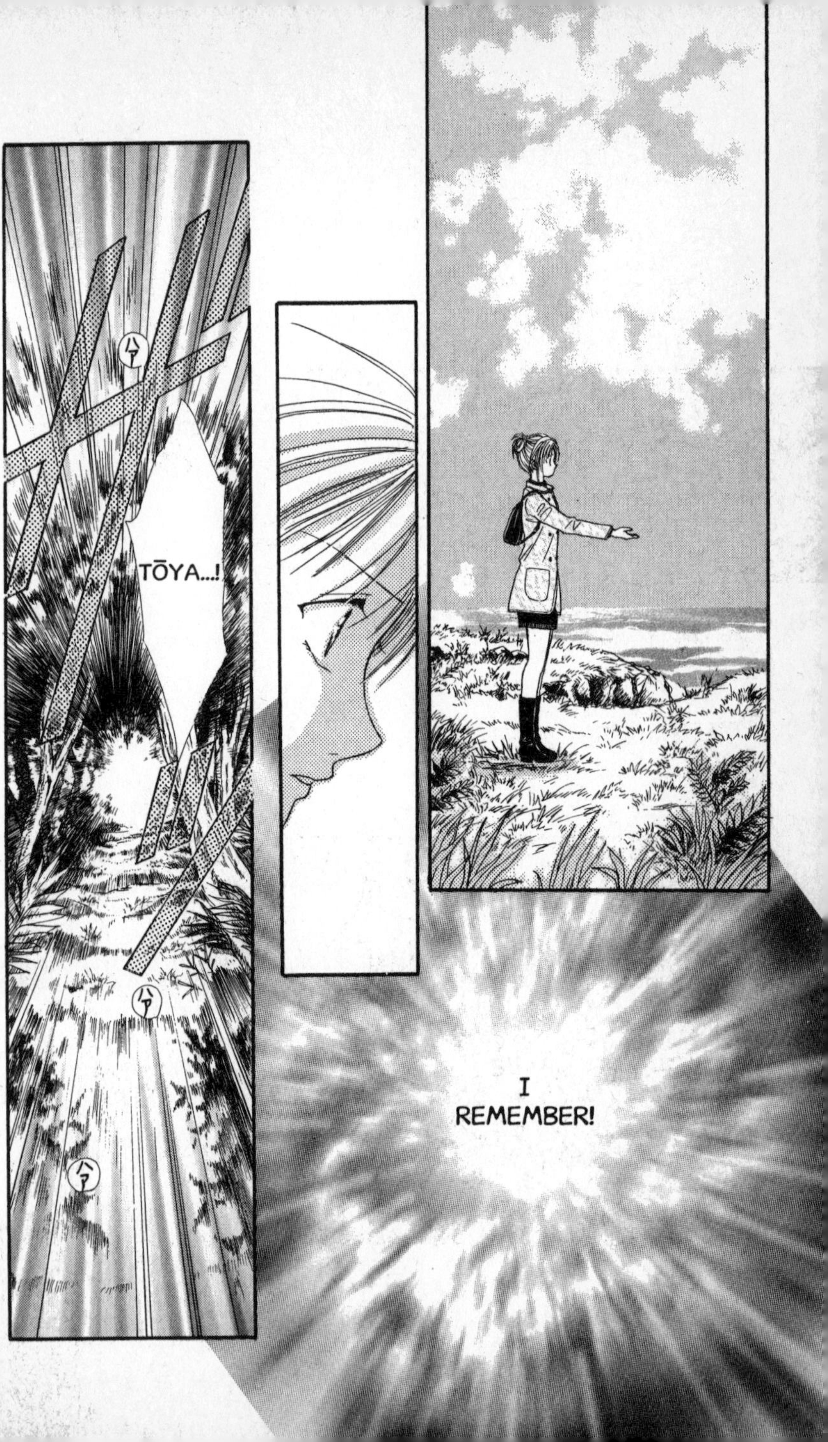
TŌYA...!
I REMEMBER!

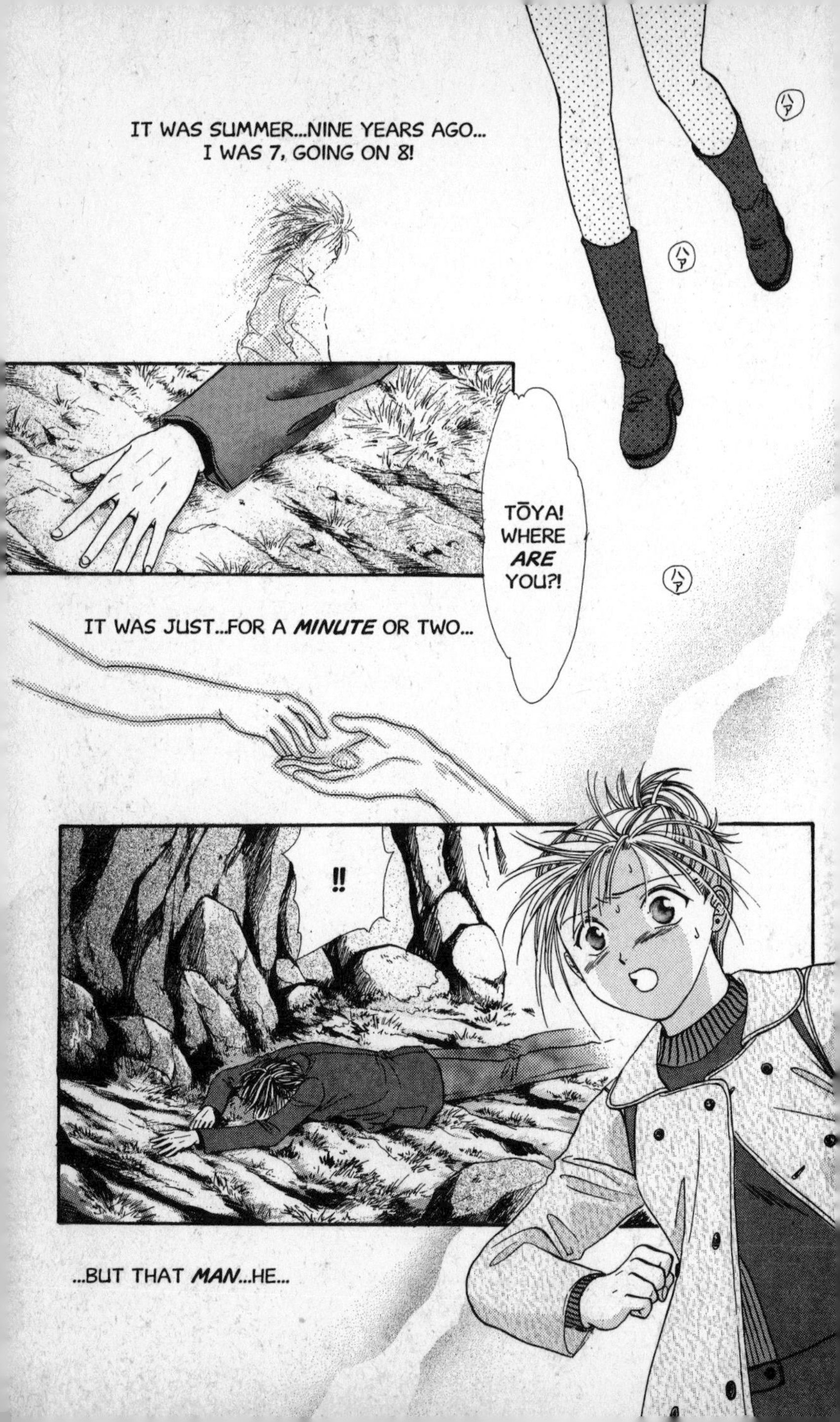
ハァ
ハァ
IT WAS SUMMER...NINE YEARS AGO... I WAS 7, GOING ON 8!
TŌYA! WHERE *ARE* YOU?!
ハァ
IT WAS JUST...FOR A *MINUTE* OR TWO...
!!
...BUT THAT *MAN*...HE...

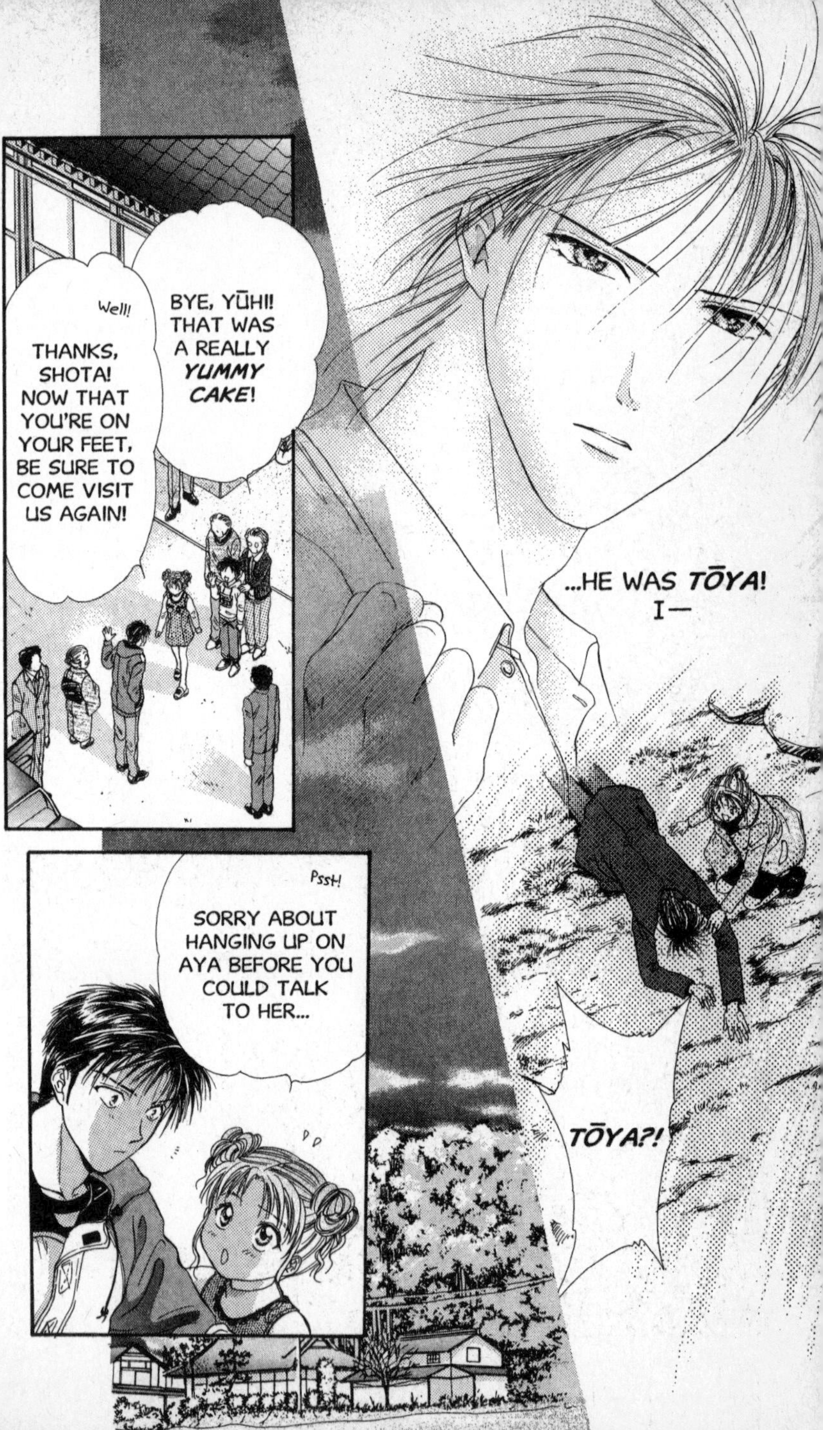
...HE WAS *TŌYA*! I—
TŌYA?!
BYE, YŪHI! THAT WAS A REALLY *YUMMY CAKE*!
Well!
THANKS, SHOTA! NOW THAT YOU'RE ON YOUR FEET, BE SURE TO COME VISIT US AGAIN!
Psst!
SORRY ABOUT HANGING UP ON AYA BEFORE YOU COULD TALK TO HER...

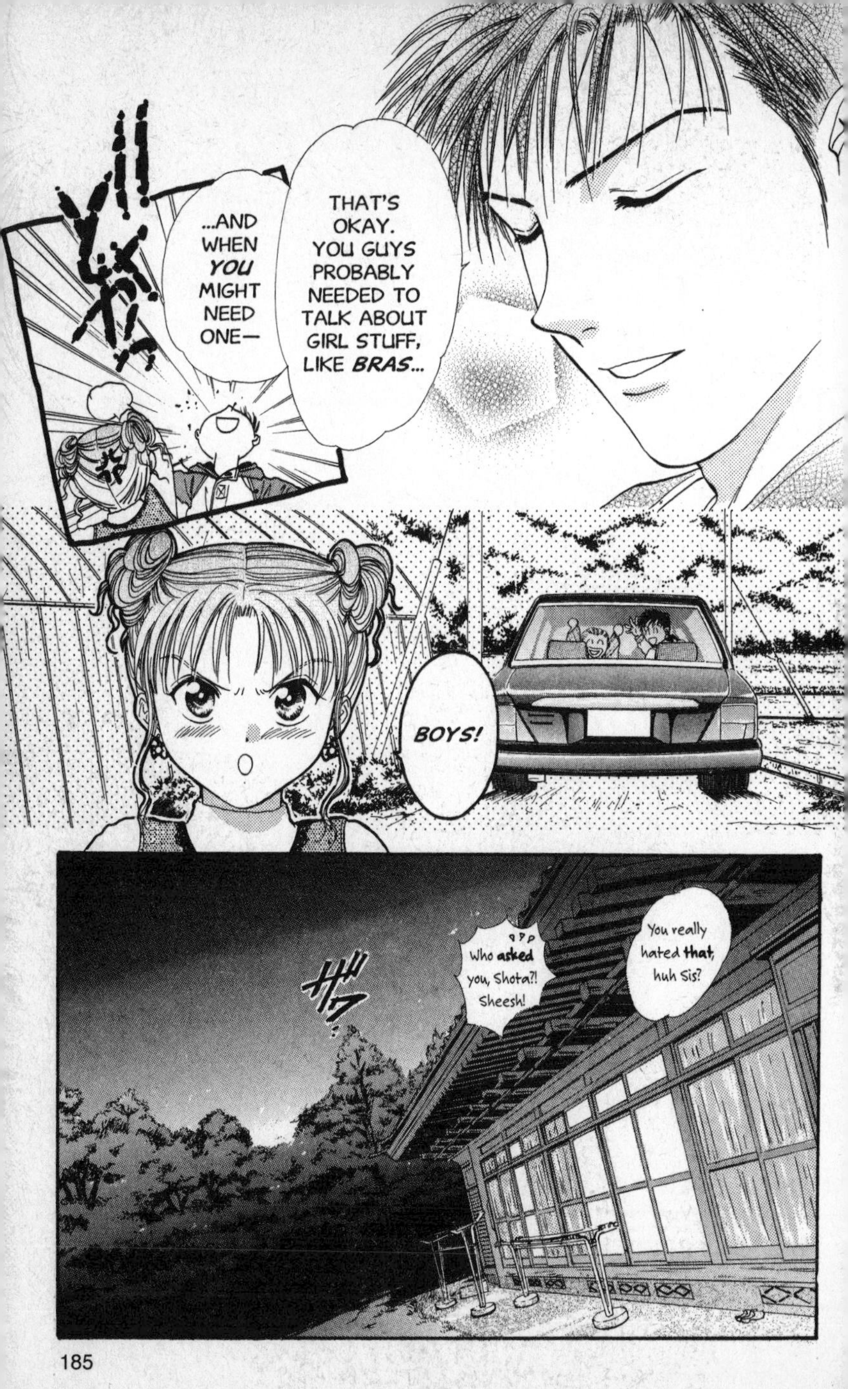
THAT'S OKAY. YOU GUYS PROBABLY NEEDED TO TALK ABOUT GIRL STUFF, LIKE *BRAS*...
...AND WHEN *YOU* MIGHT NEED ONE—
BOYS!
You really hated **that**, huh Sis?
Who **asked** you, Shota?! Sheesh!

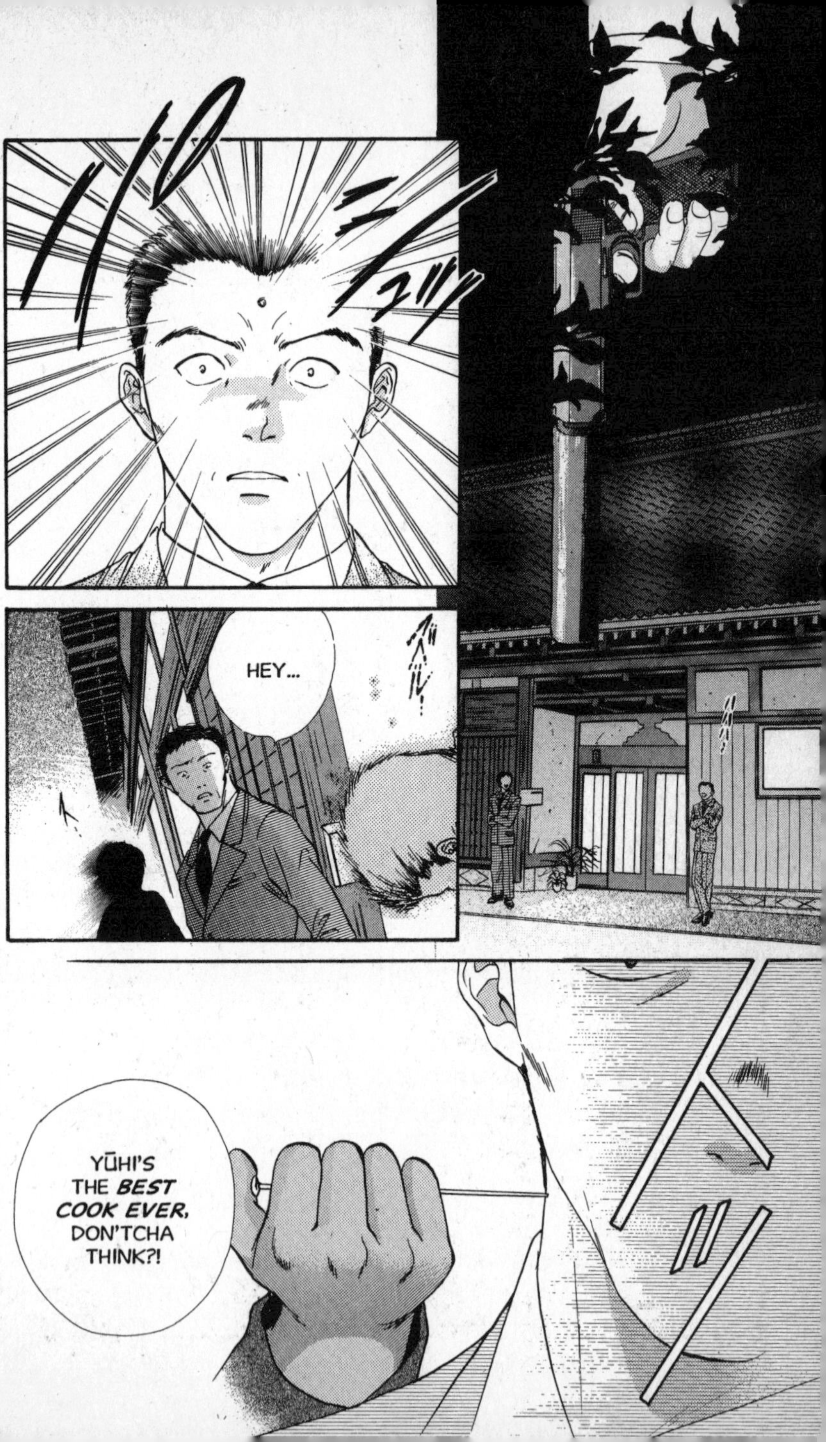
HEY...
YŪHI'S THE *BEST COOK EVER*, DON'TCHA THINK?!

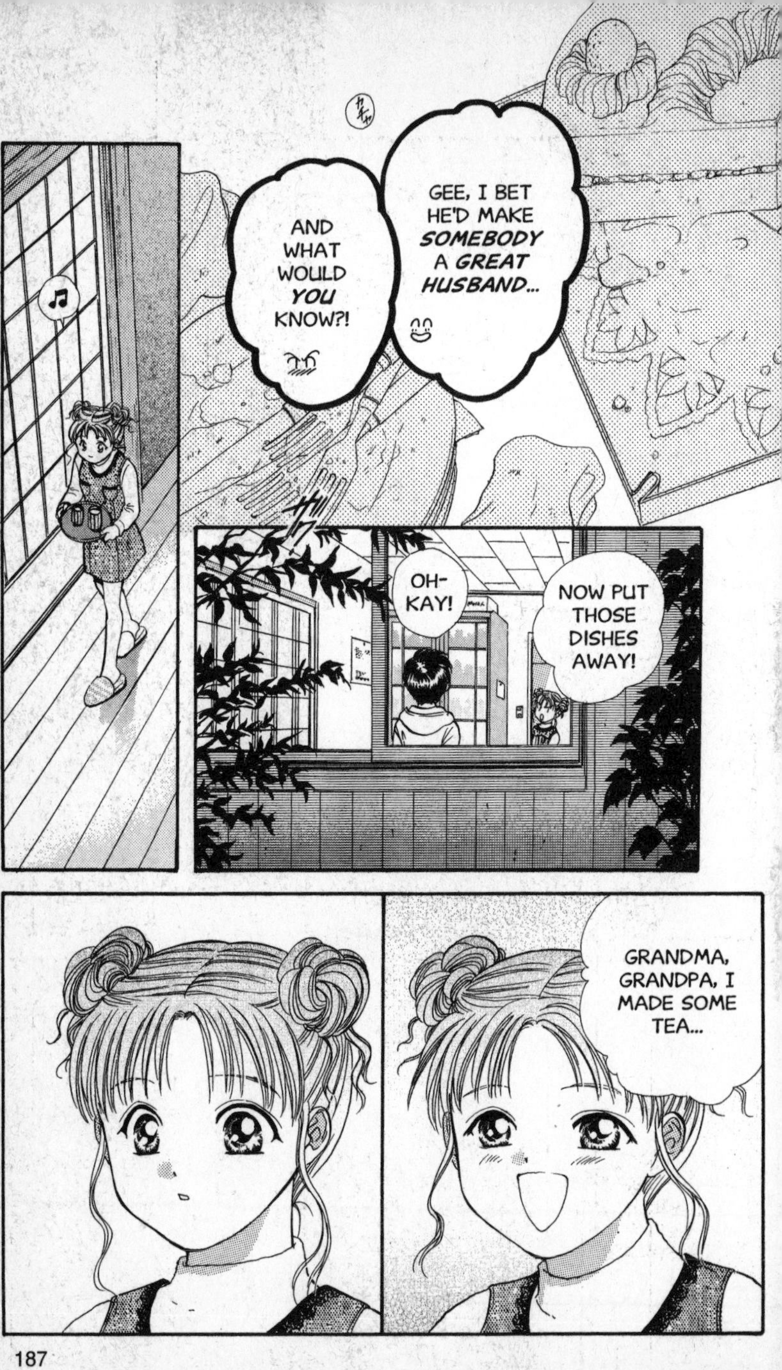
GEE, I BET HE'D MAKE *SOMEBODY* A *GREAT HUSBAND*...
AND WHAT WOULD *YOU* KNOW?!
NOW PUT THOSE DISHES AWAY!
OH-KAY!
GRANDMA, GRANDPA, I MADE SOME TEA...

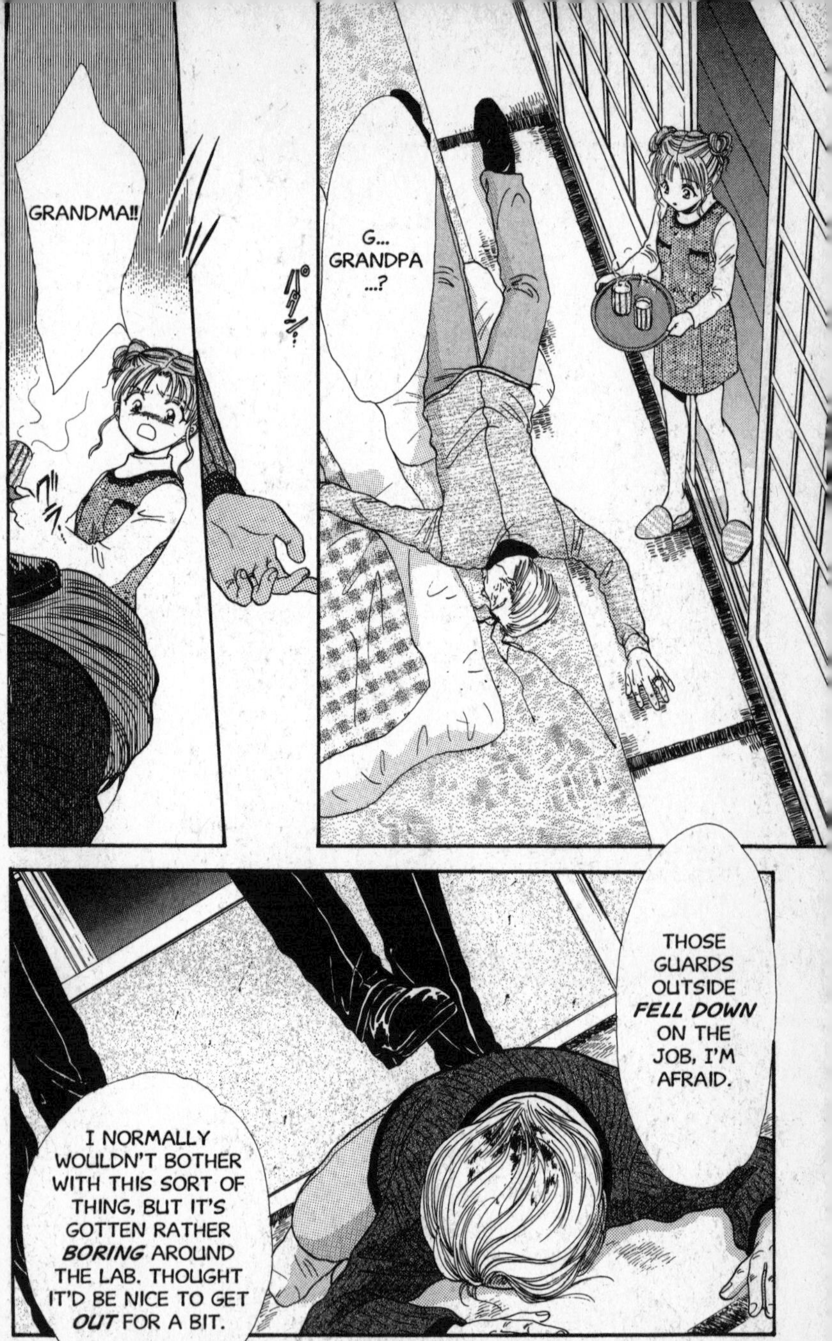
G... GRANDPA ...?
GRANDMA!!
THOSE GUARDS OUTSIDE FELL DOWN ON THE JOB, I'M AFRAID.
I NORMALLY WOULDN'T BOTHER WITH THIS SORT OF THING, BUT IT'S GOTTEN RATHER BORING AROUND THE LAB. THOUGHT IT'D BE NICE TO GET OUT FOR A BIT.

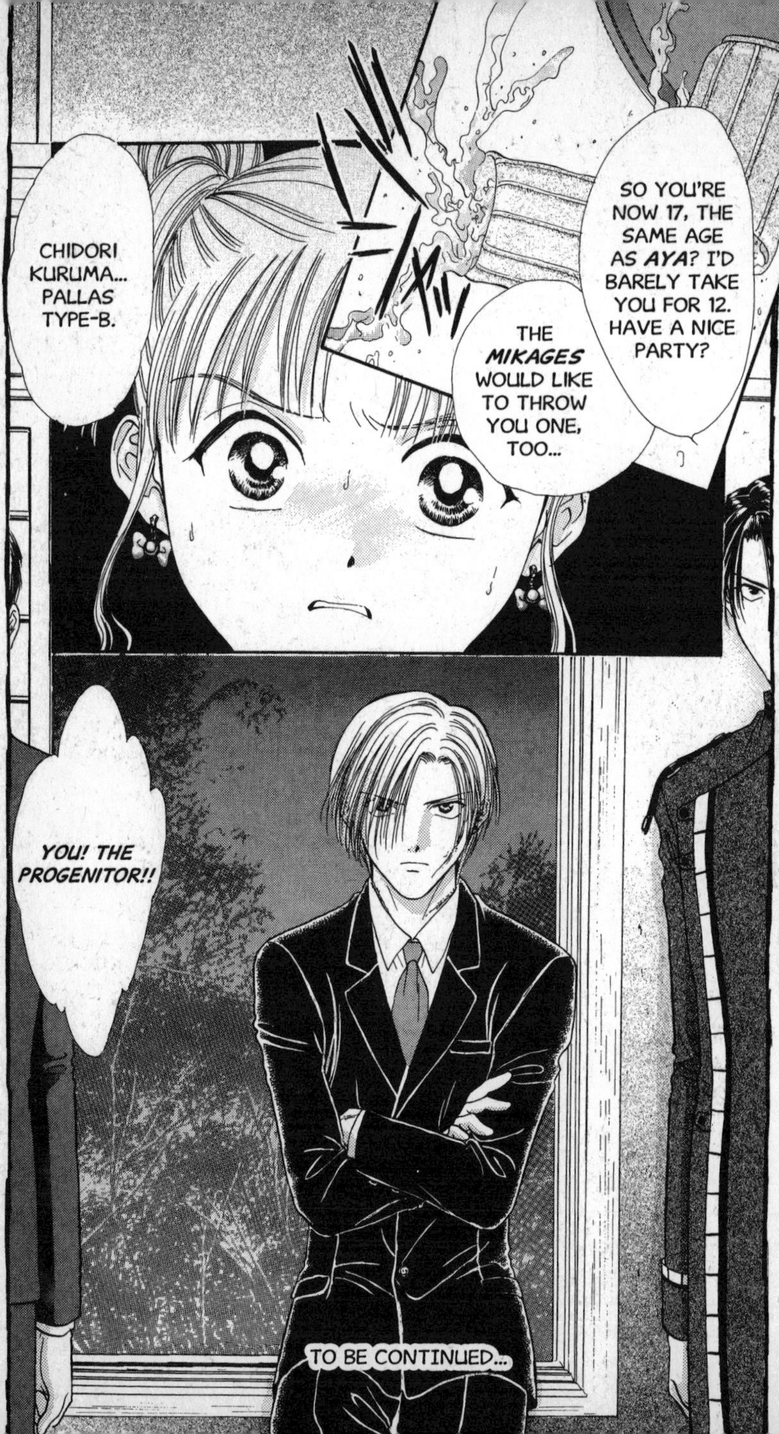
SO YOU'RE NOW 17, THE SAME AGE AS *AYA*? I'D BARELY TAKE YOU FOR 12. HAVE A NICE PARTY?
THE *MIKAGES* WOULD LIKE TO THROW YOU ONE, TOO...
CHIDORI KURUMA... PALLAS TYPE-B.
YOU! THE PROGENITOR!!
TO BE CONTINUED...

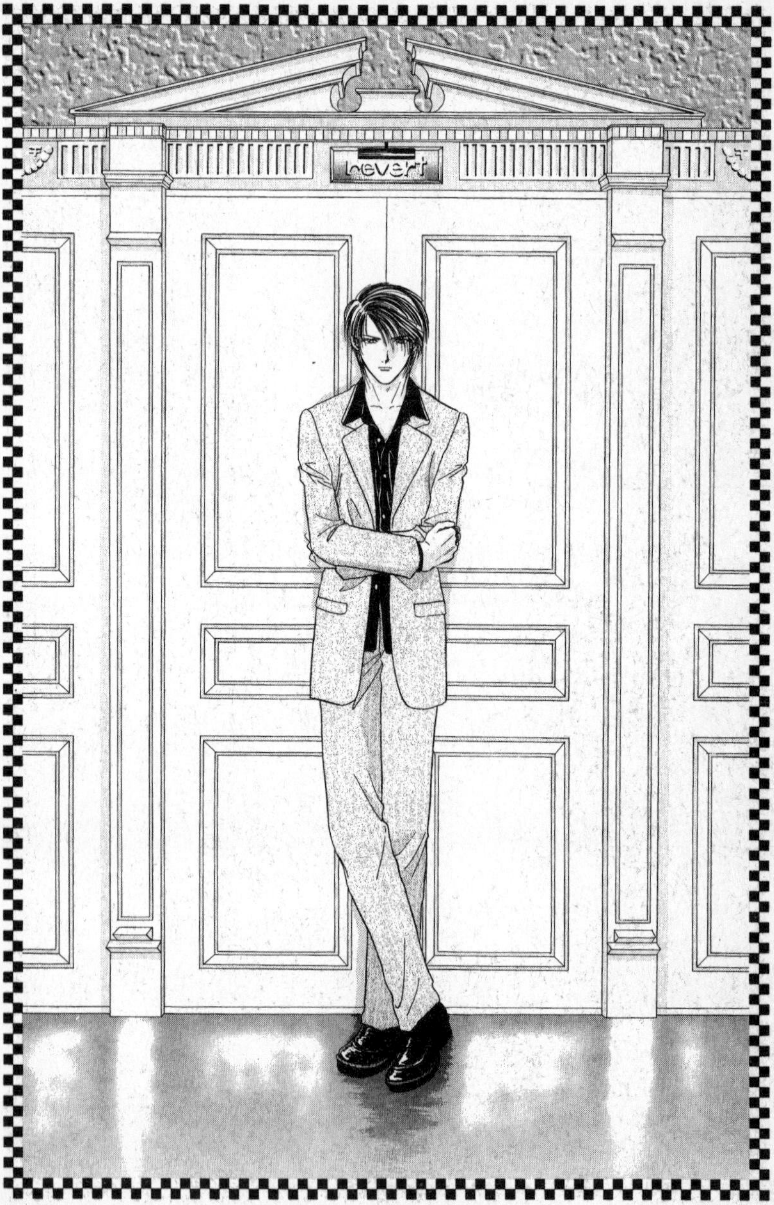
Levert

The CERES Guide to Sound Effects

We've left most of the sound effects in CERES as Yuu Watase originally created them—in Japanese. VIZ has created this glossary to help you decipher, page-by-page and panel-by-panel, what all those foreign words and background noises mean. Use this guide to impress your friends with your new Japanese vocabulary. The glossary lists the page number then panel. For example, 3.1 indicates page 3, panel 1.

047.3 FX: Patan (softened "thud" of a door)
048.2 FX: Gasshi ("glomp" of a hug)
048.3 FX: Gui gui (hasty shove, or tug down)
048.4 FX: Kokun (nod)
053.2 FX: Gushu (sniffle)
054.2 FX: Garari (clatter of sliding door)
058.5 FX: Su (light, caress-like movement)
065.3 FX: Ha ha (laughter)
068.2 FX: Ka (footstep)
068.3 FX: Ka (footstep)
069.1 FX: Kacha (opening "klik" of door)

006.5 FX: Kakun (sleepy "nod")
007.2 FX: Pi pi (electronic "beep")
007.2 FX: Kashan ("clank")
008.1 FX: Bochan (device thrown into water)
010.2 FX: Giku (startled, unpleasant flinch)
011.9 FX: Chi ("tic" of watch-hand)
013.1 FX: Chi chi ("tic-tic")
013.2 FX: Chi chi ("tic-tic")
013.4 FX: Chi chi chi chi ("tic-tic-tic-tic")
018.1 FX: Gyu (squeeze)
018.4 FX: Zawa (rustling, as of foliage)
020.3 FX: Basa (hair falling, after a cut)
030.2 FX: Gyu (squeeze)
034.2 FX: Geho geho (deeper, from the chest "koff, koff")
036.1 FX: Bata bata (tantrum kicks)
037.2 FX: Piku (twitch, or flinch)
038.4 FX: Ba (bursting forward, or up, or out)
040.2 FX: Fu (soft laugh)
040.5 FX: Patan (the softened "thud" of a door)
041.1 FX: Fu (soft laugh)
042.2 FX: Kii ("screech" of brakes, or tire on pavement)
042.2 FX: Ban ("slam" of a door)
043.5 FX: Uchu (sloppy "smooch")
045.3 FX: Niko (easy smile)

069.4 FX: Ka (footstep)
070.2 FX: Butsu butsu
(unintelligible mumbling)
070.5 FX: Kata ("klunk" or "skud"
of chair leg)
071.1 FX: Butsu butsu
(unintelligible mumbling)
072.1 FX: Pan pan
("clap! clap!" applause)
072.2 FX: Gyu (squeeze)
072.4 FX: Pan pan
("clap! clap!" applause)
078.1 FX: Shu-ta-ta-ta-ta-ta (rushing
movement, stomping step)
078.3 FX: Peko (bow)
079.1 FX: Guri guri (grinding
or "noogie" sound)
079.2 FX: Ka—an ("klong" of can
against skull)
080.3 FX: Ha— (heavy exhale)
082.2 FX: Fu (soft laugh)
083.1 FX: Gashi gashi
(equivocating head scratch)
083.2 FX: Kyoton (stupefaction,
"gobsmackery")
083.3 FX: Bi (Aya's hand snapping up)
085.4 FX: Guri guri guri
(grinding or "noogie" sound)
085.5 FX: Za ("sloosh" of waves)
088.3 FX: Gu (clasping hand)
091.4 FX: Za za za ("sloosh" of waves)
095.3 FX: Su— (soft exhale of sleep,
or snuggling head)
098.5 FX: Kya-ha-ha-ha-ha
(careless, girlish laughter)
104.2 FX: Pi-po-pon, pi-po-pon
(doorbell)
104.5 FX: Doka ("slam")
105.1 FX: Pata pata (flailing arms)
106.1 FX: Gutsu gutsu gutsu
(bubbling of stew in *nabe* pot)
106.2 FX: Kacha
("klak" of rested chopsticks)
106.4 FX: Pi-po-pon, pi-po-pon
(doorbell)
107.1 FX: Kacha
(opening "klik" of door)
107.4 FX: Ban ("slam")
109.6 FX: Kura— (wavering swoon)
110.5 FX: Hogya hogya hogya
(newborn wails)
111.2 FX: Pii-po— pii-po—
(siren-wail of ambulance)
119.2 FX: Ha ("gasp!")
120.4 FX: Gachi gachi
(strongly chattering teeth)
120.4 FX: Su
(tug of fabric against fabric)
122.4 FX: Zan ("sloosh" of wave)
122.5 FX: Gura (tossing upheaval)
123.4 FX: Zaza (choppy waves)
124.3 FX: Gura (tossing upheaval)
125.2 FX: Zan ("sloosh" of wave)
126.1 FX: Zuzu (glow of light)

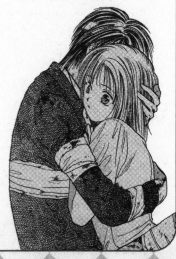

126.2 FX: Gabo gabo
(drowning sounds)
126.4 FX: Za ("sloosh" of waves)
127.1 FX: Gobobobo
(drowning "burble")
127.2 FX: Ha ("gasp!")
128.3 FX: Zaza (choppy waves)
128.3 FX: Zapu zapu ("splup"
of waves against hull)
129.1 FX: Ha ("gasp!")
129.3 FX: Ha ("gasp!")
130.3 FX: Geho (deeper,
from the chest "koff, koff")
130.3 FX: Geho geho (deeper,
from the chest "koff, koff")
130.4 FX: Su— (light brush of hair,
or soft sighing breath)
130.5 FX: Giku
(startled, unpleasant flinch)
131.1 FX: Do do ("b-bmp, b-bmp")
131.2 FX: Do do ("b-bmp, b-bmp")
131.3 FX: Do do ("b-bmp, b-bmp")
131.4 FX: Do do ("b-bmp, b-bmp")
132.1 FX: Zaza—an
(long crash of waves)
133.1 FX: Zuru (sudden slump)
133.2 FX: Ka (footstep)
133.3 FX: Ka ka (footsteps)
133.4 FX: Ka (footstep)
133.5 FX: Ka (footstep)
134.2 FX: Dokun dokun dokun
(heavy heartbeats)
136.1 FX: Vun (sudden flash)
137.1 FX: Ku (scornful laugh)
138.1 FX: Zaza (choppy waves)
139.3 FX: Mogu mogu (chewing)
139.7 FX: Gara (rattle of door)
140.1 FX: Shi— (extreme
"taken aback" reaction)

141.1 FX: Za ("sloosh" of waves)
141.2 FX: Gu (clenched hand)
141.4 FX: Basa ("fwap" of coat flap)
142.1 FX: Basha basha
(splashing-walk in water)
142.3 FX: Ha ("gasp!")
143.1 FX: Za ("dash" movement
through sand)
143.4 FX: Kura (fainting swoon)
144.1 FX: Zapa zapa ("spash, spash"
of running step)
145.3 FX: Pita
(movement, frozen in time)
146.2 FX: Doki
(startled "thud" of heartbeat)
149.3 FX: Gyu (squeeze)
153.1 FX: Fu (soft laugh)
154.1 FX: Do ("b-bmp")
154.3 FX: Do do ("b-bmp, b-bmp")
154.4 FX: Do do do
("b-bmp, b-bmp, b-bmp")
155.2 FX: Kachi kachi kachi
(chattering teeth)
156.1 FX: Ga ("tug")

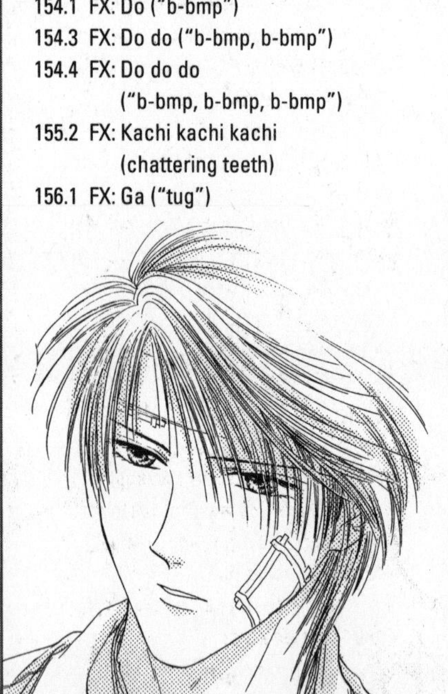

156.4 FX: Ha ("gasp!")
159.3 FX: Kacha kacha kacha ("clacking" of keys)
159.4 FX: Kachi kachi (mouse clicks)
159.4 FX: Kachi kachi (mouse clicks)
165.1 FX: Kusun ("sniff")
165.2 FX: Kacha kacha ("clacking" of keys)
168.2 FX: Zu (slow, sluggish movement)
168.3 FX: Buru buru buru (shuddering)
168.4 FX: Gaku (slump)
169.4 FX: Biku (tongue-swallowing flinch)
171.3 FX: Ka (footstep)
172.2 FX: Ha ("gasp!")
172.3 FX: Gachan (slam of receiver into cradle)
172.4 FX: Tsu— Tsu— (dial tone)
172.4 FX: Doki doki (heavy heartbeats)
172.5 FX: Ta ("trot"-like step)
173.1 FX: Suta suta suta ("tromping" step)
173.2 FX: Pita (movement, frozen in time)
174.1 FX: Go— (roar of jet engines)
174.3 FX: Gyu (squeeze)
176.2 FX: Za ("sloosh" of waves)
177.2 FX: Gu (clenching rail)
178.1 FX: Dokun dokun dokun (thudding heartbeats)
178.2 FX: Ta ("trot"-like step)
178.4 FX: Gyu (squeeze)
178.5 FX: Zaza (choppy waves)
179.1 FX: Za ("sloosh" of waves)
179.2 FX: Do do ("b-bmp, b-bmp")
179.4 FX: Do do do ("b-bmp, b-bmp, b-bmp")
180.1 FX: Do do do ("b-bmp, b-bmp, b-bmp")
180.3 FX: Do do ("b-bmp, b-bmp")
180.4 FX: Do ("b-bmp")
182.4 FX: Za ("sloosh" of waves)
182.4 FX: Ha— ha— ha— (labored, heavy breathing)
183.1 FX: Ha— ha— ha— (labored, heavy breathing)
185.2 FX: Doka ("pow!")
185.4 FX: Zawa (rustling, as of foliage)
186.1 FX: Ha ha ha (laughter)
186.2 FX: Pashu ("funt" of silencer)
186.3 FX: Zuru (sudden slump)
186.3 FX: Su (almost imperceptible movement)
186.4 FX: To (touch of stiletto against flesh)
187.1 FX: Kacha (opening "klik" of door)
187.2 FX: Zawa (rustle, as of foliage)
188.2 FX: Patan (softened "thud" of a door)
188.3 FX: Ha ("gasp!")
188.3 FX: Gura (wavering slump)
189.1 FX: Basha (spilling splash of tea)

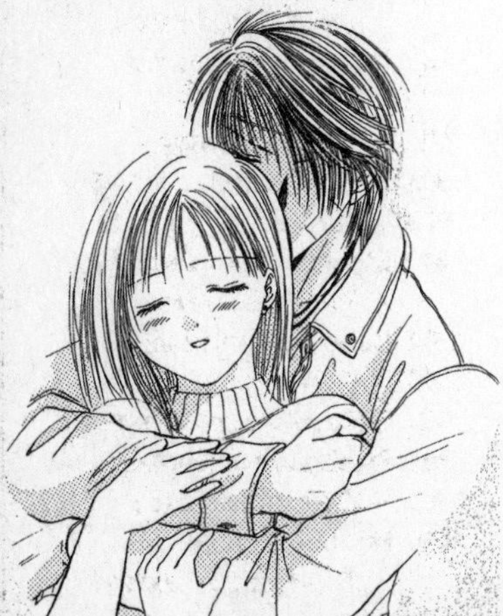

Yuu Watase was born on March 5 in a town near Osaka, Japan, and she was raised there before moving to Tokyo to follow her dream of creating manga. In the decade since her debut short story, *PAJAMA DE OJAMA* ("An Intrusion in Pajamas"), she has produced more than 50 compiled volumes of short stories and continuing series. Her latest work, *ZETTAI KARESHI* ("Absolute Boyfriend"), has recently completed its run in Japan in the anthology magazine *SHÔJO COMIC*. Watase's other beloved series *CERES: Celestial Legend, Fushigi Yûgi, Imadoki! (Nowadays),* and *ALICE 19TH* are now available in North America in English editions published by VIZ.

COMPLETE OUR SURVEY AND LET US KNOW WHAT YOU THINK!

☐ Please do NOT send me information about VIZ products, news and events, special offers, or other information.

☐ Please do NOT send me information from VIZ's trusted business partners.

Name: _____

Address: _____

City: _____ State: _____ Zip: _____

E-mail: _____

☐ Male ☐ Female   Date of Birth (mm/dd/yyyy): ___ / ___ / ___   (Under 13? Parental consent required)

What race/ethnicity do you consider yourself? (please check one)

☐ Asian/Pacific Islander   ☐ Black/African American   ☐ Hispanic/Latino

☐ Native American/Alaskan Native ☐ White/Caucasian   ☐ Other: _____

What VIZ product did you purchase? (check all that apply and indicate title purchased)

☐ DVD/VHS _____

☐ Graphic Novel _____

☐ Magazines _____

☐ Merchandise _____

Reason for purchase: (check all that apply)

☐ Special offer   ☐ Favorite title   ☐ Gift

☐ Recommendation   ☐ Other _____

Where did you make your purchase? (please check one)

☐ Comic store   ☐ Bookstore   ☐ Mass/Grocery Store

☐ Newsstand   ☐ Video/Video Game Store ☐ Other: _____

☐ Online (site: _____)

What other VIZ properties have you purchased/own? _____

_____

How many anime and/or manga titles have you purchased in the last year? How many were VIZ titles? (please check one from each column)

ANIME	MANGA	VIZ
☐ None	☐ None	☐ None
☐ 1-4	☐ 1-4	☐ 1-4
☐ 5-10	☐ 5-10	☐ 5-10
☐ 11+	☐ 11+	☐ 11+

I find the pricing of VIZ products to be: (please check one)

☐ Cheap ☐ Reasonable ☐ Expensive

What genre of manga and anime would you like to see from VIZ? (please check two)

☐ Adventure ☐ Comic Strip ☐ Science Fiction ☐ Fighting
☐ Horror ☐ Romance ☐ Fantasy ☐ Sports

What do you think of VIZ's new look?

☐ Love It ☐ It's OK ☐ Hate It ☐ Didn't Notice ☐ No Opinion

Which do you prefer? (please check one)

☐ Reading right-to-left
☐ Reading left-to-right

Which do you prefer? (please check one)

☐ Sound effects in English
☐ Sound effects in Japanese with English captions
☐ Sound effects in Japanese only with a glossary at the back

THANK YOU! Please send the completed form to:

NJW Research
42 Catharine St.
Poughkeepsie, NY 12601

All information provided will be used for internal purposes only. We promise not to sell or otherwise divulge your information.